P9-CDD-497

The Computer as an Educational Tool

Productivity and Problem Solving

Second Edition

Richard C. Forcier
Western Oregon University

Merrill,
an imprint of Prentice Hall

Upper Saddle River, New Jersey   *Columbus, Ohio*

Library of Congress Cataloging-in-Publication Data

Forcier, Richard C.
    The computer as an educational tool: productivity and problem
solving / Richard C. Forcier.—2nd ed.
        p.   cm.
    Rev. ed. of: The computer as a productivity tool in education.
c1996.
    Includes bibliographical references and index.
    ISBN 0-13-741968-6
      1. Education—Data processing—Study and teaching (Higher)
2. Computers—Study and teaching (Higher) 3. Computer managed
instruction. 4. Computer-assisted instruction. I. Forcier,
Richard C. Computer as a productivity tool in education.
II. Title.
LB1028.43.F67   1999
371.33′4—dc21   98-2888
                                     CIP

Editor: Debra A. Stollenwerk
Developmental Editor: Gianna M. Marsella
Production Editor: Mary Harlan
Photo Coordinator: Anthony Magnacca
Design Coordinator: Karrie M. Converse
Text Design and Production Coordination: Carlisle Publishers Services
Cover Designer: Susan Unger
Cover Art: © Marjorie Dressler
Production Manager: Pamela D. Bennett
Director of Marketing: Kevin Flanagan
Marketing Manager: Suzanne Stanton
Marketing Coordinator: Krista Groshong

This book was set in Garamond by Carlisle Communications, Ltd. and was printed and bound by R. R.
Donnelley & Sons Company. The cover was printed by Phoenix Color Corp.

 © 1999, 1996 by Prentice-Hall, Inc.
Simon & Schuster/A Viacom Company
Upper Saddle River, New Jersey 07458

Previous edition entitled *The Computer as a Productivity Tool in Education.*

Photo credits appear on page xvi.

Excerpts from *Principles of Instructional Design,* Fourth Edition by Robert M. Gagne, Leslie J. Briggs, and
Walter W. Wager, copyright © 1992 by Holt, Rinehart and Winston, reprinted by permission of the publisher. "Cone of Experience" from *Audio-Visual Methods in Teaching,* Third Edition by Edgar Dale, copyright © 1969 by Holt, Rinehart and Winston, reproduced by permission of the publisher.

Printed in the United States of America

10 9 8 7 6 5 4 3

ISBN: 0-13-741968-6

Prentice-Hall International (UK) Limited, *London*
Prentice-Hall of Australia Pty. Limited, *Sydney*
Prentice-Hall of Canada, Inc., *Toronto*
Prentice-Hall Hispanoamericana, S. A., *Mexico*
Prentice-Hall of India Private Limited, *New Delhi*
Prentice-Hall of Japan, Inc., *Tokyo*
Simon & Schuster Asia Pte. Ltd., *Singapore*
Editora Prentice-Hall do Brasil, Ltda., *Rio de Janeiro*

Preface

The Computer as an Educational Tool: Productivity and Problem Solving, Second Edition, is based on the author's long-held view that technology should be as transparent as possible—that is, that the use of technology should not call attention to itself. Technology, specifically computer technology, should be a means to an end—not the end in itself. The computer should empower the user to solve problems effectively and efficiently.

The goal of this book is to lead teachers and those aspiring to be teachers to become proficient at applying the computer to solve problems, to infuse the computer into the curriculum in order to help students do the same, and to encourage both teachers and learners to integrate technology into their professional, academic, and personal lives in useful and meaningful ways. Those who are successful in doing this will indeed come to see the computer as an extension of their human capability. The computer will allow them to do more, to do it faster, and to do it more creatively and more accurately.

A PROBLEM-SOLVING FOCUS

The Computer as an Educational Tool: Productivity and Problem Solving, Second Edition, provides a current, comprehensive look at the computer's role in education and problem solving, as well as the application of the computer as a tool of the mind. As the text examines the computer's various roles in education, topics are broken down into specific areas of interest to encourage an understanding of the computer's contribution to solving problems. Problem-solving models are included in the text to encourage an increase in computer productivity and to clarify the application of the computer in a thoughtful and deliberate manner, reinforcing the concept of the computer as a mind tool.

NEW IN THIS EDITION

Teachers and students will find that the strengths of the book in its first edition remain:

- A balance of *factual information, research, theory, and application*
- *Highly readable, student-friendly prose*
- *Technical matters explained clearly and accessibly* for the nonexpert audience
- *Examples drawn from both PC-based Windows and Macintosh platforms*

With the help of feedback from professors and student users delivered via e-mail and in teleconferences, this book has been revised extensively. Meaningful changes have been made to more effectively demonstrate the computer's capacity as an educational tool for problem solving and to show to a greater extent the range of classroom applications of computer technology available to teachers and learners. Highlights of this revision include

- *A new chapter on the Internet* (Ch. 11), which includes discussion of resources on the Internet (including e-mail, electronic conferencing, and LISTSERVs), Internet navigation and retrieval tools (including search engines and bookmarks), and applications of the Internet for both teachers and students. It also includes crucial information on "netiquette" and how to critically evaluate web sites.
- *A new chapter dedicated entirely to multimedia technologies* (Ch. 12), including information on, and classroom applications for, multimedia authoring tools, presentation software, and virtual reality.
- *A reorganized table of contents* that better contextualizes computer use in educational settings and *reflects a deeper integration of problem solving* throughout the book. In this edition, the text treats theory and current issues in technology first, discusses strategies for using computers in educational settings next, shows practical applications, and then discusses management and administrative concerns.
- *A better, more comprehensive explanation of the computer as a problem-solving tool that increases our productivity as learners and educators*. Along with improved definitions of key concepts such as "productivity tool" and "constructivism," this edition devotes an entire chapter to linear and nonlinear problem-solving processes early on in the book (Ch. 3), where the discussion can contextualize the more technical information and the applications of the problem-solving model in later chapters.
- *A greater emphasis on curriculum applications,* with numerous examples, model lessons, and suggestions for integrating the computer into educational curricula added.
- *A greater emphasis on social contexts for computer use* in the classroom, including treatment of issues such as assistive technologies for students with disabilities, selecting software to use when teaching gifted students and students with limited English proficiency or special needs, equity in computer access, and gender equity.
- *An updated research base, new screen captures, and discussion of new and emerging technologies* in a rapidly changing field.

TEXT ORGANIZATION AND SPECIAL FEATURES

Woven throughout this text is the use of the computer as a personal productivity and problem-solving tool for the teacher in both an instructional and a management role, as well as for the student in a learning role. The text, therefore, is organized with the following thematic frameworks:

- *Issues in information technology.* A number of issues are examined, including copyright, information ownership, equitable computer access, and gender equity. The computer's role in the educational reform movement is discussed, as well as its place in current and future trends in information technology.
- *Learning theory and instruction.* Theoretical structures are established to look at the computer's role in teacher-centered instruction and to examine student-centered learning. Both *behaviorist* and *constructivist* perspectives are examined. Underlying principles and theories of education and communication are reviewed and applied to discussions of computer applications in instruction and learning. Implications of emerging technologies are discussed.

- *Strategies for computer use.* The computer as a productivity tool is applied to tutorial, drill and practice, simulation, and multimedia formats. The Internet, word processing, graphics, databases, and spreadsheets are seen as problem-solving tools. New and emerging technologies are examined, and their roles in education are discussed.
- *Selecting, evaluating, and managing a software collection.* A unique examination of the process of developing and sustaining a software collection is included to meet the information needs of teachers and students. The management of a software collection on *FileMaker Pro*™ is discussed, a complete *template* appropriate for both Windows and Macintosh platforms is developed, and then complete field definitions are presented in Appendix M.

Furthermore, the text is organized to provide thorough coverage of computer knowledge and educational applications, including the following:

- *The computer itself and its user interfaces.* An explanation of computer hardware commonly found in schools is presented. A look at current and emerging user interfaces is examined.
- *Word processing.* Applications are suggested and examples are used to illustrate them.
- *Graphics.* Bit-mapped and vector graphics are explored and examples given. Proper selection of chart types and the interpretation of data represented by graphs are analyzed. Information on the use of the computer to generate display graphics for charts and graphs, signs, posters, bulletin boards, and overhead transparencies is presented.
- *Spreadsheets.* Problem-solving models are applied to the development of spreadsheets. Applications are suggested and examples are used to illustrate them.
- *Databases.* The organization and retrieval of information are examined. Problem-solving models are applied to the development of databases. Applications are suggested and examples are used to illustrate them.
- *Telecommunications.* Networking schemes are explored, as are the fundamental concepts of telecommunications. Applications are suggested and examples are used to illustrate them. An introduction to the Internet is presented, followed by an in-depth look at the World Wide Web.

CHAPTER FEATURES

This edition maintains the style of the first edition, which drew acclaim from students for presenting important and useful information in a highly readable format. The following features are included in each chapter:

- Each chapter begins with an *advance organizer.*
- *Charts and line drawings* are used to illustrate concepts in a concrete manner.
- *Screen displays* illustrate concepts and application software in, as much as possible, a nonspecific hardware platform.
- *Exercises* allow the student the opportunity to process the information presented in the chapter and apply it in a practical manner, using higher-order thinking skills.
- *Important terms are printed in boldface* when they are introduced to the reader. They are then defined in the chapter glossary and are included in the index at the end of the book to facilitate reference.
- The *appendixes* serve as a ready reference to the student. They include sample software evaluation forms, a sample parental permission form for telecommunications, a

practical listing of Internet resources and their addresses, field definitions for a software database, and a list of software publishers, with a statement of each one's sales and support policies. These forms are perforated for ease of use.

ACKNOWLEDGMENTS

I would like to acknowledge the significant contributions that the following people made to the creation and development of this text:

- Peggy Forcier, manager of the Washington County (Oregon) Cooperative Library Services, as well as my wife and best friend, for her unflagging support and thoughtful consideration of every idea presented.
- Gianna Marsella, a development editor at Prentice Hall, whose tireless efforts made this book as good as it could be.
- Melanie Wallis, a library media specialist in McMinnville, Oregon, for her delightful story that concludes this text in the Afterword.
- Nancy Powell, an international consultant on library collection assessment, for her thoughtful review and many suggestions that contributed greatly to the strength of Chapter 12. Figure 12–1 is an adaptation of a model she suggested.
- Jim Long, a colleague who has managed a U.S. West grant, training teachers and students to effectively access the Internet, for his assistance with Chapter 11.
- Al Mizell and his students in computer education at Nova Southeastern University for including me in their stimulating teleconferences.
- All of my graduate students, especially Sylvia Sandoz for her clever design of a model representing virtual reality, and Susan Arnold for her well-executed study of multimedia's impact on elementary school students.

I would also like to express my gratitude to the reviewers who so thoughtfully read and offered constructive criticism to the work in progress. Their expertise contributed greatly to the strength of this book and to its potential usefulness in a course dealing with computers in education. They include Sylvia S. Bienvenu, University of Southwestern Louisiana; David Edyburn, University of Wisconsin, Milwaukee; Teresa J. Franklin, Ohio University; Jho-Ju Tu, University of Southwestern Louisiana; Bonnie H. Keller, Valdosta State University; Lee McCanne, Boston University; Al P. Mizell, Nova Southeastern University; and Lynn Pachnowski, University of Akron.

Brief Contents

Contents

A Message to the Reader

We often encounter trite sayings such as "We are living in the Information Age." This term has been overused to the point that we do not appreciate what it really means. I believe, though, that each one of us will have our own "aha!" moment, where we will reach a personal understanding of the true impact of its meaning. I venture to guess that this personal understanding will relate in some manner to shifting paradigms associated with teaching and learning and to the pertinent use of technology. We will fully realize that we cannot teach in the manner that we ourselves were taught.

It is my fervent hope that each and every one of you, as readers of this text, will sharpen your skills related to information creation, storage, access, retrieval, analysis, and dissemination. Do not take the term *Information Age* at face value, but dig deeply to derive your own personal understanding. Let this insight guide your teaching behaviors.

The title of this book should challenge you to seek a deeper definition of productivity than the one based on the factory model of the efficient creation of products. Think of productivity as encompassing effectiveness as well. Include quality, quantity, time, and space in your definition. Think of productivity when you read the quote that begins Chapter 1. Examine your knowledge base as you conceptualize productivity before you encounter the concept put forth in Chapter 2.

In our profession, change is not only inevitable, it is rapid and significant and it is upon us as a new generation of teachers. Allow me to share an inscription that is carved in the stonework above the entrance to the Instructional Technology building on our campus at Western Oregon University: "Who dares to teach, must never cease to learn." We must always seek the unknown so that we can provide the information and the guidance that will allow our students to create new knowledge and understandings. Let us allow the computer to become for us the productivity tool that extends our human capability as we teach and continue to learn.

Richard C. Forcier

Photo Credits

Chapter 1

Historical and Social Contexts for Computer Use

ADVANCE ORGANIZER

1. How are shifting paradigms of computer use affecting the classroom?

2. How has computer technology evolved and what is its potential impact on you as a user?

3. Do those who have home access to a computer have an unfair advantage over those who do not?

4. Do students who attend schools in affluent neighborhoods have an unfair advantage over those who do not?

5. How should we as teachers strive to promote gender equity in our classrooms? What actions must we take to affirm this goal?

6. What can the computer provide to students with special needs?

7. What are some of the current and future trends in information technology?

All media are extensions of some human faculty.
Marshall McLuhan (1967)

The word *media* has been defined in many ways. Its most popular definition in our culture refers to the mass media of communications: radio, television, newspapers, and magazines. Some teachers see media as new audiovisual aids; some see media as relating to library and **information technology.** A definition gaining favor in recent years identifies the media as a tool. Consider the word *media* itself. *Media* is the plural form of the word *medium,* a term broadly understood as being in the middle. Something is medium if it is neither hot nor cold, neither fast nor slow, neither large nor small. Medium implies in the middle or between two extremes or two points. This understanding is the ideal foundation for defining a medium as a tool between the user and **information** to be created, received, stored, manipulated, or disseminated. A tool is in the middle between the user and the task being addressed. Information technology is the application of the tool to solve problems related to information.

Tools are what McLuhan was referring to as extensions of our human capability. From the study of archeology, we know that humans have always been tool makers and tool users. Consider, during our existence on this planet, how we have created and adapted physical tools such as the lever, the wheel, and the engine to amplify our physical abilities and figurative tools such as language and mathematics to enhance our cognitive abilities. Some would define *technology* as this deliberate ingenious effort to create, select, adapt, and apply tools to a task or problem at hand.

Among our ancestors, women were some of the earliest technologists as they fashioned agricultural and homemaking tools.

The computer is one of our most recent tools in education. When we consider technology in education we include, among other things, the application of the computer as a multifaceted tool. Not being limited to a single tool, we select from a variety of tools, perhaps adapt, and then apply the tool to the problem at hand. Alan Kay (1991) refers to the computer as a *metamedium* able to imitate all other existing media. He states, "Constructions such as text, images, sounds, and movies, which had been almost intractable in conventional media, are now manipulatable by word processors, desktop publishing, and illustrative and multimedia systems" (146). We, as teachers apply the computer system as a tool to the instructional, management, or action research task at hand.

The way we view computing has shifted in at least four significant areas. Figure 1–1 illustrates this shift radiating outward from the past, shown in the innermost circle, to the present and to the near future, represented by the outermost circle. Beginning in the upper left quadrant and progressing in a clockwise fashion, the areas represented may be summarized by the words *Where, How, Who,* and *What.*

The *Where* has been a transition from a computer room to the users' desktops in the classroom, in the office, or at home. The transition has now progressed to users themselves as they transport computers with them wherever they go as personal assistants in the form of **laptops, palmtops,** and **personal digital assistants (PDAs).** The *How,*

Figure 1-1

Shift in computer paradigms (Adapted from Greene, 1988)

or under what conditions, has been a shift from a tightly controlled, centralized, and in-stitutionalized environment such as a school district office or a service bureau provid-ing computer services to the school to a highly personalized one with the user in com-mand of the computer and increasingly to a truly interpersonal one that lets users interact with one another. In addressing the *Who* of computing, we have seen a distinct move from the **computer operator** (often a technician somewhat remote from the problem) to the **end user** (the person deriving direct benefit) interacting directly with the computer. The near future will witness a networked community of users intercon-nected electronically with one another. Teachers and students will communicate with peers around the globe. Finally, the *What* demonstrates a move from a fascination with huge amounts of stored **data** to a concern for the value of the information that can be extracted from it. Teachers and students alike are developing increasingly sophisticated skills in the creation of, access to, and manipulation of information.

Keeping in mind these shifting paradigms of the student or teacher personally ex-changing information with another user in the same neighborhood or around the world, the goal of this chapter is to help educators gain perspective on current com-puter usage by understanding historical contexts (past, present, and future trends in information technology) and social contexts for computer use in the classroom.

EVOLUTION OF COMPUTER TECHNOLOGY

Yesterday

Rapid changes in computer technology have resulted in greatly improved and ex-panded applications. Early applications were computational in nature, and early pro-gramming was done in a numbering system other than our familiar decimal one. Thus, a misconception arose that, to be a programmer or even a competent user, one had to have an extensive mathematical background. We now realize that the com-puter is a tool for everyone.

As we review the history of computer technology, we become aware of a tremen-dous simplification in operation: a vast improvement of the machine/human inter-face and a dramatic reduction in equipment size. Both of these elements contribute significantly to the expanding computer utilization in society in general and in edu-cation in particular. Nine significant occurrences are identified in Figure 1–2 and dis-cussed in the following sections.

1890. The 1880 census took seven years to process manually and, with a growing pop-ulation, the 1890 census posed a serious problem. It appeared that it would take more than 10 years to process the census information unless some new method were em-ployed. Herman Hollerith solved the problem with a machine that stored data printed as holes punched on cards. The machine sorted and counted the cards. The 1890 cen-sus was processed in just three years. Hollerith manufactured his invention, then merged with another company. The new firm was called International Business Machines (IBM).

1945. The first general-purpose electronic **digital** computer was introduced in 1945. The ENIAC occupied 3,000 cubic feet of space, weighed 30 tons, contained over

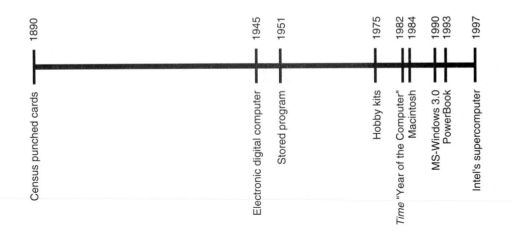

Figure 1–2

Significant events in computer evolution

18,000 vacuum tubes, and drew 140,000 watts of power when it was running. The **vacuum tube** acted like a gate, passing or blocking an electric current in a digital circuit. As current was passed or blocked, it was translated into a binary code of 1s and 0s. The ENIAC could do only simple addition, subtraction, multiplication, and division operations in a programmed sequence. To change the sequence to address a new problem, the ENIAC had to be rewired by hand.

1951. The first electronic computer to use a stored program entered the market in 1951. One **transistor,** a half-inch square, replaced the vacuum tube, allowing the computer itself to be reduced from building size to room size and then to the size of several large file cabinets.

Programs stored in computers were written in machine language as **binary** code. Think of the vacuum tube for a moment. It can be "on" and passing current or it can be "off" and blocking current. This on or off state could be represented by a 1 or by a 0. Zeros and ones are gathered in groups of eight. As shown in Figure 1–3, eight **bits** in this case form one **byte,** representing an alpha or a numeric character.

Fortunately, although today's computer still understands only binary code, we do not have to use this code to communicate with it. Computer languages have been developed that allow us to employ English-like words, which are then translated into a binary form. These are called "higher level" languages because they resemble English, as opposed to the "lower level" languages at the machine level of 0s and 1s.

1975. Microcomputers marketed in kit form for the hobbyist were introduced in 1975. Within two years, Apple, Commodore, and Radio Shack microcomputers were on the market and the microcomputer explosion was under way. Remember the vacuum tube and the transistor that replaced it? The **integrated circuit,** or **chip,** found in microcomputers is approximately one-quarter inch square and may contain millions of transistors.

1982. *Time* magazine proclaimed 1982 as "The Year of the Computer" because of the significant contributions that personal computers made in complementing human abilities. In explaining their proclamation, the editors said, "A new world beckons,

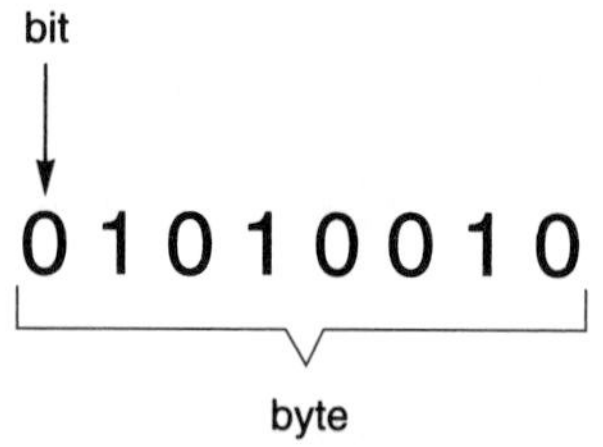

bit

$\downarrow$

0 1 0 1 0 0 1 0

byte

Figure 1–3

Byte composed of eight bits

created by a technological upheaval that is bringing computers to millions" (Friedrich, 1983). The desktop-size personal computer can not only do the automated tasks necessary to keep a business operating efficiently, but, as it is operated by the person responsible for a given task, it performs as an extension of that person.

This is also the year that Microsoft released the MS-DOS operating system for IBMs and compatibles.

1984. Apple Computer introduced the Macintosh computer, successor to its Lisa, introduced the year before. The "Mac," as it became known, featured a **graphic user interface (GUI)** complete with a mouse, icons, screen windows, and pull-down menus.

1990. After a few setbacks (Windows 1.0 and 2.0), Microsoft released Windows 3.0, a successful competitor to the Macintosh operating system. Windows, in its recent versions, has become the best-selling computer program, or **software,** of all time and the dominant operating system in almost all market segments.

1993. Unlike the 30-ton ENIAC that occupied 3,000 cubic feet of space, laptops such as the PowerBook introduced in 1993 weighed about seven pounds and occupied less than one-seventh of a cubic foot of space. The ENIAC had an internal memory capacity of 12K, storing about 12,000 characters in its memory. In comparison, laptops introduced in 1993 had a 4 **megabyte (MB)** memory, expandable to 36 MB (about 36 million bytes); about 3,000 times greater than the ENIAC, and 100,000 times more reliable. Today's laptops are significantly more powerful yet.

1997. Intel Corporation developed a supercomputer for the U. S. Department of Energy capable, for the first time, of breaking the trillion-calculations-a-second barrier. It can sustain a speed of 1.06 trillion operations a second. The four-ton computer can perform 667 million calculations in the time it takes a bullet to fly one foot, or 40 billion calculations in the blink of an eye (Manning, 1996). These most astonishing developments have taken place in a little more than 50 years. What astounding advances in technology will the next 50 years bring?

Today

How do learners of today differ from learners of yesterday? It could be argued that one of the most dramatic changes is the amount of information available to them and their greatly enhanced access to it. Much of this information is packaged in a visual form and presented in an interactive manner at a rapid rate. Consider the way television, magazine, billboard, and radio ads bombard our senses as consumers. As viewers, readers, and listeners, we have adapted to "consume" information differently. Similarly, as the amount of information available to learners multiplies, the process of learning must evolve. Consequently, schooling is changing dramatically and, with it, the role of the teacher.

Yesterday, learners were at times seen as containers, or vessels, needing to be filled with factual information. Teachers were dispensers of information, and memorization was equated with learning. An "educated person" was one who was well read and in possession of facts in a variety of fields. With the explosion of information and widespread and immediate access to it, today's learners are faced, like never before, with the need to develop problem-solving skills. Today's educated person is one who knows how to access information efficiently and evaluate it and apply it effectively as that individual constructs appropriate knowledge.

How do changes in schooling relate to the paradigm shifts in computing just described? Centralized information dispensing by the teacher has shifted to individualized information retrieval by the student. The evolution of computer technology has enabled those paradigm shifts as equipment, or **hardware,** has become smaller, more portable, more affordable, more powerful, and easier to use.

As new technology is making vast amounts of information available to teachers and students, a need for highly developed information literacy skills has been recognized. Teachers and students must learn how to conduct effective searches, how to critically evaluate the results of the search, and how to create new knowledge from the information distilled. The American Association of School Librarians (AASL) and the Association for Educational Communications and Technology (AECT) have developed joint national guidelines for information literacy. Several states have adopted their own in conjunction with the national guidelines. The Oregon guidelines, as an example, can be examined on the Oregon Educational Media Association web page (http://www.teleport.com/~oema/infolit.html).

Change seems to be the hallmark as we enter the twenty-first century. Social and economic struggles of the present have thrust educational and school reform from the theoretical realm of educators into the public arena. Legislators, businesspeople, parents, and other taxpayers are demanding fundamental changes from schools, teachers, and administrators. Each has a unique interpretation of what these changes should be and how they will best occur. Businesses have created, have funded, and are managing for-profit schools, some within the public school system. School choice is an issue that has been the subject of both political rhetoric and informed debate. Some parents advocate more government support of home schooling, while others expect help from the school system with child care, parenting advice, and social services. Taxpayers are dissatisfied with the performance of public schools in relation to the amount of tax money spent. Significant changes in the whole structure of the educational system and our philosophies of education and learning are occurring, a paradigm shift discussed in greater detail in the next chapter.

As schools have gradually adopted the use of computers and related technology, they have undergone some degree of instructional change. According to Allan Collins (1991), these trends include the following:

1. A change from whole-class to small-group instruction
2. A move from lecture to coaching
3. A move from working with better students to spending more time working with weaker students
4. A shift toward students becoming more engaged in their learning
5. A change to assessment based on products and outcomes
6. A shift from a competitive to a cooperative atmosphere in the classroom
7. A shift from all students attempting to learn the same thing at the same time to different students learning different things at their own rate
8. A move from an emphasis on verbal thinking to the integration of visual and verbal thinking

Tomorrow

We find ourselves in the midst of a powerful information revolution. Combined with the significant restructuring in education occurring in this country, the way we use computers in the classroom is changing as well. What role might the computer play in school restructuring? Much will depend on you and teachers like you who recognize the potential of the computer as an intellectual tool.

In order for schools to keep up with the demands of the students, the demands of the community, and the demands of the government, there will have to be a philosophical shift in the public's perception of education. Often the public's perception is based on the past, on what education was like, rather than the reality of what it is like today or its potential. Technology, with its frequent innovations and pervasive influence, provides an impetus for that shift. It also provides the tools educators need to implement change now.

The U.S. Department of Education has adopted four national technology goals, and funding is being provided from a variety of sources to help schools install the necessary infrastructure and to train teachers in the use of technology to meet those goals. The goals are:

- All teachers and students will have modern computers in their classrooms.
- Every classroom will be connected to the information superhighway.
- Effective and engaging software and online resources will be an integral part of every school curriculum.
- All teachers will have the training and support they need to help all students learn through computers and through the information superhighway.

Any lasting changes and reforms will need to be preceded by a vision of what future learning environments will be like. What will be the expectation placed on the learner? What will be the role of the teacher? What will be the physical structure of the learning environment? How will library media centers fit into this new environment? How will technology affect learning?

The basic curriculum will change as schools focus on information and thinking skills, and as the use of tools such as computers, sophisticated information storage and retrieval systems, holograms, and virtual reality simulations becomes the norm rather than the exception. Teaching methods will change as these tools are incorporated. Instructional materials will reflect the tools being used in learning. Expectations and outcomes will be different for children, teachers, parents, and administrators. The physical structure and internal organization of the school will certainly differ as these changes are assimilated.

In the future, the amount of time children spend in school may well become more flexible as technology provides new tools and inspires new teaching and learning methods. Networking will allow students to work at multiple sites while interacting with the class or the teacher. As students begin taking more responsibility for their own learning, the pace of that learning will have a more natural rhythm dictated by the individual student's needs instead of an imposed districtwide schedule. Some students may choose to work in the early morning, at night, or on weekends. Even younger children may choose to work on an absorbing project for extended lengths of time rather than having the day segmented into predetermined bits of learning.

Technology will provide students with access to information and the tools to produce substantial work. Each student will have a computer available at school. This may be in the form of a personal computer workstation, a shared terminal for database and networking access, or a portable computer. The computers would all have networking capabilities and be linked by a worldwide network to teachers, parents, homes, databases, electronic bulletin boards, library and information centers, and other people all over the world.

The most exciting use of technology by the students of the future will be an enhancement of their production of authentic, meaningful work. Students will write, illustrate, publish, program, and create models, movies, music, stories, poetry, artwork, and other products of research and learning. They will utilize integrated technologies involving optical disks, computers, multimedia, virtual reality, and holographic imaging. Given access to information and technology, the skills to use them, and the freedom to learn and explore, children will be able to produce work that is barely imaginable to adults today.

Schools are under pressure to provide more than just a limited-use building with a single mission. Taxpayers complain about expensive buildings and equipment that are virtually deserted for up to a fourth of the year and are available only during school hours for the rest of the year. Teachers find themselves unable to teach academics when children are more in need of a nurse, counselor, social worker, or parent. The school of the future will have to address those needs. A multiple-use neighborhood facility combining education with the traditionally separate fields of child care, health care, social services, and fitness will more successfully meet the needs of the children and the community. Professionals in each of those fields would staff the facility, working as a team to provide the best possible environment for children and their parents.

A study entitled "The Effectiveness of Using Technology in K–12 Education (Birman, Kirshstein, Levin, Matheson, & Stephens, 1997) has recently been completed by the American Institutes for Research. It reviews current research demonstrating the impact of technology on educational reform. Along with school reform, a number of trends dealing with technology's impact on schools are becoming apparent. The following trends seem to be emerging and very likely will assert themselves in the twenty-first century:

1. Private enterprise will play an increasing role in schools and will hasten the infusion of technology. This will occur as private enterprise targets education as a lucrative market, developing better and more powerful computer and video software and installing no-cost or low-cost technology in the schools that will be funded by advertising revenues. It will also occur as private enterprise develops partnerships with schools to provide funding and increased opportunities for job training and career development.

2. Multimedia will show significant growth as a tool for supporting students' construction of their knowledge. This will occur as teachers increasingly develop a comfort level with interactive computer technology. It will occur along with a paradigm shift from teachers defining what students should learn and students memorizing what they read or are told, to teachers facilitating and coaching students as they learn and students constructing their own meanings and solutions to problems (Cowart & Schalock, 1994).

3. Optical technology will become the storage medium of choice and will be accessible over networks. The low cost, durability, and random access characteristics of optical media such as **CD-ROM** or its logical successor, **DVD,** make it a winner. The technology will continue to improve, providing better compression/decompression techniques and a faster data transfer rate. Publishers will have to work out problems with fee structures for networked products simultaneously accessible by large numbers of users.

4. Libraries will become automated information centers. Public and school libraries will continue to provide recreational reading, viewing, and listening but will also provide outstanding electronic reference services by using networked CD-ROM encyclopedias and databases with provisions to dial in from home computers. Libraries will provide high-level telephone support to reference questions and direct access to the Internet.

5. Telecommunications will become a major factor for delivery of information to the school and to the home. This will increase home schooling opportunities, but it will also change the nature of the classroom to support the paradigm shift previously mentioned and many others as well.

Few school patrons would deny the essential nature of pencils, paper, and books in a school. They are the tools and resources children use to learn, explore, and apply new ideas and concepts, to communicate with others, to express themselves artistically, and to produce work. These materials will be important components in education far into the future, yet technology provides us with powerful tools that serve the same educational purposes and that allow us to achieve even more. Why not integrate technology's tools so completely that they become indispensable as well?

SOCIAL CONTEXTS FOR COMPUTERS IN THE CLASSROOM

Thus far, we've discussed advances in technology since Hollerith's census counting machine a little more than a century ago, as well as historical contexts for computer use. If you look back to Figure 1–1, you'll recall that not only are the *What, Where,* and *How* of computer usage changing, but so is the *Who.* As the technology for computers changes, so do the people who use computers and the contexts in which they use them. No longer are building-size computers used to crunch numbers for an elite coterie of scientists and mathematicians. Now, more than ever, computers are mobile, and information is accessible to many people. Adults and students in a wide range of disciplines and with vastly different levels of expertise use computers for thousands of professional, educational, and recreational applications.

Today's computer-savvy and Nintendo-habituated learners have vastly different expectations for their educational experiences than learners of the not-too-distant past. The techno-literate MTV generation is less inclined to sit still and listen to a slow-paced lecture when stimulating, interactive educational and recreational experiences offer other, multisensory options. Today's students have a high comfort level with things electronic, digital, and wired. Their level of visual literacy—a result of living in a visually rich and exciting environment—is a distinct factor in how today's students acquire and process information.

Because of their versatility and capability for individualization, computers—when they are accessible—can help teachers challenge and educate all students, including those with special needs.

Students with Special Needs

Students with special needs have often been called "at risk," because many are in danger of dropping out of school. Factors that contribute to this potential risk include "low teacher expectations, lack of motivation, academic difficulty, and lack of meaningful experiences" (Poirot & Canales, 1993–1994). Students who are thought of as learning disabled, culturally and linguistically different, or talented and gifted are considered potentially at risk.

As the restructuring of U.S. education progresses, many paradigm shifts will occur. One such shift is that schools will move from students with special needs being separated from their regular classmates for instruction to educational programs and practices that have as their aim "full inclusion from the child's perspective, that is, where a teacher adapts the learning environment to meet the diverse needs and backgrounds of the children being taught" (Cowart & Schalock, 1994). Another shift will be that schools will move from being organized on a grade-by-grade and course-by-course basis to being organized to accommodate developmental levels of learners. The computer has a significant role to play in both of these changes.

Students with Disabilities   Structuring a suitable learning environment for a physically challenged student requires providing the appropriate learning tools to achieve sensory and communication compensation. Research indicates that technology "can be adapted for use by disabled students and can result in higher achievement and improved self-image" (Kober, 1991). Assistive devices of all kinds that provide visual,

The computer can help remove barriers that students with disabilities may encounter.

aural, or tactile support greatly extend the capabilities of impaired students to use the computer effectively. The computer-based Kurzweil Reading Machine scans printed documents and converts text into electronic speech. Speech synthesizers, speech recognition devices, image magnifiers, specially designed keyboards with exchangeable overlays, and a variety of switches have made the computer a tool useful to the physically impaired.

Though a good deal of attention has been paid to hardware for special education, software also plays a key role in making the computer accessible. The following list adapted from Karen Armstong (1995) presents software features that can be helpful to users with disabilities.

- Easy-to-read screens—Simple, legible text and menu items are represented in graphics and text.
- Consistency—Consistent placement of menus and objects on the screen make programs more intuitive and predictable.
- Logical labels—Easily understandable names in lists and menus give a reasonable sense of what will happen when they are selected.

- Graphics—Graphics encourage interaction and support nonreaders and beginning readers.
- Support for inclusion—Software that appeals to all users promotes inclusion.
- Documentation—Instructions are available in large print, Braille, electronic text, or recorded form.
- Audio/visual cues—Prompts and feedback can provide important support and keep users on track.
- Built-in access—Alternative access methods allow users to select appropriate input devices such as a joystick or touch screen.

A student with a learning disability often harbors feelings of inadequacy. As computers have become increasingly user-friendly, they offer that student a chance to be in control, a chance to excel. One day, while visiting my son's high school, I observed a remarkable sight—"exceptional children," working as computer lab assistants, helping the "normal" students as they encountered difficulties. Those lab assistants exhibited a very positive self-concept.

Computers are patient tutors and provide simulated environments in which students with mild physical disabilities and students with learning disabilities can work. Malouf (1991) mentions the limitation of errors, the unhurried pace, the repetition of missed items, and the provision of remedial feedback as characteristics of good computer software that meets the needs of students with disabilities. Problems develop for the exceptional child when these same characteristics are not found in the classroom.

Students with Limited English Proficiency. The computer is a valuable tool in teaching written and spoken communication to students who are culturally and linguistically different. The computer's engaging visual feedback can be especially appealing to students with limited English proficiency. Graphics software allows the students to express themselves in ways reflective of their own culture. The right software transforms the computer into a patient tutor that allows students to make mistakes and to proceed as slowly as necessary in each case. Other software creates a microworld in which a student responds and practices newly acquired language skills. A word processor using a standard typeface or a special typeface such as Kanji might allow the students to express themselves in their native language and to teach their classmates a few words and expressions in that language.

Some tutorial, drill and practice, and simulation software is becoming available in non–English-language versions. The most commonly available languages at this time are Spanish, French, and German. Some software allows the user to toggle between English and a second language. Some of the Discis™ interactive storybooks distributed on CD-ROM allow the selection of English or another language and include the ability to have the words showing on the screen read to the user. Spell checkers, dictionaries, and thesauruses are now available in other languages for a number of word processors.

Cooperative learning strategies appear to work well with children who are culturally or linguistically different by integrating them into small groups and then facilitating their integration into the class as a whole. The computer is a tool that lends itself well to a number of cooperative learning strategies.

Computers provide endless opportunities for students to express their creative abilities. This student created a multimedia piece for a school report.

Students on the Hoopa Indian Reservation spent a year constructing a dictionary in their native language of the plants and animals indigenous to their area (Berney & Keyes, 1990). The project proved to be a challenge for them, since their native language is an oral, not a written, language. The computer, with its graphics capability, afforded them a concrete experience.

Students Who Are Talented and Gifted. It is important to acknowledge that even children who are recognized as talented and gifted may be at risk. Boredom, slow pace of instruction, lack of challenge, lack of recognition of a sometimes unique learning style—any and all of these factors may contribute to the talented and gifted child being at risk of dropping out of school or of getting far less out of school than might be possible. Enter the computer: a tool with which to experiment and test hypotheses, a tool with which to analyze information and draw conclusions, a tool with which to express oneself by drawing as well as by writing, a tool with which to explore a wide, wide world!

The computer has many times been called the ultimate individualized instruction tool. The disabled and the gifted represent the opposite ends of an ability continuum. A case can be built supporting computer use as a means of reaching individual students at either end of the scale. Both types of students will derive satisfaction from constructing a worthwhile product as evidence of their creativity and knowledge.

Most gifted students are inquisitive and academically uninhibited. When introduced to computer programming, they often develop a high degree of problem-solving skills and abilities. These skills stand them in good stead in other disciplines.

Many talented and gifted children have difficult social adjustments to make because of their superior intellectual abilities. They are sometimes viewed by other students as uninteresting, overly academic, and with few social skills. They sometimes view other students as uninteresting, unchallenging, and flighty. Once again, the computer, used wisely as part of a cooperative learning strategy, can provide a positive social experience and help in the development of interpersonal skills. To build interpersonal skills, for example, these students might experiment with telecommunications software, programs that contain interactions with characters in simulations and adventures, programs about social issues, group participation/decision-making programs, and games that involve two or more players.

Computer Access and Equity

What if you gave your students an essay to write and some wrote in pencil, some typed, some used a typewriter with a correcting ribbon, and some wrote on a computer using a word processor complete with spell checker, full dictionary, thesaurus, and grammar checker? You would, of course, expect the products to be different regardless of the individual students' skills and aptitudes. Why? Because of the tools used. The essay prepared in pencil would probably have a number of erasures. You might well find some correction fluid applied to the typed essays. Those typed using a correction ribbon would certainly present a good appearance. However, the essays prepared on the computer with full control over all elements of the font have the potential of presenting the best visual appearance. Not only will they appear the best, but they should also be free of typing and spelling errors. They also will probably make the best use of words. Why couldn't the students using pencils and typewriters use a dictionary and thesaurus? They could, of course. Doing so, however, would add a considerable amount of time and effort beyond that spent by the students on the computers. The conclusion to be drawn is that the computer, with its support for easy editing, revision, and text presentation, is a significant tool in the writing process.

The student writing an essay on a computer is at a distinct advantage. If you consider all of the various types of computer software through which the computer can extend the user's capability, you see that the use of this tool has a significant impact. Equal access to that tool is then a serious concern. We currently have a class of "haves" and a class of "have nots," those with good access to computers and those without.

There are schools in more affluent neighborhoods or with staff possessing grant-writing expertise that are well equipped with computers. They have a reasonably high ratio of computers to students. The computers are located in individual classrooms, in a library media center, and in open computer labs available before, during, and after school hours. Students can search for information, practice skills and concepts, and create their own products.

However, because of a scarcity of resources, apathy toward technology, or lack of leadership, other schools have an inadequate number of computers and a poor selection of software. Students at these schools are deprived of the richness of the resources found elsewhere. After visiting a number of schools in various parts of the country, Charles Piller (1992) stated,

"Computer based education in poor schools is in deep trouble. . . . Although some affluent schools also have lackluster computer-based learning programs,

The many uses of the computer empower students to express themselves and use new tools to achieve their goals.

students from these schools usually enjoy supportive, well-educated families that supplement school-based training with home computers. Federal surveys suggest that whites are about three times as likely to have computers at home as are African Americans or Hispanics; affluent students are nearly four times as likely as poor students."

Recent estimates of computer availability in U.S. homes range from 25 percent to 33 percent. This means that up to one-third of all U.S. students have access to a computer at home. It stands to reason that most of these homes are reasonably affluent. Among the most common reasons given for purchasing a home computer is to assist in the education of children. A recent contact with a leading educational software publisher revealed that the volume of its sales to the home market was significantly greater than that to schools. Unfortunately, some home computers turn into simple game machines, with very little software to help the children learn. Students with access to a home computer having a word processor and other productivity software constitute an elite group, one with a distinct advantage that over two-thirds of the student population does not enjoy. This variability of access should influence a teacher's expectation when it comes to the quality of product prepared by the students.

Differences in achievement for students with and without access to home computers exist. Allen and Mountain (1992) report that, in their study of inner-city African American children with access to computers and an on-line service, one of the primary factors in increased test scores appeared to be whether the children perceived themselves as "haves" or "have nots." A study by Nichols (1992) suggests that higher achievement scores for students with access to home computers might be the result

What actions should we as teachers take to promote gender equity in our classrooms?

of those children having an increased desire to succeed. Regardless of the reason—higher self-esteem, higher motivation, or simply more powerful tools with which to work—students with computers tend to achieve higher outcomes.

How can access be improved? Teachers in schools with inadequate computer resources should demand access to such an important educational tool. They should make the administration, the school board, and community groups aware of the need. Teachers in schools with reasonable computer resources should work toward making the computers available with an acceptable measure of security and supervision outside of normal school hours to students, parents, and community groups.

Gender Equity

Gender equity should be a continuing cause of concern to educators. Computer usage suffers from an inherited gender bias that holds that math and science are not "feminine things." Although efforts to remedy this bias are certainly under way, it is difficult to overcome the fallacy that girls cannot excel in math and science. This bias has its roots in the seventeenth century, when inventions in science and technology began to be made not by aristocrats but in the monastic environment of the universities, which were under the control of the male-dominated political and religious forces of the time. The elite created an aura of a quasi-priesthood of science and technology and erected barriers to keep others, primarily women, out (Noble, 1992). From that point until the mid-twentieth century, women were basically told that math and science were not for them.

Courses dealing with the use of computers are often taught by math or science teachers. If girls believe they are not good in these subjects they often draw the conclusion that they also would not do well in the use of computers (Culley, 1993).

It is interesting to note the equal participation of boys and girls in computer literacy and application activities in the elementary and middle-level grades. Girls and boys appear to be equally enthusiastic when it comes to using the computer. As students move into high school, stereotypes exert themselves. Girls continue to refine word processing skills and other business (read "clerical") skills, while boys overwhelmingly populate the computer science classes. High school girls tend to develop negative attitudes regarding computers (Kirk, 1992).

Studies have shown that males do not necessarily outperform females in computer courses (Massoud, 1991). In spite of this evidence, some teachers demonstrate gender bias. The more difficult computer class assignments tend to be given to the boys, who therefore receive more personal attention and time from the teacher. According to Koch (1994), teachers ask boys technical questions and are more likely to answer a boy's questions, but they take over and complete a task for a girl. This kind of teacher behavior fosters learned helplessness rather than self-sufficiency in girls.

In a typical school computer lab, computers are available on a first come, first served basis. With more students than computers, the more aggressive students usually get them. Many boys spend countless hours playing video games as preadolescents and gravitate toward the use of computers.

Software itself can contribute to gender iniquity. For example, research shows that clip art libraries severely underrepresent women and ethnic minorities, and they reinforce gender stereotypes about sex roles and work (Dyrud, 1996). Additionally, recreational software tends to be loud, flashy, violent, and based on competitive win/lose situations. Even educational software has at times exhibited some of these characteristics. Females tend not to be drawn to this type of software and, therefore, spend less time at the computer as an enjoyable diversion.

Parental encouragement is another factor influencing gender bias. Parents often envision their sons in scientific or technical careers and encourage them to take computer science classes and attend computer camps. Parents are more likely to buy computers for use by their sons than their daughters. Boys get the message that spending time at a computer is a worthwhile activity.

How should we as teachers strive to promote gender equity in our classrooms? What actions must we take to affirm this goal? We should go out of our way to praise girls' accomplishments on the computer. We must be sure to include them in any special computer-based projects. We can encourage equal access to computers by instituting sign-ups, rotation schedules, and other democratic systems. We should include girls' names in computer examples we give. We must also buy and use gender-equitable software and avoid programs that aren't. We should encourage girls to consider careers involving computer use beyond standard clerical applications. We must provide more female role models by inviting women who are computer scientists or who make extensive use of the computer in their professions to speak to our classes. We must continually examine our own actions and guard against any subtle, even unintentional, actions we might take that would in any way diminish girls' interest or discourage them from interacting with the computer in a meaningful way.

SUMMARY

The advent of the twenty-first century has thrust educational and school reform into the public arena. Businesses have created, have funded, and are managing for-profit schools, some within the public school system. In order for schools to change, there will have to be a philosophical shift in the public's perception of education. Technology provides a turning point for that shift, as its influence pervades so much of our daily lives. Any lasting changes will need to be preceded by a vision of what future learning environments will be like. The basic curriculum will change as schools focus on information and thinking skills and as the use of tools such as computers, information storage and retrieval systems, holograms, and virtual reality simulations becomes the norm rather than the exception. Teaching methods will change as these tools are incorporated. Instructional materials will reflect the tools being used in learning.

Technology will provide students with access to information and the tools to produce substantial work. The computers will be linked by a worldwide network to teachers, parents, homes, databases, electronic bulletin boards, library and information centers, and other people all over the world. The most exciting use of technology by the students of the future will be the production of meaningful work. Students will write, illustrate, publish, program, and create models, movies, music, stories, poetry, artwork, and other products of research and learning. They will utilize integrated technologies involving optical disks, computers, multimedia, virtual reality, and holographic imaging.

Students with special needs, who are sometimes thought of as learning disabled, culturally and linguistically different, or talented and gifted, are often at risk of dropping out of school. As the restructuring of U.S. education progresses, educational programs and practices will have as their aim "full inclusion from the child's perspective," and schools will be organized to accommodate the developmental levels of learners. Structuring a suitable learning environment for a physically challenged student requires providing the appropriate learning tools to achieve sensory and communication compensation. A student with a learning disability often harbors feelings of inadequacy. As computers have become increasingly user-friendly, they offer that student a chance to be in control and to excel. Computers are patient tutors and provide simulated environments in which students with mild physical disabilities and learning disabilities can work.

The computer is a valuable tool in teaching written and spoken communication to students who are culturally and linguistically different. Graphics software allows the students to express themselves in ways reflective of their own culture. Other software creates a microworld in which a student responds and practices newly acquired language skills. A word processor might allow students to express themselves in their native language. Some software is becoming available in non-English-language versions, with the user allowed to toggle between English and a second language.

Boredom, slow pace of instruction, and lack of challenge may contribute to the talented and gifted child being at risk of dropping out of school. The computer can be used as a tool with which to test hypotheses, to analyze information and draw conclusions, to express oneself by drawing as well as by writing, and to communicate around the world. Talented and gifted children often have difficult social adjustments to make because of their superior intellectual abilities. The computer, used wisely as part of a cooperative learning strategy, can provide a positive social experience and can help in the development of interpersonal skills.

Students using computers are at a distinct advantage in that they use a tool that can extend their capabilities. Some schools are well equipped, with a high ratio of computers readily available, and others are not. Whites are about three times as likely to have computers at home as are African Americans and Hispanics; affluent students are nearly four times as likely as poor students. Students with access to a home computer having a word processor and other productivity software constitute an elite group with a distinct advantage that over two-thirds of the student population does not enjoy.

While there is fairly equal participation between boys and girls in computer application activities in the elementary and middle-level grades, as students move into high school boys overwhelmingly populate the computer science classes. Parents are more likely to buy computers for use by their sons than by their daughters and encourage boys to take computer science classes and attend computer camps. Teachers must actively seek out software without gender biases and continually guard against any subtle actions that would in any way diminish girls or discourage them from interacting with the computer in a meaningful way.

CHAPTER EXERCISES

1. Describe your personal use of any tool outside of the educational setting. Now describe how you might use the computer as a tool. Compare your two examples and demonstrate how a tool extends your human capability.

2. Do a bibliographic search in the library on the topic "Computer Access: In School and at Home." Select only articles written in the past four years. Using a word processor, write a report of at least two double-spaced pages on the issues. Cite references and include a bibliography. Your name followed on the next line by the course number and name must be in the top left corner of the first page. The title must be centered on a line, in a larger size than the body text, and in boldface.

3. Do a bibliographic search in the library on the topic "Computers and Gender Bias: Cause and Effect." Select only articles written in the past four years. Using a word processor, write a report of at least two double-spaced pages on the issues. Cite references and include a bibliography. Your name followed on the next line by the course number and name must be in the top left corner of the first page. The title must be centered on a line, in a larger size than the body text, and in boldface.

4. Examine vendor catalogs and locate three programs, in at least two different subject areas, that use a language in addition to English.

5. Locate available graphics software. Make three different 8 1/2-by-11-inch signs to be placed in the computer lab reminding students of copyright rules.

GLOSSARY

binary Consisting of two parts; limited to two conditions or states of being. Computer memory is designed to store binary digits symbolized by 0s and 1s in a code. The computer circuitry is designed to manipulate information in an on/off state.

bit The single digit of a binary number, either 0 or 1; derived from the words b*inary dig*it.

byte Usually a grouping of eight bits (by eight); the code representing one character of data.

CD-ROM Compact disk–read only memory. A 5-inch optical disk connected to a computer that reads or plays back text, graphics, sound, and movies.

chip A small piece of silicon housing an integrated circuit that may contain tens of thousands of transistors and other electronic components.

computer operator A technician trained in the operation of a large computer system who is interposed between the user and the computer.

data Vast amounts of stimuli than can be perceived in any given environment. We are constantly inundated with data in our daily lives, most of which we tend to ignore until we perceive a need.

digital Pertaining to a single state or condition. A digital circuit controls current in a binary on/off state.

DVD (Digital Versatile Disc) A digitally recorded optical disk medium with many times the storage capacity of CD-ROM and a faster transfer rate.

end user The individual who ultimately benefits from the computer application.

graphic user interface (GUI) The on-screen use of pictorial representations (icons) of objects. The user can move a screen pointer onto an icon and click a mouse button to issue a command to the computer.

hardware A term used to describe physical equipment (e.g., computer, monitor, printer).

information Data selected and organized to produce meaning.

information technology The process of creating, storing, organizing, accessing, and displaying information.

integrated circuit An electronic component made up of circuit elements constructed on a single piece of silicon.

laptop A portable, lightweight, battery-operated computer with an LCD screen that usually folds down onto the keyboard for ease of carrying.

MB The symbol for megabyte, equated with approximately 1 million.

megabyte One million bytes, used as a reference to memory capacity.

palmtop A lightweight, battery-operated computer considerably smaller than a laptop.

personal digital assistant (PDA) A very small battery-operated computer, usually with limited but very specific built-in functions.

software Computer program(s) preserved on a recording medium and usually distributed on floppy disks or CD-ROM.

transistor A small electronic device that controls current flow and does not require a vacuum to operate.

vacuum tube A sealed electronic device designed to regulate current flow.

REFERENCES & SUGGESTED READINGS

Allen, A. A., & Mountain, L. (1992, November). When inner city black children go online at home. *The Computing Teacher, 20*(3), 35–37.

Armstrong, K. (1995, October). Special software for special kids. *Technology & Learning, 16*(2), 56–61.

Berney, T., & Keyes, J. (1990). *Computer writing skills for limited English proficiency students*. Brooklyn, NY: Report to the New York City Board of Education.

Birman, B. F., Kirshstein, R. J., Levin, D. A., Matheson, N., & Stephens, M. (1997, January). *The effectiveness of using technology in K–12 education: A preliminary framework and review*. Washington, DC: American Institutes of Research.

Brown, J. M. (1997, March). Technology and ethics. *Learning & Leading with Technology, 24*(6), 38–41.

Collins, A. (1991, September). The role of computer technology. *Phi Delta Kappan,* 28–36.

Connecticut State Department of Education, Hartford (1991). *Learning resources and technology. A guide to program development*. ERIC Document Reproduction Service Number ED 338 223.

Cowart, B., & Schalock, D. (1994). *Concepts, practices, and research pertaining to Oregon's new design for schools*. Monmouth, OR: Teaching Research Division, Western Oregon University.

Culley, L. (1993). Gender equity and computing in secondary schools: Issues and strategies for teachers. In John Beynon & Hugh Mackay (Eds.), *Computers into classrooms: More questions than answers*. Bristol, PA: Farmer Press, 147–159.

Dyrud, M. (1996, November). *An exploration of gender bias in computer clip art*. Paper presented at the Association for Business Communication annual conference, Chicago, IL.

Friedrich, O. (1983, January 3). The computer moves in. *Time, 121*(1), 12–24.

Greene, S. (1988, September 26). Redwoods and hummingbirds. *Apple Viewpoints, 2,* 1–3.

Kay, A. (1991). Computers, networks, and education. *Scientific American, 262*(3), 138–148.

Kirk, D. (1992, April). Gender issues in information technology as found in schools: Authentic/synthetic/fantastic. *Educational Technology, 32*(4), 28–35.

Kober, N. (1991). What we know about mathematics teaching and learning. Washington, D.C.: Council for Educational Development and Research.

Koch, M. (1994, November). Opening up technology to both genders. *Educational Digest, 60*(3), 18–22.

Malouf, D. B. (1991, Spring). Integrating computer software into effective instruction. *Teaching Exceptional Children,* 54–55.

Manning, J. (1996, December 17). Intel machine zips to speed record. *The Oregonian,* MNW 1.

Massoud, S. L. (1991, July). Computer attitudes and computer knowledge of adult students. *Journal of Educational Computing Research, 7*(3), 269–291.

McLuhan, M. (1967). *The medium is the message*. New York: Bantam Books.

Mendrinos, R. (1994). *Building information literacy using high technology: A guide for schools and libraries*. Englewood, CO: Libraries Unlimited, Inc., 190.

Nichols, L. M. (1992, August). Influence of student computer-ownership and in-home use on achievement in an elementary school computer programming curriculum. *Journal of Educational Computing Research, 8*(4), 407–421.

Noble, D. E. (1992). *A world without women: The Christian culture of modern science*. New York: Knopf.

Norris, C. A. (1994, February). Computing and the classroom: Teaching the at-risk student. *The Computing Teacher, 21*(5), 12–14.

Parette, H. P., Hourcade, J., & VanBiervliet, A. (1993, Spring). Selection of appropriate technology for children with disabilities. *Teaching Exceptional Children*, 18–22.

Piller, C. (1992, September). Separate realities. *Macworld, 9*(9), 218–231.

Poirot, J. L., & Canales, J. (1993–94, December/January). Technology and the at-risk—An overview. *The Computing Teacher, 21*(4), 25–26, 55.

Speziale, M. J., & LaFrance, L. M. (1992, November). Multimedia and students with learning disabilities: The road to success. *The Computing Teacher, 20*(3), 31–34.

Thornburg, D. (1991). *Education, technology, and paradigms of change for the 21st century*. San Carlos, CA: Starsong Publications.

Chapter 2

Instruction, Learning, and Problem Solving

ADVANCE ORGANIZER

1. What are the basic tenets of behaviorism?

2. What are the basic tenets of constructivism?

3. How can the computer support each perspective?

4. What is problem solving?

5. How is the computer broadly defined as a productivity tool?

6. How is information acquired?

7. What is the relationship between concrete and abstract experiences?

8. How does motivation relate to instruction and learning?

9. How can the presentation of the message be enhanced in computer software?

This chapter will establish the groundwork for looking at the computer's role in instruction and will examine its role in student learning. Recognizing that there are several theories of instruction, that classroom practice is often based on one or more of these theories in combination, and that this text does not purport to be an instructional theory textbook, we will review behaviorist and constructivist theories of instruction and learning covered in greater depth in courses dealing with pedagogy. The intent here is to demonstrate that the computer can be a practical tool used in concert with teaching strategies that have a solid theoretical basis.

Acknowledging that there is a growing interest in constructivist theories of learning, this chapter will present an overview of a moderate constructivist perspective so that the use of the computer as a productivity tool can be better understood. The thoughtful application of the computer can make students more productive in the construction of their knowledge through problem solving.

Many of the problems faced by educators could be solved with the assistance of a computer. If the computer is to be an effective tool in increasing productivity, fundamental questions to be answered by the teacher are "When do I use a computer?" "Will using a computer save time?" "Will it allow me to perform tasks that might otherwise be beyond my skills?" and "Can I get better, more complete, and more accurate information by using a computer or will it just complicate my life?"

Using computers in education depends upon the effective use of software that can increase productivity. As computer users, we need to be thoroughly familiar with the process of problem solving. Most of us will never choose to become computer programmers, but as educators we need to be good users of computer programs, and we need to acquire skill to develop problem-solving specifications.

Looking beyond our own needs as educators, problem-solving proficiency is an essential skill that we must help our students develop. The constructivist point of view holds that students interact with the real-life experiences that surround them and construct mental structures that provide an understanding of their environment. If students are to build these mental structures, they must refine skills needed to solve problems they will encounter, whether they are working individually or in co-operative learning groups.

Not all people's thinking patterns and learning styles are alike, although many different cognitive processes and intelligences are valid and should be valued. This chapter will give an overview of perception, communication, and motivation in order to emphasize the importance of analyzing our student population and matching instructional materials to student needs.

PERSPECTIVES ON TEACHING AND LEARNING

Every learning environment has an implied method of information presentation. Learning activities are based on a belief of how students best learn. Of the many philosophical doctrines, two stand out rather clearly as examples related to software development, selection, and use.

Behaviorists view the teacher as the manipulator of the environment that is experienced by the learner. B. F. Skinner, well known for his work in behavior modification through operant conditioning, was a proponent of programmed instruction. Skinnerian-style lessons use carefully planned steps of stimulus-response pairing and reinforcement to reach a goal. The lessons and their accompanying drills are administered in small, incremental steps to minimize the likelihood of incorrect responses. The techniques used reflect a belief that, by tightly structuring the environment, the behavior of the organism (the student) can be shaped to achieve desired changes (learning). Linear programmed instruction is an example of this concept of education, where the accumulation of knowledge is preparing the student for predicted future needs. Traditional classroom instruction has included strong components of this behaviorist theory, which has been referred to at times as **objectivist**. The teacher, with the prescribed textbook, is the source of information. Behavioral objectives are identified, lessons are planned, instruction is delivered, guided practice is provided, retention and transfer of learning activities are encouraged, and testing the information taught is the standard means of assessment.

In direct contrast to the behaviorist viewpoint is the perspective espoused by constructivists, who view education as inseparable from ordinary life. Through developmental exploration and play, students assume control of educational activities by making choices related to individual interests. The students discover rules and concepts during the course of interactions in an environment that encourages the use of problem-solving strategies, which in turn are developed while learning how to think. The teacher learns along with the students and becomes a guide, a facilitator, and a supportive partner in this educational process. Education is considered to be a guided tour of preparatory experiences in which students practice making decisions by simulating real-world situations. The teacher becomes the facilitator of education by selecting the experiences that offer the appropriate practice to the students. In this way students construct their own knowledge and gain skills that will be needed in a future environment, which may be quite different from the present one. If reduced to a single overriding distinction, it could be said that constructivism encourages the learner to pose a problem and then solve it, while behaviorism sees the role of the teacher or other external source to pose the problem to be solved. It should, therefore, be noted that the teaching of problem-solving strategies is important to both perspectives.

Software may reflect one or both of these approaches and may make assumptions about the teaching/learning style that will be used in the classroom. Different techniques are selected to achieve educational goals in relation to different philosophical perspectives. Teachers must learn to identify the instructional approaches embodied in particular software, if they are to effectively harness the power of the computer in their classrooms.

THE BEHAVIORIST PERSPECTIVE ON LEARNING

Robert Gagné (Gagné, Briggs, & Wager, 1992, pp. 54–66) lists types of intellectual skills in a **linear** scheme, ranging from simple discriminations to the complex problem-solving process. This approach is predicated on the belief that the acquisition of knowledge at any stage depends on what has been learned at an earlier one. Thus, a learner must master the lower-level abilities before tackling the higher orders.

Elements of a Good Lesson

A great deal of research has gone into identifying the components of a good learning situation. Gagné views learning theory as technology—that is, there is a set of rules that can be followed in the design of instructional events. His point of view draws on many theories of outstanding psychologists and resulted in the formulation of the following instructional events as elements of a good lesson (Gagné, Briggs, & Wager, 1992, p. 190):

1. Gaining attention
   Stimulation to gain attention to ensure the reception of stimuli
2. Informing learner of the objective
   Informing learners of the learning objective to establish appropriate expectancies
3. Stimulating recall of prerequisite learning
   Reminding learners of previously learned content for retrieval from long-term memory
4. Presenting the stimulus material
   Clear and distinctive presentation of material to ensure selective perception
5. Providing learning guidance
   Guidance of learning by suitable semantic encoding

6. Eliciting the performance
Eliciting performance involving response generation
7. Providing feedback about performance correctness
Informing students about correctness of responses
8. Assessing the performance
Following the opportunity for additional responses, inform the learner of mastery and give further directions
9. Enhancing retention and transfer
Arranging variety of practice to aid future retrieval and transfer of learning*

Wedman (1986) found it quite revealing to examine the elements of a good lesson related to the instructional functions provided by CAI software. By describing common ways in which software provides each of the instructional events, he offers a method of software analysis of a program's strengths and weaknesses relative to the elements in a good lesson as described by Gagné, Briggs, and Wager. Wedman then examines the teacher's role in complementing the instruction provided by the software to provide a complete instructional unit. The chart presented in Figure 2–1 displays the CAI software and teacher techniques related to each instructional event.

A diagram of these events as they might occur in a computerized lesson using the program *Odell Down Under* (The Learning Company, Inc.) is provided in Figure 2–2. This example, set in Australia's Great Barrier Reef, is a worthy successor to the award-winning *Odell Lake* and uses all the instructional events described by Gagné, Briggs, and Wager. Figure 2–3 is an example of the high-quality graphics used to gain attention. Animation is also present on the computer screen. Some software, of course, uses only some of the instructional events. In such cases, the teacher must provide the missing events for the lesson.

Human Factors

A great deal of attention has been given to individual responses to interaction with computers. These effects are critical to the effectiveness of a program because they influence the learning events of a good lesson. Early writings by Gagné and Briggs (1974, p. 11) recognized six human factors affecting the learning event. These factors, identified as external stimulus factors and internal cognitive factors, are listed in Figure 2–4. The three external factors are contiguity (time relationship between stimulus and response), repetition (frequency and rate of exposure to a stimulus), and reinforcement (follow-up to the reception of a stimulus). The three internal cognitive factors are factual information (from memory or external sources), intellectual skills (ability to manipulate information), cognitive strategies (ability to process or interpret into meaningful information). Added to these are the internal affective factors of inhibition (reluctance to react to a stimulus) and anxiety (a tension often stemming from a lack of confidence).

---

*Excerpts from *Principles of Instructional Design,* Fourth Edition by Robert M. Gagne, Leslie J. Briggs, and Walter W. Wager, copyright© 1992 by Holt, Rinehart and Winston, reprinted by permission of the publisher.

Events of Instruction	CAI Techniques	Teacher Techniques
1. Gaining attention	Graphics Sound Games	Demonstrate relevance of content. Present high-involvement problems. Use related, highly attractive media. Assign groups to use software.
2. Informing learner of objectives	Pretest Textual statement of objectives Graphic illustration of objectives Brief interactive demonstration	Pretest Tell the learner what is expected. Demonstrate use of the content.
3. Stimulating recall of prerequisites	Pretest for prerequisites Textual review of prerequisites Graphic display of prerequisites	Test prerequisite content. Review prerequisite content and vocabulary.
4. Presenting stimuli	Textual display of new content Graphic display of new content Learner control over presentation sequence and display rate Reference to non-CAI material	Use other media to present new content.
5. Providing guidance	Attention-focusing devices (e.g., animation, sound, pointers) Help screens Examples and illustrations	Organize peer tutoring. Cross-reference difficult content to examples and remediation in other materials.
6. Eliciting performance	Questions on new content Applications of new content to solve problems or control situation (e.g., flight simulator)	Ask questions. Create performance tasks to let the learner apply the new content (e.g., lab experiment).
7. Providing feedback	Display score and/or correct answer Help screens for incorrect answers Additional information or examples	Provide answer keys. Provide reference materials coordinated with correct answers. Provide outcome guides coordinated with performance tasks (e.g., lab experiment check sheet).
8. Assessing performance	Test questions Limited response time (for memory-level questions) Record keeping	Give paper-and-pencil tests. Conduct performance tests. Use computers for context rich testing.
9. Enhancing retention and transfer	Repeating content not mastered Applying new content to a different but related situation	Provide alternative instructional materials for content not mastered. Create situations (not involving a computer) to let students apply new content.

Figure 2–1

CAI and teacher techniques related to events of instruction (Wedman, 1986. Courtesy of *The Computing Teacher*)

Gaining Attention
A reef is shown, with fish swimming around and music playing.

Stating the Objective
The student is informed that the object is to discover the relationship between fish, which to eat, which to avoid, and which will clean off parasites.

Stimulating Recall of Prerequisite Learnings
The student is reminded to use all of the information presented in the picture and to make choices. The student can interrupt the program at any time to review information about the various reef dwellers.

Presenting the Stimulus Material
When the student has chosen a fish and has read the given information, the computer generates a picture of the reef, with the chosen fish shown in some situations.

Eliciting the Performance
The student is asked to control the fish's behavior by moving the mouse, clicking when appropriate, or pressing the spacebar.

Assessing the Performance
The computer indicates whether the chosen behavior was correct, incorrect, or indifferent.

Providing Feedback About the Performance
The action in the given reef situation is carried out, demonstrating the behavior chosen by the student.

Enhancing Retention and Transfer
Another situation is presented to the student based on past performance.

Figure 2–2

Elements of a good science lesson demonstrated in Odell Down Under, *a simulation of a predator/prey model*

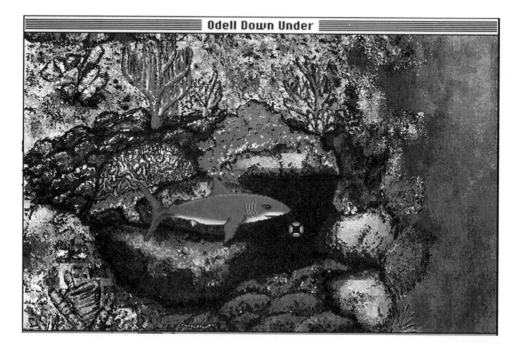

Figure 2–3

A screen from Odell Down Under (Courtesy of TLC Properties Inc., a subsidiary of The Learning Company, Inc.)

External Stimulus Factors

- Contiguity
- Repetition
- Reinforcement

Internal Cognitive Factors

- Factual information
- Intellectual skills
- Cognitive strategies

Internal Affective Factors

- Inhibition
- Anxiety

Figure 2–4

Eight human factors affecting the learning event

These factors relate to a theory of how information is stored in and retrieved from short-term and long-term memory. Gagné and Briggs believe that information that is sensed is held in the auditory, visual, or tactile register for only a second before it is disregarded or sent to short-term memory. There it is encoded for about one-half minute before storage in long-term memory. Because of the short periods involved, a *stimulus* must be limited to one idea, and there must be enough time to process and store the information without interference or overload. Meaningful repetition is believed to contribute to control of the processes and, in turn, to learning. The effectiveness of a lesson depends on the internal responses to a stimulus, the senses used, and the ease of use to minimize distractions during computer-assisted learning.

THE CONSTRUCTIVIST PERSPECTIVE ON LEARNING

Cognitive psychologists as early as Whitehead (1929) have insisted that learning is an active and highly individualized process. They clearly point out that learners must actively construct new knowledge based on their own individual experiences and understandings. This constructivist model of learning is based on the concept that knowledge is produced by the individual learner rather than processed from information received from an external source. The student becomes the producer rather than the consumer of information. The teacher becomes the guide and facilitator of learning rather than the director of instruction. Goals are still set, but the learner is given significant freedom in how to attain them. Assessment is still performed, but benchmarks are established and the teacher employs authentic measures such as evaluating a product or examining a portfolio.

A foundation for some of the current constructivists' beliefs can be found in the work of Jean Piaget. He is best known for proposing four stages of development in a child's cognitive abilities: (1) from birth to about age two, the sensorimotor stage (when children begin to explore their environment and to differentiate themselves from the world around them); (2) from age two to about seven, the preoperational stage (when language and intuitive thought develop); (3) from age seven to about 12, the concrete operational stage (when classifying and ordering of items and inductive reasoning develop); and (4) from about age 12 on, the stage of formal operations (when more abstract and formal thought, control of variables, and proportionality can be managed). Piaget attributed these stages to a naturally occurring process of maturation and the appropriate exposure to experiences that encourage development.

The idea that children learn without being taught is central to this learning theory. Long before children enter school, they have mastered the complexities of language and speech enough to understand and communicate with those around them. They have gained a sense of intuitive body geometry that enables them to get around in space, and they have learned enough logic and rhetoric to convey their desires to parents and peers. Children learn all these things effectively without formal teachers and a curriculum, and without explicit external rewards or punishments. They learn by simply interacting with their environment, relating what is new to what they know from past experience.

For example, a very young child can build a cognitive structure or a concept of "dogness": dogs look, feel, sound, and smell a certain way. Whenever a dog is encountered, the child attempts to make sense of the experience by calling on a previously formed cognitive structure of "dog." Piaget calls this assimilation. But a new dog may be different from the one met before. As new elements are encountered (a curly tail instead of a straight one; long, shaggy hair instead of short hair; and so on), the cognitive structure for "dog" must be modified and enlarged to encompass the new information, a process Piaget called accommodation.

If we think of learners in Piagetian terms, as the active builders of their own cognitive structures, we should consider the kinds of experiences and material our culture provides for use in this building process and examine the potential contribution of the computer.

Figure 2–5 summarizes the predominant differences between the behaviorist and constructivist perspectives. They should be viewed as points on a continuum, not as absolutes. Though the trend in the United States is toward constructivism, most classrooms exhibit some characteristics of both.

PROBLEM SOLVING

Saunders (1992) illustrated the constructivist perspective with the model shown in Figure 2–6. He states: "Constructivism can be defined as that philosophical position which holds that any so-called reality is, in the most immediate and concrete sense, the mental construction of those who believe they have discovered and investigated it." In Figure 2–6, the conflict between expectations (what we think will happen) and observations (measures of what actually happens) causes disequilibration. The problem is resolved through accommodation, or learning—the process of reconciling new information with previously held ideas and beliefs. Explained this way, it becomes clear that constructivism is a philosophy in which problem solving is a central element.

Behaviorist	Constructivist
Teacher-centered	Learner-centered
Teacher as expert	Teacher as member of learning community
Teacher as dispenser of information	Teacher as coach, mentor, and facilitator
Learning as a solitary activity	Learning as a social, collaborative endeavor
Assessment primarily through testing	Assessment interwoven with teaching
Emphasis on "covering" the material	Emphasis on discovering and constructing knowledge
Emphasis on short-term memorization	Emphasis on application and understanding
Strict adherence to fixed curriculum	Pursuit of student questions highly valued

Figure 2-5

Comparison of behaviorist and constructivist perspectives.

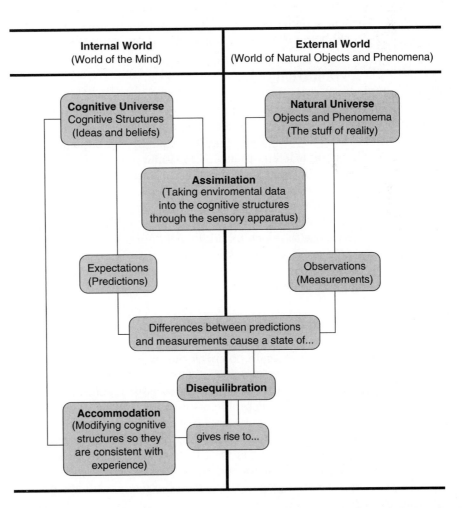

Figure 2–6

A constructivist learning model (Reprinted with permission from School Science and Mathematics.)

From a constructivist perspective, learners must be provided with a rich environment of sensory experiences, to which they will respond in a problem-solving fashion in order to build understandings. The computer, through its use of text, sound, graphics, animation, and multimedia, is ideally suited to present such a rich environment.

The shifting paradigms described in the first chapter describe a transition from a centralized environment to a personalized one, with the user in command of the computer, and to an interpersonal one, where users interact with one another. There is a distinct move from the computer operator to the end user interacting directly with the computer and to a networked community of users interconnected electronically. Finally, we have moved away from a fascination with huge amounts of stored data to a concern for the value of the information and the development of knowledge. Every one of these paradigm shifts parallels the shift in philosophical foundations of education toward a more constructivist approach emphasizing problem solving.

Compared to behaviorist approaches to instruction, in which "covering the material" is emphasized, constructivist approaches to instruction focus on students "discovering the material." When students are actively engaged with other students and teachers in the process of learning through the completion of authentic tasks, they need both problem-solving tools and problem-solving skills to assist them.

A Productivity Tool

A tool is a medium for completing some work and extending the user's ability. We either create a tool or select from a variety of existing ones and apply it to the task at hand to solve a problem (for example, we use a screwdriver to fasten something, a sewing machine to assemble clothing, an automobile to transport us swiftly and comfortably, and a word processor to record our thoughts in a quick, flexible manner). Accepting this definition of a tool allows us to see its intervention between the user and the information to be created, received, stored, manipulated, or disseminated. The student who locates and downloads information from the Internet, uses a database to search for additional information, then uses a word processor to write a report and a graphics program to draw a map for inclusion in the report is using the computer as a tool to enhance efficiency and effectiveness in response to the problem or assignment.

Productivity and Problem Solving

It's time, once again, to check our own perceptions and to ask ourselves the question "What is *technology?*" Technicians carry screwdrivers around in their pockets and tinker with hardware. Technologists understand how to use that hardware and related software as problem-solving tools. The equipment, the computer, the VCR, the camcorder, the ubiquitous overhead projector, all are the "things" of technology. They are simply the visible, tangible artifacts of technology. To be most successful as a teacher, the artifacts of technology have to become almost transparent so we don't call attention to them but rather, as technologists, focus our efforts on the problems we are trying to solve, the objective we are attempting to reach.

The factory model compared *productivity* with efficiency, defined it as producing a tangible *product,* and was often linked to the notion of accomplishing menial tasks. A more productive worker built a greater number of widgets than a less productive one. The constructivist perspective demands a broader understanding. All too often, the term *productivity tool* has been used with the limited factory model vision. In schools the term has been easily understood and readily applied to word processors, graphics, spreadsheets, and database use. A deeper understanding would apply it to learning with computers and would also compare productivity with effectiveness. Rather than limiting our view to developing a product often associated with the performance of clerical or manual tasks, we have begun to see productivity as using tools (such as computers) to maximize or extend our innate capabilities in order to surmount challenges and solve problems. Productive learners might learn more but they also learn better. Productive writers and artists are not only prolific but have a greater impact on their readers, viewers, and listeners.

Is the computer a productivity tool for the secretary? Absolutely! It enhances the performance of repetitive clerical tasks. But it is also a productivity tool for the administrator to make projections, find information, and communicate effectively. It is a productivity tool for the teacher who selects appropriate hardware or software and adapts it to the instructional, management, or research task at hand. A computer is a productivity tool whenever it is used to assist individuals in solving problems. Students are increasing their productivity by developing sophisticated skills in the creation, access, manipulation, and transmission of information in order to respond to an assignment or solve a problem. We are witnessing the evolution of some time-tested teaching and learning strategies and philosophies as they change to account for new tools and innovations. The computer is a tool that can give students a wider variety of educational experiences than has ever been offered before.

INSTRUCTION AND LEARNING

Just as problem-solving strategies vary among individuals, so do types of intelligence, perception, and motivation. Good teachers always try to individualize their instruction, even when dealing with 30 students in a classroom. They attempt to know each student as an individual, to recognize strengths and weaknesses, and to identify, accommodate, and respect different types of intelligence and different learning styles. Good teachers also understand the role of perception and motivation in learning, and how computer software can increase both faculties. Understanding students as individuals allows teachers to make intelligent and informed decisions when choosing software for their classrooms.

Types of Intelligence

Howard Gardner describes eight intelligences: linguistic, logical-mathematical, spatial, musical, bodily-kinesthetic, interpersonal, intrapersonal, and naturalist (Pennar, 1996). Your students may exhibit one type of intelligence in particular or may have several

Intelligence	Type of Software
Linguistic	Word processors, word games, software with speech output, crossword puzzle generators, books on CD-ROM
Logical-mathematical	Spreadsheets, databases, problem-solving software, computer programming, log, strategy game formats
Spatial	Graphic production; 3-D modeling; mazes and puzzles; logo; maps, charts, and diagrams; multimedia
Musical	Song creation; music concepts/skills; story and song combinations; recording music, singing, or rhymes with a microphone
Bodily-kinesthetic	Alternative input devices, keyboarding/word processing, science and math with manipulatives and probes, programs in which the user can move objects on the screen
Interpersonal	Telecommunications, interactions with characters in simulations and adventures, programs about social issues, group participation/decision-making programs, two or more player games
Intrapersonal	Tutorial, self-paced games played against the computer, self-awareness/self-improvement building programs
Naturalist	Spreadsheets, databases, image capture software

Figure 2–7

Multiple intelligences and software types. (Adapted with permission from "Hot Tips for Inclusion with Technology" by K. Eichleay and C. Kilroy, December/January, 1993-94, The Computing Teacher, *21(4), pp. 38–40. Modified by the author in 1998.*

strengths. Although many people tend to think of intelligence more narrowly, it is important to recognize and support individual aptitudes by ensuring that all students have resources to help cultivate their talents and intelligences. Reflecting on these intelligences and seeking to create a computer environment supportive of all students, Eichleay and Kilroy (1993-94) suggest types of software appropriate to each intelligence.

Not all students will react alike to the same piece of software. A study of Figure 2–7, adapted from Eichleay and Kilroy (1993-94, p. 39), and modified by this author in 1997, will suggest ways in which a variety of software can be applied to meet the needs of different learners.

Perception

What we know about the world, we have experienced through our senses. Free of any physical impairments, we normally gain information through all five senses. Infants are intrigued by the wondrous variety of sounds and sights and smells to which they are exposed, and they seek to explore every sensory stimulus. As we mature, our visual and aural senses assume an overwhelming importance in the acquisition of knowledge. Indeed, a great deal of the information we possess as adults has been acquired through the sense of sight.

Sensory stimuli are accepted by the learner and given meaning based primarily on past experiences. Thus, sensory experiences result in perceptions. Since perceptions, in turn, are organized into understandings, the quality of the visual and aural stimuli embodied in software assumes great importance.

As an infant, the concept of "fiveness" might be acquired by handling five items (units), gradually seeing them represented by five fingers (digits), and then processing the meaning as the numeral 5 (symbol). Once a child has been exposed to a variety of **concrete** experiences, pictorial and then verbal experiences are an effective and much more efficient way of building understandings. These more **abstract** expressions of ideas must have a concrete basis. Examining well-designed software, we find that computer graphics, visuals, and certainly multimedia serve as more concrete referents to meaning than does the written word. Since visuals resemble the items they represent, they offer the viewer concrete clues to meaning. To enhance the perception of visual information in software, research by Guba et al. (1964) and others has shown that, in good graphic design, distracting elements must be kept to a minimum.

Motivation

Motivation is an essential element in instruction and learning. The continuous attention focused on well-designed software is due in large measure to the continuity of thought promoted when text is coupled with graphics and at times with sound. Motivation is further heightened when the learner is asked to respond to the program overtly. Even a response as simple as clicking a mouse button or pressing a key may contribute to the learner's involvement in the act of learning, hence becoming a significant factor when software presents learning sequences of longer duration, when the learner must control the rate of presentation.

One of the challenges we face as teachers is to understand learners and to elicit maximum responses from them. As Jack Frymier (1968), a former director of the Institute for Motivational Research at Ohio State University, has pointed out:

> Motivation to learn in school is in part a function of what resides within the individual and in part a function of the external world he encounters. Some positively motivated youngsters seem to draw most heavily upon forces located within themselves to enhance their learning. They believe in learning and knowledge, for example, and the new and novel excite them. Ambiguity and uncertainty intrigue them. Other students, equally well motivated, seem to be most positively affected by the quality and quantity of stimuli which they experience in school. Exciting lectures, fascinating movies, vivid illustrations, and intense discussions are likely to spark these students' efforts.

If we understand that students may be motivated differently, we accept that some will be enthusiastic consumers of information. They are the avid readers, the television watchers, the students who sit at the computer and patiently construct elaborate searches of electronic encyclopedias, who use the computer to search remote databases and browse through on-line news services. They are often the students who don't like to call attention to themselves. They may capture stunning images and create marvelous designs on the computer but are reluctant to show them to others, especially to large groups. Other students will be producers of information. They are the students who engage in music and drama performances, who write lengthy reports on the word processor, who construct elaborate multimedia products and love to stand at the overhead display panel in the front of the room and project their work for the whole class to view.

Communication and Communication Models

The opening quote of Chapter 1 is attributed to Marshall McLuhan, a professor of English and a popular philosopher of the 1950s and 1960s. He devoted many years to the exploration of how a chosen medium affects the **message,** or structured content, being communicated. The media he studied most closely were the mass media of radio, television, newspapers, and magazines. We have defined *media* as tools between the user and information to be created, received, stored, manipulated, or disseminated. Tools are what McLuhan was referring to when he said that media are extensions of human capability. When we consider the computer as a multifaceted tool, we accept the fact that most of the communication occurs through the software. To select software that will provide appropriate vicarious experiences, we must understand the process of communication.

Communication is often defined as the transmission or sharing of ideas based on common understandings in one of three major modes: oral, visual, or written. Direct, face-to-face communication usually is oral. The visual mode often spans greater distances. This is also true of the written mode, the most abstract of the three. It is often suggested that communication implies an interaction, give-and-take, and feedback.

Since a learner cannot experience everything on a direct, purposeful, firsthand basis, a great deal of knowledge is gained through vicarious experiences. Meaning resides in the individual, not in the message—the structure of contextual clues and stimuli designed to evoke a desired response. **Instructional communication** can be seen as the transmission of this structured information organized to produce learning. The source of such a transmission might be a person speaking or demonstrating a skill or procedure. The source might also be printed, projected, or electronic materials such as textbooks, films, videos, and computer software. The computer software might take the form of drill and practice, tutorial, simulation, or interactive multimedia software that combines text, graphics, sound, and animation and controls live-action video sequences.

We will examine three communication models in order to better understand the process of instructional communication and the role of computer software. The first model, Figure 2–8, was proposed by Claude Shannon and Warren Weaver (1949), two mathematicians employed by Bell Telephone Laboratories. This linear, technical model is quite appropriate for understanding telephone or radio communication. A popular song, for example, might be selected by a disc jockey (information source),

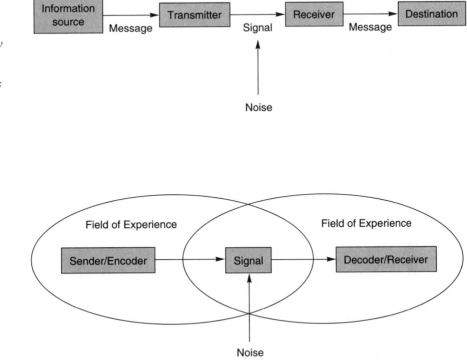

Figure 2–8

Shannon-Weaver model (From The Mathematical Theory of Communication. Copyright 1949 by the Board of Trustees of the University of Illinois. Used with permission of the University of Illinois Press.)

Figure 2–9

The Schramm revision of the Shannon-Weaver model

encoded by equipment (transmitter) into radio waves, received by a radio (receiver), and heard as music reaching your ear (destination). **Noise** might be static in the atmosphere or, as the authors defined it, anything that deteriorates the quality of the signal. It might even be visual distractions.

We might apply this linear model, well suited to examining the one-way transmittal of stored information, in the following manner. A message is stored as a file (information source) on a floppy disk, loaded into a computer (transmitter), displayed on a monitor screen (receiver), and examined by the user (destination). Noise that affects the message might be inadequate brightness and contrast levels on the monitor, restrictive screen size, glare on the monitor screen, or a flickering, unstable image. Noise affects the quality of the message being received. The user is placed in a passive mode.

Wilbur Schramm (1954), concerned with the instructional communication potential of educational television, adapted the Shannon-Weaver model to reflect the interpretation of meaningful symbols, as shown in Figure 2–9. For communication to take place, the fields of experience of the sender and of the receiver must overlap. The signal that is shared is subject to each party's perceptions. The sender encodes the message according to skills possessed, biases, cultural influences, attitudes, and so on. The receiver calls on like factors to decode (understand) the message.

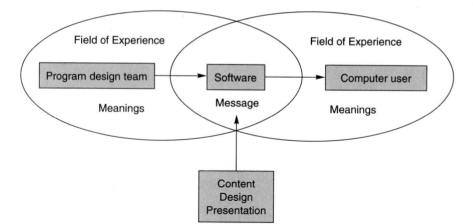

Program design team	Software	Computer user
Drawing on knowledge of content and on learning theory, the design team prepares the software for an intended audience.	The content of the message must be authentic and accurate. Its design must be pedagogically sound and its presentation must stimulate and tie to the learner's "reality."	Drawing on a concrete base of experience, the computer user extracts meaning transmitted by the software.

Figure 2–10

A software-specific communication model

A further adaptation of this model, as suggested in Figure 2–10, examines the role of computer software in instructional communications. Since meanings cannot be transmitted, the model illustrates that the message designed under the influence of meanings, which reside in the sender (the program design team), must elicit accurate and appropriate meanings in the receiver (the computer user). In turn, the message being communicated is embodied in the software. Meanings that reside in the field of experience of the program design team have a direct influence on the coding of the message. The decoding (understanding) of the message depends on meanings that reside in the field of experience of the computer user. The software carries the message, serving as a channel or bridge between fields of experience. The more truly the software expresses meanings in each field, the better the communication. The quality of the software, as the vehicle carrying the message, depends on the content and its treatment, instructional design, and manner of presentation.

The message will be degraded or distorted if the user perceives the content as incorrect, biased, or incomplete. It will suffer if the sequencing is wrong, if it is too fragmented, or if too much information is presented to be absorbed by the user. The message will be lost if the presentation is boring. Distractions will enter as noise in the communication process if the predetermined pacing is wrong (too slow or too fast) for the user or if the presentation employs verbal or visual techniques that are foreign to the user.

FROM THEORY TO APPLICATION

Good practice should be based on an understanding of sound theory. As we study theories of learning, reflect on our experiences, and examine our own motivations—as well as those of our students—we should seek to develop a knowledge base and a skill level that will enhance our application of computers to the classroom. This knowledge and skill will guide us through many decisions related to curriculum, teaching and learning strategies with the computer, equipment purchases, and computer software selection.

Appropriateness of Software

Since the learning theory on which software design is based dictates the role of the computer, the role of the teacher, and the role of the student, recognizing these elements is an important first step toward making good use of the computer in the classroom. Instructional objectives will be met only if the software and the intent of the lesson are closely related.

To understand why the computer lesson must be consistent with the kinds of learning students have come to expect, consider the following example. Imagine that you have prepared a lesson plan calling for practice on the subtraction of whole numbers less than 100. Surveying a curriculum resource guide for software to use, you find a program that presents a subtraction algorithm. This software on subtraction is designed for discovery learning. That is, when a student misses the answer, the software branches back to work that should have been mastered earlier and presents a different problem. However, if your classroom method prior to this lesson has been directive, replete with examples, some students would be frustrated by the computer lesson because it fails to give them the information they expect. Clearly, in this case, your students would be better served by software built around a more linear approach.

Effectiveness of Software

In assessing the effectiveness of software, keep in mind that the internal responses to a stimulus correspond very closely with the events of a good lesson. The student is alerted or motivated, perhaps by curiosity, to interact with the program. The objective of the program sets an expectancy for performance that interests the student. The student must be able to retrieve prerequisite information that provides meaning to the activity. The stimulus of new information must be perceived selectively over time, or through repetition, for processing to memory. Feedback in the form of favorable reinforcement should bolster self-worth. The information should have relevance to the student's environment for generalization and transfer of learning to occur. If the progression of these responses is not smooth, the chain of events is interrupted and the lesson becomes less effective.

Multiple senses can be utilized to appeal to students' interest and gain their attention. As with other classroom activities, a variety of events is more effective than one or two continuously repeated actions. Variety can be achieved by offering, for example, interaction through the tactile response of typing on the keyboard, different sounds, bright colors, interesting graphics, and new topics to challenge reasoning. In addition, students should be able to perform at the appropriate level to avoid frustration or boredom.

When evaluating software, remember that the process of interacting with the computer must be simple, so students can concentrate on the content of the program. Elements that contribute to easy use are centralized around simple means of input and simple presentations of output. To simplify input, a simple mouse click, single-key commands, and single-key selection of activities from a menu of options limit typing errors and speed up program execution. Error-free programs (no bugs) and error-trapped designs (mistakes are correctable or not accepted at all) avoid the frustration of stalled or prematurely terminated lessons.

Clarity in eliciting responses from the student also avoids confusion when interpreting what or how to respond. Output can be simplified by, for example, limiting the field of perception by presenting simple, uncluttered displays one page at a time; double-spacing text for readability; grouping ideas for easy understanding; formatting the screen to focus on one point; and highlighting major points by effectively using color, animation, and sound. Most of these features are encountered frequently in films, slides, textbooks, and other instructional materials.

Based on an understanding of learning theories and an awareness of factors dealing with intelligence, perception, and motivation, it is possible to postulate the following guidelines for effective software:

- Software must stimulate a high degree of interest in the learner.
- Software must contribute to developmental learning and thereby increase its permanence.
- Software must be based in concrete experience to enhance understanding.
- Software must make optimum use of the visual and, where appropriate, the aural sensory channels to strengthen the reality of the experience.

SUMMARY

Behaviorism views the teacher as the manipulator of the environment that is experienced by the learner. The techniques used reflect a belief that, by tightly structuring the environment, the student's behavior can be shaped to achieve learning. Constructivism views education as inseparable from ordinary life. Learning is seen as an active and highly individualized process in which learners must construct new knowledge based on their own individual experiences and understandings. Knowledge is produced by the individual learner rather than processed from information received from an external source. To maximize the constructivist learning experience, students need problem-solving tools and problem-solving skills.

We have defined *tools* as extensions of human capability. Tools allow their operators to complete some work or solve a problem with greater efficiency or effectiveness. The computer is a powerful tool that extends the user's ability to create, receive, store, manipulate, or disseminate information.

Just as problem-solving strategies can vary among individuals, so do types of intelligence, perception, and motivation. Understanding students as individuals allows teachers to make sound and informed decisions when choosing software for their classrooms. A variety of software can be applied to meet the learning needs of individuals with different types of intelligences and learning styles.

Sensory experiences result in perceptions. Sensory stimuli are accepted by the learner and given meaning based primarily on past experiences. As perceptions are organized into understandings, it becomes evident that the quality of the concrete visual and aural stimuli embodied in the software assumes significant importance. The more abstract expressions of ideas must have a concrete basis. Examining well-designed software, we find that computer graphics, visuals, and certainly multimedia serve as concrete referents to meaning. Continuous attention focused on well-designed software is due in large measure to the continuity of thought promoted when text is coupled with graphics and at times with sound. Motivation is further heightened when the learner is asked to respond to the program overtly. Communication is enhanced when fields of experience overlap.

Based on an understanding of learning theories and an awareness of factors dealing with intelligence, perception, motivation, and communication, it is possible to postulate the following guidelines for effective software: (1) software must stimulate a high degree of interest in the learner; (2) software must contribute to developmental learning and thereby increase its permanence; (3) software must be based in concrete experience to enhance understanding; (4) software must make optimum use of the visual and, where appropriate, the aural sensory channels to strengthen the reality of the experience.

As we study theories of learning, reflect on our experiences, and examine our own motivations—as well as those of our students—we should seek to develop a knowledge base and a skill level that will enhance our application of computers to the classroom. This knowledge and skill will guide us through many decisions related to curriculum, teaching and learning strategies with the computer, equipment purchases, and computer software selection.

CHAPTER EXERCISES

1. Select one piece of software in a curriculum area that is of special interest to you and analyze it in light of Gagné's events of instruction as elements of a good lesson.
2. Analyze the same piece of software from the constructivist viewpoint as described in the section "The Constructivist Perspective on Learning."
3. What attributes of that piece of software enhance the concreteness of the learning experience for students?
4. What constitutes instructional communications? Describe an example that would be applicable to software use.
5. What are the design elements of software that can increase the student's motivation to learn?

GLOSSARY

abstract Symbolizing an object, event, or occurrence, which can be observed by the learner.

communication The transmission or sharing of ideas based on common understandings in one of three major modes: oral, visual, and written.

concrete Actual, direct, purposeful happenings involving the learner as a participant.

instructional communication The encoding, transmission, and decoding of structured information organized to produce learning.

linear Proceeding in a step-by-step, sequential manner.

message A structure of contextual clues and stimuli designed to evoke a desired response (meaning).

motivation The incitement of a desire that causes a learner to act and the continued fostering of that desire.

noise In the context of a communication model, any distraction or condition that disrupts the transmission or reception of a message.

perception A learner's acceptance of sensory stimuli, given meaning based primarily on past experiences.

REFERENCES & SUGGESTED READINGS

Astleitner, H., & Keller, J. (1995, Spring). A model for motivationally adaptive computer-assisted instruction. *Journal of Research on Computing in Education, 27*(3), 270–280.

Bagley, C., & Hunter, B. (1992, July). Restructuring constructivism and technology: Forging a new relationship. *Educational Technology, 32*(7) 22–27.

Eichleay, K., & Kilroy, C. (1993-94, December/January). Hot tips for inclusion with technology. *The Computing Teacher, 21*(4), 38–40.

Foriska, T. (1993, November). What every educator should know about learning. *Schools in the Middle, 3*(2), 39–44.

Frymier, J. R. (1968, February). Motivating students to learn. *National Education Association Journal,* 37–39.

Gagné, R. (1982, June). Developments in learning psychology: Implications for instructional design, and effects of computer technology on instructional design and development (interview). *Educational Technology,* 11–15.

Gagné, R., & Briggs, L. (1974). *Principles of instructional design.* New York: Holt, Rinehart and Winston.

Gagné, R., Briggs, L., & Wager, W. (1992). *Principles of instructional design.* Fort Worth, TX: Harcourt Brace Jovanovich.

Gardner, H. (1983). *Frames of mind: The theory of multiple intelligences.* New York: Basic Books.

Gardner, H. (1993). *Multiple intelligences: The theory in practice.* New York: Basic Books.

Granat, D. (1997, February). I'm smart, you're smart. *Washingtonian, 32*(5), 60–63, 94–95.

Griest, G. (1993, April). You say you want a revolution: Constructivism, technology, and language arts. *The Computing Teacher, 20*(7), 8–11.

Guba, E., Wolf, W., DeGroot, S., Kneneyer, M., VanAtta, R., & Light, L. (Winter 1964). Eye movements and TV-viewing in children. *AV Communications Review, 12,* 386–401.

Moursund, D. (1989, May). Teacher productivity tools. *The Computing Teacher, 16*(8), 5.

Pennar, K. (1996, September 16). How many smarts do you have? *Business Week,* 104–107.

Saunders, W. L. (1992, March). Constructivist perspective: Implications and teaching strategies for science. *School Science and Mathematics, 92*(3), 136–141.

Schramm, W. (1954). Procedures and effects of mass communication. In N. B. Henry (Ed.), *Mass media and education, fifty-third yearbook of the National Society for the Study of Education, part II.* Chicago: University of Chicago Press.

Shannon, C. E., & Weaver, W. (1949). *The mathematical theory of communication.* Champaign: University of Illinois Press, 7.

Wedman, J. F. (1986, November). Making software more useful. *The Computing Teacher, 13*(3) 11–14.

Whitehead, A. N. (1929). *The aims of education.* New York: Macmillan.

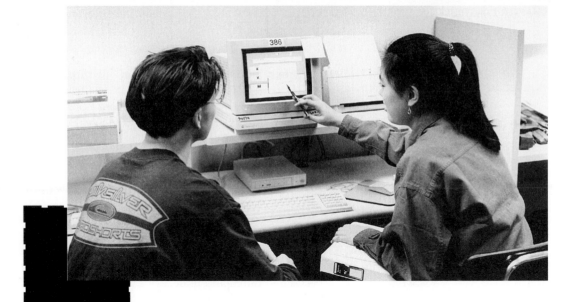

Chapter 3

Problem-Solving Strategies

1. How do problem-solving strategies relate to your learning style?

2. How might different strategies be implemented?

3. What is task analysis and how should a task be analyzed?

4. How is a flowchart constructed?

5. How can error trapping be designed into the solution to a problem?

6. How can a debugging procedure be designed into a computer-based solution to a problem?

Educators, as decision makers, must hone their problem-solving skills. Administrators are involved in the planning and implementation of curriculum decisions. They help select and provide continuing professional development opportunities for their staff. They take part in establishing rules and regulations that affect students' safety and welfare, as well as their education.

Teachers are constantly faced with the management of instructional units and the creation of teaching materials. They must analyze their student population and match student needs with instructional materials. They must then track the students through the learning material and assess their progress.

Students also must develop strategies for problem solving. Teachers have recognized that the information explosion of the past decade demands much more of students than does the memorization of facts. Information is power only to those who know how to interact successfully with it. This realization has highlighted the importance of developing problem-solving skills in students.

Problem-solving activities are part of everyday life. Many of us, however, do not approach this process systematically, and, as a result, solutions may often be hit or miss. This chapter will examine two approaches to the problem-solving process. We should be able to apply a systematic technique when confronted with the need to solve a problem, whether it be to prepare a lesson plan, develop a study guide, give a demonstration, design an assessment instrument, or effectively use application software that applies resources that provide drill and practice or simulated learning environments. The processes discussed in this chapter are appropriate for the analysis of most decisions that teachers and administrators make on a regular basis.

PROBLEM-SOLVING SKILLS

Not all people approach problem solving in the same fashion. There is no single best approach. Extensive work done by Anthony Gregorc in the development and application of his Style Delineator (Tompson & O'Brien, 1991) suggests that the human mind has mediation abilities—namely, perception and ordering—through which it receives and expresses information most efficiently and effectively. Perception can be measured along two continua, *abstract* to *concrete*, and ordering can be measured from *sequential* to *random*, yielding the four polar attributes of *abstract random, abstract sequential, concrete random*, and *concrete sequential*. In reality, most individuals possess all four traits to some extent, though most exhibit a predominant tendency toward one. Linear-thinking, sequential individuals feel comfortable with problem-solving strategies that follow a neat, orderly, step-by-step process. Divergent-thinking randoms feel stifled by those strategies and tend to use some that are less confining and more holistic. Both approaches are valid and should be valued.

In both cases, when examining problems for which the solution may be partly carried out on a computer, we must first be sure that we truly understand the task and then determine what the computer and the software must do to address the solution. Only then can we select the appropriate program and apply it effectively.

A Nonlinear Approach to Problem Solving

The process of problem solving might be approached by an individual with a **random** learning style in a manner similar to the simple, three-part process illustrated in Figure 3–1. "Given" is the information in our possession. What do we know about the situation or job at hand? What are its component parts? What are the restrictions or limitations with which we must cope? "To Find" is the information we are seeking. What output do we need? What are the results we are trying to achieve? When will we know that we have achieved them? While it is the answer to the factual question, it may also be knowledge that needs to be constructed. Hence, we might want to substitute "To Develop" or "To Create" for the term "To Find." Finally, "Procedure" is the method we are going to use to reach our goal. How will we achieve results? What strategy should we develop? What tool should we use?

Apply the process just described to the following simple word problem: A boy takes home $6.00 an hour from a weekend job. How many hours must he work in order to be able to purchase a $350 bicycle?

Given: Take-home pay is $6.00 per hour.
              Cost of the bicycle is $350.
              (All other information presented is not relevant to solving the problem.)

To Find: Number of hours of work required to earn enough to purchase the bicycle.

Procedure: Divide the cost of the bicycle ($350) by the hourly take-home rate of $6.00 ($350 \div 6.00 = ?$).

Figure 3–1

*A random-style
individual's
approach to problem
solving*

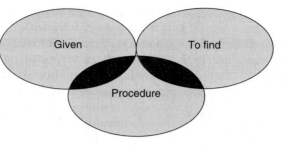

Applying the computer as a tool to solve this problem would entail first choosing the software application. It is evident that, since we must deal with numbers in this problem, a word processor or a graphics program would be inappropriate. Since we are not recording numerous facts that we would then manipulate, we wouldn't choose a database manager. We know, however, that spreadsheets are designed to manipulate numbers and to make comparisons. We enter the known data into the spreadsheet and seek to determine the number of hours needed. Examining that figure, we invoke the forecasting power of the spreadsheet and contemplate, "If I were to purchase a more expensive bike, how long would I have to work to pay for it? What if I were to find a better paying job?" Our problem-solving strategy is to determine what we are seeking, how to proceed to find it, and then choosing the most appropriate computer application software to solve the problem accurately, quickly, and easily.

Consider, as an example, you assign your students to write an article on a particular topic. How would you help them to understand the tasks related to writing a successful article? You would probably ask them to consider what they know, what they believe, and what they feel about the topic. You would ask them to identify resources that would give them additional information. You would then discuss the style that their writing should take. By introducing them to the Given/To Find/Procedure problem-solving method, you could help them analyze the problem of writing a clear, concise, and convincing article along the following lines.

Given:	Background information on the topic
	Range of thoughts on the topic
	Viewpoint or bias on the subject matter
	Writing skills
To Find:	Clear, concise, and convincing article
Procedure:	Seek additional information needed.
	Choose a presentation format and style.
	Organize thoughts clearly.
	Prepare a draft copy.
	Revise draft until satisfied.

In this case, dealing with the dissemination of ideas primarily through written expression, the word processor and related modules is the obvious choice of computer software. It would facilitate the procedure previously outlined by allowing your students to create a draft document, to check the spelling, and to refine it through the use of a thesaurus. It permits your students the painless revision of the document until a clear, concise, and convincing article is achieved.

Consider another example: the creation of a computerized grade book to report student progress in a classroom. What is involved in this problem? What are the related tasks?

Given: Student names
            Student performance on a variety of measures
            Target audience of students and their parents
To Find: Complete, accurate report of student progress in a timely manner
Procedure: Select presentation format.
            Choose software that facilitates the selected presentation format.
            Organize relevant data clearly.
            Summarize performance measures appropriately.

This approach to problem solving allows divergent-thinking individuals room to determine their own pattern without having a hierarchical structure imposed on them. They can contemplate the information in their possession and examine it in light of what they understand to be the desired goals. They can then consider an alternative from several options. They can reject an alternative that at first seems appealing and go on to another one.

A Linear Approach to Problem Solving

A problem-solving strategy that might appeal more to a **sequential** learner is illustrated in Figure 3–2. It consists of two phases, the *analysis* phase and the *synthesis* phase. In the analysis phase, we develop a clear definition and understanding of the problem and of the component tasks that relate to the problem. In the synthesis phase, we plan our strategy and carry out the solution to the problem. Evaluation provides feedback that could modify decisions made in both the analysis and synthesis phases.

If the problem is for one of the students in your government class to give a speech on the Bill of Rights, the analysis phase would consist of defining the Bill of Rights within the context of the speech. That is, will the speech be a recitation and explanation of the 10 amendments or will it address historical and social issues? The analysis phase would also include assessing the knowledge level of the audience and de-

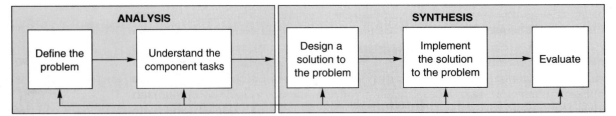

Figure 3–2
A sequential-style individual's approach to problem solving

termining what points must be made and how to make them. The synthesis phase would be the researching of information and the writing, polishing, and delivery of the speech. Audience reaction, or feedback, would be a measure of whether or not the goal was reached.

To more clearly understand the process, let's take a look at both phases in greater detail.

Analysis Phase. **Analysis** is defined as the separation of a whole into its component parts for the purpose of examination and interpretation. As shown in Figure 3–3, we need to clearly examine the problem, define what must be done, and clearly identify the specific tasks involved during the analysis phase.

Defining the Problem. The first step is to make sure that we understand the nature of the problem and exactly what is expected in its solution. One of the biggest mistakes made in solving problems is to make assumptions about what is supposed to happen and to neglect the verification of those assumptions. In defining the problem, we will establish a need. A need is the discrepancy between the present state and the desired state. It is an evaluation of the "what is" and the "what ought to be."

Imagine a person saying, "It's springtime! I guess I'll have to get the soil in my garden ready for planting." What does this statement signify to you? What need is expressed? Careful—don't jump to unwarranted conclusions! Do you know anything about the person's physical characteristics? Are there unstated limitations that might affect the conditions suggested in the statement? Often we formulate a solution without even understanding the problem. We have an answer before really understanding the question.

In the statement in the previous paragraph, the implication is that the soil is not in a proper state. The soil has probably become too compacted over the winter and must be loosened and its texture smoothed in order to facilitate planting. If that is indeed the case, we need to till the soil in some manner to change its present undesirable state to a desired state. To achieve this goal, we must analyze the task at hand. A reasonable knowledge of gardening would tell us that the person intends to grow plants and that some form of soil preparation is in order. We don't know much else. Is the garden a window flower box, a 2 ft. by 4 ft. flower bed on a city lot, or a half-acre vegetable garden? Without being able to determine this, we certainly could not select the proper tool to till the soil prior to planting. Try turning over a half-acre of soil using nothing but a hand trowel! How about tilling a 2 ft. by 4 ft. flower bed with a 7-hp power tiller! In order to select the proper tool, we must understand the task that it is being called upon to perform. We must assess the need and perform a task analysis.

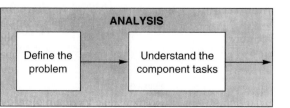

Figure 3–3

Analysis phase of problem solving

Understanding the Component Tasks. When first examined, many problems seem to be so complex that they defy solution. Should you find yourself in this situation, start by examining the output required and determine what is necessary to produce this result. A top-down outlining approach is one that proceeds from global to specific concerns and facilitates systematic analysis. In order to better understand a complex task, we should attempt to simplify the problem and to break it down into subtasks. When we have achieved what we believe to be the subtask's simplest form, we proceed to the synthesis phase and design a solution to address that simple task. We expand the solution to cope with the relationships between the subtasks until we are effectively addressing the complex problem.

Let's apply the outlining method shown in Figure 3–4 to better understand the statement that we encountered previously, "It's springtime! I guess I'll have to get the soil in my garden ready for planting." The following questions would be addressed: Is the soil ready to till? Has debris been removed? Is the soil dry enough so that it will turn over in a fine, smooth consistency? What size is the garden and are there any time considerations? What are the physical limitations of the gardener, if any? What tools are available? Considering answers to the previous questions, what is the proper tool to use? The component task analysis might resemble Figure 3–5.

In an effort to bring the problem-solving process into sharper focus and to understand component tasks, let's consider the task of recording student progress in a computerized grade book. The following questions must be answered before you can sit down at a computer and begin to solve the problem:

- How many different classes will be entered in the grade book?
- How many students will be in each class?
- How will student names be entered (last name first)?
- How many different activity types will be allowed for each class (e.g., quiz, test, project, portfolio, lab)?

Problem Statement

1. **Task 1**
   - Subtask 1
   - Subtask 2
2. **Task 2**
   - Subtask 1
   - Subtask 2
3. **Task 3**
   - Subtask 1
   - Subtask 2

Figure 3–4

Using an outline to understand component tasks

Till the Garden

1. **Prepare the soil.**
   - Remove any debris.
   - Test moisture content of the soil.
2. **Select the tool.**
   - Determine time constraints.
   - Evaluate physical limitations of gardener.
   - Assess area of garden.
   - Choose from available tools.

Figure 3–5

Analyzing component tasks

- How many different grades will be entered into each activity type?
- How are grades to be calculated (will they be weighted)?
- How are grades to be reported?

These tasks could certainly be further expanded, refined, and organized in an outline fashion, similar to the one suggested in Figure 3–4. As we attack the problem of preparing a computerized grade book, we must make sure that we understand what is required of the software before attempting to solve the problem. We may otherwise select the wrong software or spend a lot of time and effort producing something that will not meet expectations.

Synthesis Phase. **Synthesis** is constructive and is defined as combining elements to form a coherent whole. As indicated in Figure 3–6, the primary purpose of the synthesis phase of problem solving is to help ensure that solutions designed to address the identified tasks are carried out in an effective and efficient manner and that the results are evaluated. When solutions involve use of the computer, we must ascertain that the software chosen will meet the specified need and that it will be applied in such a way as to produce the necessary results. Any solution to a problem should be examined to see if the solution is practical. Almost every problem can be solved in more than one way. The user must decide on the best way for the given situation.

Designing a Solution to the Problem. Top-down design requires that, having identified our broad goal, we formulate the execution of each identified task and subtask that relates to the goal and prescribe the proper sequence of action. We develop each task fully and tie the tasks together in a fashion that effectively addresses the major goal.

The solution to the problem consists of a sequence of actions. There are certain tasks that must be done first, second, third, and so on. We develop a list and check out alternate sequences of actions. A common mistake made in solving problems is the tendency to neglect to check perceptions and to jump to conclusions without the proper examination of alternatives and the proper analysis of the preferred solution. Except for the simplest of problems, the solution will not be composed of a single task but of many interrelated ones. Our responsibility is to outline an acceptable sequence of actions and to establish an order of events that will lead to the solution of the stated problem.

After we have described the order of tasks to be accomplished, we have a good idea of what must be done, but we may not know how to carry out the tasks in order to achieve the desired result. We must now break down each task into individual steps. Two excellent outlining tools, the written outline and the flowchart, are at our disposal. Let's first examine the use of the written outline, a tool for the development of a sequence of executable steps that can be used to accomplish the tasks.

Figure 3–6

Synthesis phase of problem solving

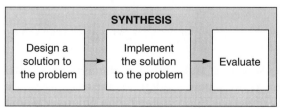

The Written Outline. In writing the proper outline to accomplish our task, we must carefully examine the alternatives. Most tasks that we will assign to the computer (e.g., entering course names, student names, and student grades and sorting lists) can be done in a number of ways. We need to select the best choice. In choosing a plan to solve a problem, we must state the plan in a sequence of steps. This implies a defined starting point, a prescribed means of moving to the next step in the sequence, and a defined ending point. The written outline, with its major headings and subheadings, provides us with a highly structured, linear organization tool.

The Flowchart. A **flowchart,** another often-used structured organization tool, is a visual representation of the problem-solving process. It is often referred to as a logic diagram and sometimes called an iconic outline. Being visual, it is constructed out of symbols of various shapes. Each symbol represents a unique function within the diagram. A starting point as well as the ending point, both represented by an oval symbol, must be identified for the process. The operation, denoted by the rectangular symbol, describes an action. At any point in the process where a decision must be made, the diamond is used to indicate that decision point. Arrows emanating from different points of the diamond allow for multiple paths reflecting the decision made. Figure 3–7 demonstrates the use of both outlining techniques. It offers a side-by-side comparison of their application to solve the problem of preparing soil for planting.

Once we have satisfactorily completed the outline and have written outlines for each task, we are ready to select the appropriate application software. Excellent software can be found to accomplish most communication and management tasks. After the software has been chosen, the data input routines, processing procedures, and output requirements can be developed according to our design.

Error Trapping. **Error trapping** is a process of designing safeguards into a solution. In tilling the garden, we might pause after every second pass to check the soil consistency. If certain values must be excluded when using the computer, then a technique must be employed to ensure that the unwanted data cannot be entered into the file. An example of common error trapping in drill and practice software is a program asking the student to press the Y key to indicate yes or the N key to indicate no in response to a question and not accepting any other key press but the Y or N. This prevents potential errors that could cause the program to execute incorrectly. An example of error trapping data entry in a student records database is to designate a range of values from 4 to 0 in a field designed to store a numerical equivalent of an *A* to *F* course grade. Limiting data entry to this range would catch typing errors such as a double key press that might attempt to enter a nonsensical value of thirty-three, for example.

Implementing the Solution to the Problem. Having analyzed the problem and then having designed an acceptable solution to the problem, we must now execute the tasks to solve it. We must till the garden, write the article, or enter grades in our computerized grade book and print reports.

Debugging the Solution. **Debugging** is the process of correcting logic and construction errors. As we till the garden, we make minor adjustments to the depth of the tilling tines or decide to pass over the same area a number of times. After writ-

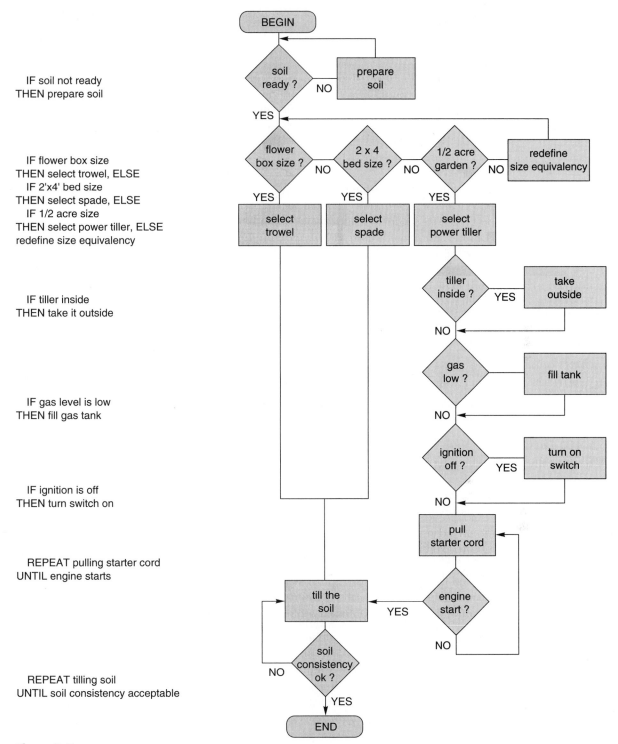

IF soil not ready
THEN prepare soil

IF flower box size
THEN select trowel, ELSE
   IF 2'x4' bed size
THEN select spade, ELSE
   IF 1/2 acre size
THEN select power tiller, ELSE
redefine size equivalency

IF tiller inside
THEN take it outside

IF gas level is low
THEN fill gas tank

IF ignition is off
THEN turn switch on

REPEAT pulling starter cord
UNTIL engine starts

REPEAT tilling soil
UNTIL soil consistency acceptable

Figure 3–7

The written outline (left-hand column) and the flowchart (right-hand column) represent outlining techniques

ing a paper, we proofread the document, noting all errors and awkward expressions. Then we revise and reprint the paper in a final, correct form. Sometimes, under the pressure of time, we may be satisfied with a less than perfect paper because we know that our reader can overlook a few minor errors and still decipher our meaning. Computers, on the other hand, cannot understand what is not there. The software cannot determine what you have written unless it is expressed in exactly the correct form.

An often-used debugging procedure is to give the program some test data that will produce known output over the entire range of use. Before entering our students' actual scores into our grade book, we might enter score values that we can compute easily and verify that the computer results are as expected. If the results are other than expected, debugging allows us to verify the correctness of our formula, the appropriateness of the functions we employed, and the logic of our design. This testing determines whether or not the program will always run correctly.

Evaluating the Results. In tilling the garden, we now examine the soil and determine if it has reached the consistency desired for planting. If the consistency is not yet acceptable, we till once more. In writing an article, this is the review or criticism phase. We might ask a friend, who has some knowledge of the subject covered in our article, to read the paper and to criticize it. Reacting to the criticism, we might decide to make additional modifications to the article. Once the computer program application has been debugged, we must verify that the program produces the desired output. We must determine if our logic was correct.

CURRICULUM APPLICATIONS OF PROBLEM SOLVING

Rather than attempt to address all of the problem-solving applications (should we call them opportunities?) across the entire curriculum, let's concentrate on information technology, since it is the focus of this book. The term ***information technology*** was defined in the first paragraph of Chapter 1 as the application of a tool to solve problems related to information to be created, received, stored, manipulated, or disseminated. As teachers in an information-rich society we must strive to encourage students to develop their information skills and to realize that information is power.

Figure 3–8 may be helpful as a lesson planning tool to develop problem-solving skills in your students. Identifying available resources describes the "Given," and specifying the performance indicators establishes the "To Find." The analysis phase is completed. Specifying the need to create, record, access, analyze, and synthesize information suggests "Procedure" to solve the problem and completes the synthesis phase of problem solving. The examination of the one or more component parts to the procedure will reveal the information skills that need to be learned by the students. The content dealt with becomes the vehicle for the acquisition of the problem-solving skills.

Unit of Study _____

Performance Indicators: _____
_____
_____

Resources Available: _____
_____
_____

Information Needs:

- Creating (writings, drawings, maps, charts, etc.)
_____
_____
_____

- Recording (facts, opinions, and impressions for future reference)
_____
_____
_____

- Accessing (from student- or teacher-created reports and data files, from bound references, from electronic encylopedias and atlases, etc.)
_____
_____
_____

- Analyzing (comparing and contrasting text, numerical, and picture data in order to form conclusions)
_____
_____
_____

- Synthesizing (reflecting on available data to create new information)
_____
_____
_____

Figure 3–8

Information techonology problem solving

SUMMARY

Individuals' thinking patterns and learning styles can be measured along the continuum sequential to random. In reality, most individuals possess traits that place them somewhere between the extremes, though they usually exhibit a predominant tendency toward one end of the scale or the other. Linear-thinking, sequential individuals feel comfortable with problem-solving strategies that follow a neat, orderly process. Divergent-thinking randoms feel stifled by those strategies and tend to use some that are less confining.

The analysis phase of problem solving supports developing a clear understanding of the problem and its component tasks. An outlining strategy is often helpful in reaching a better understanding of a problem's component tasks. The top-down outlining approach is one that proceeds from global to specific concerns and facilitates systematic analysis. In order to better understand a complex task, attempt to simplify the problem and to break it down into subtasks.

The synthesis phase is the planning of strategy and carrying out of the solution to the problem. A description of a structured sequence of clear and effective actions will help to produce a result. Evaluation provides feedback that could modify decisions made in both the analysis and synthesis phases.

Error trapping is a process of designing safeguards into a solution. It is often accomplished by controlling data entry in computer programs. Debugging is the process of correcting logic and construction errors. An often-used debugging procedure consists of giving the program some test data that will produce known output over the entire range of use.

Problem-solving skills related to information to be created, accessed, stored, manipulated, or disseminated may be taught following either the linear or nonlinear models suggested. The academic content becomes the vehicle for the acquisition of the problem-solving skills.

CHAPTER EXERCISES

1. Using the nonlinear model suggested in Figure 3–1, analyze the following case. Given a grade book with students' names and scores already entered, write a report showing students' progress.
2. Using the linear model suggested in Figure 3–2, perform the task analysis for the following case. Given a grade book with students' names and scores already entered, write a report showing students' progress.
3. Using the linear model suggested in Figure 3–2, perform the task synthesis for Exercise 2.
4. Explain why you feel more comfortable with the linear or with the nonlinear model.
5. Using either the linear or nonlinear model as a guide, design your own grade book.

6. Choose an activity that you are familiar with. Design a flowchart that represents the steps you follow to complete this activity. See if a partner can improve your chart and complete the activity.

7. Using either the linear or nonlinear model as a guide and a word processor as a tool, write a report on the computer's impact on the curriculum.

GLOSSARY

analysis The separation of a whole into its component parts for the purpose of examination and interpretation.

debugging The process of removing all logic and construction errors.

error trapping The provision for the treatment of incorrect data entry in such a way that it is either refused or ignored by the program.

flowchart A visual representation of the problem-solving process. It is often referred to as a logic diagram.

random An attribute that allows your mind to perceive and organize information in a nonlinear, holistic manner.

sequential An attribute that allows your mind to perceive and organize information in a linear, methodical, step-by-step manner.

synthesis Combining elements to form a coherent whole.

REFERENCES & SUGGESTED READINGS

Fagella, K. (1992, January). Solid gold problem solving. *Instructor, 101*(5), 35–37.

Gregorc, A. F. (1982). *An adult's guide to style.* Columbia, CT: Gregorc Associates.

Harris, J. (1994, April). *Opportunity in work clothes: Online problem solving project structures.* http://www.ed.uiuc.edu/Mining/April94-TCT.html

Ivers, K. (1996-97, December/January) Desktop adventures: Building problem-solving and computer skills. *Learning and Leading with Technology, 24*(4), 6–11.

Lamb, A., & Johnson, L. (1997, April). Wondering, wiggling, and weaving: A new model for project- and community-based learning on the web. *Learning and Leading with Technology, 24*(7), 6–13.

Tompson, M. J., & O'Brien, T. P. (1991, April). *Learning styles and achievement in postsecondary classrooms.* Paper presented at the annual conference of the American Educational Research Association, Chicago, IL.

Wheeler, P. J. (1991, April). *Style mismatch or learning disability: A case study.* Paper presented at the annual conference of the American Educational Research Association, Chicago, IL.

Zelazek, J., & Lamson, S. (1992, February). *Action research and the student teacher: A framework for problem solving and reflective thinking.* Paper presented at the annual meeting of the Association of Teacher Educators, Orlando, FL.

Chapter 4

Computer Applications in Education

ADVANCE ORGANIZER

1. What are some functional categories of computer applications in education?

2. How do the categories in school management relate to tasks you might commonly perform as a teacher, school library media specialist, or administrator?

3. How does the application of the computer to instruction and learning relate to teacher- or student-centered strategies?

4. What is a typical drill and practice lesson format and how can the computer be used in such a lesson?

5. What is a typical tutorial lesson format and how can the computer be used in such a lesson?

6. What is a typical simulation lesson format and how can the computer be used in such a lesson?

7. What are the roles of the student and the teacher in those three strategies?

8. What constitutes multimedia and what does it have to offer the learner?

9. What is computer literacy and what is its future?

10. What does computer-managed instruction offer you as a teacher?

11. How can the computer enhance your capability as a teacher to design teaching materials?

12. How can the computer be used as an information tool by the student?

13. How is the computer a research tool?

The title of this book is *The Computer as an Educational Tool: Productivity and Problem Solving*. As discussed in a previous chapter, too often the term *productivity* has been used with a limited vision. But the deeper understanding we seek demonstrates its applicability not only to word processors, graphics, spreadsheets, and database use, but to computer-assisted instruction and to computer-enhanced learning as well. If we believe that education is in the business of fostering student learning, computer applications that help students to learn more easily should be seen as productivity tools.

Changes are occurring in education, as well as in technology, with school restructuring suggesting a different way of looking at and measuring teacher effectiveness. Pupil learning gains are being included in a discussion of productivity. Tutorial instruction, drill and practice, and simulation, all time-tested teaching strategies, are being joined by multimedia instruction and learning. If computer software implements these strategies in an effective and efficient manner, should not this software be seen as a teacher productivity tool?

The intent of this chapter is to demonstrate that the computer can be a practical tool used by the student and by the teacher in concert with various teaching and learning strategies. Therefore, this chapter will present an overview and classification of computer applications in education so that we may gain an improved perspective of the breadth of applications and better understand their relationships. The classification proposed is hierarchical, with divisions made according to function. Classification schemes, no matter how well reasoned, are somewhat arbitrary. Some applications may not fit neatly in the pigeonholes of the structure but may cross boundaries and overlap, much as the subjects we teach our students cross boundaries and overlap. Thus, this chapter recognizes the importance of multidisciplinary curriculum integration.

COMPUTERS IN EDUCATION

Any classification is an attempt to group like items together in order to study them, noting their similarities and their differences. Early software classifications described **computer-assisted instruction (CAI)** and **computer-managed instruction (CMI).** They, by themselves, are no longer adequate. The software classification model proposed in Figure 4–1 emphasizes function. It places primary emphasis on how software is used.

In this model, the functional use of computers in education has been divided into three categories: *management, instruction and learning,* and *action research.* The management category includes school and classroom applications in budgeting, accounting, record keeping, printed and electronic communication, and information retrieval. The category of *instruction and learning* has been subdivided into *teacher-centered instruction* to take in software functions interacting directly with students under the teacher's control in the design, development, and delivery of instruction, as well as *student-centered learning,* recognizing functions related to the student involved in constructive activities that lead to learning. Categories are further subdivided to recognize common computer applications. The *action research* category includes applications in data storage and statistical analysis and must be recognized for the contribution it makes to teaching and learning by placing the teacher in the role of researcher, often examining some aspect of classroom practice.

Software classification permits the identification and comparisons of like programs. Organization schemes other than the one proposed in this chapter are, of course, possible and should be encouraged if they will facilitate the study of software and its application. The development and use of classification methods to identify software will facilitate the task of teachers, who ultimately decide which material to use in the classroom. It will promote a better understanding of software selection, evaluation, and collection management. Classification methods can also

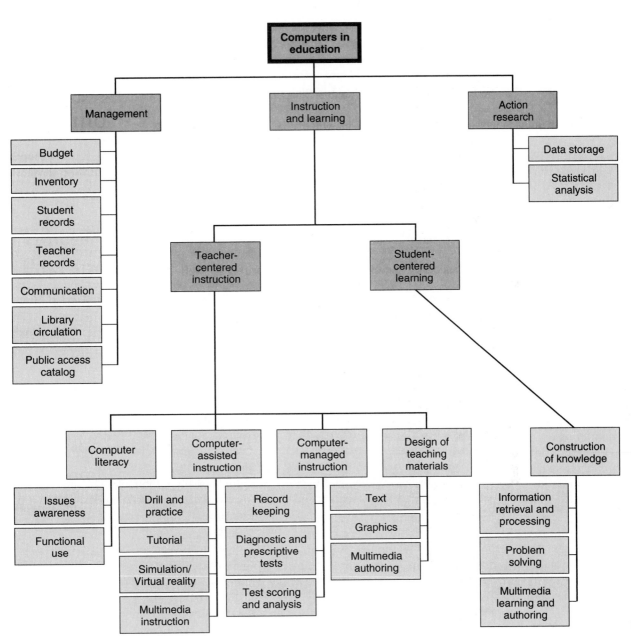

Figure 4–1

Classification of computers in education

promote better communication between teachers and publishers. Teachers can more clearly explain their needs to publishers, and publishers can better describe their available products. The software classification must reflect accepted theories and practices in education. More information on developing and managing a software collection can be found in Chapter 12.

The emphasis in this text will be on the management category and the instruction and learning category, although the category of action research is briefly covered as well. The elements of teacher-centered instruction are addressed most thoroughly. Learning theories and the continued evaluation of new technologies are increasingly placing strong emphasis on the growth and development of student-centered learning.

MANAGEMENT

The chart presented as Figure 4–2 suggests that there are several areas in the realm of school and classroom management that are well suited to computer applications. In each area, the computer used as a tool can save the user some time, can improve the accuracy of information, and can efficiently handle large amounts of data.

Budget

Budgets must often be built by teachers, department heads, and other administrators to deal with instructional materials, field trip costs, student club activities, personnel, and departmental needs. In preparing a budget, school administrators and teachers depend on records of historical information. With the exception of zero-based budgeting (a technique that assumes that every budget category begins at zero each year), past budgets form the foundation for future budget development. It is necessary to understand past practices, allocations, and expenditures. It is equally important to be able to project ahead in areas of school and program enrollment, staffing needs, curriculum changes, and inflation. Computer-based **file managers** and **spreadsheets** are particularly useful tools to accomplish tasks relating to budget preparation and management. On the one hand, they provide the user with current, accurate records in a timely fashion and, on the other, with the ability to reflect changes dynamically as the user manipulates variables to look at projections. Spreadsheets have earned their well-deserved reputation as being "what if . . . " tools. They immediately reflect the results when the user asks, "What if this amount were changed? What impact would this have?"

Inventory

School personnel are accountable for a wide variety of items, ranging from food and janitorial supplies to textbooks, curriculum materials, and instructional equipment. A computer-based file manager can record use, track inventory levels, record the location of items and their condition easily and accurately, and make information available at a moment's notice.

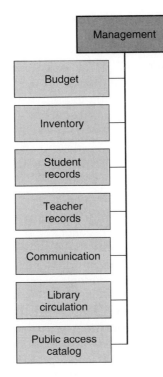

Figure 4–2

Computers in school and classroom management

Student Records

A school is required to keep many different records concerning students. Many of these are ideally suited for electronic storage. Health and immunization records begin in the primary grades. Information about home and parents/guardians is recorded. Attendance is closely followed. Grades are calculated and stored; then grade reports are generated from these electronic gradebooks. Individual Education Programs (IEPs) are tracked, and students' growth in ability and performance levels is monitored. Student portfolios may contain numerous artifacts or samples of student work that can be easily stored, organized, and retrieved electronically. Participation in athletics, music programs, talented and gifted programs, and extracurricular activities is noted. In the past, manual record-keeping systems were used. They worked but they were time consuming and yielded limited additional information, since cross-referencing was difficult. Well-designed computer-based systems again prove to be quicker and more efficient, and they yield more potentially useful information by creating a more complete profile of the student.

Teacher Records

Teachers manage information on students, but they also need to manage their own information: syllabi, lesson plans, test banks, evaluation notes, worksheet masters, handouts, etc. They can also correspond with other educators via e-mail, participate in LISTSERV discussions, and use their computer to download information from the Internet for classes. They can even enroll in credit courses offered over the Internet. They can record their participation in professional growth activities that may generate district credit toward advancement. As teachers develop their continuing professional development plans, they may want to use a word processor to keep a reflective teaching journal or to use database managers to store audio or visual artifacts in their own electronic professional teaching portfolios.

Communication

Parental involvement can increase student achievement and improve the parents' relationship with the school. Written and electronic communication is greatly facilitated by the computer. Personalized letters to parents generated by a word processor save a great deal of clerical time and tend to increase the amount of correspondence between school and home. A **desktop presentation** program allows teachers and administrators to enhance their presentations to students, as well as to parent and community groups, by projecting text and graphics on a screen. Modems allow schools throughout a district to communicate by exchanging memos, notices of important events, and attendance data. Teachers can access lesson plans stored on electronic bulletin boards. Some schools have home pages, where students can check class assignments and use e-mail to ask classmates or school-provided tutors questions on homework assignments. Students, sitting at computers with modems, can reach across the miles to others and can begin to truly understand the term *global village*.

Library Circulation

Manual library circulation systems have existed for a long time in schools and public libraries. A manual system, though acceptable for recording the checkout and return of books and other materials, is time consuming and provides little additional information of benefit to the user. An automated circulation system employing a computer and bar codes on the circulating materials can record the checkout and return of materials and can generate lists of the library's holdings, record borrowers' transactions quickly and efficiently, generate lists of overdue materials, provide inventory control to a level that was never before possible, and calculate use statistics. A computerized library circulation system performs existing tasks quicker and more accurately than a manual system and provides the user with information not easily acquired in the past.

Library Public Access Catalog

Just as an automated library circulation system can enhance the distribution of materials, an online **public access catalog (PAC)** of a library media center's materials collection can greatly improve access to information. Such a system should allow a user to browse the collection electronically and to perform author, title, subject, and

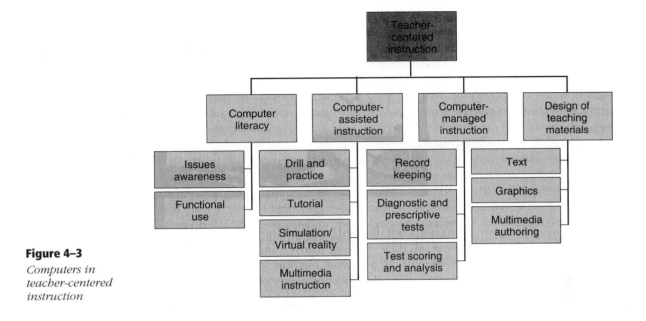

Figure 4–3

Computers in teacher-centered instruction

keyword searches. Most sophisticated systems allow the use of the Boolean operators AND, OR, and NOT to facilitate more complex searches. Beside supporting direct queries, an automated system can generate highly specialized bibliographies.

INSTRUCTION AND LEARNING

The category of instruction and learning is separated into *teacher-centered instruction*—dealing with those functions that directly include the student in either an individual or a group setting and that take into account teacher planning, preparation, and delivery of instruction—and *student-centered learning*—including the functions that deal with the student involved in constructive activities that lead to learning.

Teacher-Centered Instruction

As seen in Figure 4–3, teacher-centered instruction includes the areas of computer literacy, computer-assisted instruction, computer-managed instruction, and design of teaching materials.

Computer literacy acquaints the student with the computer and its functional use. The presentation of information through computer-assisted instruction under the control of the teacher and the management of the student's performance and interaction with that information through computer-managed instruction, though viewed separately for the purpose of functional examination, sometimes overlap. As a design tool, the computer has become widely used by teachers to create hard copy, as well as projected instructional materials.

Computer Literacy. The subject of **computer literacy** focuses on the computer as the object of instruction. This topic is not to be confused with computer science instruction, which studies hardware, operating systems, and computer languages. In computer literacy, a scope and sequence of curriculum goals is usually developed within a school district that specifies what is to be learned about the use of the computer and about its role in society. Computer literacy often examines the history of computing and computer awareness and functional use, as well as the broader role of the computer as it relates to societal issues such as computer access, gender relationships, software copyright, rights of privacy, data security, and information ownership. Some of these issues were introduced in Chapter 1; others will be addressed in later chapters.

Some educators argue that, as computers become commonplace items in homes and schools, the need for computer literacy will be diminished in the curriculum. Some feel that while teaching scope and sequence of skills may no longer be necessary, computer-related issues will still need to be discussed.

Computer-Assisted Instruction. *Computer-assisted instruction* is a term applied to a teaching/learning situation that involves the direct instructional interaction between computer and student. In this teacher-centered approach, the teacher, ultimately having responsibility for all instruction in the classroom, sets up the learning environment through careful selection and analysis of the instruction material; ensures that each student has the necessary entry-level knowledge, skills, and attitude to engage in a particular activity; monitors the learning activities, adjusting them according to the students' needs; and follows up with activities designed to promote retention and transfer of learning.

Regardless of the underlying philosophy in the classroom, *tutorial instruction, drill and practice,* and *simulation* are time-tested instructional strategies. They are strategies that behaviorists can apply in a teacher-centered instructional situation and that constructivists can apply in a student-centered learning environment. Depending on how they are employed, they are strategies that can gain attention, stimulate recall of prior learning, and present new information in ways that approximate real-life situations at a more concrete level than most media used in the classroom.

They are strategies that address the right or the left hemisphere of the brain. They can be tailored to support activities favored by students with concrete-sequential, concrete-random, abstract-sequential, or abstract-random preferred styles, and they can be appealing to students with diverse strengths and intelligences. Teachers who understand the individual needs of their students will tailor their strategies and the computer applications to meet those needs.

Al Mizell (1997) at Nova Southeastern University states forcefully, "I don't believe enough attention is focused on the value of using computers where they are strongest; e.g., as patient tutors, competent analysts, master presenters of stimulus material, and evaluators of consequences of various decisions made by the student. In other words, they are more valuable for higher level thinking and processing skills than when they are used as electronic page turners."

Tutorial Applications. A **tutorial** program exposes the student to material that is believed not to have been previously taught or learned. A tutorial program often includes a placement test to ensure student readiness and sometimes a pretest on specific objectives to validate the placement test. The computer usually assesses a student's prior learning, determines readiness for the material, and presents material for student observation, note taking, and other interaction. New material is commonly provided in small increments, replete with instructional guidance and appropriate feedback to encourage correct student response.

Tutorial instruction often follows a **linear** programmed instruction model mainly because it is difficult, time consuming, and therefore expensive to write **branching** programs that would attempt to remediate incorrect responses. Both linear and branching formats present information and questions that lead toward an identified goal. Linear programs (Figure 4–4) present information in a sequential manner and

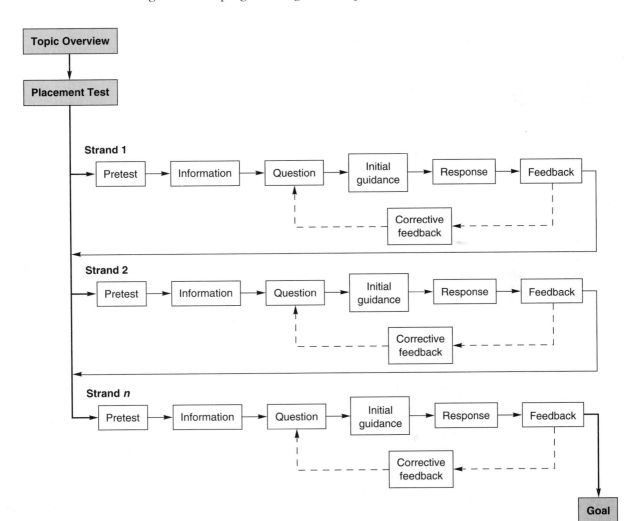

Figure 4–4
A typical tutorial format

do not attempt to remediate errors made. Tutorials often include initial guidance in the form of prompts to encourage the student to answer correctly, especially at the outset of the lesson. The diagram in Figure 4–4 illustrates a representation of a linear format often used in tutorial programs. Some programs employ modest branching techniques to provide alternative paths, or branches, for remediation or acceleration. Tutorials must record student responses and allow for teacher analysis of the student's progress to determine if the goal has been met.

Tutorial programs, such as the example in Figure 4–5, are often used to help students who have been absent from class. They may also be effective when assigned as independent study to students exhibiting difficulty with specific skills and concepts.

In a behaviorist model, the teacher identifies the proper lesson objectives, selects the appropriate computer program, maintains a reasonably comfortable environment free from unnecessary distractions, and, where needed, provides additional resources

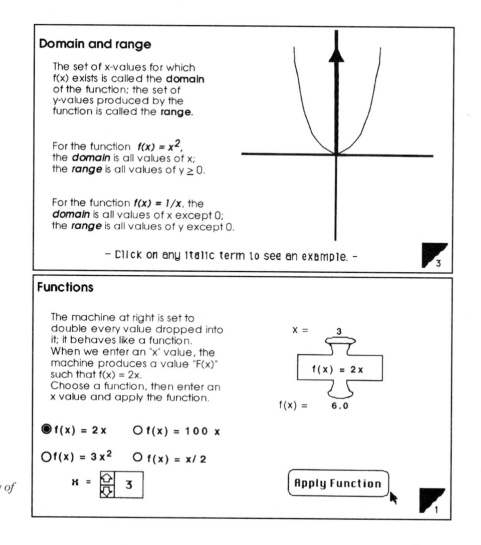

Figure 4–5

Calculus (Courtesy of Broderbund Software, Inc.)

and encouragement to the student. The teacher must also monitor the progress made by the student by interpreting data collected by the computer program and must be prepared to intervene if necessary. In a constructivist model, tutorial software may be suggested by the teacher as a way for the student to acquire a particular skill or concept once its value is recognized. The teacher's role is to ascertain readiness on the part of the student, to select the appropriate software, to assess the student's performance as the newly acquired skill or concept is applied to a meaningful task, and to determine if further practice is required.

Working directly at a computer on a tutorial program can provide interest and motivation, if the teacher keeps in mind that it is only one alternative among various strategies to teach specific skills or concepts. The educational quality of the program must be ascertained and, to maintain its effectiveness, the strategy should not be overused.

Drill and Practice Applications. **Drill and practice,** a time-honored technique, is used by teachers to reinforce instruction by providing the repetition necessary to move acquired skills and concepts into long-term memory. It assumes that the material covered has been previously taught. In the past, teachers have used flash cards, worksheets, board games, and verbal drills to achieve results. Computer programs present an additional and, if used well, a more powerful alternative.

Criticism leveled in the past at drill and practice software was really aimed at poorly designed software that was boring, that treated all users the same regardless of ability, and that employed undesirable feedback. Teachers tell of students deliberately giving incorrect responses in order to see flashy animated graphics on the screen. The reward offered by that software for making correct responses was the presentation of another boring problem. A typical format used in drill and practice programs is illustrated by the diagram in Figure 4–6.

Whenever this technique is used, the assumption is made that the topic has already been introduced to the student and that some prior instruction has taken place. In a behaviorist model, the teacher's role, in addition to determining the appropriate lesson objective and to delivering the initial instruction, is to select the appropriate software, to monitor the student's progress through the material, and to assess the student's performance. In a constructivist model, drill and practice software may be suggested by the teacher as a way for the student to refine a particular skill or concept once its value is recognized. The teacher's role, in addition to determining that the student understands and accepts an agreed-upon goal, is to ascertain that initial information has been acted upon by the student, to select the appropriate software, and to assess the student's performance as the skill or concept is applied to a meaningful task.

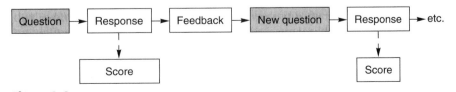

Figure 4–6
A typical drill and practice format

"Many students choose to spend considerable time on the computer performing drill and practice writing lessons in a game format. They get immediate feedback on anything they do. It makes learning exciting for them."

Becky Benjamin, 7th Grade Language Arts Teacher
Carrollton Junior High, Carrollton, GA

The student must interact with the computer by responding to screen prompts and by providing appropriate keyboard or other input. The student should request teacher or peer assistance if necessary and examine the results of the activity. The computer presents material for student interaction, provides appropriate feedback to student responses, and usually records the rate of success, often displayed as a score or percentage. Effective software requires the student to respond based on deductions and inferences, as well as recall.

Figure 4–7 illustrates screens from a popular drill and practice program from MECC called *Number Munchers*. In the top half of the illustration, the number muncher is seen in the second row of the second column. The user guides the character to those boxes that contain numbers that are multiples of 9. Beware of the Troggle, though, that eats number munchers. The entertaining video game format encourages users to spend extended time at the keyboard, practicing skills they have acquired.

A number of factors influence the effectiveness of drill and practice software. The teacher must know the program well enough to determine the accuracy of the content and the match between the presentation of the material and an individual student's learning style. If the software is to be used in a group setting, are intrinsic gaming strategies employed or can external gaming strategies be used by the teacher? **Gaming,** though often found in drill and practice programs, can be found in all computer-assisted instruction categories. The technique includes a set of rules and a clear contest. Students or groups of students may compete against each other or against the computer or another fixed standard. Students must find the material and its presentation interesting enough to be willing to become mentally and emotionally involved. The program's use of basic graphic design, as well as a variety of stimuli such as color, sound, and animation, in both its presentation and feedback screens greatly enhances its effectiveness.

The drill and practice program called *Math Blaster* provides practice of higher-level thinking skills. See the word problem presented in Figure 4–8. Each screen guides the learner through a problem-solving strategy.

The three screens shown in Figure 4–9 reward the student by presenting a graphic, by listing the student's performance, and by printing a certificate of accomplishment.

Simulation/Virtual Reality. **Simulation** is another time-honored teaching strategy used to reinforce instruction by the teacher. It can also function effectively in a student-centered environment by providing a climate for discovery learning to take place or for newly acquired skills and concepts to be tested. A simulation can pre-

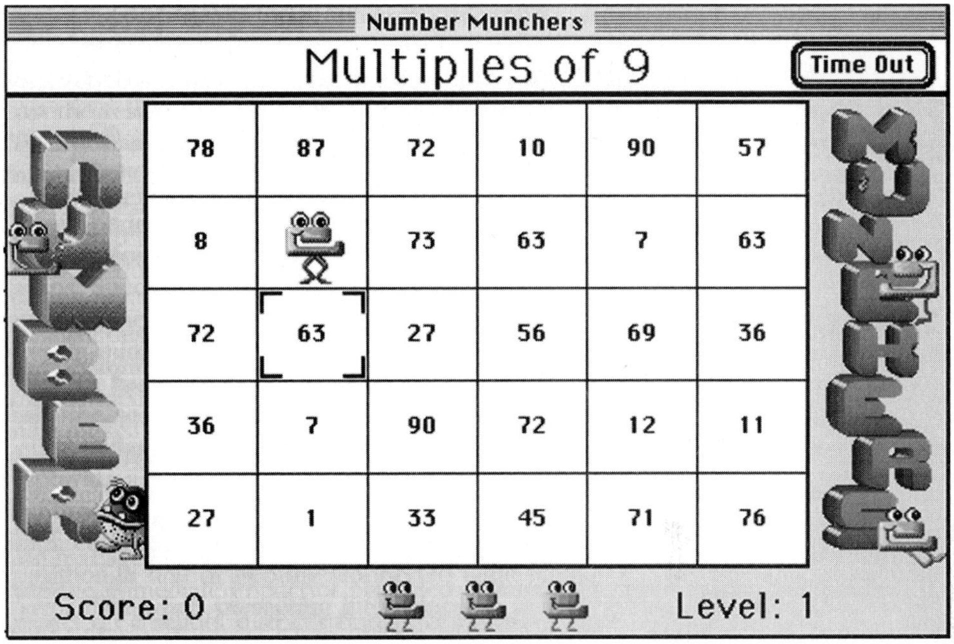

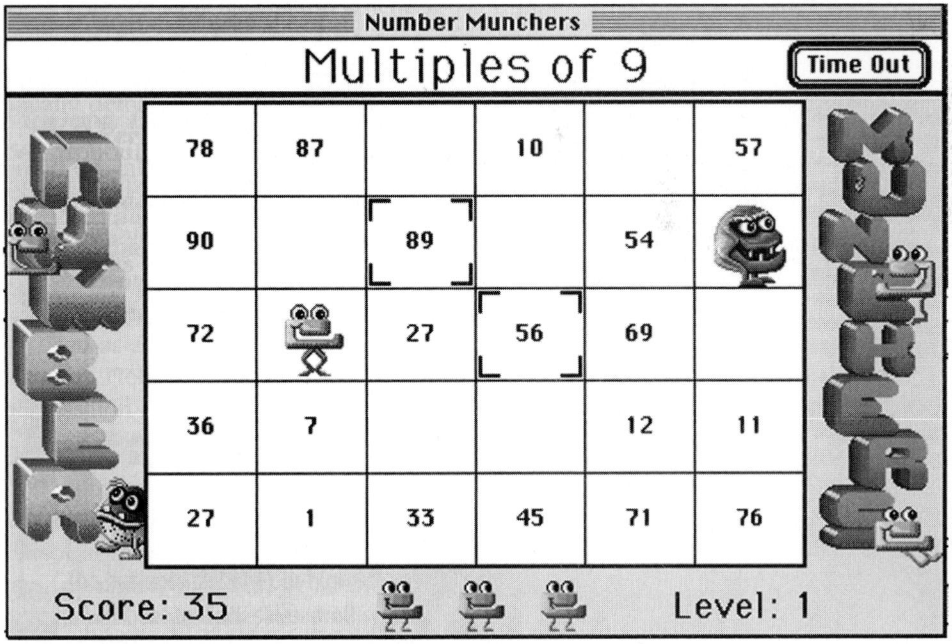

Figure 4–7

Screens from Number Munchers (Courtesy of TLC Propertiers, Inc., a subsidiary of The Learning Company, Inc.)

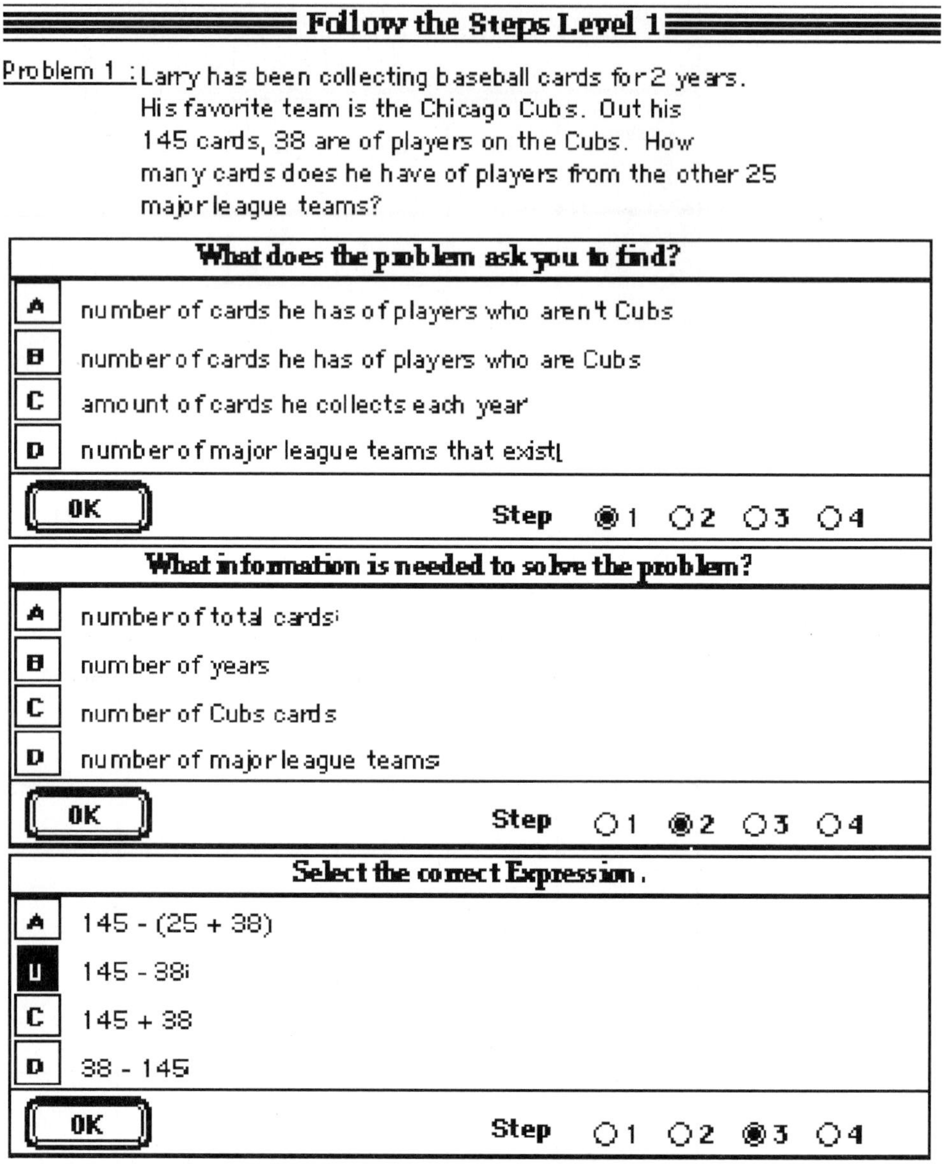

Figure 4-8

Math Blaster Mystery (Courtesy of Davidson & Associates, Inc.)

sent a sample of a real situation and can offer genuine practice at solving real problems unhampered by danger, distance, time, or cost factors. Simulations call for decisions made by the student. In the past, teachers have used board games, drama, and role playing to implement the simulation technique. The computer is a useful tool to manage this technique.

A sophisticated simulation can present the facts and rules of a situation in a highly realistic manner without the limiting factors of time, distance, safety, and cost and

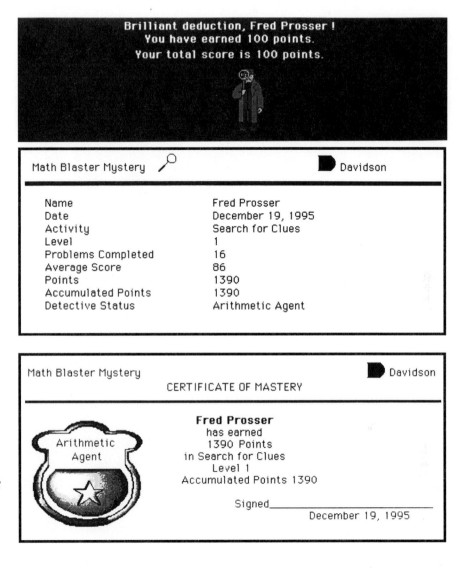

Figure 4–9

*Math Blaster Reward
Screens Mystery
(Courtesy of
Davidson &
Associates, Inc.)*

then can adjust these factors to respond to interaction by the student. High levels of cognitive skill are involved in the synthesis of facts, rules, and concepts in solving problems. Simulation permits this synthesis to take place within the classroom.

Consider, for example, the teacher who wants to teach the concept of free elections in a representative democracy. Figure 4–10 suggests a common flow of events in a typical simulation. A classroom simulation might call for the creation of class offices, including development of a nomination process, establishment of platforms, identification of a polling place, preparation of secret and secure ballots, and agreement on term of office for the successful candidates. The simulation just described has been conducted for years without a computer. A computer program, however,

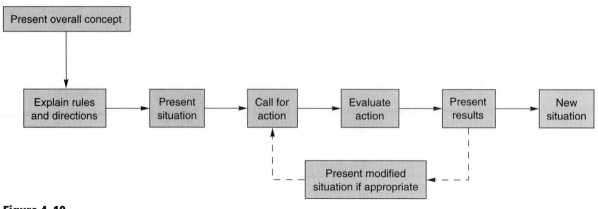

Figure 4–10

A typical simulation format

can increase the sophistication of the simulation and can extend it into a broader context. For instance, it could introduce a number of historical variables that might influence decisions made in the running of a presidential election campaign. In this case, the program could store a wealth of data that can be called upon as needed and cross-referenced to demonstrate cause and effect.

Simulation software can provide highly realistic practice at solving real problems in the classroom without many of the limiting factors often found in real life.

> "I use Sim Earth on the one computer I have in my classroom along with an LCD panel on an overhead projector. The first team of students designs their environment to maximize population expansion; the second to maximize plant life; the third to maximize sustainable growth; and the fourth to factor in natural disasters. Each team presents to the whole class. Ensuing discussion examines consequences of each choice."
>
> *Jim Long, Marine and Environmental Science Teacher*
> *North Salem High School, Salem, OR*

As in any use of CAI, the role of the teacher is to identify the proper lesson objectives and to select the appropriate computer program. When using simulation software in a behaviorist model, the teacher often provides background information and may be called upon to teach related skills and concepts and to provide additional resources where needed. The teacher must also monitor the progress made by the student or by the group of students and assess their performance. Simulations, lending themselves to group use, promote social interaction and can often be used as an introductory activity for a unit. In a constructivist model, simulation software may be suggested by the teacher as a way for the student to develop a particular skill or concept in a manner that is close to a real-life situation. The teacher's role is to ascertain readiness on the part of the student, to select the appropriate software, to discuss the student's performance in the simulation, and to suggest a real-world application.

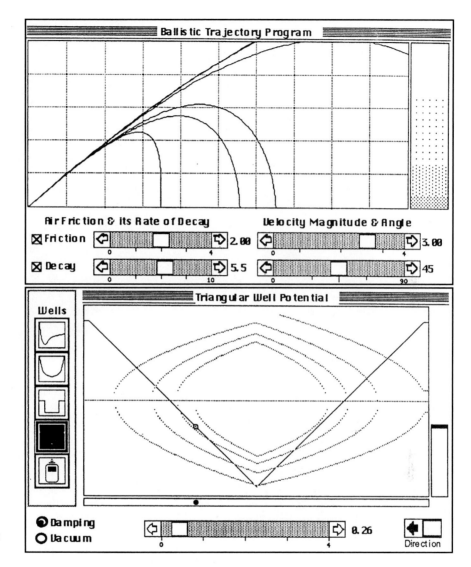

Figure 4–11

Physics Simulation Series, 2 screens (Developed by Blas Cabrera, Stanford University, and published by Intellimation, Santa Barbara, CA.)

The top screen in Figure 4–11 is from a program called *Ballistic*. The user sets initial parameters of initial velocity, angle of projection, and drag medium. By turning on the Friction control but leaving the Decay control turned off, a medium of constant density is simulated. Turning on the Decay control simulates a medium whose density decreases with altitude. Once launched, the projectile leaves a trace in the display window. By varying the parameters of initial velocity, angle of projection, air friction as the drag medium, and altitude-related decay, the user can compare the results of these combined factors as traces in the display window.

The bottom screen in Figure 4–11 is from a program called *Potential*. Users choose from four one-dimension potential wells or create their own. The illustration

Figure 4–12

Oregon Trail II General Store (Courtesy of TLC Properties, Inc., a subsidiary of The Learning Company, Inc.)

represents a triangular well: a ball travels downward along the left slope, reaches bottom, rolls a certain distance upward on the right slope, then reverses its direction. This is repeated with diminishing distances until all energy is spent. A damping effect can be employed to observe the effect of various dissipating conditions. Kinetic and potential energies are continually displayed in a column at the right of the screen. Velocity or acceleration can be plotted for each travel of the ball.

Both of these examples are intrinsic simulation models that create an artificial environment for the user to explore. In these microworlds, elements of the environment operate according to a regular set of rules. The student manipulates things to learn what their characteristics are within the artificial environment.

In *Oregon Trail,* an award-winning program now available with sophisticated graphics on CD-ROM as *Oregon Trail II* from The Learning Company, Inc., the user is placed in the position of traveling the 2,000-mile Oregon Trail from Independence, Missouri, to Oregon's Willamette Valley. Having declared an occupation and thereby receiving an allocation of available funds, the user begins preparing for the journey by carefully purchasing supplies, as shown in Figure 4–12.

The screen of Figure 4–13 is a typical one seen as the program progresses. A log, or diary, of the journey appears below the map. Four buttons are arranged at the bottom of the screen, presenting the user with options. The Guide button reveals pertinent information about the geography of the region in a separate window. The user is encouraged to keep a diary. The health status of the party can be revealed by pressing the appropriate button. As the journey progresses, the user can change the pace of travel and adjust the rationing of food. Hunt calls forth an arcade-type

Figure 4–13

Traveling the Oregon Trail (Courtesy of TLC Properties, Inc., a subsidiary of The Learning Company, Inc.)

game, allowing the user to collect food. At each stop along the way, the user can see who's around and choose to talk to one or more people, often revealing clues or historical facts.

A Wagon Score is displayed only if the user successfully crosses the trail. A value is placed on the people and supplies that complete the journey. Some occupations receive a smaller allocation of funds than others, so have a more difficult time successfully completing the trip. A factor is, therefore, employed depending on the user's chosen occupation.

The program has a management option protected by a password that allows the teacher to clear the List of Legends, adjust the simulation speed and hunting time, and determine network use, if any. A new network version of the program allows a number of users to interact simultaneously with one another on their journey.

The award-winning Carmen Sandiego series of programs (Where in the U.S.A. . . . , Where in the World . . . , Where in Europe . . . , etc.) is the all-time best-selling software in grades K–12. The premise of each program is that as a detective you must pick up the trail of one of Carmen's villainous gang and, following geographic (or historic) clues, deduce the identity of the villain, follow the trail, and ultimately apprehend the culprit (Figure 4–14). The program is so popular that it spawned a television program and Carmen Sandiego clubs all over the country. It simulates actions that might be taken in the real world and calls upon the user, often working cooperatively with others, to make decisions based on facts gathered. Each program provides an appropriate reference book such as Fodor's *USA*. The computer's role usually is to create a realistic environment and present material for student interaction, to

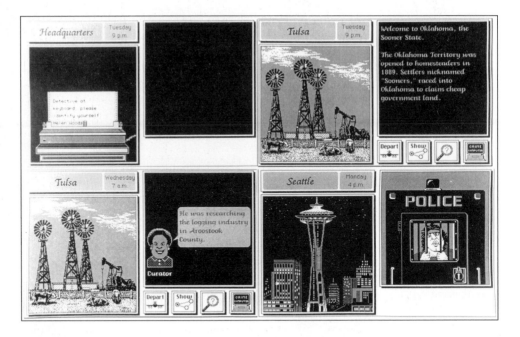

Figure 4–14

Four scenes from Where in the USA is Carmen Sandiego? (Courtesy of Broderbund Software, Inc.)

provide appropriate feedback to student responses, and, based on decisions made by students, to modify the environment and present new material, allowing the students to witness the results of their decisions.

Students might be asked to trace their travels in the simulation on a map and list the countries through which they travel. Students could be named as "ambassadors" representing each country. They would research the country they represent and present brief reports or hold a mock United Nations meeting and discuss issues of importance to them.

Virtual reality (VR) is a computer-based technology that creates an illusion of reality, in which the participants interact with, and in fact are immersed in, an artificial environment to the degree that it appears real; it is highly interactive, multisensorial, and vivid enough for the participants almost to think it is reality. If virtual reality achieves perfection, participants will not recognize the difference between reality and virtual reality. Virtual reality, according to Furness (Miller, 1992, p. 14), is "just like you're walking into another world, and you're perceiving it as if it becomes reality itself."

As you might guess, this form of simulation requires a great deal of computing power and a phenomenal amount of programming. The remarkable increase in the power of affordable computers is one factor contributing to the rapid advances made by virtual reality during the past few years.

Virtual reality offers teachers and students the opportunity to explore reality in a new way. We can generate a model and then manipulate it in ways that were not previously possible. For example, we can travel through our model and view it from angles that would be impossible in our physical reality. We can also put abstract ideas into a form that can be perceived and manipulated. Theoretically, anything represented by a computer can be placed within a virtual framework for interaction within a virtual reality context.

Educational applications might be found in a number of disciplines, or, better yet, they may exist in a cross-disciplinary framework. The phenomena of physics might be explored as virtual objects to manipulate in a vastly extended simulation. Virtual molecules might be examined in chemistry. Imagine the pleasure of dissecting a three-dimensional virtual frog (hopefully, without the virtual smell of formaldehyde). Current and historical cultures experienced in a virtual environment might lead to a better understanding and acceptance. Students with physical disabilities or motor impairments could participate in a virtual downhill ski race or perform an intricate virtual surgical procedure.

Designing virtual worlds for education may become a whole new field of specialization. "It is one thing to present a richly textured world for immersion and exploration, it is entirely another matter for educators to properly structure this kind of a setting for profitable learning" (Woodward, 1992, p. 4). Woodward (1992, p. 5) goes on to state that unless we "do a better job of directing the learner toward explicit, measurable outcomes—it is likely that the value of simulations as educational techniques will remain modest." Woodward also feels that the same may be true for the highly promising virtual reality systems.

There are mixed opinions about the future of virtual reality in the classroom. Some seem excited about the possible educational applications, while others appear more concerned with what seem like the insurmountable technical and financial challenges. Clearly, virtual worlds could be used in many different ways in schools if the challenges can be overcome.

In a simulation, students interact with the environment and perhaps with each other, make decisions based on the material presented by the computer, and make choices they deem appropriate. As part of the overall activity, they may discuss results of the simulation. Since the learning theory on which software design is based dictates the role of the computer, the role of the teacher, and the role of the student, recognizing these elements is an important first step toward making good use of the computer in the classroom. Since virtual reality is such a complicated technology with so many possible applications, it is discussed at greater length in Chapter 12.

A table summarizing the teacher, student, and computer roles in CAI is presented for your review as Figure 4–15.

Multimedia Instruction. Few, if any, pieces of software are "pure" drill and practice, tutorial, or simulation. Some are predominantly one type but embody elements of other approaches. **Multimedia instruction,** more than any other category of software, blurs these lines of distinction. It is also closely related to **multimedia learning.** If you refer back to Figure 4–1, you will notice that multimedia learning is a subcategory of construction of knowledge under the category of student-centered learning.

Multimedia programs are often used to control the presentation of video information from external sources such as videotape or videodisc, as well as graphic, audio, or textual information from CD-ROM. Although the majority of these programs are designed for individual instruction, they may be adapted for group use by the instructor. Typically, audio and video material (still frames, sounds, and/or moving

	Tutorial	**Drill and Practice**	**Simulation**
Teacher	Determines objectives	Determines objectives	Determines objectives
	Selects materials appropriate to students	Selects materials appropriate to students	Selects materials appropriate to students
	Monitors progress	Teaches original skills or concepts	Teaches related skills
	Assesses student performance	Monitors progress	Often prompts students to discover concepts
		Assesses student performance	May take active role in a group
			Assesses student performance
Computer	Presents original material	Presents material in form of problems or questions	Presents a situation
	Assesses progress	Displays feedback	Elicits student response
	Displays feedback	May assess performance	Modifies situation
	Provides guidance	May record performance	May assess performance
	May assess performance		Demonstrates result of student action
	Records performance		
	Tests for objectives		
Student	Interacts with computer	Interacts with computer	Reacts to situation
	Responds to feedback	Responds appropriately	Refers to external resources if needed
	Controls pace of presentation	Examines results	Confers with others as needed
	Examines results		Makes choices based on information

Figure 4–15

Role comparison in CAI

images with sound) is presented to the viewer accompanied by computer-generated text in a true multimedia fashion. The instructional designer uses the computer to se-lect the video segment and present it on the screen, often interspersed with com-puter-generated question frames. Depending on the response to the question, the designer can program the computer to repeat the segment, present another one in a remediation mode, or move on to new information.

Multimedia instruction in a computer-assisted instruction format is blossoming rapidly in business and industry as an effective and efficient training tool. It is re-ceiving a good deal of attention at the college and university level and is making rapid inroads in K–12 education as better software becomes commercially available and as teachers develop increasing confidence and skill in designing their own lessons. In an information tool format, multimedia allows students to create their own visuals and incorporate them into their products or to create their own navigation through existing resources. Because of the breadth of classroom applications possible with this technology, multimedia, hypermedia, and virtual reality are discussed in greater detail in Chapter 12.

Curriculum Integration. A danger in examining discrete elements and in categorizing software or computer applications is that we neglect the whole as we examine the separate parts. Much software available today spans more than one category. Tutorial software may well have drill and practice components. Simulation software may well introduce new concepts and repeat previously learned material. Classification schemes can become counterproductive if they interfere with an understanding of the potential application of software.

The somewhat arbitrary classification of curriculum over the past decades, especially at the secondary school level, into specific subject matter areas is now breaking down in favor of the integration of disciplines to foster richer learning environments. As we consider computer applications, then, we should keep in mind the concept of integration. The following discussion by David Thornburg (1991) in his book *Education, Technology, and Paradigms of Change for the 21st Century* is an excellent example of classroom application of the computer in an integrated curriculum:

> Suppose you are a teacher who is exploring California for social studies. One way to do this is to present the students with material right from the textbook. This familiar approach takes a fascinating topic and makes it boring. It causes some students to say, "Who cares?"
>
> On the other hand, in the same period of time, a teacher who really cares about the subject may try a different approach. After exploring California's location on the planet and talking about the geologic upheavals that created some of the spectacular landscape, the students might be encouraged to imagine themselves as members of an ancient tribe of Indians, the Ohlones, for example. Student research on this tribe would allow them to think about the rich civilization these Indians had when the pyramids were being built in Egypt.
>
> As the students learned more about these ancient people, they could learn how to identify animals from their tracks. For this task, students could use Animal Trackers, a program from Sunburst Communications that provides clues from which the students must identify a particular animal. Because this program supports databases for grasslands, desert and wooded areas, it can be used all over the country. Each clue provides information of a different sort—habitat, nesting, food, and footprints. After working with this program for a while, students will have learned a lot about native American animals, as well as honing their higher order thinking skills. This activity provides an opportunity for science to become integrated with social studies.
>
> As the year proceeds, the students might see a new animal through Indian eyes—the strange creatures with two heads and four legs (the Spanish explorers on horseback). At this point some students might want to retain the Indian perspective and others might want to join forces with Portola or Father Junipero Serra as the colonization of California took place.
>
> Later on in the course, the teacher might show the film Dream West, showing the life of Fremont as he explored the West and paved the way for the United States to ex-

pand its boundaries. At this point, students could use the Oregon Trail simulation from MECC to see how well they might fare on their own journey across the country. (pp. 22–23)

Computer-Managed Instruction. Although computer-assisted instruction, especially tutorial software, sometimes includes some management and record-keeping function, its emphasis is on the presentation of information or instruction. Computer-managed instruction, on the other hand, stresses the management of student performance in a direct, on-line approach, with the student working directly at the computer or in an off-line approach, as suggested by Figure 4–16. This category includes programs that are *diagnostic and prescriptive tests,* programs that *analyze test scores,* and programs that *keep student records.* Spreadsheet and database management software is playing an increasing record-keeping and analysis role in computer-managed instruction.

Most teachers believe in the concept of individualized instruction. With great effort, many succeed. Individualized instruction is not to be confused with independent study. Individualized instruction means that a teacher knows all students well on the basis of their personal, cultural, experiential, and academic background, scholastic ability, and learning style. It further signifies that, knowing the students in this manner, the teacher is capable of providing for this diversity in the classroom. Given current typical student/teacher ratios, the mainstreaming of students with special needs into the regular classroom, and the attendant, legally mandated IEPs, the record keeping involved in individualizing instruction is a monumental task. It is

Figure 4–16

Two approaches to computer-managed instruction

On-Line Approach	Off-Line Approach
Database of goals and performance indicators is established.	Database of goals and performance indicators is established.
Test items are stored in computer.	Printed tests are constructed.
Student takes a test "online" at the computer.	Student responds to test on optical scored cards.
	Optical scanner records student responses.
Computer analyzes student performance on test items related to established goals.	Computer analyzes student performance on test items related to established goals.
Computer presents tutorial, drill and practice, simulation, or interactive video instruction to student.	Computer directs student to learning activities based on the performance analysis.
Supplementary "off-line" activities may also be suggested.	
Teacher retrieves a student profile from the computer.	Teacher retrieves a student profile from the computer.

however, a task well suited to the computer. Student progress can finally be tracked effectively and efficiently.

Design of Teaching Materials. Many teachers have relied heavily on commercially prepared teaching materials in the form of bulletin board materials, overhead transparency masters, printed masters for worksheets, and other handouts. At times this has resulted in an accommodation between the teacher's perceived needs and the materials available designed by a third party. This reliance on commercial materials could at times be attributed to teachers' lack of confidence in their own creative ability, as well as to the time demanded for the production of original materials. Teachers are learning that the computer can significantly increase their ability and dramatically decrease production time demands.

Text. The computer is ideally suited to creating display materials, and users are presented with a wide variety of software from which to choose. A word processor can be used to prepare practice exercises for the student to complete in school or at home. By selecting a large type size, this same program can prepare an overhead transparency master. Color can be used to highlight key words by separating the components of the transparency into two masters and printing them in different colors. Special attention might be paid to programs that allow the easy integration of graphics and sound with text.

Graphics. Many individuals do not have a high degree of confidence in their artistic drawing ability. Graphics programs level the playing field. They allow the creation of respectable illustrations and often bolster the self-esteem of self-prescribed nonartists. Programs such as *Freehand™, Illustrator™, Corel Draw™, ClarisWorks™, ClarisDraw™, Kid Pix™, PC Paint™,* and *Print Shop™* facilitate the creation of bulletin board and display graphics and text. *Persuasion™* and *PowerPoint™* allow the creation and projection of a series of images containing both text and graphics. Programs such as *ClarisWorks™, DeltaGraph™, Excel™,* and *Microsoft Works™* generate line graphs, bar graphs, and pie charts from numeric data.

Multimedia Authoring. You may have noticed in Figure 4–1 that multimedia appears as a subcategory under teacher-centered instruction, as well as under student-centered learning. Much multimedia software is not procured from commercial sources but created locally by teachers and students. When creating lessons in the multimedia format, the teacher controls audio and video information, as well as text from internal and external sources. Sophisticated yet easy to use software such as *HyperCard™, ToolBook™,* and *HyperStudio™* turn the teacher into a multimedia author.

Programs and video boards are available that allow computer screens to be recorded on videotape to serve as titles, credits, animated graphics, and instructional text screens. A variety of scene transitions that allow one image to fade or to merge into another lends sophistication to the recording. Desktop presentation software permits the projection of computer screens by either a video projector or a video display panel placed on the stage of an overhead projector. Software that supports the design of teaching materials serves as an extension of the creative teacher. Although these materials can be created in other ways, the computer makes it easier and less time consuming and thereby stimulates teachers to maximize their creative efforts.

Student-Centered Learning

Student-centered learning is an approach that views the computer as an information tool for the student to use to create, access, retrieve, manipulate, and transmit information. One or more students can approach a computer on a needs basis in a classroom, school library, or computer lab environment.

Any diagram of computers in education is by nature arbitrary. Every teacher could draw a unique diagram based on experiences, knowledge, skills, and beliefs. When you examine this portion dealing with student-centered learning, know that many facets referred to under teacher-centered instruction may apply in varying degree to this section as well. The effort here, however, is to focus attention on the student as the user, creator, and disseminator of information and as the builder of knowledge.

Construction of Knowledge. As can be seen in Figure 4–17, student-centered learning encourages students to view the computer as a tool similar to a pencil, brush, or calculator in order to solve a problem. The techniques embodied in student-centered learning are found in subsequent chapters dealing with the computer as a word processing, spreadsheet, database, graphics, or Internet tool. The computer is not only a productivity tool for the teacher but also a tool that enhances the productivity of the student.

The word processor allows the student to express ideas and, with the teacher's guidance, refine the quality of that expression with a reasonable amount of effort in a short period of time. Inquiry strategies can be mapped, content outlines prepared, and detailed reports written. Simple skill-building exercises can become pleasurable. Classroom and school newspapers can be published with word processors and desktop publishing software. Students of all ages can become authors and their books placed in the school library for others to read.

We live in an environment where visual images are constantly bombarding our sense of sight. The advertising industry has made a science of using graphics. Computers have emerged as devices to manipulate visual images and to create forms of video animation. Having recognized the power of visuals to communicate ideas and to persuade the viewer, this industry remains at the forefront of computer graphics applications.

Paint and draw programs allow students not only artistic expression but also powerful nonverbal communication to communicate an idea as they prepare signs relating to a cocurricular activity, maps for a social studies project, posters promoting a candidate in a school election, and banners proclaiming significant events. They allow students to explore the spatial relationships of an idea. Graphing programs allow students to examine abstract numeric relationships in a more concrete manner.

Information Retrieval and Processing. Telecomputing on the Internet, research on the World Wide Web, database searching, and spreadsheet forecasting allow a student to investigate information in depth. By developing powerful search strategies, a student can find answers to perplexing questions, connect related facts, and derive new information. By sorting information, a student can examine precedence and develop a better understanding of linear relationships or hierarchical order. By altering vari-

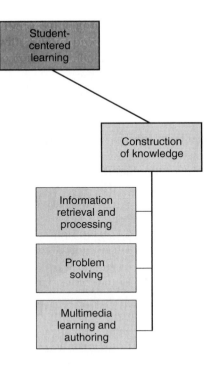

Figure 4–17

Student-centered learning

ables in a problem, a student can explore cause-and-effect relationships and forecast results of a decision. The computer is indeed a tool that amplifies a person's ability to build knowledge.

Problem Solving. The use of the computer as a problem-solving tool is a major focus of this book, and the following chapter will be devoted to this topic. Problem-solving strategies revolve around having a certain background knowledge, understanding the material at hand, knowing what is expected, developing a solution strategy, and reflecting on its effectiveness. Both linear and nonlinear strategies will be discussed. The computer can provide background knowledge and can provide a tool to explore solution strategies. It can organize and manipulate information, allowing the user to test tentative solutions before adopting the most appropriate.

Multimedia Learning and Authoring. Multimedia learning gives the student control of powerful tools in the exploration and creation of information. Multimedia tools allow a student to compose a complex statement that might include computer-generated sound, graphics, and animation, along with sound and visual forms stored in another medium such as videodisc, videotape, and CD-ROM or downloaded from a source on the Internet. Multimedia allows the student to explore communication through multiple senses and become the creator, the artist, the storyteller as vivid mental images are painted. Students learn to access and organize information; display text, graphics, audio, and video information; and present the products as evidence of knowledge they have constructed.

ACTION RESEARCH

The functional application of the computer to classroom action research, as addressed in Figure 4–18, includes data storage and statistical analysis. Once again the computer is seen as a tool. It is a tool that supports **action research,** placing the teacher in the role of the researcher, often examining some aspect of classroom practice.

The state of Oregon has required for several years that student teachers demonstrate their ability to impact pupil learning as a requirement for initial teacher licensing. Faculty at Western Oregon University have developed a work sample methodology to address that requirement. Simply described, the methodology requires student teachers to gather appropriate data to describe the learning environment as fully as possible and to prepare a sample of their work. Community, school setting, grade level, class size, gender ratio, number of exceptional students [talented and gifted youngsters, children with learning disabilities, those for whom Individual Education Programs (IEPs) have been written, those with limited English proficiency (LEP), at-risk youth, etc.], and available classroom resources all are described as the context in which instruction and learning take place. A two- to five-week unit of instruction is then designed. Unit goals and objectives are developed based on Oregon Common Curriculum Goals and district specific goals. A pretest based on the unit's objectives is developed and administered to the class. Appropriate scoring guides are written for the test items and a **quartile analysis** performed. Lesson plans are written. Following the two- to five-week period of instruction, a posttest is administered. The student teacher is required to compare the test results, analyze the level of learning outcomes, reflect on the instruction given within the described context, and draw conclusions.

All teachers are now required to demonstrate their ability to impact pupil learning as a requirement for continuing or advanced teacher licensing in Oregon. The methodology just described may prove to be of assistance to teachers as they fulfill this licensing requirement.

The personal computer behaves as a number cruncher, providing for the storage and analysis of relevant data in the work sample. Pupil names and pretest scores may be entered in a spreadsheet and sorted in descending order of scores. The teacher may separate the resulting list into four groups and have the spreadsheet calculate the average score for each quartile. Later, individual posttest scores are entered. Once again the spreadsheet can calculate the average score for the previously established quartiles and

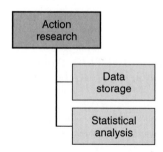

Figure 4–18

Computer applications in action research

can calculate the change in quartile averages as well as in individual scores and present the information in graph form based on the data. Reflecting on the demands and support of the teaching context, the teacher can then rate the level of progress toward desired learning outcomes and the equity in the level of progress across the four quartiles.

Data Storage

As seen in the example just given on work sample methodology, data storage integrates with other functions dealing with the management of information. Stored data accumulated from various sources can be called upon in the future to examine correlations on SAT scores, GPA, and individual student performance. With the help of a personal computer and appropriate software, the teachers/researchers probing a specific topic can analyze data collected on their sample populations and gleaned from student records. Although this certainly could have been done before the advent of the personal computer, now it can be done more easily and cost effectively.

Statistical Analysis

The advent of statistics programs available on personal computers has allowed teachers to analyze data and draw conclusions. This ready access will especially encourage the growth of action research at the K–12 level. Numbers plugged into spreadsheets can yield simple to complex analyses. Even a simple grade book designed on a spreadsheet can reveal mean, range, and standard deviation of scores. As teachers move toward new product-oriented, criterion-based methods of assessment, they are also attempting to understand and compare student performance through new and different means.

SUMMARY

This chapter examined a framework for software in three major categories: school management, instruction and learning, and educational research.

School management was divided by data processing and information retrieval functions into seven functional categories: budget, inventory, student records, teacher records, communication, library circulation, and library public access catalog.

Instruction and learning was divided into two major areas, teacher-centered instruction and student-centered learning. "Teacher-Centered Instruction" examined the computer as the object of instruction, as well as a tool of instruction and the management of instruction. It was subdivided into the categories of computer literacy, computer-assisted instruction, computer-managed instruction, and design of teaching materials.

Computer literacy was recognized as addressing both issues awareness and functional use. As the computer becomes easier to use and more commonplace, less time and effort will go into teaching how to use it. Societal issues related to the computer such as access, copyright, rights of privacy, data security, and information ownership may well continue to command attention in the classroom.

Computer-assisted instruction was subdivided into categories that parallel learning theory. Computer software might take the form of drill and practice, tutorial, simulation, or interactive multimedia software that combines text, graphics, sound, and animation and that controls live-action video sequences.

A tutorial software program is designed to introduce new information to the student and often includes a placement test to ensure student readiness. Drill and practice is a technique used to reinforce previous instruction and newly introduced concepts by providing the repetition necessary to move skills and concepts acquired into long-term memory. Simulation software supports the problem-solving learning that all students must go through to connect concepts into major clusters of knowledge.

Simulations provide an environment for discovery learning to take place or for newly acquired skills and concepts to be tested. Lending themselves to group use, they promote social interaction and can often be used as an introductory activity for a unit. Simulation can be a method of holding a student's attention while not adversely interfering with the lesson's intent. Virtual reality (VR) is a computer-generated simulated environment delivered directly to the user. This computer-based technology creates an illusion of reality in which the participants interact with, and in fact are immersed in, an artificial environment to a degree that appears real. The possibilities for virtual reality applications in education are great, although so are the technological and financial challenges associated with it.

Multimedia instruction combines the computer with other instructional devices to control the presenting, analyze the responses, and store the results of instructional events. Multimedia employs more than one way of conveying information in a multisensory manner.

The distinguishing characteristics that separate the different categories of computer-assisted instruction are beginning to blur, because strategies are being combined to achieve a wider range of objectives. We must keep in mind that we are witnessing the adaptation of time-tested teaching strategies to a different medium. This adaptation gives students a wider variety of educational experiences than has ever been offered before.

Computer-managed instruction was discussed as a category of software that helps the teacher track students' progress. If this time-consuming work can be done more efficiently with the aid of the computer, then the teacher will have more time to help students. This alone can make for a more effective learning environment.

Design of teaching materials deals with the design, development, and creation of teaching materials. A vast array of tools are available to the creative teacher to design and produce materials that communicate effectively.

Student-centered learning views the computer as a tool for the student to use to create, access, retrieve, manipulate, and transmit information in order to solve a problem. Understanding the concept of the computer as an information tool relies on accepting the fact that the computer is a productivity tool for the student and teacher alike.

Classroom action research includes functions relating to information gathering and processing. The teacher/researcher may examine student performance data in new and revealing ways.

The somewhat arbitrary classification of curriculum over the past decades, especially at the secondary school level, into specific subject matter areas is now breaking down in favor of the integration of disciplines to foster richer learning environments. As we consider computer applications, then, we should keep in mind the concept of integration. The complexity of hardware and software design will increase because of technological advances, greater sophistication in programming, and innovative discoveries. As this happens, programs will address multiple skills embedded in more intriguing activities that may change the way we learn.

CHAPTER EXERCISES

1. Create a mock budget for a student activity club in an area of personal interest. List income and expenditures. How could a computer assist you in managing this budget?
2. Identify as many tasks as you can that are included in library circulation. Which of these tasks might be facilitated by a computer? Which would not?
3. Compare the instructional intent of drill and practice, tutorial, and simulation software and describe how a teacher might employ all three types of programs within a unit of instruction.
4. Describe a drill and practice format. Apply this description to a piece of software you have examined and explain in detail how it employs that technique. Identify the role of the teacher, the student, and the computer.
5. Describe a tutorial format. Apply this description to a piece of software you have examined and explain in detail how it employs that technique. Identify the role of the teacher, the student, and the computer.
6. Describe a simulation format. Apply this description to a piece of software you have examined such as *Oregon Trail*™ by MECC or *Where in the World is Carmen Sandiego*™ by Broderbund and explain in detail how it employs that technique. Identify the role of the teacher, the student, and the computer. What does the program simulate and how does it do it? Does it also employ any drill and practice techniques? Explain.
7. Describe how the use of gaming strategies might enhance or detract from drill and practice software. How might they affect a simulation?

GLOSSARY

action research The teacher as researcher investigates a problem, usually arising from some classroom practice. Results are applicable only to the setting in which the research was conducted.
branching A design of some programs that employs techniques to provide multiple alternative paths, or branches, for remediation or acceleration.
computer-assisted instruction (CAI) The direct instructional interaction between computer and student designed to produce the transmission of information.
computer literacy The study of the development and functional use of the computer, as well as related societal issues.

computer-managed instruction (CMI) Use of the computer as a diagnostic, prescriptive, and organizational tool to gather, store, manipulate, analyze, and report information relative to the student and the curriculum.

desktop presentation The display of screens (images or text) of information stored in a computer. The display device is often a video projector or flat panel overhead projection device.

drill and practice A category of computer software that employs the teaching strategy to reinforce instruction by providing repetition necessary to move acquired skills and concepts into long-term memory. Problems are presented and feedback provided to the student's response.

file manager Software that is designed to create and to manage data files. Current usage employs this term synonymously with database manager.

gaming A strategy that can be incorporated into all instructional software categories. Includes the elements of a set of rules and competition against others or against a standard.

linear Linear programs present information in a sequential manner and do not attempt to remediate errors made. New material is commonly provided in small increments, replete with instructional guidance and appropriate feedback to encourage correct student response.

multimedia instruction The technique of accessing and displaying textual, graphic, audio, and video information stored in electronic, magnetic, or optical form under the control of a computer to meet objectives specified by the teacher by conveying information in a multisensory manner.

multimedia learning The technique of accessing, organizing, and displaying textual, graphic, audio, and video information stored in electronic, magnetic, or optical form under the control of a computer to meet student needs by conveying information in a multisensory manner.

public access catalog (PAC) A computer-based system that provides user access to a library's holdings.

quartile analysis The ranking of performance measures from high to low and the separation of the measures into four groups to study performance by high, medium, and low achievers.

simulation A category of computer software that employs a teaching strategy based on role playing within structured environments. It provides an environment for discovery learning to take place and for newly acquired skills and concepts to be tested.

spreadsheet Software that accepts data in a matrix of columns and rows, with their intersections called cells. One cell can relate to any other cell or ranges of cells on the matrix by formula. Often used with numeric data to forecast results of decisions.

tutorial A category of computer software that employs the teaching strategy in which the student's level of knowledge is first determined before new information is introduced along with learning guidance. The computer usually assesses a student's prior learning, determines readiness for the material, and presents material for student observation, note taking, and other interaction.

virtual reality A computer-generated simulated environment with which a user can interact.

REFERENCES & SUGGESTED READINGS

Barron, A. E. (1993, March). The marriage of computers and TV. *Media and Methods, 29*(3), 10.

Brown, J. (1992, Spring). A computer based cooperative learning project for preservice teachers. *Journal of Computing in Teacher Education, 8*(3), 11–16.

Dillon, R. (1997, September). Strategies for the one computer classroom. *Learning and Leading with Technology, 25*(1), 32–33.

Griest, G. (1993, April). You say you want a revolution: Constructivism, technology, and language arts. *The Computing Teacher, 20*(7), 8–11.

Hill, W. F. (1977). *Learning: A survey of psychological interpretations*. New York: Harper & Row, 214–216.

Maley, D. (1993, Summer). Technology education: A natural for middle level students. *Schools in the Middle, 2*(4), 10–14.

Miller, C. (1992, November) Online interviews: Dr. Thomas A. Furness, III, virtual reality pioneer. *Online, 16*(6), 14–27.

Mizell, A. (1997, July). Unpublished review, Nova Southeastern University, Miami, FL.

Norton, P. (1992, March). When technology meets the subject-matter disciplines. *Educational Technology, 32*(3), 3–5.

Saunders, W. L. (1992, March). Constructivist perspective: Implications and teaching strategies for science. *School Science and Mathematics, 92*(3), 136–141.

Thornburg, D. (1991). *Education, technology, and paradigms of change for the 21st century*. San Carlos, CA: Starsong Publications.

Woodward, J. (1992, June). *Virtual reality and its potential use in special education*. Washington, D.C.: Cosmos Corp. (ERIC 350 766).

Zelazek, J., & Lamson, S. (1992, February). *Action research and the student teacher: A framework for problem solving and reflective thinking*. Paper presented at the annual meeting of the Association of Teacher Educators, Orlando, FL.

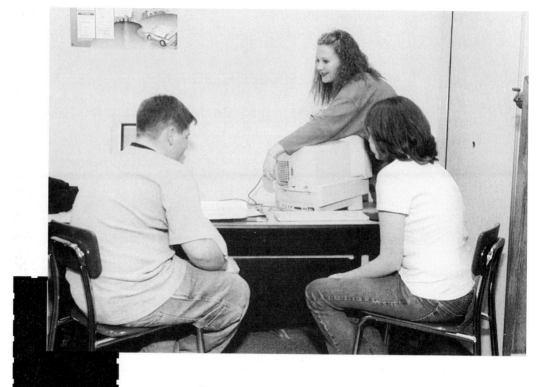

Chapter 5

Examining the Tool

1. What are the primary processes involved in a computer system (input of data, operations performed on the data, and output of information)?

2. The input process: what hardware exists today to facilitate your entering data?

3. What is a CPU?

4. What are the different types of memory and how do they differ?

5. The output process: what hardware exists today to facilitate your extracting information?

6. How has the user interface evolved and what is the potential impact on you as a user?

An understanding of the computer as a tool requires an awareness of its component parts and an appreciation of what each part may contribute as we attempt to solve problems encountered. A discussion of computer equipment can never be truly current, for as this is being written a new product is undoubtedly entering the market. The goal of this chapter is to acquaint you with fundamental concepts related to equipment, or hardware, and to describe in modest detail the equipment that has found some measure of acceptance in schools.

This chapter offers a brief look at the evolution of computer hardware and an explanation of the various components of a computer system. It will show how their interrelationship allows a user to put data into a system, manipulate those data, and retrieve information in an appropriate manner, and then the chapter highlights particular applications in school settings. It also introduces you to the concept of an operating system. The majority of references can be generalized to all major brands of microcomputers.

Once again the shift in computer paradigms identified in Chapter 1 becomes apparent as we trace the development of the technology and in particular the development of computer hardware. Now the mobile user employing a personal computer is able to interconnect with a network of other users in order to search a labyrinth of databases to access valuable information.

WHAT IS HARDWARE?

Hardware is a term commonly used to designate the equipment components of a computer system. A monitor, a keyboard, a mouse, a joystick, a printer, a disk drive—all are examples of **hardware.** Not all tangible objects are encompassed by this term, however. For instance, floppy disks, which are tangible objects, are usually termed "magnetic media" or just "media" and are considered consumable supplies. Recording a program on a floppy disk changes the terminology of the **disk** to **software.** More precisely, the actual recording of the program itself on the magnetic medium is the software, but you can see that at some point it is impossible to separate the two. To unravel the confusion related to equipment specification, this chapter is organized according to the three processes involved in a computer system and will examine the hardware related to each.

WHAT PROCESSES ARE INVOLVED IN A COMPUTER SYSTEM?

When we refer to "a computer system," we are taking into account all components necessary to perform a designated task. The actual pieces of hardware may vary, but a computer system, as illustrated in Figure 5–1, has three basic processes: input, operation, and output.

The **input** is the process of entering data into the computer system. The **operation** is the process of manipulating the data in a predetermined manner by the computer itself or, more precisely, by the **central processing unit (CPU)** under the control of a program. The **output** is the process of retrieving the information once it has been acted upon by the CPU. All hardware other than the computer itself is referred to as peripheral equipment. The computer system as illustrated in Figure 5–1 groups equipment in clusters that parallel the input, operation, and output processes.

Input Peripherals

Input peripherals are all the hardware items whose function is to enter data into the computer through tactile, audio, video, or electronic means (Figure 5–2). Specialized cables and connectors are used to transfer electronic impulses between the peripheral devices and the computer. Keep in mind the relationship of the various hardware elements so that you will more easily understand the functioning of the computer system.

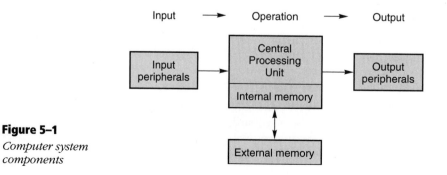

Figure 5–1

Computer system components

The **keyboard** is the primary device through which data are entered into a personal computer system. This typewriter-like device's function is to generate a digital code that can be entered into the computer's memory and be understood by the microprocessor. The binary code used in personal computers is **ASCII** (American Standard Code for Information Interchange, pronounced "askee").

The **mouse** is a small, hand-held input device that a user moves left, right, up, or down on a flat surface such as a desk. It depends on a software interface (a program) to move a cursor on the screen, replicating the motion of the mouse. The software constantly monitors the position of the cursor on the screen. Pressing a button on the mouse results in one of several actions, depending on the program being used.

The **trackball** is a stationary device that some say resembles a mouse on its back. With the mouse, the user grasps a frame that rolls around the desk surface on a ball. With the trackball, the user rolls a movable ball fixed in a stationary frame.

The **trackpad,** usually found on laptop computers, is a pressure-sensitive pad about two inches square. By pressing a finger to the pad, the user moves a pointer on the screen.

Printed bar codes similar to the **UPC** (Universal Product Code) found on many products make data entry extremely fast and accurate. The codes are read by devices that sense the sequence of thick and thin lines and their spacing. Two commonly used **bar code readers** are the hand-held wand and the stationary reader similar to those commonly employed at grocery checkout counters. The bar code readers generate light, which reflects from the bar code in a light and dark pattern. The reader, sensing the pattern, generates the appropriate matching digital code, thus eliminating the need for time-consuming keyboard entry, with its inherent typing errors.

A school library's circulation system could be based on a bar code applied to each student's identification card, with appropriate bar codes placed on book spines or card pockets. Information can be read into a computer by a bar wand and in seconds the checkout procedure is completed.

Most models of **digital cameras,** as shown in Figure 5–3, are easy to use and store between 30 and 96 digital images. When connected to a computer, the images may be downloaded and stored to be later manipulated in a variety of ways by appropriate software. They are great tools for incorporating photographic images into presentations to the class, as well as to parent groups. They make a wonderful contribution to the preparation of newsletters.

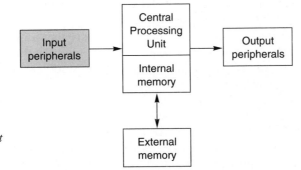

Figure 5–2

A schematic indicating the input peripherals component

Figure 5–3

*A digital camera
(Courtesy of Eastman
Kodak.)*

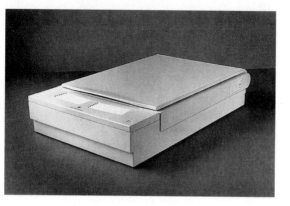

Figure 5–4

*An optical scanner
(Courtesy of Apple
Computer, Inc.)*

Optical scanners, as shown in Figure 5–4 operate by reading light reflected from the surface of an object such as a photograph, line drawing, or printed page of text. The scanner is accompanied by software that allows it to exercise some degree of control over the scanned image. It is often possible for the user to vary the image's size by **cropping** (adjusting only the outside dimensions) or **scaling** (proportionally enlarging or reducing the entire image) and to adjust brightness and contrast.

Graphics tablets similar to those depicted in Figure 5–5 are input devices that allow the user to create or trace figures or drawings of any kind. A student can draw a picture with a stylus provided on the surface of the tablet and see it replicated on the monitor screen. The stylus allows the user far greater control than the mouse in drawing intricate designs. The accompanying software translates the stylus's position and displays it as a point on the monitor screen. The series of points are the representation of a straight or curved line segment making up a total picture. You can also fill in solid areas of color, as well as enlarge or reduce the drawing. Again, using the software, the user can select certain shapes, shadings, and line widths or "paintbrush" effects. An art teacher might choose to have students use this device to execute lessons in perspective, line, or contour drawing. With its inherent ability to trace existing material, the graphics tablet is also an excellent device to facilitate the production of maps for a social studies lesson.

Although **voice entry devices** have been available for a few years to interface with personal computers, it is only recently that they have gained ready acceptance. Most current applications allow command words (e.g., New, Bold, Italic, Save) to be

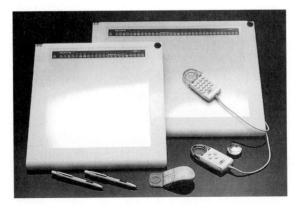

Figure 5–5

*Graphics tablets
(Courtesy of Kurta®.)*

spoken into a microphone that, through the appropriate software, conveys the command to the computer, which interacts with the word processor in use. Broader applications are on the horizon, however. Voice entry has the advantage of eliminating the need to learn keyboarding skills. It offers speed, ease of use, and the potential for voice recognition security. A great deal of research and development is occurring in this area, and dramatic new software product announcements are expected.

The telephone **modem** (MOdulator-DEModulator) is both an input device and an output device. It translates digital computer information into **analog** signals of varying frequency that can be transmitted over telephone lines and analog signals into a digital form that can be processed by a computer. The relatively inexpensive modem is playing a major role in making the information revolution a reality. It is a vital link allowing computers to exchange information. Depending on their speed of transmission, modems are now commonly available in 33,600 or 56,000 bps (bits per second). Modems that operate over cable or specialized phone lines are far faster yet. **Bps** has replaced the former designation of **baud rate.**

With telefacsimile (fax) machines becoming so commonplace in businesses and schools, the advent of the **fax-modem** came as no surprise. It allows a computer to communicate with another computer or with a fax machine. Fax machines send and receive information in a type of graphic format so that pages of text are transmitted as images. Faxes received by fax-modems are stored in the computer as graphic documents unless software is used to convert them into text files that can be edited.

Daily attendance figures could be gathered at each school, entered into a computer, and transmitted by modem to a computer at a central office, where the data could be analyzed and stored. With the use of modems, electronic mail within a school district is a reality. Modems facilitate the sharing of computer resources among schools and school districts, as well as public schools and colleges.

Central Processing Unit

A computer program is a series of executable instructions and related information conveyed as a digital signal in binary form. The heart of the computer system through which all instructions and information flow is the central processing unit

(CPU) (see Figure 5–6). This term is a throwback to large mainframe jargon, when the CPU was in fact a separate piece of equipment. The CPU is now often referred to as the microcomputer chip or the **microprocessor.** It is usually the largest chip on the computer's circuit board. The two predominant families of microprocessor chips are manufactured by Intel (e.g., 80486, Pentium series), used by the computers operating under MS-DOS and Windows, and by Motorola and IBM (e.g., 68040, PowerPC 604), used by Macintosh and a new line of cross platform referenced computers developed by IBM.

Internal Memory

The **internal,** or working, **memory** of the computer (Figure 5–7) can be examined in two basic categories, constant and temporary. The manufacturer stores instructions that govern the fundamental operations of the computer in the constant memory, or **ROM** (read-only memory). Integrated circuits contain the ROM, which consists of instructions that, once encoded by the manufacturer, cannot be erased, written to, or modified in any way. ROM is not dependent upon a supply of power to maintain itself. Since the user has no control over the ROM, little attention is usually paid to it.

The **temporary memory** is the category of internal memory available and accessible to the user. When you write an original program, load a prepared program from a diskette, type a letter using a word processor, or enter information into a database management program, you are in fact entering instructions or data and placing them in temporary memory called random-access memory, or **RAM.** RAM is often called **volatile memory** because it requires a constant source of power to maintain itself. Should power fail for even a brief moment, the contents of RAM are lost forever. Users who are concerned about power outages or interruption usually connect their computer to a backup or uninterruptible power supply (**UPS**). Figure 5–8 is a reminder of the different types of internal memory.

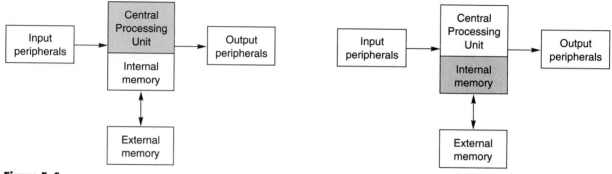

Figure 5–6

A schematic indicating the central processing unit component

Figure 5–7

A schematic indicating the internal memory component

There are times when the user is employing the computer (and its internal temporary memory) in a direct, immediate mode, perhaps to communicate by electronic mail or as a supercalculator to solve a mathematical problem. In most other instances, however, it is important to save work done on the computer. When the program being written or the information being entered should be preserved, RAM is really only a temporary holding area, where the ideas are manipulated and the data organized before being passed on and stored permanently in external memory. In the case of RAM, bigger is indeed better. The more temporary memory available (RAM), the larger and more sophisticated is the application program that can be run and the larger is the file that can be processed. Graphics files, for instance, can consume a very large amount of RAM. The amount of RAM is measured by counting the potential bytes of information. Remember that a byte is the amount of memory required to represent one alphabetic or numeric character. The amount of RAM may be expressed in units of 1,000 bytes, represented by the symbol **K,** as in **kilobytes** or in units of 1 million by the symbol **MB,** as in **megabytes.** Computers today are sold with millions of bytes of RAM.

External Memory

The **external memory** apparatus (Figure 5–9) can really be considered as both input and output devices. Information such as programs can be copied into or read by the computer (input), and files can usually be saved (output) to this hardware to be later retrieved (input) from it. External memory, as its name implies, is *not located on the main internal circuit board of the computer.* It is the auxiliary storage of programs and data, often on a removable medium such as a magnetic disk or CD-ROM, housed in a piece of equipment sometimes separate from the computer cabinet itself. The term can be somewhat confusing, though, insofar as the peripheral memory equipment is now often housed in the computer's cabinet.

A type of external storage widely available in the past was the **floppy disk,** a small wafer of flexible polyester film coated with an emulsion having magnetic properties similar to audio or videotape. It was encased in a 5¼″ square, flexible protective plastic jacket that was lined with a nonwoven fabric liner designed to clean the diskette as it rotated smoothly. It had a large center hole designed to accept a spindle, which spun the disk at high speed within its protective jacket.

The 3½″ microdiskette format (Figure 5–10)—with its smaller size, improved protection against dirt and physical damage, and far greater storage capacity—has re-

Figure 5–8

A schematic identifying types of internal memory

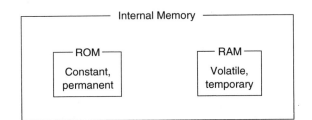

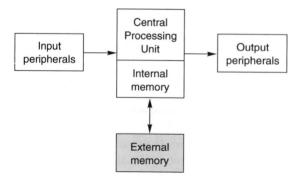

Figure 5–9

A schematic indicating the external memory component

placed the 5¼″ floppy disk. The **microdiskette** is not only much smaller than the original 5¼″ floppy, but it is housed in a rigid plastic protective case; nevertheless, the term *floppy disk* has persevered. The hub opening is nearly covered by the metal hub piece, and the read-write head access slot is protected by a spring-loaded, sliding metal cover. Write protection is accomplished by sliding a small plastic tab located near one corner on the bottom of the diskette toward the edge of the case. When the slot is open, the disk is protected. When the tab covers the hole, information can be stored on the disk or erased from it.

The disk drive's function is to save data to and retrieve data from the floppy disk. It does this by engaging the disk and rotating it at high speed on a motor-driven spindle while the magnetic read-write head scans the surface, sensing or creating magnetic domains (Figure 5–11). This aspect is, in fact, similar to audiotape recording and playback. When a song is played from a tape, it is not removed from the tape. Likewise, when a program is read from a disk, it is only copied into RAM and not removed from the disk. The actual process of searching for and loading a program

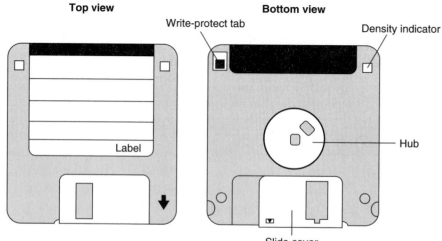

Figure 5–10

A 3½″ microdiskette now commonly referred to as a floppy disk

As disk rotates . . .

Figure 5–11

Disk read-write access

. . . head moves back and forth

(copying it into RAM from external memory) is much more analogous to playing an audio CD than playing an audiotape, however. The computer disk and the audio CD are random-access devices with multiple access points. Many different programs can be stored on the same diskette. Each program has a unique identifier stored in a diskette directory or catalog track. When selecting a song to play from an audio CD, you can punch in a code number that will select the beginning of a particular song as the CD is spinning. When you instruct the computer to load a particular program from a diskette, the spindle rotates the disk while the read-write head scans the surface, looking for the beginning of the program you selected, which it then loads into RAM. Combining the two factors of spinning the disk at high speed and quickly moving the read-write head in and out across its surface results in rapid random access to any information on the disk.

It is necessary to prepare a blank floppy disk to receive data. This **formatting,** or **initializing,** process allows you to save your programs later onto the disk. In preparing a disk, the computer lays out an indexed map on the disk so it will know where to write the programs and files to be saved. Programs on floppy disks are indexed by track and sector number. When the disk is formatted, a directory is created and concentric circles called **tracks** are laid out on the surface of the disk (Figure 5–12). These are the major divisions of the disk. Each circular track is divided into units called **sectors.** Each sector is capable of storing a certain number of bytes of information. Newer operating systems allow much greater storage density than did previous ones.

This format directory, or computer-created map, on the disk can be compared to a road map. You can find a city on a map by looking up its horizontal and vertical location coordinates in the map index. The index may also tell you the population of that city. The disk map, or directory, tells the computer where to find a specific file and its memory size.

Figure 5–13 gives pointers on the care and handling of floppy disks.

Another common form of external memory is the **hard disk.** It is a rigid platter coated with a magnetic emulsion similar to that used on a floppy diskette. The hard disk is often enclosed in the computer's case and is then called an internal hard disk. It is referred to as an external hard disk if it is enclosed in its own separate case and connected by cable to the computer. It is usually fixed, whether inside or outside of the computer, but may also be removable for portability, a new, popular trend set by the Iomega Zip and Jaz drives. A variation on removable cartridges is the magneto-optical ones, in which, in addition to magnetic recording, a laser distends a recording surface by heating it and thereby encoding a message.

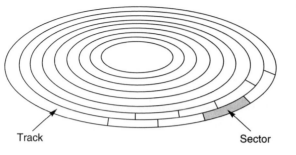

Figure 5–12

Tracks and sectors established by formatting

The hard disk's main advantage over the floppy diskette is its far greater memory storage capacity. A secondary advantage is faster access time when loading programs. Hard disks often offer over a **gigabyte** (1,000 megabytes) of storage. This amount of memory allows users to place programs permanently on the hard disk drive rather than having to work from floppies.

The **laser videodisc** is making some contributions in school applications. The recording is stored on a rigid platter either 8 or 12 inches in diameter and is read by a laser. It is used mainly to store text, pictorial and audio information, and moving images to be presented under the control of a computer. By taking advantage of its two separate audio tracks, recordings can be presented in English and in a second language; the user can select which track to listen to. This feature has drawn considerable attention in bilingual education. Thanks to the videodisc's success in the consumer entertainment market as a medium for feature films, players are now readily available and reasonably priced. It is important to recognize that it is strictly a playback medium. Teachers must depend on the commercial availability of recorded videodiscs.

Another laser-read medium has gained ready acceptance in the consumer as well as the education market. The CD-ROM is currently available as a 5″ diameter disk. Remember that the acronym CD-ROM stands for compact disk–read only memory. Publishers have released encyclopedias, dictionaries, atlases, and many other books and databases in this format. Connecting a CD-ROM player to a computer and using the software provided, the user can perform rapid and sophisticated searches. Many new products, ranging from specialized databases to titles of works in children's literature, have been introduced in this format. Software is now readily being distrib-

---

- Do not lay the disk down on a dirty or greasy surface.
- Keep the disk away from liquids and excessive chalk dust.
- Do not write on disk label in pencil. Stray bits of graphite could cause read errors.
- Do not store disks in direct sunlight or next to a heater. Protect them from extremes of temperatures.
- Keep all magnets away from the disk. Do not place a disk on a TV or monitor; the picture tube's magnetic field may destroy the information on the disk.
- Do not retract the metal shutter and touch the resulting exposed disk surface.

Figure 5–13

The care and handling of disks

uted in the CD-ROM format. While the original format was read only, newer formats sometimes referred to as CD-R or CD-RW and the Digital Video Disk (DVD) format allow the user to read, write, and erase.

Output Peripherals

Output peripherals (Figure 5–14) are all the hardware items whose function it is to display information from the computer through audio, video, print, and electronic means. Specialized cables and connectors are used to transfer electronic impulses between the peripheral devices and the computer. Once again, it is important to keep in mind the relationship of the various hardware elements in order to understand the functioning of the computer system. Without one or more output peripherals, the computer system would be incomplete and of little value.

The **video monitor** accepts a computer's video signal directly and is capable of displaying a picture of much higher resolution than a television receiver; therefore, it is the standard for computer applications. With so much software depending on color, color monitors are now the norm for use with computers.

Although one or two interconnected large-screen (25″ or larger) video monitors may suffice when presenting information to a small group of viewers, they are not ideal in front of a large group. **Video projectors** such as the one shown in Figure 5–15 are capable of displaying a large (10-foot diagonal or larger) projected image. They accept a video signal directly from a computer. Their main drawback is the need for better light control than is the case when using monitors. The projected image's lower level of brightness and the presence of ambient room light striking the screen usually demand a darkened room to maximize the impact of the projected image.

The **overhead display panel,** as shown in Figure 5–16, is a portable, lightweight liquid crystal display **(LCD) panel** that is designed to sit on the stage of an overhead projector. Many panels are multiscan and accept video signals of different bandwidths from computers such as the Macintosh and IBM compatibles. One model, PC Viewer, even has its own internal, battery-supported RAM to store up to 75 screen images so

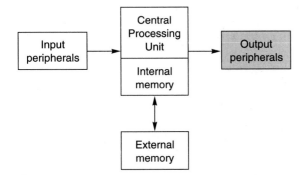

Figure 5–14

A schematic indicating the output peripherals component

Figure 5–15

A video projector (Courtesy of Sharp Electronics.)

Figure 5–16

An overhead display panel (Courtesy of InFocus, Inc.)

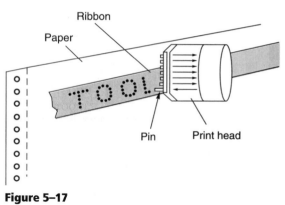

Figure 5–17

A dot matrix print head

that the computer doesn't even have to be connected during the presentation. Screen brightness and image size are functions of the overhead projector and screen placement. The projected image is usually less bright than that of a video projector.

For many years, the most popular type of printer in schools has been the **dot matrix printer** that prints on regular bond paper. Most models accept cut sheets such as letterhead, as well as continuous form fan-fold tractor paper, and are available with friction feed as well as adjustable tractors. The printing, at a resolution of 72 dots per inch (dpi), is somewhat jagged and is recognizable as being computer generated. Some dot matrix printers achieve greater than 72 dpi resolution and are promoted as being "near letter quality." Print size and density can easily be manipulated, achieving compressed, expanded, darkened, and emphasized print. This is achieved by sending commands from the computer to the printer. Dot matrix printers are also capable, through dot-addressable graphics, of printing pictures, charts, and other graphics on paper.

The dot matrix print head (Figure 5–17) consists of one or more columns of pins, which are activated, or fired, separately to strike an inked ribbon, printing dots, which, when viewed at a normal distance, appear to form a letter. With each firing of the pins, the print head forms part of the letter as it travels across the paper. Most printers use nine pins, but a few use 24 smaller pins to enhance the detail quality and resolution of the print.

The low-cost **ink-jet printer** shown in Figure 5–18 also prints on regular bond paper or letterhead and is quickly becoming the printer of choice in schools. Rather than firing pins to strike an inked ribbon, the print head of an ink-jet printer squirts a dot of quick-drying ink through precisely controlled nozzles onto the paper. Ink-jet printers can achieve a resolution of 600 dpi or greater and are much quieter than dot matrix printers in their operation. Best of all, ink-jet printers print in full color. With their low cost, ease of maintenance, high resolution, and color, it's no wonder that they are quickly replacing dot matrix printers for many school applications.

At the higher end of the printer cost scale are **laser printers** (Figure 5–19), which use a laser beam to create an image on a photosensitive drum surface. The image is transferred by means of a carbon toner to produce letter-quality (approaching type-

Figure 5–18
An inkjet-printer (Courtesy of Hewlett Packard Co.)

Figure 5–19
A laser printer (Courtesy of Hewlett Packard Co.)

set quality) printing of text and graphics onto plain bond or letterhead paper at a very high resolution, exceeding 1,200 dots per inch (dpi). This technology is very similar to the one employed by sophisticated photocopiers. As the price continues to drop, this may well become the printer of preference for many school applications. It is now commonly found in school offices and on networks where several computers can use it.

A laser printer receives information from a computer and stores it temporarily in its internal memory. It transfers this information as a code that governs the operation of a laser that strikes a photosensitive drum, as illustrated in Figure 5–20, setting up electrical charges on its surface. The drum rotates past a carbon particle toner reservoir, where toner is attracted to the charged areas. A sheet of paper is pressed against this toner-bearing drum and the toner transfers to the paper. Before exiting the printer, the paper passes through a thermal fuser section, which hardens and fixes the toner on the paper.

When considering printers, we must also consider interfacing, or the ability to transmit information from the computer to the output device. An interface is a two-part device; one part is built into the peripheral device and the other part into either the computer or a firmware card that plugs into one of the expansion slots on the computer's main circuit board. A cable attaches the card to the printer or plotter.

Interfaces are available in either *parallel* or *serial* mode (Figure 5–21), depending on the particular printer used. A **parallel interface** sends the seven or eight bits of data comprising the byte simultaneously along eight different wires in a flat ribbon cable. In addition, other wires in the cable carry communication signals between the computer and the printer. This cable is limited to a short length of only a few feet. The **serial interface** sends one bit at a time in a continuous sequence along one wire, inserting a code to separate the bytes. The cable may be a simple **twisted pair** of wires and may run for many, many feet. The important thing to remember is that the printer used determines the interface mode. A parallel printer will not accept serial transmission and vice versa. Some printers have both serial and parallel ports built in and therefore can communicate in either mode.

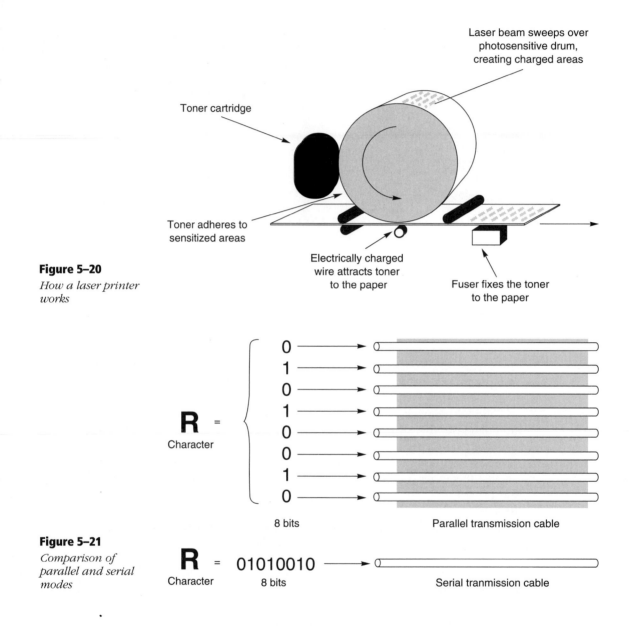

Figure 5–20

How a laser printer works

Figure 5–21

Comparison of parallel and serial modes

USER INTERFACE

The **user interface** can be thought of as the interaction between human and machine. It is receiving a good deal of attention in the design of new operating systems. Early interfaces progressed from mechanical (throwing switches) to text based (typing command words). One of the most widely used **operating systems** of all time, Microsoft's MS-DOS, uses a text-based command line interface which gives the user a great deal of control over the functions of the computer, but is complex, requiring the memorization of command words.

Apple Computer introduced the Macintosh in 1984. It capitalized on research done by Xerox and was the first commercially successful computer to substitute a **graphic user interface (GUI)** for the command line interface. Since 1984, graphics have become much more important to the manner in which humans interact with computers. Microsoft introduced a graphic interface called Windows that ran once MS-DOS was loaded. It has followed that with Windows 95 and Windows NT and their current derivatives. All computer operating systems are substituting the use of **icons,** or pictorial representations, for complex verbal commands. Instead of typing a command to retrieve a file from external memory, you might simply move a screen arrow to point to the icon of a file folder and click the mouse button to open the folder. The file can be opened immediately by pointing to it and double clicking the mouse button. Should you decide later that the file is no longer needed, you can drag its icon to an icon of a trash can, thus "throwing away" the file. Here the screen action replicates kinesthetic behavior associated with everyday occurrences in the work environment.

In examining Figure 5–22, it is easy to see that folder icons look very much like manila file folders used in a filing cabinet. Software publishers design their own unique icons to represent their software and the files or documents created by their software. Program and document icons can be dragged to folder icons in order to store them in that folder. Folders may be placed inside other folders.

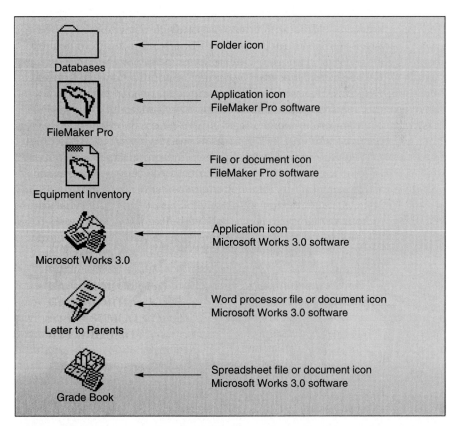

Figure 5–22

Various types of icons

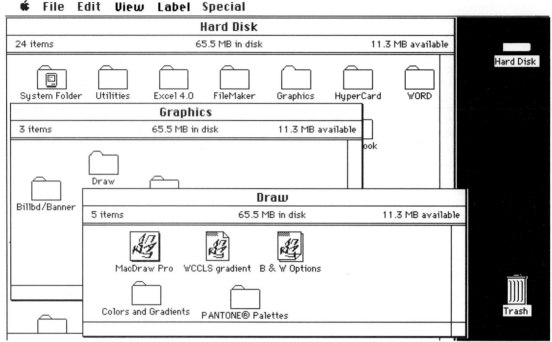

Figure 5–23
Overlapping windows, open folders, and icons

Figure 5–23 illustrates overlapping windows, open folders, and icons. The *Hard Disk* window is in the background on the patterned desktop. The pattern on the *Graphics* folder indicates that it is open and its window is therefore also open, over-lapping the *Hard Disk* window. The pattern on the *Draw* folder indicates that it is open and its window is therefore also open, overlapping the *Graphics* window. Notice that, in the *Draw* window, the program *MacDraw Pro™*, two files, and two additional folders are found. Two icons, one representing the hard disk drive and one representing the trash, are located on the desktop to the right of the open windows.

In September 1993, Apple Computer released its first personal digital assistant (PDA), called the Newton MessagePad. This small, hand-held computer (the size of a paperback book and weighing one pound) organizes information interactively in an address book, a list of things to do, and a calendar. It also communicates information to the outside world by modem, fax, radio pager, infrared beam, serial port, and LAN connection. One of the most exciting features of the Newton, however, is its pen-based operating system, which recognizes cursive handwriting. It borrows concepts from the graphics tablet. As illustrated in Figure 5–24, the user writes with a plastic stylus, which presses against a protective cover layer. This pressure is transmitted to conductive layers, which allow current flow at the pressure point. The information is transferred to an LCD pixel matrix layer, which creates shapes in what is being called digital ink. The operating system attempts to recognize the shapes as letters or common objects. Users can increase the likelihood of the system recognizing letters by teaching it their hand-

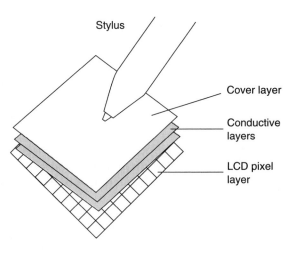

Stylus

Cover layer

Conductive layers

LCD pixel layer

Figure 5–24

How a pen-based system works

writing. It recognizes shapes and transforms roughly drawn circles, for instance, into perfect ones of an equivalent diameter.

Just as the GUI and pen-based systems have revolutionized the use of the computer, the next generation user interface may take us into brand new territory. The next interface may revolve around voice entry, allowing the user to speak command words to the computer. The new interface may be able to recognize many different voices and, depending on the voice recognized, would allow or deny certain operations or access to certain files.

The research and development in improving the user interface is focused on making use of the computer as natural and as easy as possible so that the hardware use becomes transparent to the purpose at hand. Rather than being overly conscious of the hardware and concerned with how to perform a computer task, the user should be allowed to concentrate on the content and nature of the problem being addressed. The most significant question posed by teachers and students will become not "How do I use this computer?" but "What can I do with a computer?"

SUMMARY

Rapid changes in computer technology have resulted in greatly improved and expanded applications, as well as a tremendous simplification in operation, a vastly improved user interface, and a dramatic reduction in equipment size.

When we refer to "a computer system," we are taking into account all hardware components necessary to support the processes of input, operation, and output. The input is the process of entering data into the computer system. The operation is the process of manipulating the data in a predetermined manner by the computer itself under the control of a software program. The output is the process of retrieving the information once it has been acted upon by the CPU.

The internal memory of the computer can be examined as constant, or read-only, memory (ROM) and temporary, or random-access, memory (RAM). The manufacturer stores instructions that govern the fundamental operations of the computer in the constant memory. The ROM cannot be changed by the user employing ordinary means, nor is it dependent upon a supply of power to maintain itself. The RAM is available to the user and is often called volatile memory because it requires a constant source of power.

External memory is the auxiliary storage of programs and data, often on a removable medium, such as magnetic disk or CD-ROM, housed in a piece of equipment sometimes separate from the computer cabinet itself. The formatting, or initializing, process prepares a blank floppy disk to receive data, allowing the user to save programs or files onto the disk. In preparing a disk, the computer lays out an indexed map of track and sector numbers on the disk so it will know where to write the programs and files to be saved.

Output peripherals are all the hardware items that display information from the computer through audio, video, print, and electronic means. Specialized cables and connectors are used to transfer electronic impulses between the peripheral devices and the computer.

A parallel interface sends the seven or eight bits of data comprising the byte simultaneously along eight different wires in a flat ribbon cable that is limited to a short length of only a few feet. The serial interface sends one bit at a time in a continuous sequence along one wire, inserting a code to separate the bytes. The cable may be a simple twisted pair of wires and may run for long distances. Some printers have both serial and parallel ports built in and therefore can communicate in either mode.

Hardware represents a substantial investment of a school district's financial resources and is constantly in a state of flux. Today's new and exciting item may be old next year. A careful analysis of computer applications in the curriculum will allow a school to develop an acquisition program and build on its established equipment base without having to replace everything and start from scratch as new technological developments occur.

Early user interfaces progressed from mechanical to text-based ones. Graphic user interfaces (GUIs) that substitute the use of icons for complex verbal commands have now become the norm for human interaction with computers. Pen-based operating systems recognize cursive handwriting, allowing the user to write with a plastic stylus. The GUI and pen-based systems have revolutionized the use of the computer. The next generation user interface may revolve around voice entry, allowing the user to speak command words to the computer and allowing or denying certain operations or access to certain files. Each progressive improvement in user interfaces makes the use of the computer as natural and as easy as possible so that the hardware use becomes transparent to the purpose at hand.

CHAPTER EXERCISES

1. Examine computer magazines, journals, and catalogs. List advertisements for the various entry devices available for the computer. Discuss briefly the features that are being promoted.

2. List the different types of external storage devices for the microcomputer. Discuss the advantages and disadvantages of each in a school setting.
3. Examine computer journals and magazines and list, by brand names, the variety of external storage devices available for the type(s) of computer(s) found in your school.
4. What two computer output devices are essential in a classroom setting? What other device would be useful? Discuss how this other device would be particularly useful.
5. Many programs in the school setting currently use keyboard input from students. At what grade level would you begin teaching keyboarding skills? Defend your position.

GLOSSARY

analog Signals of a continuous nature that vary in frequency and amplitude. Analog signals can be transmitted over telephone lines.

ASCII The acronym for American Standard Code for Information Interchange. A code in which the numbers 0 to 127 represent alphanumeric, symbolic, and control characters.

bar code reader A device that translates the sequence of spaced thick and thin lines to the computer, enabling it to identify an object.

baud rate A term that has been replaced by bps (see the following entry).

bps A measure of data transmission speed between computers in *bits per second*.

central processing unit (CPU) The point (a chip) in the computer where all parts of the system are linked together and where the calculations and manipulation of data take place (may be referred to as a microprocessor).

cropping Controlling the size of an image without affecting the size of any of its components. Cropping an image smaller than the original eliminates some of the content.

digital camera A device that captures and stores images in a digital format.

disk An external storage medium consisting of a rigid platter (hard disk) or a flexible one (floppy disk) coated with a magnetic emulsion.

dot matrix printer An impact printer that uses a series of electrically hammered pins to create characters composed of a pattern of dots.

external memory The auxiliary storage of programs and data, often on a removable medium such as magnetic disk or tape, housed in a piece of equipment usually separate from the computer cabinet.

fax-modem A device that allows a computer to communicate by phone lines with a facsimile (fax) machine or with another modem-equipped computer.

floppy disk An external storage medium made of flexible polyester film with magnetic properties, similar to audiotape.

formatting Preparing a blank disk to receive information.

gigabyte 1,000 megabytes, used as a reference to memory storage capacity.

graphic user interface (GUI) The on-screen use of pictorial representations (icons) of objects. The user can move a screen pointer onto an icon and click a mouse button to issue a command to the computer.

graphics tablet A peripheral input device used with accompanying software that allows the user to create or trace figures, maps, graphs, and drawings with a finger, a stylus, or another instrument on the tablet and to see it replicated on the screen.

hard disk An external storage medium consisting of a rigid platter coated with a magnetic emulsion and not removable from the disk drive; three to five times larger than a floppy disk, it has far greater memory storage capacity.

hardware The equipment components of a computer system.

icon A pictorial representation of an object.

initializing See *formatting*.

ink-jet printer A printer that uses a series of electronically controlled nozzles to create characters composed of a pattern of dots squirted onto the paper.

input The process of entering information into the computer system.

input peripherals Equipment whose function is to enter data into the computer.

internal memory The storage facilities in a computer system in which data and programs are placed immediately before execution; usually the highest-speed memory in the system.

k The symbol for kilo, equated with 1,000 (actually 1,024 in computer terms).

keyboard The primary input device for the computer; it generates a digital code that can be understood by the microprocessor.

kilobyte One thousand bytes, used as a reference to memory capacity.

laser printer A printer that uses a laser beam to create an image on a photosensitive drum and transfers this by means of carbon toner to paper.

laser videodisc A laser-read rigid platter in either 8″ or 12″ diameter, mainly used to record pictorial and moving images, as well as accompanying sound.

LCD panel Liquid crystal display panel (see also *overhead display panel*).

MB The symbol for megabyte.

megabyte One million bytes, used as a reference to memory capacity.

microdiskette A 3½″ format that houses a magnetic disk in a rigid plastic protective case. It typically has much higher storage capacity than the 5¼″ floppy disk.

microprocessor See *central processing unit*.

modem A device that translates digital computer information into analog signals that can be transmitted over telephone lines and analog signals into a digital form that can be processed by a computer.

mouse A hand-held device connected to the input port of a computer, which, if moved up, down, left, or right on a flat surface, moves a pointer on the screen that selects functions or options.

operating system An operating system enables the central processing unit (CPU) to control and communicate with internal and external devices.

operation The process of manipulating information in a predetermined manner by the central processing unit of the computer system.

optical scanner An input peripheral that reads an image by reflecting light from its surface.

output Information that a computer sends out to a screen, printer, or mass storage device.

output peripherals Equipment whose function is to display information from the computer.

overhead display panel A liquid crystal panel designed to sit on the stage of an overhead projector, allowing a computer image to be projected onto a screen.

parallel interface A method of transmitting data a byte at a time, using a separate line for each bit being transferred to achieve a high rate of speed.

RAM Random-access memory; temporary internal memory that is erased if power to the computer system is interrupted.

ROM Read-only memory; constant memory contained in an integrated circuit or chip that cannot be modified by the user.

scaling Controlling the size of an image and, in direct proportion, all of its components. Scaling an image reduces or enlarges all of its elements.

sector A segment of a track as determined by the disk operating system.

serial interface An input or output device that affects both data transmission and reception, transforming parallel output data into a sequential string of pulses and transforming input data from a sequential string of pulses into parallel binary words.

software A computer program (information and directions to control the computer) preserved on a recording medium (e.g., floppy disk) and usually accompanied by written documentation.

temporary memory Internal memory that is available and accessible to the user and requires a constant source of power to maintain itself; also called RAM, or volatile memory.

track The path followed by a disk drive read-write head, on which data are recorded to or read from a disk.

trackball A device in which the user rolls a movable ball in a stationary frame in order to move a pointer on the screen.

trackpad A pressure sensitive pad on which a user presses a finger in order to move a pointer on the screen.

twisted pair A cable consisting of one or more pairs of conductors running side by side.

UPC Universal Product Code; a sequence of thick and thin lines on consumer products spaced to identify a specific item, read by an optical bar code reader.

UPS An uninterruptible power supply is a device that provides emergency power from batteries in the event of an AC power failure.

user interface The interaction between human and machine.

video monitor A television set that has been manufactured to accept a video signal directly and is capable of displaying a picture of much higher resolution than a standard television receiver.

video projector A device that accepts a video signal and projects an image onto a screen.

voice entry device A computer input peripheral that converts human voice or sounds into a digital signal.

volatile memory See *temporary memory*.

REFERENCES & SUGGESTED READINGS

Bortman, H. (1992, February). Is there a pen in your future? *MacUser,* 144–148.

Brady, H. (1992, March). IBM raises the bar. *Technology and Learning, 12*(6), 34–37.

Davis, F. (1992, December). Electrons or photons? *Wired, 1*(1), 30–32.

Lu, C. (1993, September). A small revelation. *Macworld, 109*(9), 102–106.

Malfitano, R., & Cincotta, P. (1993, May). Network for a school of the future. *T.H.E. Journal, 20*(10), 70–74.

McMullen, (1993, September). Unleash your LAN. *Macworld, 10*(9), 209–212.

Pittelkau, J. (1989, January). Through the liquid glass. *MacUser, 5*(1), 213–221.

Schultz, E. (1991, January). Putting it all together. *Teacher Magazine, 2*(4), 44–49.

Tessler, F. (1992, April). Review: Voice express and voice navigator II. *Macworld, 9*(4), 180–182.

Van Winkle, B. (1996, August). Video for classroom multimedia instruction. *Syllabus, 10*(1), 10–11.

Chapter 6

Word Processing

ADVANCE ORGANIZER

1. What is a word processor?

2. What are some common features of word processors?

3. What are some editing functions found in word processors?

4. Why is lettering important and what are some guidelines for its effective use?

5. How might the word processor be a productivity tool for you as a teacher or an administrator?

6. How is the word processor a productivity tool for the student at different grade levels?

When asked where they would really like some help, teachers often respond "with the paperwork," the preparation of supplementary materials and tests, the recording of scores and other measures of student performance, the preparation of grades, the communication with parents, and the finding and filing of resource materials. Every teacher maintains a set of resource materials, yet, each time these materials are used, they seem to require a little revision. These activities do not involve students directly and are often done outside actual class time. If the time required to perform these tasks could be decreased, the teacher would have more time to devote to planning and preparing lessons and to working directly with students.

Obviously, classroom teachers are not the only educators who can make use of word processors. Library media specialists can use them to maintain bibliographies of the print and nonprint materials available. Special educators can use word processors to maintain individual student correspondence files that are continually updated. They can build a student's IEP and later recall the IEP to update it easily.

Principals and administrative office staff can use word processors in many of their tasks, since they maintain the ongoing records and reports for the school. Some documents must be updated every year, yet only parts of each form are actually changed. A document kept on the computer can be amended at any time and reprinted when needed without having to reconstruct it in its entirety.

Word processing has also become a powerful tool in the hands of students. Research studies in computer applications consistently show that the use of word processing improves students' attitude toward writing by making them want to write more and making them feel better about their writing (Roblyer, 1988). Studies have shown a positive relationship between word processing and a desire to write (Woodruff, Bereiter, & Scardamalia, 1981). According to Riedesel and Clements

(1985), students are also more eager to write, claiming it is "easier to get down ideas with a word processor," and they use a larger vocabulary because they find it easy to correct spelling.

WORD PROCESSORS

The term word *processor* is used to denote a whole category of software whose primary purpose is to facilitate written communication. As indicated in Figure 6–1, word processing is a systematic organization of procedures and equipment to display information efficiently in a written form and to preserve it electronically. This section focuses on computer software available to assist in the creation of written material.

Word processing programs usually consist of two basic, interacting parts—a text editor to manipulate text and a print formatter to deliver the text file to the printer—and, depending on the individual software, several additional parts such as a spell checker, a dictionary, a thesaurus, and even a grammar checker. The **text editor** is the most visible part of the program and is the one that allows the user to manipulate text on a screen display. It is used during the text entry phase to help you add, change, and delete text, as well as to locate words and phrases and to embed the format commands needed to control the print formatter. From the editor, you can insert the commands to determine the print font, margins, and line spacing. The editor also contains the means to save, merge, copy, and insert text from one file to another. The **print formatter** delivers the text file to the printer and ensures that it is printed correctly on paper. A word processor will send control characters to the printer that govern the margin settings, lines per page, length of page, and special commands to enhance the printed text.

Word Processor Features

There are many good word processors from which to choose. Selecting the one that is best for you depends on your computer system, but most of all on your individual needs. Figure 6–2 presents a list of features that might be considered when choosing a program. Selection of a word processor will also be explored in Chapter 12.

The following is a brief discussion of the features found in word processing programs.

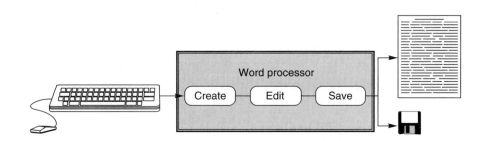

Figure 6–1
Word processing

Column Formatting	Orphan/Widow Control
Dictionary	Outlining
Footnotes	Pagination
Glossary	Preview Document
Header/Footer	Save as ASCII Text Files
Help Screens	Spell Checking
Hyphenation	Style Sheets
Index	Table of Contents
Mail Merge	Thesaurus

Figure 6–2

Features found in word processing programs

column formatting In addition to specifying top, bottom, and side margins, many word processors allow the user to format a page in more than one column. Multiple columns yield shorter line lengths, which may at times improve the readability of the text.

dictionary This feature provides word definition and syllabication, as well as allowing the user to confirm spelling.

footer Similar to a header, a footer is automatically added to the bottom of each page and can be suppressed on a title page.

footnotes Some programs allow the user to mark words in the text to be referenced automatically as footnotes at the bottom of the page or as endnotes at the end of the document.

glossary Often-used words and phrases such as a return address or closing of a letter can be created and stored in a glossary to be called up at any time by a simple keyboard command.

header A header is a brief message that may include text or a date, time, or page display that is automatically added to the top of each page. Usually, the header can be suppressed on a title page.

help screens Help screens are designed into some programs to present information to the user about the operation of the word processor and its functions as the need arises. The better ones are context sensitive, which means that the information presented applies closely to what the user has been attempting to do.

hyphenation Since **word wrap** can leave lines of varying lengths, thereby creating a ragged right margin, some word processors allow the user to turn on a hyphenation feature that will generate a hyphen at the most appropriate syllable break in a word at the end of a line. This function can also be turned off at will.

index The creation of an index can be greatly facilitated by a feature that allows a user to mark words that are then automatically copied, along with a page reference, to an index at the end of the document.

mail merge An almost indispensable feature when sending form letters that appear to be personalized with appropriate names and addresses is the ability to merge data from one file to another at the proper place in the document.

orphan/widow control Orphans are single lines of text that occur at the bottom of a page. Widows are single lines of text that occur at the top of a page. Some word processors will not allow these to occur but, instead, will force the appropriate page break so that at least two lines of text will appear together.

outlining Some of the more powerful word processors have integrated outliners built into them, allowing the user to create an outline of the document and to expand or collapse various levels.

pagination Once a user sets the page length of the document by prescribing top and bottom margins on a specified size of paper, this feature allows a word processor to generate page breaks and indicate them on the screen automatically and to number pages and renumber them when editing is performed.

preview document All worthwhile word processors allow the user to see the document on the screen as it will look when printed. The better programs allow document editing in this page view and closely approach a WYSIWYG (What You See Is What You Get) state.

save as text Word processors usually save documents created in their native format. Saving them also as a file in an **ASCII text** format allows the documents to be transported between word processors produced by different publishers. This can be done by exchanging disks, by transmission over a network, or as an attachment to an e-mail message.

spell checking Contrary to a dictionary, a spell checker does not display definitions but, rather, compares all words found in the document against its master list. Any word not matching is called to the user's attention and, if possible, a replacement word is suggested. Most allow the user to add frequently used unusual words (proper nouns, acronyms, etc.) to a custom list.

style sheets A style is a set of format characteristics (left aligned, 10 point, Times, .5 inch first line indent, for example) that can be applied to text. A style sheet is a collection of styles used in a document. Choosing a style for text about to be entered is a time-saving device.

table of contents This feature facilitates the creation of a table by allowing a user to mark words that are then automatically copied to a table of contents at the beginning of the document.

thesaurus This feature soon becomes a writer's favorite tool. A selected word is compared with a list in the thesaurus and a number of synonyms are suggested to avoid undue repetitions or to adjust a subtle nuance in the writing.

A grammar checker is another feature that has drawn some interest. It may be integrated into the word processor or used as a separate, add-on program. It attempts to identify wordiness, awkward constructions, singular/plural agreement, and the use of passive voice, among other things. Some writers feel that grammar checkers are slow and cumbersome to use, have rather limited capability, and are not of much use.

An essay grader is a somewhat related product. Research on computer grading of written essays began 30 years ago, but only in the past few years have the hardware and software really been up to the task (Page & Petersen, 1995). Recent developments show interesting promise, holding out hope to English teachers everywhere that help in grading student essays may well be on the way.

Word Processing Functions

Word processors are commonly available either as individual programs or as integrated software that may also contain a spreadsheet, a file manager, and even graphics and telecommunications components. Word processing may be categorized into the following three major categories: short, simple documents; longer, complex documents; and desktop publishing.

Short, Simple Documents. Programs in this category are for people who do not do much writing and for users who are willing to sacrifice power because they need only limited functions. Most of these programs stress well-designed ease of use rather than a wealth of complex features. Some programs aimed at the grade school student also fit this category. Programs in this category are usually used to write letters, memos, brief reports, and simple handouts. Features normally found in this category include format ruler, search and replace, spelling checker, and perhaps graphics placement.

Longer, Complex Documents. Some programs in this category are for the serious user who does not, however, need (or want) the full, extended features of the page layout programs. For example, programs in this category may not be able to allow for multiple document editing with a split screen and for text wrap around graphic images. These programs do, however, contain all of the necessary functions for work on full reports, position papers, and article manuscripts. In addition to the features mentioned in the first category, these programs include headers and footers, a thesaurus, and usually the ability to build a table of contents, an index, and footnotes automatically, as well as mail merge, so that form letters personalized with names and comments can be printed.

Desktop Publishing. The term *desktop publishing* implies the ability to create sophisticated printed documents. Programs in this category contain the most extensive set of commands and include advanced page layout capabilities. These programs may require an investment of time and/or training to take full advantage of their many features, as well as continual use to maintain skill level. They contain all of the necessary functions for work on full reports, newsletters, brochures, and documents that include **text-wrapped graphics.** In addition to the features mentioned in the first two categories, these programs include the ability to create a master page layout or design that is repeated on every page, to format variable-width columns, to use drop caps at the beginning of paragraphs, and to import and format graphics, as well as to wrap lines of text around their irregular edges.

Desktop publishing really takes advantage of the power of the printed page. Embodying all of the features of less-powerful word processing programs, it adds to the writer's expressive ability by improving the visual presentation of text and visuals by controlling their juxtaposition. By careful control of the white space on the page, the writer controls the overall appearance of the document and gives added impact to the intended message.

A number of tools are used to organize the appearance of text. Notice those presented in Figure 6–3. Margins create a white space surrounding the text, which af-

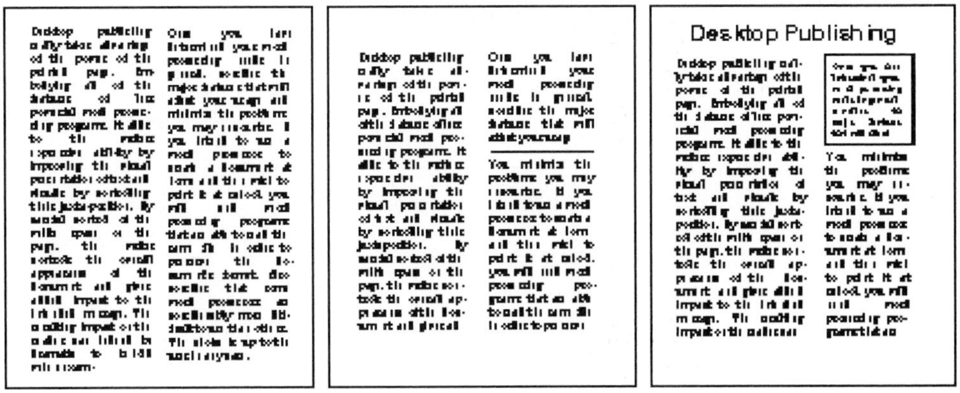

Figure 6–3

*Examples of desktop
publishing tools*

fects a document's *feel.* Wider margins result in a *lighter* document. The width of the space between columns, called the gutter, also contributes to the feel of the document. Horizontal rules may separate parts of a document. Thin rules are used when the document contains a lot of text. Boxes also separate the parts of a document. They are usually used to isolate specific information, sometimes called *sidebars.* Columns may be of different widths, often with artwork extending across one or more columns. Headlines grab attention and encourage the viewer to become a reader of the article. To be effective, headlines should be concise and delineated from the body of the text by use of the same or contrasting typeface in a larger size and different style.

Full-featured, desktop publishing programs can be expensive and quite complex for the average user. Less-expensive desktop publishing programs are available with a reduced set of features, making them easier to use. These have found favor with teachers and students who use them to prepare newsletters and bulletins and even lay out yearbooks.

Once you have determined your word processing needs in general, consider the major features that will affect your usage and will minimize the problems you may encounter. If you intend to use a word processor to create a document at home and then wish to print it at school, you will need word processing programs that are able to read the same file in order to preserve the document's format. Also consider that some word processors are considerably more difficult to use than others.

Editing Functions

A representative sample of editing functions is presented in Figure 6–4. The user can navigate through the document, adding, deleting, finding, replacing, inserting, and moving information at will. Operating in the Macintosh or Windows environments, many editing features are invoked through pull-down menus, but most have shortcuts that are keyboard equivalents or double key presses so that the program can distinguish a command from text entry. A double key press simply means that the user holds down a designated key such as the Command or Alt key and presses a second key.

Block moves		New
Copy		Open
Cut		Paste
Delete		Save
Find and Replace		Save As
Insert		Word wrap

Figure 6–4

Some word processor editing functions

Let's briefly review the most significant functions that make the word processor the powerful tool it is. Most word processors allow you to create a document by invoking the New command. As you enter text, you realize that a word that cannot completely fit at the end of a line is automatically moved down to begin a new line. This feature is called word wrap. It requires you to type a return only at the end of a paragraph or to create a blank line. As you reach the bottom of the screen, the program automatically scrolls your text upward to allow you to continue typing without hesitation. The following are the most often used editing functions.

block moves The selection of any amount of text and/or graphics to reposition it elsewhere in the existing document or in another document, as explained in the Cut, Copy, and Paste command definitions.

copy The Copy command allows the duplication of selected text and graphics. The duplicated item is stored in temporary memory, however.

cut This command allows the removal of selected text and graphics. This removed item is stored in temporary memory.

delete The removal of text can be accomplished in a number of ways. Placing the cursor immediately following a text character and pressing the key usually labeled Delete or Backspace erases the character to its immediate left, one character at a time. Many word processors allow the user to easily select and delete an entire word or even an entire line at a time. The remaining text is automatically rearranged properly, with word wrap and page breaks taken into account.

find and replace This feature allows one to find a particular word or phrase by searching for it from the beginning of the document. Once found, the item can be replaced with a new word or phrase.

insert Placing the cursor anywhere in a line of text; additional typing spreads apart the existing text to accommodate the new entry. The material being inserted may be as little as a single letter or many paragraphs long.

paste This command allows whatever is stored in temporary memory to be duplicated and inserted in the document at the location of the cursor.

word wrap Automatically moves a word to the next line without splitting the word.

In addition to the editing commands, there is a set of commands to determine the format of the printed output. These print commands, of course, are not printed out as text; they are the embedded control commands giving instructions to the printer being used. These allow the user to describe paper size; margins; character typeface, size, and style; right, left, center, or full line justification; and more.

Desktop publishing programs are used as tools by students to prepare publications such as newsletters and to layout yearbooks.

Lettering

Word processing has added a new graphic dimension to communicating in print. It's not only what you say and how you say it but how it looks on the page. Word processing has placed at our disposal the ability to affect the appearance of the printed word easily yet markedly. Reflecting on the adage that "a picture is worth a thousand words," word processing has now added somewhat of a "picture" quality to the text medium and requires us to attend to some terms and some guidelines concerning the appearance of text.

Font. The *collection of characteristics* applied to a typeface in a particular size and style is called a font. Sample fonts are illustrated in Figure 6–5.

Size. The *height* of a letter is expressed in points (1 point equals 5½"). Figure 6–6 illustrates a progression from 9 to 24 point type. Different typefaces vary in letter width and thickness of line, sometimes giving the appearance of a variation in size.

Style. *Style* refers to the *appearance* of a particular typeface as visual modifications are applied, as illustrated in Figure 6–7.

Typeface. A **typeface** is the design of the letter and the name given to the design. New designs are constantly emerging and are usually copyrighted by the creator. Typefaces affect the feeling imparted by the message, as well as its content. Some employ harsh, angular lines, while others use soft curves. Some are narrow and condensed; others are round or broad. Some use thick lines and convey a heavy or dark

Bookman in 14 point bold
Helvetica in 12 point italic
Palatino in 18 point plain text

Figure 6–5
Sample Fonts (combining typeface, size, and style)

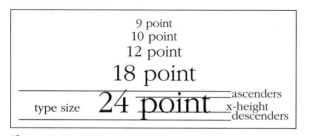

Figure 6–6
Sample point sizes

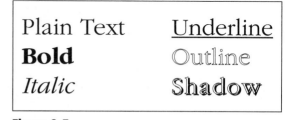

Figure 6–7
Sample styles

impression to a body of text, while others use thin lines, resulting in a light text. Sample typefaces are illustrated in Figure 6–8.

Serif typefaces such as those illustrated in Figure 6–9 have fine lines that finish the major strokes of the letters. These serve as decorative yet functional connectors that appear to join adjacent letters, thereby helping the reader to perceive groups of letters as words. Therefore, serif typefaces enhance the speed and ease with which text can be read. This textbook is printed in a serif typeface.

As you study Figure 6–9, notice that some typefaces occupy more line length in the same point size because of the rounder shape of their letters. The rounder shape of the lowercase letters in Bookman make this most apparent in Figure 6–9.

Sans serif typefaces, such as those illustrated in Figure 6–10, should not be used in body text. Their clean lines and lack of connectors make them somewhat difficult and tiring to read in body text. Sans serif typefaces should be used primarily in a bold style and larger size as headlines and titles. As you study Figure 6–10, notice that different typefaces use a thicker line, thereby making a stronger statement.

Ornate typefaces, such as those illustrated in Figure 6–11, are certainly attention getting and effective if used sparingly. They are as much graphic as they are text. The message embodied in the ornate design should support the written words.

Every text example shown thus far has been a **proportional-spaced** typeface. That is to say, its design attempts to achieve **optical spacing** by allowing the surface area of the space between each letter to be roughly the same. The distance will, therefore, vary between each letter, depending on its shape. A **monospaced** typeface such

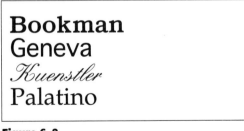

Figure 6–8

Sample typefaces

Times	An analysis of factors that influence
Palatino	An analysis of factors that influe
Bookman	An analysis of factors that inf

Figure 6–9

Samples of serif typefaces shown in 18 point plain text

Avant Garde:	An analysis of factors that influen
Geneva:	An analysis of factors that influe
Chicago:	**An analysis of factors that i**

Figure 6–10

Samples of sans serif typefaces shown in 18 point plain text

Brush Script:	*An analysis of factors that influence typeface selection*
UMBRA:	AN ANALYSIS OF FACTORS THAT INFLUENCE
Snowcap:	An analysis of factors that influence typeface selection

Figure 6–11

Samples of ornate typefaces

Palatino (proportional)
    An analysis of factors that influence typeface selection must incl
Courier (monospaced)
    An analysis of factors that influence typeface

Figure 6–12
Proportional and monospaced typefaces

as Courier is sometimes referred to as achieving **mechanical spacing.** Its design allows each letter to be equally distant from the next, regardless of the letter shape. As you examine Figure 6–12, which illustrates the difference between the two types of spacing, pay particular attention to the letters *i* and *l* and their adjacent letters.

Lettering Guidelines

- Select a suitable typeface to enhance readability and the expression of your words.
- Use sans serif typefaces in a larger size for headlines or titles. Used sparingly, they have a simplicity that commands attention. Large amounts in body text are difficult to read.
- Use serif typefaces for body text. The decorations on the letters help to guide the reader's eye movement from one letter to the next, thereby helping the reader to perceive words rather than letters.
- Use ornate text sparingly for special visual effects.
- Avoid mixing typefaces within the same document except for a distinct purpose. Rarely should you mix more than two typefaces in the same document.
- Select a letter size appropriate to the message and its intended impact. Consider that not all output is intended for 8½-by-11-inch paper. Consider the optimum viewing distance and the medium (e.g., a minimum of 18 point size should be used for overhead transparencies and 24 point or larger for presentation slide shows).
- Allow ample leading (space) between lines of text so that ascenders and descenders do not touch.
- Use style (plain, bold, italic, outline, shadow, underline) for emphasis.
- Allow plenty of white space around a block of text. A block of text takes up space, so be sure to consider it in your overall design.

WORD PROCESSOR APPLICATIONS

As stated in the introduction to this chapter, teachers want help in alleviating the paperwork demands made on them. They want help in accomplishing activities that do not involve students directly and are quite often done outside of actual class time. If the time required to perform these tasks could be decreased, teachers would have more time to devote to working with students.

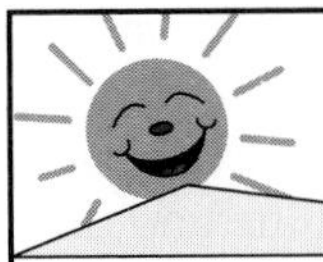

Sunrise Elementary School
575 Redondo Rd.
Pleasantville, NY 10570

{TODAY'S DATE}

Dear {PARENTS' NAMES},

{CHILD'S NAME}'s class will be going on a field trip to the Museum of Science and Industry next Tuesday, February 17th, to view the exhibit on computer technology and robotics. Two parent volunteers will assist your child's classroom teacher in supervising the field trip. Transportation will be by school bus departing at 10:00 A.M. and returning to the school by 2:00 P.M. We ask that you provide your child with a sack lunch and money to purchase a beverage, if you wish. Please sign, date, and return the lower portion of this notice, giving permission for your child to participate.

Sincerely,

{TEACHER'S NAME}

- -

{CHILD'S NAME} has permission to participate in the field trip to the Museum of Science and Industry next Tuesday, February 17th.

(signed) : ______________________________

(today's date) : ____________

Figure 6–13
Sample personalized form letter

Teachers create some written classroom material that changes very little from one year to the next. An exercise sheet or another resource material such as a game or puzzle used once in a unit plan may be used the following year with only slight modification. Material, once designed, can be easily modified to serve a similar purpose in another unit of study. By using a word processor, the teacher could develop a few standard templates and then make appropriate changes as needed.

In addition to the preparation of instructional materials, consider the writing that is expected of a teacher. Ask yourself how a teacher might save time and effort and still accomplish the writing tasks effectively. One example of these writing tasks might be asking parents to allow their child to participate in a school-sponsored field trip. The task might be accomplished by sending home an impersonal request form and asking the parents to fill in the name of their child and sign the form. Using a word processor and merging information from a data file, this process can be personalized, as shown in Figure 6–13. Labels in curly brackets { } indicate an item to be inserted from the data file.

In addition to appearing as a personal communication to the parents, the form letter could be used as a **boilerplate** for any other field trip permission form, with a minimum of retyping. *Boilerplate* is a term that comes from the legal profession and signifies material that can be used repeatedly without modification. The term **template** is becoming a popular replacement for boilerplate.

We often think of a word processor as a tool that enhances an individual's personal productivity, and indeed it is. Collaborative writing, however, is a technique that allows more than one student to engage in a writing activity together. The technique often calls for students to agree on an outline and then to parcel out the writing tasks. The written documents are then merged together, and the students edit each other's work and rewrite the composition. If the writing is done in a computer lab, students can brainstorm a story idea and then begin drafting the story on their own computers. After 15 to 20 minutes, students can exchange places and continue writing where the previous student ended. New software allows students sitting at computers on a network to write and to edit each other's documents in real time.

For many years teachers have promoted the teaching of writing as a process of drafting, revising, editing, and publishing. Teachers need to guide students' composition and provide necessary feedback for revision. The word processor supports writing instruction by making the writing process less tedious, thereby encouraging a far more positive attitude toward writing and motivating students to experiment with language. A study of elementary school students (Raef, 1996) identified as having weak writing skills indicated that the students' motivation to write increased with the use of word processing.

Figures 6–14 through 6–25 depict activities to illustrate how a word processor might be used as a tool by students to explore creative writing—to write reports, compositions, and poetry. These examples can be modified to serve in a variety of subject areas and grade levels. Word processing objectives, writing objectives, and subject matter objectives often dovetail. If students are to capitalize on the power of the word processor as a tool and employ it with confidence, they must develop an understanding of its application and a reasonably high level of skill in its use. Using this tool, they will enhance their written communication as they acquire and construct knowledge in various content areas.

Commercially published "Big Books" are in a large format that lends itself to being read and displayed in front of a group of students. They usually contain one story, some of them with repetition on each page, as illustrated in Figure 6–14. The example in Figure 6–15 is a continuous story, with each child responsible for writing and illustrating one page. Books created by children can range over a wide variety of topics and can integrate a number of subject matter disciplines. Consider the following ideas:

- Write about endangered animals: an illustration and facts about the animals that would require some research.
- Use alliteration with names from your hometown or state to foster recognition of place names, cities, towns, rivers, and so on: "Suzy Smith from Seaside sings in the shower" or "Terrific Terry from Troutdale travels along the Trask River."
- Report on a classroom activity: "What I learned about raising quail chicks in school."
- Read a story such as "Alexander and the Magic Pebble" and respond to it: "If I had a magic pebble, I would. . . ."
- Engage in wonderful word problems. Write and illustrate math word problems. Place answers to the student-written problems on the last page.

Billie, Billie, what do
you see?
I see a white bunny
rabbit looking at me.

Suggested Use: Children use "Big Books" in primary grades to acquire simple language skills. Following the pattern of a "Big Book," children could dictate one page of a story to the teacher or to a parent volunteer, who would enter it into a word processor file, leaving space for an illustration. In this example, children were asked to name an animal and a color, along with their name in a rhyme.

Children would be encouraged to draw a picture illustrating their words. Drawn on a simple graphics paint program, the image then could be inserted into the word processor file. If it were drawn by hand on paper, the drawing could be scanned into an electronic form and then this image inserted into the word processor file. Stories could be bound and placed in the school library media center to be read by others.

Figure 6–14

"Big Book" sample page authored by students

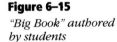

| Frog and toad swam in the pond. | Later they rode bikes. | "Would you like to come to my house for dinner?" said frog. | "Sure,. . .," etc. |

Figure 6–15

"Big Book" authored by students

... He had told all hands that they ought to see to their equipment; once they got on the trail, opportunities for repair work might be scarce. The Spettle brothers, for example, had no equipment at all, unless you called one pistol with a broken hammer equipment. Newt had scarcely more; his saddle was an old one and he had no slicker and only one blanket for a bedroll. The Irishmen had nothing except what they had been loaned.

"Lonesome Dove"
Larry McMurtry

Suggested Use: Using a word processor, the teacher types a selection from a popular novel, eliminating the first topic sentence and running two or more paragraphs together, then saves it as a word processing file.

Class discussion reviews topic sentences and getting the main idea of a paragraph. Students are assigned to load the teacher's file, create a topic sentence, and separate the paragraphs. They then print out their modified file.

Discussion follows, in which the teacher indicates the correct paragraph breaks and students listen to each other's topic sentences, discussing their merits. The teacher then reads the original selection from the book.

Figure 6–16
Topic sentence

I have a 1978 Chevrolet Caprice station wagon to sell. Considering its age and its 178,000 miles, it's in good shape. The 400 cu. in. engine runs very well, no doubt because I have changed its oil and filter faithfully every 3000 miles. It averages 12 to 14 miles per gallon of gas. The automatic transmission is original and had been serviced at regular intervals. The body has no rust on it and only a few minor scratches and small dents. The fuel pump, rear wheel bearings, universal joints and all four brakes are about one year old. The water pump is original. I would estimate that the tires have at least a good year of wear left on them. The car has a heavy-duty load-equalizing trailer hitch attached to its frame. I am asking $350 in cash but would not refuse any reasonable offer. You must see it to fully appreciate it.

Suggested Use: The teacher prepares a lengthy and verbose paragraph describing an article for sale and saves it as a word processing file.

Class discussion reviews topic sentences and getting the main idea of a paragraph.

Students are assigned to load the teacher's file and to (1) underline the main idea, (2) eliminate extraneous elements, and (3) prepare a succinct classified advertisement from it. Students then print the teacher's modified file and their original advertisement. Discussion would follow to select the best ads.

A follow-up activity would be to select classified ads from the newspaper, improve them, and write more descriptive paragraphs.

Figure 6–17

Classified advertisement

Mrs. Prosser's Classroom News
May 21, 1995

School Built on Site of Indian Village

Mr. Gerald Girod showed his collection of arrowheads to Mrs. Prosser's fifth grade class. He grew up here in Chicopee Falls and started his collection when he was a young boy. He found his first arrowheads in what is now the school playground years before the school was built. He found some small arrowheads that he thinks were used to hunt birds.

Mr. Girod also showed some broken pieces of pottery that he found down on the river bank. The pottery shards, the arrowheads, and pictures of what the playground area looked like before the school was built will be placed in the display case in the school library.

Suggested Use: The teacher serves as guide and advisor as students published a class newspaper. They discuss events of the past week and decide which to report. They focus attention on the importance of the headline and take turns writing the stories. They edit each other's stories for content, spelling, grammar, and creative expression.

An extension of this activity could have the teacher encourage students to interview local business and civic leaders, examine local occupations, or record stories told by old-timers in the community.

Student photographs and drawings could be scanned and inserted in the document. Modest page layout software could eventually replace the word processor and give the publication a more sophisticated look as the students gain skills and experience.

Figure 6–18

Classroom newsletter

'Twixt optimist and pessimist
——————————————
The optimist sees the doughnut;
    The pessimist sees the hole.
          The pedigree of honey
          Does not concern the bee;
          A clover, any time, to him
               ——————————————

                   Dogs in the country have fun.
                   ——————————————
                   But in the city this species
                   Is dragged around on leashes.

Suggested Use: Using a word processor, the teacher types selections from several poems, eliminating one line from each poem, then saves the document as a word processor file.

Class discussion reviews rhyme and meter. Students are assigned to load the teacher's file and create the missing line. Each student then prints a copy of the completed poems.

Discussion follows, in which the students listen to each other's poems, discussing their merits. The teacher then reads the original selection.

Figure 6–19

Poem

What would the Oregon Country be like, she wondered as she gazed at her child burning with fever. Would this interminable trek ever end? Would they find the answer to their prayers? Would she, Abner and their children ever see the green valleys and rushing streams they had heard about?

The parching heat and blowing dust make every mile seem like ten. The slow creaking of the wagon wheels and plodding of the oxen add to the monotony. The scout says there's a river an hour away where we will make camp for tonight. The thought of water and some rest lift my spirits and give me the energy to keep going.

Suggested Use: Students agree on a story outline. Using a word processor, they develop some ideas as they write paragraphs into a file. Students merge their separate files into one document.

The example above shows two students' files merged together. Each student then takes a copy of the document and rewrites the entire segment to give the paragraphs coherence and unit of expression.

Students print their own file when they are finished and exchange papers to compare writing styles. Students are then given the opportunity to modify their own document.

Figure 6–20

Collaborative exercise

A student approached Mrs. Alderson after class with a request for help. She said that she was confused between the terms latitude and longitude. She couldn't remember which was which.

Mrs. Alderson responded with a comparison of the similarity in the words latitude and altitude pointing out their North-South or "up-down" and height relationship. She concluded by suggesting that latitude be thought of as a ladder that she would climb up and down and pointing out the alliteration, ladder and latitude.

Suggested Use: The purpose of the lesson is to rewrite sentences, eliminating the gender-specific pronouns *he* and *she* when they do not refer to an identifiable person in the story.

Using a word processor, the teacher prepares a paragraph, using several pronouns and saves the document as a word processor file.

Class discussion reviews pronouns and antecedents. Students are assigned to load the teacher's file and to rewrite the paragraph, replacing gender-specific pronouns where appropriate. Students print the modified file. Discussion would follow, in which the modified paragraphs were examined.

Figure 6–21
Gender-neutral style

1. The child enters the classroom.
   The <u>child</u> enters the classroom.

2. The kitten loves to chase the ball of yarn.
   The <u>kitten</u> loves to chase the ball of yarn.

3. The man waits patiently for the store to open.
   The <u>man</u> waits patiently for the store to open.

4. The woman sits quietly while eating her lunch.
   The <u>woman</u> sits quietly while eating her lunch.

Suggested Use: Using a word processor, the teacher prepares a file containing sets of sentence pairs and distributes it on disk or by a file server to student workstations.

Students read the sentences on the computer screen. Using the editing capabilities of the word processor, students modify the second sentence in each pair by replacing the underlined words with a plural form.

Care must be given to making appropriate changes to assure correct verb forms and pronoun agreements.

Students print the modified copy and either check each other's work or submit it to the teacher.

Figure 6–22
Plural forms

It was a * and * night. The moon was * hidden behind a * cloud and a * wind was blowing from the North. It was a night when imaginations could * run * .

* Jim and Gwenda heard an * sound coming from just outside their campground. They wondered if their * sister, Margaia, had heard it too. They heard it again. This time it seemed * .

Suggested Use: Using a word processor, the teacher prepares a file consisting of a selection with missing modifiers replaced by asterisks.

After reading the selection, students replace the asterisks with one or more adjectives or adverbs. Students underline the modifiers that they inserted, rename the file, and save it to a diskette or to a folder assigned to them on a hard disk or file server.

In a follow-up activity, students load each other's files and substitute other modifiers for all underlined words in order to change the mood or meaning of the selection. A discussion should follow on how modifiers can alter the meaning of a story.

As a further creative writing activity, students could be asked to complete their story.

Figure 6–23
Modifiers

I predict for America, not despair but rather great hope. I believe that anything is possible if people want it badly enough.

I see America, not in the setting sun of a black night of despair ahead of us, I see America in the crimson light of a rising sun fresh from the burning, creative hand of God. I see great days ahead, great days possible to men and women of will and vision . . .

—Carl Sandburg

Suggested Use: The teacher finds a quotation that illustrates expressive language. Using a word processor, the teacher paraphrases the quotation in a direct style and, after spacing down the page, enters the quotation. Using a large monitor or an overhead display panel, the teacher shows the first section to the class.

After reading the first section, students rewrite the selection, using a more expressive style. They may then read their selection aloud or display it for the class to read. The teacher then displays the original quotation and leads the class in analyzing the style.

In a follow-up activity, students load each other's files and edit each other's work in an attempt to influence the mood of the selection.

Figure 6–24
Whole-class writing exercise

The state of Oregon was founded.

John Jacob Astor established a flourishing fur trade.

Andrew Jackson became president.

Wagons completed the first journey over the Oregon Trail.

The Oregon Territory was created.

The Civil War ended.

The first missionaries arrived in the Willamette Valley.

Lewis and Clark reached what is present-day Astoria, Oregon.

Suggested Use: Using a word processor, the teacher prepares a file consisting of a series of historical events in a scrambled chronological order.

Students read the statements on the computer screen. Using the cut and paste function of the word processor, students arrange them in the correct chronological order and print the file. Using reference tools in their classroom and in the library, students verify the correctness of their printout.

In a follow-up activity, students assign dates to each event and identify names of important people and places related to the events, where appropriate.

A slight variation of this activity might mix local, state, national, and world events in the file prepared by the teacher. Another variation might mix events from social studies, science, and the arts in order to foster cross-curriculum integration.

Figure 6–25
Chronological order

"When students write using the word processor, they tend to examine their work and 'fix things that are broken.' It really encourages them to rewrite."

Becky Benjamin, 7th Grade Language Arts Teacher
Carrollton Junior High, Carrollton, GA

THE WORD PROCESSOR AS A PRODUCTIVITY TOOL

The computer is a tool, and word processing is one of the most popular and powerful tool uses. Seat work, homework, exercise sheets, lesson plans, bibliographies, class notes, reports, essays, compositions, memos, letters to parents—the list of practical word processing applications goes on and on. It is easy to understand why most people purchasing a personal computer do so primarily to use it as a word processor.

The argument can be built that the word processor and not the computer itself is in fact the productivity tool. Software indeed transforms the hardware. Using the best software appropriate for a given task makes the computer far more effective or productive than using poorly designed or inappropriate software. Once software is loaded into the hardware, perhaps we should no longer refer to it as a computer but, rather, call it a word processor, database manager, drawing table, and so on.

To gauge the word processor value as a productivity tool, the following questions must be answered. Does using the word processor increase my accuracy? Does it ease my task? Does it increase the speed at which I can complete a task? Does it allow me to accomplish something that I might otherwise find impossible? In other words, does it contribute to my efficiency or effectiveness?

SUMMARY

This chapter addressed the value of using a word processor in the classroom as a tool to facilitate written communication. Studies have shown that the use of word processing by students increases their motivation to write and expands their vocabulary. Applications by students, teachers, library media specialists, administrators, and clerks were discussed.

Features that might be considered when choosing a word processor were examined. The more sophisticated, and usually more expensive, programs are expected to contain a greater number of features. After writing needs are determined, a program can be selected that has an appropriate set of features.

Representative editing functions were examined that allow the user to navigate through the document, adding, deleting, finding, replacing, inserting, and moving information at will. In addition, print commands were acknowledged that allow the user to describe paper size; margins; character typeface, size, and style; and right, left, center, or full line justification. Lettering guidelines were suggested in order to take full advantage of the visual impact of print generated from a word processor.

Teacher applications were explored, using the word processor as a tool to save time and effort and to personalize communications. A process called mail merge integrates information from a data file into a word processed document. Material that is used repeatedly without modification is known as a boilerplate and can be incorporated into documents, thereby saving a good deal of time.

Collaborative writing, a technique that allows more than one student at a time to engage in a writing activity, is greatly facilitated by a word processor. New software allows students sitting at computers on a network to write and to edit each other's documents as they write them.

Examples of student applications were presented in a cross-disciplinary fashion in order to stimulate the reader's imagination and encourage unique creative applications. Instructional, or teacher-centered, applications were differentiated from student-centered applications of the word processor as a learning tool.

CHAPTER EXERCISES

1. Many programs in the school setting currently use keyboard input from students. There has been a good deal written in the past several years on the subject of keyboard instruction. Write a two- to three-page paper discussing the issue of teaching typing starting at an early level. Cite your sources.
2. Describe at least five examples of how you might use word processing in your work as a teacher. Develop a sample of one of them.
3. Using a word processor, write a two- to three-page reaction paper to the concept of collaborative writing. Include a bibliography listing at least three sources.
4. Using a word processor, write a few paragraphs about the motivation that is prompting you to enter the teaching profession and save the file. Exchange your file with a friend who has written a similar one. Finish the document you have received by adding a few paragraphs of your own describing what you hope to accomplish as a teacher. Edit the entire document for consistency of style. Once again exchange it with your friend and compare the documents.
5. Pick a partner and together choose a topic on which to write. After agreeing on an outline, divide the writing task between yourselves. After completing your independent writing assignment, merge your files. Edit the entire document for consistency of style.

GLOSSARY

ASCII text A format that allows text files or documents to be transported between word processors produced by different publishers.

boilerplate A paragraph or section of a document that is used repeatedly with little or no modification when inserted into word processed documents.

desktop publishing Usually refers to the use of software that contains an extensive set of text and graphics manipulation commands and includes advanced page layout capabilities.

font The collection of characteristics applied to a typeface in a particular size and style.

footer A brief message that may include a date, time, or page display that is automatically added to the bottom of each page.

header A brief message that may include a date, time, or page display that is automatically added to the top of each page.

mechanical spacing Letter spacing that requires letters within a word to be equally distant from each other regardless of the letter shape. This results in unequal surface areas in the spaces between letters.

monospaced See *mechanical spacing*.

optical spacing Letter spacing that requires letters within a word to have equal surface areas in the spaces between each other, thereby taking letter shapes into account. Distances between letters will vary.

orphans Single lines of text that occur at the bottom of a page.

print formatter The part of a word processing program that delivers the text file to the printer and ensures that it is printed correctly on paper.

proportional-spaced See *optical spacing*.

size The height of a letter expressed in points (1 point equals $5\frac{1}{2}$ of an inch).

style (1) A set of format characteristics (left aligned, 10 point, Times, 0.5 inch first line indent, for example) that can be applied to text in a word processor.
(2) When dealing strictly with the appearance of text, style pertains more narrowly to the appearance of a particular typeface (plain, bold, italic, outline, shadow, and underline).

style sheet A collection of styles used by a word processor.

template See *boilerplate*.

text editor The part of a word processing program that allows the user to manipulate text on a screen display. It is used during the text entry phase to help add, change, and delete text, as well as to locate words or phrases.

text-wrapped graphics The format feature that allows the program to wrap lines of text around the edges of graphics.

typeface The design or appearance of a particular letter type and the name given to that design (Bookman, Geneva, Times, New Century Schoolbook, Palatino, etc.).

widows Single lines of text that occur at the top of a page.

word processor Software, with accompanying hardware, used primarily to facilitate the creation, editing, formatting, saving, and printing of information in electronic and hard copy form.

word wrap A process of monitoring the entry of words so that words are not split on the right side of the screen. If a complete word will not fit on the current line, the complete word is moved to the next line.

WYSIWYG (What You See Is What You Get, pronounced WHIZ-EE-WIG) The exact screen replication of what will be printed on paper.

REFERENCES & SUGGESTED READINGS

Aker, S. Z. (1992, June). Key words. *MacUser, 8*(6), 18–28.

Beaver, J. F. (1992, February). Using computer power to improve your teaching. *The Computing Teacher, 19*(5), 5–9.

Griest, G. (1993, April). You say you want a revolution: Constructivism, technology, and language arts. *The Computing Teacher, 20*(7), 49–51.

Koppelman, J. (1988, October). Introductory computer literacy skills for students and faculty through word processing. *Tech Trends, 33*(5), 34–36.

Landau, T. (1992, September). The right word processor. *MacUser, 8*(9), 101–110.

Levin, M. (1997). *Kids in print: Publishing a school newspaper.* Parsippany, NJ: Good Apple.

Marcus, S. (1991, May). Word processing: Transforming students' potential to write. *Media and Methods, 27*(5), 8.

McCain, T. D. E. (1993, March). There's more to reading than reading. *The Computing Teacher, 20*(6), 5–9.

Page, E. B., & Petersen, N. S. (1995, March). The computer moves into essay grading. *Phi Delta Kappan, 76*(7), 561–566.

Raef, C. (1996, April). *Improving student writing skills through the use of technology.* M.A. thesis, St. Xavier University, ERIC NO: ED399537.

Riedesel, C. A., & Clements, D. H. (1985). *Coping with computers in the elementary and middle schools.* Englewood Cliffs, NJ: Prentice-Hall.

Roblyer, M. D. (1988, September). The effectiveness of microcomputers in education: A review of the research 1980–1987. *T.H.E. Journal,* 85–89.

Woodrow, J. F. J. (1991, Summer). Teachers' perceptions of computer needs. *Journal of Research on Computing in Education, 23*(4), 475–493.

Woodruff, E., Bereiter, C., & Scardamalia, M. (1981). On the road to computer assisted compositions. *Journal of Educational Technology Systems, 10*(2), 133–148.

Wresch, W. (1990, October). Collaborative writing projects: Lesson plans for the computer age. *The Computing Teacher, 18*(2), 19–21.

Chapter 7

Graphics

ADVANCE ORGANIZER

1. What are some tools you might use for creating computer graphics?

2. What are bit-mapped graphics?

3. What are vector, or object-oriented, graphics?

4. What is clip art and how can it be used?

5. What is a practical application of computer graphics that you might use as a teacher in designing instructional materials for your classroom?

6. What are some basic rules to follow when designing overhead transparencies on the computer?

7. What are desktop presentation programs and how might you use them?

8. What are some tools you might find useful for displaying computer-generated graphics?

The adage "A picture is worth a thousand words" is an appropriate beginning to any basic discussion about graphics. Teachers appreciate the value of this statement because pictorial representations have always been an important means for communicating ideas and concepts to students quickly and accurately.

Many different graphics tools have been employed in instructional situations. The chalkboard, drawings, flowcharts, diagrams, print of different sizes, underlining, and arrows are common tools for enhancing the communication of ideas to students. Film projectors, video recorders, overhead projectors, slide projectors, photographs, posters, maps, textbooks, video, and television have also added different dimensions to our capabilities in using visuals to affect the learning experience. Each tool expands the user's ability to refine the presentation of ideas and to emphasize key parts through motion, color, size, and blank space. The computer is a visual tool that can present many of these capabilities interactively, adding more power to graphic communication.

Schools have recognized the uniqueness of visual literacy, and many include visual literacy skills training as part of their curriculum. A scope and sequence of visual literacy skills as they apply to still images often proceeds along the following continuum:

Naming—recognizing objects and elements and labeling them or calling them by name

Describing—sorting out details and delineating them verbally or in writing
Interpreting—studying details; deciphering visual clues; inferring probable past, present, and future actions and the relationships among people, objects, and events

Music and language have discrete systems of notation. Visuals have a complex code system composed of color, texture, size, medium, realism, etc. These codes combine to make visuals powerful tools. Teachers have recognized that students are surrounded and constantly bombarded by visual stimuli and, often as part of a visual literacy skills curriculum, have attempted to teach them effective **decoding** skills in order to derive accurate meaning from these stimuli. Computer-generated graphics also provide students the opportunity to learn powerful **encoding** skills as they analyze the symbols they choose in order to communicate effectively.

Still images can stimulate interest and assist the understanding of verbal materials. Line drawings, easily prepared in a computer graphics program, can sometimes simplify a complex visual reality. Projected as an overhead transparency, these graphics can reach a large group through conventional delivery methods or through the electronic projection process called desktop presentations.

TOOLS FOR CREATING GRAPHICS

ClarisDraw®, *PC Paint*™, *CorelDRAW*™, *MacBillboard*™, and other graphics programs are available for Macintosh computers and for computers running Windows to facilitate the creation of bulletin boards and display graphics and text. *Crossword Magic*™ simplifies the creation and printing of crossword puzzles to drill students in vocabulary, terminology, and definitions in any subject area. Programs such as *Microsoft*® *Excel*™, *DeltaGraph*™, *ClarisWorks*®, and *Microsoft*® *Works* automatically generate line graphs, bar graphs, and pie charts from numeric data. Software in this category serves as an extension of the creative teacher. Although these materials can be created in other ways, the computer makes it easier and less time consuming and thereby stimulates teachers to reach out and maximize their creative efforts.

Programs and video boards are available that allow computer screens to be recorded on videotape to serve as titles, credits, animated graphics, or instructional text screens. A variety of wipes and dissolves that allow one image to merge into another lends sophistication to the recording. Various input peripherals were discussed in Chapter 5. They were defined as the hardware items that enter data into the computer. Of those discussed, the ones most important as graphics tools are optical scanners and graphics tablets.

Optical scanners, somewhat resembling small photocopiers, operate by reading light reflected from the surface of an object such as a photograph, line drawing, or printed page of text. Flatbed scanners, depending on the model, accept originals with dimensions up to 11 by 14 inches. Scanners are usually accompanied by software that allows control over brightness, contrast, resolution, and image size.

The graphics tablet was discussed as an input device that allows the user to create or trace figures and drawings. The user can draw a picture on the surface of the tablet with a stylus, which provides far greater control than a mouse. Using the software that accompanies the tablet, certain shapes, shadings, and line widths or "paintbrush" effects may be selected by the user. With its inherent ability to trace existing material, the graphics tablet is an excellent device to facilitate the production of state, regional, and even local maps, which can then be projected and are so often in demand in the classroom.

Employing the video digitizer, it is possible to record still images through the use of digital cameras and video camcorders. By using appropriate firmware cards in the computer and accompanying software, recorded images can be transmitted into the computer, manipulated, and stored on disk as graphic files.

Bit-Mapped Graphics

There are two basic ways in which graphics are created by the computer. For **bit-mapped graphics,** the computer-generated image is composed of bits, or screen picture elements called pixels, that are turned on (black or colored) and bits that are off (white or clear). A pixel is the smallest dot a computer can display. Most programs that incorporate the name "paint" in their titles produce bit-mapped graphics. This has led to the practice of calling bit-mapped programs paint programs. Programs such as *MacPaint*™, *PC Paint*™, and *Kid Pix™* often were the user's first introduction to computer graphics and as such should not be disparaged, even though more powerful programs exist.

A simplified bit-mapped drawing of the side view of a child's wagon created in a paint program is presented in Figure 7–1, with a dot pattern applied to the body and a solid pattern applied to the wheels.

Figure 7–2 shows that same wagon with a section of the drawing enlarged. Horizontal and vertical lines are smooth, but notice the jagged edges of the circle (wheel) and diagonal line (handle shaft). The square shape of the pixel becomes apparent. One of the inherent drawbacks of bit-mapped graphics is that the size of the pixel limits the sharpness, or resolution, of the drawing, regardless of the resolution of the monitor or printer used to display the graphic. Normally, bitmaps are created at a resolution of 72 dots per inch (dpi). One pixel is 1/72 of an inch. Phosphor dots on a video tube are much smaller and many are required to make up a pixel. Laser print-

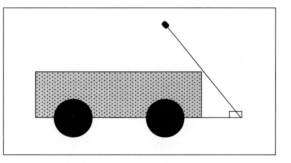

Figure 7–1

Wagon in bit-mapped graphics

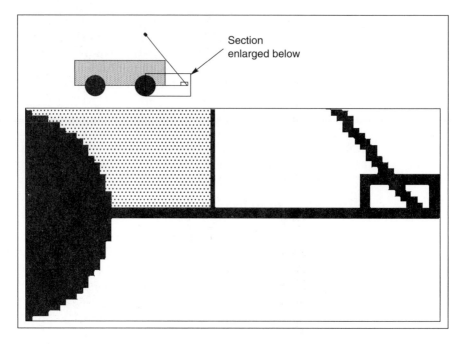

Figure 7–2

Enlargement showing the low resolution of bit-mapped graphics

ers frequently found in schools are capable of printing at 300 or 600 dpi. Unfortunately, bit-mapped images cannot take advantage of either the higher screen display or higher printing resolution.

In order to modify an existing image in a paint program, the user must turn pixels on and off individually or erase larger segments, as shown in Figure 7–3. Notice that the eraser (the white square) is turning bits off; that is, it is turning black or colored pixels white against a white background, virtually making them disappear. Whenever text is inserted, as in Figures 7–2 through 7–4, the text itself also becomes a bit-mapped graphic. Think of it as a picture of the words. Once text is fixed in position, it cannot be edited. Pixels composing the letters can be erased like any other graphic element, thereby allowing entire letters and words to be erased. Once text is inserted into a "paint" document, typing errors cannot be easily corrected, nor can typefaces, sizes, or styles be changed.

Vector, or Object-Oriented, Graphics

The other type of computer graphic is called **vector,** or **object-oriented.** The computer-generated image, instead of being composed of bits or screen pixels that are turned on and off, is determined by formulas that create discrete objects of a certain size and position. Most programs that incorporate the label "draw" in their titles such as *ClarisDraw*™ and *CorelDRAW*™ produce object-oriented graphics. This has led to the practice of calling object-oriented programs draw programs. Integrated packages such as *Microsoft Works*™ include a draw program or module.

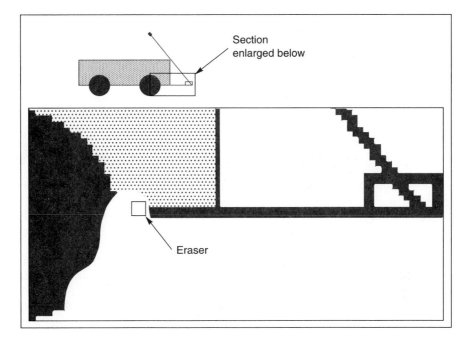

Figure 7–3

Erasing bits

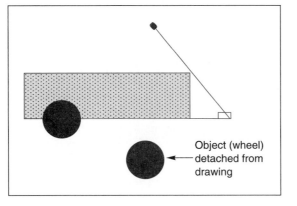

Figure 7–4

Wagon in vector, or object-oriented graphics

In Figure 7–4, the front wheel has been moved away from the rest of the drawing. Each picture element is a separate object and can be changed independently. It can be enlarged, reduced, moved, or have its pattern changed. Creating an image in a draw program is conceptually very different from creating one in a paint program. Rather than drawing freehand with a pencil or paintbrush, the user of a draw program creates objects of different shapes (e.g., lines, circles, rectangles, and polygons), adjusts line thickness and applies patterns to the objects, then organizes them into new, more complex objects.

Many draw programs allow the use of **gradient fill** patterns similar to those shown in Figure 7–5 that begin with a certain density of pattern or opacity at a determined

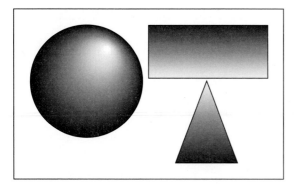

Figure 7–5
Sample use of gradient fill

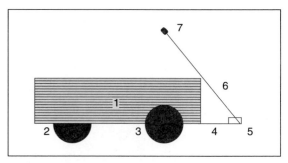

Figure 7–6
Objects making up the drawing in vector graphics

point and gradually fade to a less-dense pattern or increase to a denser one. Gradient fills can create the appearance of a third dimension on an object and are a dramatic background for text.

Once objects are created in draw programs, their shape, size, and position can be changed. Two or more objects may be linked or grouped together to form a new object. Text inserted in a drawing remains an editable text object. Typing mistakes can be easily corrected, and typefaces, sizes, and styles can be changed at any time. Being a discrete object, text may also be repositioned at will.

Count the objects making up the wagon in Figure 7–6. There are seven objects: (1) the shaded body of the wagon, (2) the rear wheel, (3) the front wheel, (4) the steering plate, (5) the handle tongue, (6) the handle shaft, and (7) the handle. Since the drawing is composed of independent objects, they may overlap or be layered on top of one another. Notice that the rear wheel is placed underneath the body of the wagon in this illustration and that the shading of the body has been changed from Figure 7–4. Some graphics programs include both bit-mapped and draw layers so that the user can take advantage of what each approach has to offer.

The Tools of Paint and Draw Programs

Figure 7–7 illustrates tools that are common to a number of paint and draw programs. Notice that a number of tools are common to both types of programs. If a paint or a draw program is truly to become a productivity tool, the user must become comfortable with the individual program and adept at using it. The following lists and descriptions help to introduce you to these tools.

Paint Tools. Paint tools are those that create bit-mapped images in paint programs.

marquee selection tool Selects a rectangular area, including any white background present.
lasso selection tool Selects an irregular shape without any extraneous background.
magic wand Selects adjacent pixels of the same color.

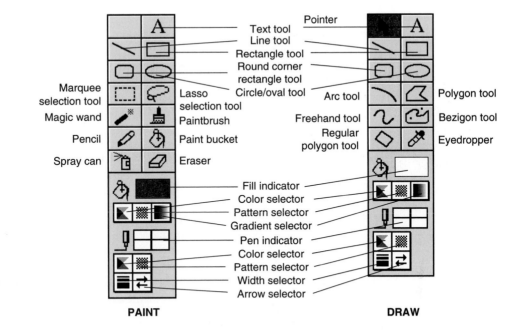

Figure 7–7

Tools commonly found in several paint and draw programs

paintbrush Paints strokes of various sizes and shapes.

pencil Paints fine lines in a freehand manner. One of the first tools people learn to use in a paint program.

paint bucket Used to fill an enclosed shape with color, pattern, or gradient.

spray can Used to create a spray-painted effect.

eraser Erases part of an image, pixel by pixel.

Draw Tools. Draw tools are those that create objects in draw programs.

pointer Selects, moves, and resizes objects.

arc tool Draws an arc curving between two points.

polygon tool Draws closed shapes made up of straight lines and angles.

freehand tool Draws irregular lines in the manner similar to a pencil.

bezigon tool Draws shapes, with the user selecting specific points. The tool draws smooth curves through those points.

regular polygon Draws polygons of equal sides.

eyedropper Picks up colors, patterns, and gradients from any object drawn and adjusts the proper selection tool. The result appears in the Fill indicator.

Common Tools. These tools are employed by both types of programs, though they behave somewhat differently in each.

text tool Inserts text on the screen in a selected font.

line tool Creates straight lines.

rectangle tool Creates rectangles and squares.

round corner rectangle Creates rectangles and squares with round corners.

circle/oval tool Creates ovals and circles.

color, pattern, and gradient fill selectors Allow user to select specific color, pattern, or gradient to fill a shape or an object.

color, pattern, width, and arrow pen selectors Allow user to select specific color, pattern, width, and arrow style for the pen.

fill and pen indicators Display the specific fill and pen characteristics that have been selected.

CLIP ART

For many years graphic artists have subscribed to services that have provided them with black-and-white or color line drawings and half-tone images. The artists clipped out any illustration that suited their needs and incorporated it into their own original work. **Clip art** files on disk are also available for use in computer graphics programs. The files are specifically available in the draw or paint format. Purchase of clip art entitles users to copy images or parts of images to use in their own drawings.

Examine the various illustrations in Figure 7–8. Some clip art files are composed solely of borders such as those shown in the upper and lower left-hand corners. There are clip art files of the flags of every nation. The chick and would-be ballplayer are simple line drawings. Notice the effective use of shading in the eagle, the kitten, and Santa. Clip art is a great time saver for all and an exceptional resource for those of modest or limited artistic skills and talents.

DESIGN OF INSTRUCTIONAL MATERIALS

In designing any communication, whether it be oral, written, or graphic, the sender of the message must know the anticipated audience that is to receive it and design the communication appropriately. The user must know what will capture the audience's attention and get the information across clearly and convincingly.

Line drawings are the most common type of graphics created on the computer. When considering line illustrations, a few simple rules apply:

- Present one topic or main idea per illustration.
- Use thick (bold) lines.
- Keep the use of text to a minimum and use a bold style.

Desktop presentation software permits the projection of computer screens by either a video projector or a video display panel placed on the stage of an overhead projector. Either projection can be in black-and-white or in color, depending on the equipment used. Some view these desktop presentation tools on the computer as "high-tech overhead or slide projectors." Computer graphics allow the user to enhance "low-tech" presentations as well. Signs, posters, maps, and banners can be created easily; so can overhead transparency masters.

Although equipment for other forms of projected media require some effort and setup time, the overhead projector sits ready to use in the front of most classrooms. This availability and its ease of use have contributed to its widespread popularity

ANIMALS
©1984 Vol# 1 McPic! by MAGNUM

Canada

FLAGS 1
©1984 Vol#2 McPic! by MAGNUM

Christmas 1
ClickArt™ Holidays

Borders #1
from Mac the Knife™ / A Macintosh™ Clip-Art Treasury
©1984 Miles Computing, Inc. / Drawn by Cliff Joyce

Figure 7–8
Samples of clip art (Courtesy of T-Maker, Magnum Software Corp., and Miles Computing, Inc.)

with teachers and increasingly with students. Unfortunately, the medium has not always been used most effectively. Computer graphics present a tool for improving the preparation of transparencies and increasing the effectiveness of their use.

When designing overhead transparencies, keep in mind the following six design rules:

1. Use landscape (horizontal) rather than portrait (vertical) orientation for your layout.
2. Lettering must be at least 1/4″ high (18 point) and should be simple, bold, and easy to read. This will allow the projected screen image of the text to be viewed comfortably from the rear of a typical classroom.
3. Lettering and drawings should be large enough to fill most of the transparency sheet, leaving enough blank space to emphasize the design elements.
4. Color should be used where appropriate. Different colors can be used to highlight keywords by separating the components of the transparency into two masters and printing them in different colors of thermal film.
5. Text should be kept to a minimum and should present only an outline or key points rather than specific details. Key points might be bulleted or presented as a list. Key words can be emphasized by using bold, underline, or italics but avoid a mixture of the elements. Remember that this is an ephemeral medium in that, once a projector is turned off, the projected information is gone. Significant text and detail require a printed hard copy in the hands of the students.
6. Divide complex topics into "overlay cells" so that the concept may be presented in a logical sequence. "Overlay" transparencies allow items to be added progressively to develop the finished product or complete idea.

For many years, teachers have created thermal transparencies using the 3-M Thermofax™ copier. This heat process uses thermal film that is chemically treated on one side with an emulsion that will produce a black, red, green, blue, or purple line. It is a line medium in that it will not reproduce solid areas, fine patterns, or photographic halftones well.

The original, or master, being copied must have a significant amount of carbon in its ink in order to reflect the heat to the film's emulsion in the copier. Prints from laser printers work well as transparency masters but those from dot-matrix printers must be photocopied. The copies then serve as transparency masters.

Designing transparency masters in computer graphics is a fairly straightforward task. The first step requires the user to create the entire drawing and save the document. In Figure 7–9, the process of plant growth was drawn in its entirety as a file named Master. The second step involves deciding what elements of the total drawing should be presented first. All other elements are deleted from the drawing and the file is saved under a different name. This file was saved as Base Cell in Figure 7–9. The files should be saved in such a way that the user will easily recognize the contents. The third and subsequent steps require the user to open the original complete document (e.g., Master in Figure 7–9), delete unwanted elements, and save the results as a new file with a different name (e.g., 1st Overlay and 2nd Overlay in Figure 7–9).

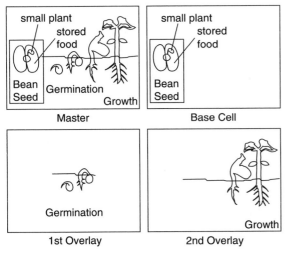

Figure 7–9

Design of an overlay transparency

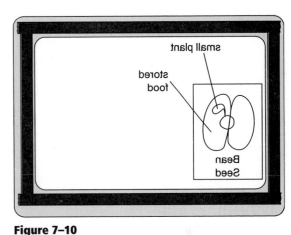

Figure 7–10

Mounting the base cell

Multiple cell transparencies should be mounted on a cardboard frame. The first, or base, cell is securely fastened with masking tape on all edges on the underside of the frame, as shown in Figure 7–10.

Overlay cells should then be mounted on the top surface of the frame, as illustrated in Figure 7–11. They may be mounted all on the same edge or on different edges.

If the concept being presented calls for information to be added in the same order (e.g., fixed sequence, progressive growth, sequential development of an idea), then overlay cells may be mounted all on the same edge of the frame so they can never be shown in the wrong order. If, on the other hand, an overlay cell is placed, adding information to the base cell, and then removed to allow a subsequent overlay cell to be placed, showing contrasting information, the cells must be mounted on different edges of the frame to allow for this flexibility.

In examining the process just described, it is apparent that the user, once having acquired a certain degree of skill and comfort level with a computer graphics program, can use it as a tool that extends abilities in a low-tech environment. Other examples include banners that can be created on continuous-form computer paper by programs such as *Print Shop*™.

Some programs take an original (either scanned into the computer or created in a paint program) and allow the user to enlarge it to huge dimensions. The image is printed in segments on four to 16 (or more) standard 8 1/2-by-11-inch sheets of paper that are tiled, or assembled, into the finished product. The example in Figure 7–12 shows an image printed on 16 sheets of paper. The sheets are assembled and fastened to each other to form a poster approximately 34 inches by 44 inches. Graphics programs such as these enhance the creative ability of students and teachers and facilitate visual communication.

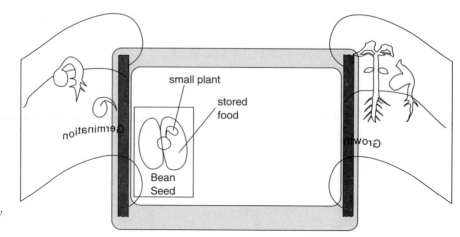
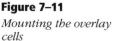

Figure 7–11

Mounting the overlay cells

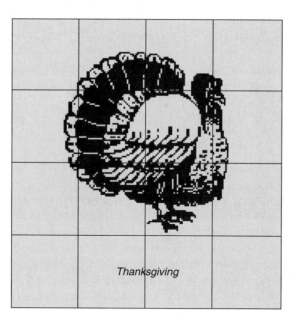
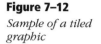

Figure 7–12

Sample of a tiled graphic

SUMMARY

Some graphics programs facilitate the creation of graphics for bulletin boards and other displays. Some generate drawings; others automatically generate line graphs, bar graphs, and pie charts from numeric data. Programs and video boards are available that allow computer screens to be recorded on videotape to serve as titles, credits, animated graphics, and instructional text screens. Although these materials can be created in other ways, the computer makes it easier and less time consuming and thereby stimulates teachers to maximize their creative efforts.

Optical scanners read light reflected from the surface of an object to be copied. Graphics tablets allow the user to create or trace figures and drawings on the surface of the tablet with a stylus, which provides far greater control than a mouse. A video digitizer accompanied by a digital camera or a video camcorder allows the user to record still images that can be transmitted into the computer, manipulated, and stored on disk as graphic files.

In bit-mapped graphics, the computer-generated image is composed of bits, or screen picture elements called pixels, that are turned on and bits that are off. One of the inherent drawbacks of bit-mapped graphics is that the size of the pixel limits the sharpness, or resolution, of the drawing, regardless of the resolution of the monitor or printer used to display the graphic.

In vector, or object-oriented, graphics, each picture element is a separate object and can be changed independently. The user of a draw program creates objects of different shapes, adjusts line thickness and applies patterns to the objects, then organizes them into new, more complex objects. Text inserted in a drawing remains an editable and movable object. Clip art is available as files in paint or draw formats on disk for use in computer graphics programs.

In designing any communication, whether it be oral, written, or graphic, the sender of the message must know the anticipated audience that is to receive it and design the communication appropriately in order to capture attention and get information across clearly and convincingly.

Signs, posters, maps, and banners can be easily created; so can overhead transparency masters. There are six basic design rules to keep in mind when creating overhead transparencies. For many years teachers have created thermal transparencies using a process employing thermal film that is chemically treated on one side with an emulsion that will produce a black, red, green, blue, or purple line. It is a line medium in that it will not reproduce solid areas, fine patterns, or photographic halftones well. The original, or master, being copied must have a significant amount of carbon in its ink in order to reflect the heat to the film's emulsion in the copier. Prints from laser printers work well as transparency masters but those from dot-matrix printers must be photocopied.

The first step in designing transparency masters in computer graphics requires the user to create the entire drawing and save the document. The second step involves deciding what elements of the total drawing should be presented first. All other elements are deleted from the drawing and the file is saved under a different name. The third and subsequent steps require the user to open the original complete document, delete unwanted elements, and save the results as a new file with a different name.

CHAPTER EXERCISES

1. Using a paint program, create a cover page for a report. How does the graphic you created heighten the reader's interest in the report?
2. Write a brief report on a topic of current national interest and use a graphic captured from a scanner to illustrate your report.

3. Using the draw component of an integrated package or a stand-alone draw program, create a set of informational or directional signs for a school lunchroom.
4. Using the same program, create a set of bookmarks that might be placed in a school library to promote books worth reading.
5. Using a paint program, draw the outline map of your state. Add the major cities and other significant geographical features such as rivers and mountains. Print the results as a base cell and two overlays. Explain why you divided the elements the way you did.

GLOSSARY

bit-mapped graphics Computer-generated images composed of bits, or screen pixels, that are turned on (black or colored) and bits that are turned off (white or clear).

clip art Prepared files of black-and-white or color line drawings and halftone images available on disk in the draw or paint format for use in computer graphics programs that are intended to be incorporated into the user's own original work.

decoding The process of giving meaning to data being communicated.

encoding The process of selecting symbols and other elements to communicate desired information.

gradient fill A pattern that begins with a certain opacity or density of pattern at a determined point and gradually fades to one that is less dense or increases to one that is more dense.

object-oriented graphics Computer-generated images determined by formulas that create discrete objects of a certain size and position.

vector graphics See *object-oriented graphics*.

REFERENCES & SUGGESTED READINGS

Duren, P. (1990-91, December-January). Enhancing inquiry skills using graphics software. *The Computing Teacher, 18*(4), 23–25.

Kinnman, D. E. (1993, March). LCD panels: The next generation. *Technology & Learning, 13*(6), 44–50.

Lake, D. (1990, May). Patrick's visual: A book report using presentation software. *The Computing Teacher, 17*(8), 54–55.

Mathis, J. (1988, October). Turning data into pictures. *The Computing Teacher, 15*(2), 40–48.

Metzler, B. (1990, April). Who can draw with a Macintosh? *The Computing Teacher, 17*(7), 21–23.

Robinson, P. (1993, March). How to warm up a crowd: Desktop presentation software. *New Media, 3*(3), 60–69.

Williams, S. K. (1991, January). Something for everyone. *Teacher Magazine,* 40–43.

Chapter 8

Spreadsheets

ADVANCE ORGANIZER

The term **spreadsheet** originated in the accounting world to refer to data entered in a column on a large, wide sheet of paper and related, component, or derivative data "spread" across columns in the same row. This ledger sheet, or spreadsheet, as it became known, was in fact a two-dimensional paper matrix of rows and columns. Spreadsheets can be used for a wide variety of activities, but most applications of spreadsheets focus on generating numeric information from other numeric information such as creating budgets and income projections and forecasting needed amounts of equipment or supplies based on a number of factors.

In 1979, Daniel Bricklin and Robert Frankston developed the first electronic spreadsheet for computers. They looked upon it as a visible calculator and thus named their product *VisiCalc*™. Because the accountants who saw *VisiCalc*™ demonstrated recognized it as a highly efficient 63-column by 254-row electronic simulation of their favorite paper-and-pencil tool, they began putting computers on their desks. *VisiCalc*™ became known as the program that sold computers. The present-day electronic spreadsheet or simply spreadsheet, as we will now refer to it, has greatly increased its power, size, sophistication, and ease of use. It lets the user enter text and values and create formulas that set up relationships between values, which may be governed by the simple arithmetic operators of +, −, *, and / or by sophisticated functions that are expressions of more complex mathematical and statistical formulas. The spreadsheet automatically recalculates all values as the data entries are made, thereby revealing relationships instantaneously.

Why would a teacher use a spreadsheet? One of many classroom applications of spreadsheets is to manage grades. Why not use a commercial grade book program? Teachers manage grades in many different ways. All too often, the adoption of a grade book program forces teachers to change their grading methods to adapt to the software purchased. A spreadsheet, on the other hand, can be custom-designed to the teacher's system.

Consider the example in Figure 8–1. As the classroom teacher uses this grade book spreadsheet, it will continually calculate the students' total point accumulation and display a final score in column G. It is also designed to keep the statistics on each class activity, identifying the highest, lowest, and average score on the activity, giving the teacher information by which to assess the activity. The rows may be sorted in alphabetical order by the student names in column A at any time so, as new students are added, the grade book is sorted once again.

USING A SPREADSHEET

The illustrations used in this chapter to explain the operation of spreadsheets are actual screens of *Microsoft Excel*™. It is important to note that most spreadsheets, regardless of program or operating system platform, look and act very much alike. To help visualize the capability of a spreadsheet, consider a grid or matrix made up of many columns and many rows. A spreadsheet is this matrix of lettered columns and numbered rows. As illustrated in Figure 8–2, the intersection of a column and a row is called a **cell** and is named by first the column and then the row designation. The

	A	B	C	D	E	F	G
1	Name	Lab 1	Lab 2	Test	Midterm	Portfolio	Grade
2		10	10	100	100	100	100
3	Adams, Laura	9	7	78	75	80	78
4	Alderson, Kathy	10	9	98	90	95	95
5	Alvarez, Manuel	10	8	85	80	85	85
6	Drexler, Richard	9	8	80	80	90	84
7	Kersey, Clyde	6	7	75	70	80	73
8	Prosser, Peggy	10	10	98	90	95	96
9	Prosser, Walt	8	8	90	80	80	83
10	Williams, Andrea	9	9	80	85	80	83
11	Highest Score	10	10	98	90	95	96
12	Lowest Score	6	7	75	70	80	73
13	Average	8.88	8.25	85.50	81.25	85.63	85

Figure 8–1

A spreadsheet used as a grade book

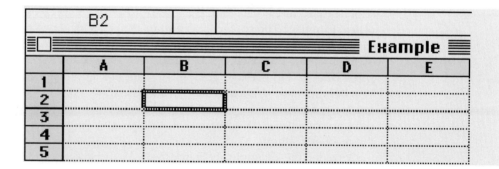

Figure 8–2

A cell named B2

cursor can be moved around through this grid and positioned in any cell. When you click in a cell, an outline appears around it, indicating that it has been selected as the **active cell**. In the illustration, the active cell is B2. Notice that the name of the cell also appears in the upper left-hand corner. The primary task when working with spreadsheets is specifying the relationship between the cells.

When an entry (text or a value) is made from the keyboard, it appears in an area at the top of the screen called the formula bar. As illustrated in Figure 8–3, B2 is identified as the active cell and the value that has been typed in that cell, 17, also appears in the **formula bar**, the area across the top of the screen. For obvious reasons, this area is sometimes also referred to as the data entry bar.

Once text, a value, or a formula is entered into a cell, the program must know that you are finished working in that cell and some signal must be given denoting that entry has ended. Fortunately, most programs adhere to the same conventions. In Figure 8–3, the Enter key was pressed. Notice that this action, while denoting the end of data entry in the cell, does not move the cursor from the active cell.

A second way to indicate that you have finished entering data or a formula in the cell is to press the Return key. As shown in Figure 8–4, this will also move the cursor to the next cell down in the same column. Notice that the active cell is then B3 and that its name appears in the top left-hand corner.

A third way to indicate that you have finished working in the cell is to press the Tab key. As shown in Figure 8–5, this will also move the cursor to the next cell to the right in the same row. Notice that the active cell is then C2 and that its name appears in the top left-hand corner. In addition to using the Enter, Return, and Tab keys, you may also press one of the arrow keys to indicate that you have finished working in a cell and wish to move the cursor to one of the four adjacent cells.

One of the real strengths of spreadsheets is the ability to relate cells to each other.

- The data in one cell can be automatically replicated in another by making cells equal to each other.
- Data in one cell can be added to, subtracted from, and multiplied or divided by data in another cell.
- Complex mathematical relationships can be expressed in a group of cells.

Formulas are created to express this ability to relate cells.

In *Microsoft Works*™, *Excel*™, and *ClarisWorks*™, formulas always begin with the *equals* sign and reference cells by their name. As you saw in Figure 8–3, the value

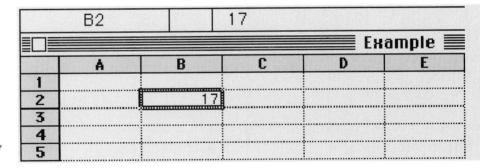

Figure 8–3

Data displayed in the formula bar

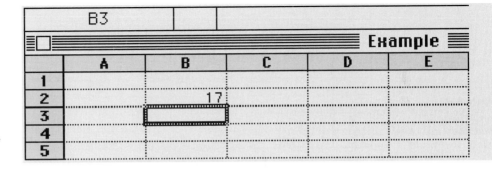

Figure 8–4

Pressing the Return key to signify end of data entry

Figure 8–5

Pressing the Tab key to signify end of data entry

17 was entered in cell B2. Figure 8–6 shows the formula =B2 entered in cell A4. This formula will replicate in cell A4 any entry occurring in cell B2.

As we see in Figure 8–7, the value 17 was entered in cell B2 and the value 2 was entered in cell C2. An additional cell, D2, was selected as the active cell and the formula entered in it was =B2*C2 [cell B2 (containing the value of 17)*(multiplied by) cell C2 (containing the value of 2)]. Notice that the result of the formula is displayed in cell D2, while the formula itself appears in the formula bar.

Formulas may contain the arithmetic operations of addition, subtraction, multiplication, division, and exponentiation. These are represented by +, −, *, /, and ^, respectively. The operations are performed in the following order: (1) perform all

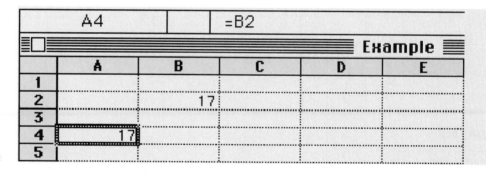

Figure 8–6

Relating one cell to another by a formula

Figure 8–7

Acting upon the contents of two other cells in a formula

operations inside parentheses, working from inside out if parentheses are nested within each other; (2) compute exponents; (3) perform all multiplications and divisions in order from left to right; (4) perform all additions and subtractions in order from left to right; and, finally, (5) perform order operations ($<$, $>$, and $=$).

In the example shown as Figure 8–7, both B2 and C2 are known as relative references in the formula, since they actually relate to cells one position and two positions to the left of the active formula cell, D2. If, on the other hand, the formula is meant to always refer to an exact cell regardless of the placement of the formula cell within the spreadsheet, the reference is called *absolute,* or *fixed.* For example, if the formula must contain a reference to the top cell in the second column, the cell would be entered into a formula as a fixed reference and in most spreadsheets would be typed as $B$1. The dollar signs indicate that the column and row will not change. Should the formula be cut or copied to any other cell, no matter where it is located in the spreadsheet, the fixed reference would remain to cell B1.

To assist the user, the spreadsheet program contains a wide variety of built-in functions that can be used simply by referencing them in the desired formula, as well as the cells containing the related data. The following are common mathematical functions often used in formulas:

SUM (of values within a cell group)
AVERAGE (of values within a cell group)
MINIMUM (value of the values within a cell group)
MAXIMUM (value of the values within a cell group)
STANDARD DEVIATION (of values within a cell group)

	A	B	C	D
1	NAME	LENGTH	WEIGHT	DIET
2	Tyrannosaurus	50 ft.	8 tons	Carniverous
3	Allosaurus	25 ft.	4.5 tons	Carniverous
4	Brachiosaurus	70 ft.	80 tons	Herbivorous
5	Triceratops	20 ft.	7 tons	Herbivorous
6	Stegosaurus	20 ft.	4 tons	Herbivorous

Figure 8–8

Using a spreadsheet to sort text

The group of cells referenced by these functions are designated as a range from the first cell in the group to the last one. Within the formula, the first and last cells in the range are usually separated by a colon or an ellipse, depending on the particular spreadsheet being used (e.g., F9:F17 or F9...F17) and enclosed in parentheses.

Spreadsheets are in fact highly specialized databases. They can store and manipulate text and numeric values and are sometimes used instead of database managers when their two-dimensional matrix format (columns and rows) lends itself to convenient data entry and when printed report requirements are minimal. The illustration in Figure 8–8 demonstrates the use of text both as **labels** in row 1 and as data to be manipulated in rows 2 through 6. Spreadsheets are often used as powerful sorting devices to examine information grouped in a variety of ways. Each row in Figure 8–8 contains information about one dinosaur. A multilevel sort has arranged the information by (1) DIET in ascending order, then within that first sort by (2) LENGTH in descending order, and then within those two levels of sort by (3) WEIGHT in descending order. This ability to nest one sort within another adds versatility to the spreadsheet.

> "I teach research skills by grouping my fifth graders into cooperative learning groups. Each group collects data from the *Sports Illustrated* CD-ROM then enters the data into a spreadsheet in order to sort it, analyze it, and draw conclusions."
>
> *Doris Holman, 5th Grade Teacher*
> *Fuqua School, Farmville, VA*

PROBLEM SOLVING WITH SPREADSHEETS

Consider the process of problem solving discussed in Chapter 3 that might be approached by an individual with a random learning style. Let us review the nonlinear method and the illustration that was presented. "Given" is the information in your possession. "To Find" is the information you are seeking. What are the results you are trying to achieve? "Procedure" is the method you are going to employ to reach your goal. How will you achieve results? This approach is illustrated in Figure 8–9.

Apply the problem-solving process just reviewed and illustrated in Figure 8–9 to the following simple word problem: A boy takes home $4.00 an hour from a weekend job. How many hours must he work in order to be able to purchase a $300 bicycle?

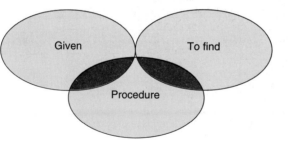

Figure 8–9

A nonlinear approach to problem solving

Given: Take-home pay is $4.00 per hour.
               Cost of the bicycle is $300.
To Find: Number of hours of work required to earn enough to purchase the bicycle.
Procedure: Divide the cost of the bicycle ($300) by the hourly take-home rate of $4.00 (300 / 4.00 = ?).

In Figure 8–10, the cost of the bicycle ($300) is entered in cell A2 and the hourly take-home rate ($4.00) is entered in cell B2. The formula = A2 / B2 (cost divided by hourly rate) is entered in cell C2. Upon completing the formula entry, the formula is displayed in the formula bar, and the value resulting from the formula as hours to work (75) is displayed in the cell.

C2		=A2/B2	
			Weekend Job
	A	**B**	**C**	**D**
1	Cost of bicycle	Hourly Rate	Hours to work	
2	$300	$4.00	75	
3				
4				
5				

Figure 8–10

Using a spreadsheet as an organizer and a calculator

C2		=A2/B2	
			Weekend Job
	A	**B**	**C**	**D**
1	Cost of bicycle	Hourly Rate	Hours to work	
2	$350	$6.00	58.33	
3				
4				
5				

Figure 8–11

Using a spreadsheet as a forecasting tool

Having discovered the number of hours necessary to earn the required amount, the boy might now wish to see the effect of moving to a higher-paying job and perhaps purchasing a slightly more expensive bike. He could play "what if" and forecast the results of change. As shown in Figure 8–11, by changing the data under "Hourly Rate" and "Cost of Bicycle," he could immediately see the impact on the number of "Hours to Work."

CURRICULUM APPLICATIONS OF SPREADSHEETS

We have described the spreadsheet as a matrix of interrelated columns and rows and have examined its operation. We understand that it can handle text and values, that it is founded on the ability to relate cells to each other, and that it has powerful built-in formulas. We are also beginning to explore some of the functional uses of spreadsheets to record, organize, and sort data (values and text); to calculate values; and to forecast results. As a recording tool, the spreadsheet allows us to alphabetize lists of names, track expenditures, analyze the performance of players in various sports, and manage a grade book. As a forecasting tool, the spreadsheet allows us to analyze the immediate impact of projected changes. We could, for instance, reveal the impact on a school district's budget of raising teachers' salaries by 5 percent, by 4 percent, by 6 percent, and so on.

The table below illustrates a number of spreadsheet applications in different curriculum areas and at various grade levels. This table summarizes the functional applications and possible curriculum areas of the examples given.

Examples of spreadsheet applications

Figure	Primary Function(s)	Curriculum
8–12	Measurement	Mathematics
8–13	Calculation	Mathematics, home economics
8–14	Calculation, analysis	Science, social studies
8–15	Recording, analysis	Social studies, mathematics
8–16	Recording, analysis	Athletics
8–17	Forecasting	Mathematics
8–18	Recording, calculation	Management
8–19	Recording, forecasting	Management
8–20	Recording, calculation	Social studies, mathematics
8–21	Calculation, graphing	Mathematics, social studies

"The business class at our high school runs a concession stand. The students use a spreadsheet to track sales, profits, and inventory. Purchase and pricing decisions are made on a spreadsheet projection of sales. "

Fred Ross, Bering Strait School District, Unalakleet, AK

	A	B	C	D	E	F
1	Group #	Length	Width	Height	Volume	
2	1	4.3	3	5	64.5	
3	2	4.4	2.8	4.7	57.9	
4	3	4.8	2.9	5.1	70.99	
5						
6						
7						
8						
9						
10						
11						
12						
13						
14						

Suggested Use: Accuracy in measurement may be encouraged by having pairs of students measure a cube. The measurements from each pair may be entered in a spreadsheet. Even a slight difference in length, width, or height can result in a considerable difference in volume.

Once the formula is entered in cell E2, students could be shown how it can be replicated down the column by first beginning in E2, then selecting the group or range of cells down the E column where the formula was to be repeated and invoking the Fill Down command.

The following formula would yield the necessary calculation in this example:

En = Bn*Cn*Dn [n represents the number of the row]

Figure 8–12

Using a spreadsheet to promote accuracy

	A	B	C	D	E	F	G
1	Ingredients	Measure	Serving Size				
2			12	20	24	30	
3	Wheat flour	Cup	2	3.33	4	5	
4	Baking powder	Tsp	2	3.33	4	5	
5	Salt	Tsp	0.5	0.83	1	1.25	
6	Egg		1	1.67	2	2.5	
7	Vegetable oil	Cup	0.25	0.42	0.5	0.63	
8	Honey	Cup	0.25	0.42	0.5	0.63	
9	Milk	Cup	0.5	0.83	1	1.25	
10							
11							
12							
13							
14							

Suggested Use: Adapting a recipe to a different number of servings is a common problem faced in preparing a meal. This illustrates how a recipe designed for a set number of servings can be adapted for any number. The example deals with servings of 20, 24, and 30, but in reality any number may be used.

The formula must first calculate the unit measure by dividing the amount by the serving size given in the recipe. It then multiplies the unit measure by the number of servings desired.

The following formulas would yield the necessary calculations in this example:

Dn = (C3/$C$2) * $D$2 [n represents the number of the row and the $ indicates an absolute reference]

En = (C3/$C$2) * $E$2

Figure 8–13

Using a spreadsheet to calculate proportions

	A	B	C	D	E	F	G
1		City: Melbourne, Australia					
2	Date	High	Low	Mean	Amount	Days	
3		Temp	Temp	Temp	Precip.	Precip.	
4	4/1/99	67	49	58	0.55	1	
5	4/2/99	69	50	60	1	1	
6	4/3/99	61	50	56	0.33	1	
7	4/4/99	66	51	58	0	0	
8							
33	4/30/99	76	55	66	0.25	1	
34	Amt. Precip.	- - -	- - -	- - -	2.56	- - -	
35	Days Precip.	- - -	- - -	- - -	- - -	6	
36	High/ Month	76	- - -	- - -	- - -	- - -	
37	Low/ Month	- - -	49	- - -	- - -	- - -	
38	Average	68	51	59	- - -	- - -	

Suggested Use: A spreadsheet could be used to record information about the weather and to calculate high, low, and average temperatures, as well as amount of and average precipitation and days of precipitation. In this example, the daily high temperature would be entered in column B; the daily low temperature would be entered in column C; and the amount of precipitation would be entered in column E. The average daily temperature would be calculated in column D. Whether or not precipitation occurred during the day would be calculated in column F. The total amount of precipitation would be calculated in cell E34. The total number of days in which precipitation occurred would be calculated in cell F35. The highest temperature for the month would be calculated in cell B36. The lowest temperature for the month would be calculated in cell C37. Averages for the month would be calculated in row 38. Discussion of relationship of weather and climate to activities and life styles could follow.

The following formulas would yield the necessary calculations in this spreadsheet:

D4 = AVERAGE (B4:C4) to average between the day's high and low temperatures

F4 = IF (E4>0,1,"") to count the day as having precipitation or not [If there is a value greater than 0 in cell E4, then enter 1 in cell F4, else leave blank]

E34 = SUM (E4:E33) to add the total precipitation for the month

F35 = SUM (F4:F33) to add the total days in which there was precipitation

B36 = MAX (B4:B33) and **C37 = MIN (C4:C33)** to calculate highs and lows

N38 = AVERAGE (n4:n33) to calculate averages [n represents columns B through D]

Figure 8–14

Using a spreadsheet to calculate sums and averages in a cross-disciplinary science and social studies context

	A	B	C	D	E	F	G	H	I	J	K
1		Total *	Died during the years				Total *	Died during the years			
2	Age	Men	1975	'74–50	'49–25	'24–00	Women	1975	'74–50	'49–25	'24–00
3	0–10	0					0				
4	11–20	0					0				
5	21–30	0					0				
6	31–40	0					0				
7	41–50	0					0				
8	51–60	0					0				
9	61–70	0					0				
10	71–80	0					0				
11	81–90	0					0				
12	91–100	0					0				
13	Totals	0	0	0	0	0	0	0	0	0	0
14	Population*										
15	Percentage										
16	* population for midpoint of each quarter century										

Suggested Use: In exploring local history, students could be made aware of the value of a local cemetery as a primary resource. Data gathered from headstones could help in the understanding of events and conditions prevalent in the local area during the last century. In order to profit from this resource, students could first discuss the type of data available in which they might have an interest and then formulate relevant questions. They might ask, for example, "How much older did women live than men? Was there a period of unusually high mortality? How did life expectancy change over time? Did it change equally for men and women?" Once prepared with data collection sheets and reminded of expected behavior in such a setting, teams of students could visit a local cemetery and gather data by walking down the rows of grave markers, tallying gender and age of the deceased and year of their death. Upon completion of the data gathering, students would enter data into a spreadsheet and search for trends and anomalies. The resulting information might generate additional questions requiring further research.

The following formulas would yield the necessary calculations in this spreadsheet:

Bn = SUM(Cn : Fn) [n represents the number of rows 3–12]
Gn = SUM(Hn : Kn) [n represents the number of rows 3–12]
n13 = SUM(n13 : n12) [n represents columns B–K]
n15 = n13/n14 [n represents the columns C–F and H–K]

Figure 8–15

Exploring a local cemetery in a math and history lesson

	A	B	C	D	E	F	G	H	I	J	K	L
1	Player	Pos	FGA	FGM	PCT	FTA	FTM	PCT	OR	DR	A	TO
2	Gwenda	C	8	5	62%	8	7	88%	3	6	4	2
3	Helen	C	12	7	58%	6	5	83%	2	5	2	0
4	Meredith	G	11	8	73%	9	8	89%	1	2	6	1
5	Nancy	G	5	3	60%	3	2	67%	2	2	5	3
6	Peggy	G	11	8	73%	10	9	90%	1	2	5	0
7	Mimi	F	18	12	67%	11	9	82%	4	5	1	0
8	Karna	F	5	2	40%	2	1	50%	0	1	2	2
9	Dovie	F	5	2	40%	1	0	0%	0	1	1	0
10												
11	SUMMARY		75	47	63%	50	41	82%	13	24	26	8
12												
13												

Suggested Use: Though this example deals with basketball, the recording and statistical analysis of player performance is applicable to all team sports. The coach or an assistant would enter data in columns A (Name), B (Position), C (Field Goal Attempts), D (Field Goals Made), F (Free Throw Attempts), G (Free Throws Made), I (Offensive Rebounds), J (Defensive Rebounds), K (Assists), and L (Turnovers) after the game. Formulas in columns E and H would calculate shooting percentages for each player. Additional columns could be added to anylyze other facets of player performance. For example, a formula that calculates the ratio of assists to turnovers could focus on the players ball-handling skills.

The following formulas would yield the necessary calculations in this spreadsheet:

En = **Dn/Cn** [n represents the number of rows 2–9]
Hn = **Gn/Fn** [n represents the number of rows 2–9]

Figure 8–16

Using a spreadsheet to analyze player performance statistics

	A	B	C	D	E	F
1	Profit	# of	List	Profit	Total Boxes	Boxes per
2	Goal	Students	Price	Margin	To Sell	Student
3	$500	30	$5.00	$2.00	250	8
4	$500	30	$6.00	$2.40	208	7
5	$500	30	$7.00	$2.80	179	6
6						
7						
8						
9						
10						
11						
12						
13						

Suggested Use: A teacher may at times supervise an activity to raise funds through a class project. Before deciding on a specific project, the class may want to consider alternatives, with the hope of finding a project that will generate the maximum income for time and effort spent. The fundamental criterion of the anaylsis would be money raised for effort spent. For example, suppose one of the projects under consideration is the sale of candy. The list price, number of available students, and target earnings could be set. The use of the spreadsheet would let the class explore the required total sales volume and the number of units each student would need to sell at each list price. With this spreadsheet, the class could play "what if" and immediately see the results. Selling a more expensive product would reduce the required sales volume and therefore require a lower minimum sales target per student in order to achieve comparable results.

After the initial values are placed in columns A, B, and C, all of the remaining cells are filled in automatically by the spreadsheet.

The following formulas would yield the necessary calculations in this spreadsheet:

D3 = C3 * .40 (40% profit)

E3 = A3/D3

F3 = E3/B3

Figure 8–17

Using a spreadsheet to forecast sales in a class activity

	A	B	C	D	E
1		Beginning Account Balance:			$1000.00
2	Date	Purchase	Transaction	Expense	Current
3		Order		Amount	Balance
4	2/17/99	B-990012	Powell's Books	$105.50	$894.50
5	3/1/99	B-990013	M & C Deli	$28.00	$866.50
6					
7					
8					
9					
10					
11					
12					
13					

Suggested Use: Many school accounts have day-to-day activity, but the general ledger printout comes out only once a month. A spreadsheet set up along the lines of this one would reveal the current status of each account.

Once the labels and formulas are designed, the template may be saved to disk and called up each month, the beginning balance entered and resaved to disk under a new name corresponding to the current month. The beginning account balance can be entered in cell E1. Information can then be entered on a new line whenever a purchase order is written, and the current balance would be displayed in cells E4–En. The formula calculating the balance is in column E.

> *The following formulas would yield the necessary calculations in this spreadsheet:*
>
> **E4 = E1 − D4** (beginning balance minus expenditure)
> **E5 = E4 − D5** (prior balance minus current expenditure)

At the end of the month this account can be reconciled against the school district's printout for the account and any differences noted and addressed.

Figure 8–18

Using a spreadsheet to keep an expenditure journal

	A	B	C	D	E	F	G	H	I	J
1	Serial	Item	Purch	Purch	Expect	Age	Replace	Inflation	Deprec	Replace
2	#	Type	Cost	Date	Life		Date	Factor	Value	Cost
3										
4	10023	OH	$389	9/9/96	7	3	9/9/03	0.03	$130	$424
5	10036	VCR	$425	8/9/97	5	2	8/9/02	0.03	$212	$450
6										
7										
8										
9										
10										
11										
12										

Suggested Use: A spreadsheet could be used to help project the cost of replacing existing instructional equipment based on the projected life of the equipment, purchase date, original cost, and inflation.

In this spreadsheet, text or values would be entered in the cells in columns A, B, C, D, and H. Some spreadsheets could post the expected life figure in column E from a look-up table containing the life expectancy of various types of equipment based on available research; otherwise, this value would also be entered manually. Formulas would generate values in columns F, G, I, and J.

The following formulas would yield the necessary calculations in this spreadsheet:

AGE.................................. **F4 = (NOW0 − D4)/365.25**

[NOW() is a function that reads the computer's internal clock/calendar. Some programs use TODAY ( ) in place of NOW(). Dividing by 365.25 converts the number of days into years, taking into account leap years.]

REPLACE DATE................. **G4 = D4 + (E4 * 365.25)**
DEPRECIATED VALUE....... **I4 = C4 * ((E4 2 F4)/E4)**
REPLACEMENT COST........ **J4 = (C4 * (F4 * H4)) + C4**

Figure 8–19

Using a spreadsheet to manage an equipment inventory and to track replacement needs

	A	B	C	D	E	F	G	H
1	Starting Date:		5/10/43			Est. days for Trip:		150
2	Date	Milestones	Current	Distance	Speed	Days	Days	% of Trip
3			State	from prior	(MPH)	from prior	elapsed	
4	May 10, 1843	Independence	MO	0	0	0	0	0%
5	May 26, 1843			400	1.5	17	17	11%
6	Jun 20, 1843			400	1	25	42	28%
7	Jul 9, 1843			300	1	19	60	40%
8	Jul 23, 1843			300	1	19	79	53%
9	Aug 13, 1843			250	0.75	21	100	67%
10	Sep 2, 1843			180	0.75	15	115	77%
11	Sep 10, 1843	Oregon City	OR	140	1	9	124	82%
12								
13								
14								

Suggested Use: In May of 1843, 1,000 emigrants in 120 wagons left Independence, Missouri, on a five-month journey to the Oregon Country. This was the beginning of the largest unforced mass migration in history. From 1843 to 1860, over 10,000 lost their lives along the trail, but over 300,000 successfully made the trip to Oregon. Stories written in pioneer diaries have contributed to making the Oregon Trail a romantic adventure in the minds of many young people. The study of the Great Migration presents a wonderful opportunity for the development of problem-solving skills in more than one discipline. Using a spreadsheet such as this one, students could study the geography of the trail and locate landmarks along the trail that posed significant hardships to the pioneers and those that provided welcomed rest. By studying the topography and climate conditions along the trail, students could adjust the speed of the covered wagons to match the progress of the pioneers in 1849 and complete the journey in about 130 days. When using the popular MECC simulation *Oregon Trail II* on CD-ROM, students could be encouraged to develop their own spreadsheets to record information and to help them make decisions.

Figure 8–20

Using a spreadsheet to record and calculate in a cross-disciplinary math and social studies context

The following formulas would yield the necessary calculations in this spreadsheet:

A5 = $C$1 + G5 [remember that the $ indicates a fixed reference]

F5 = (D5/E5) /16 [16 = the hours traveled in a day. This quickly changes to 12]

G5 = G4 + F5 [this formula is replicated down column G]

H5 = G5 / $H$1 [this formula is replicated down column H]

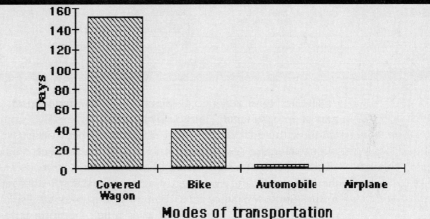

	A	B	C	D	E	F	G	H
1	Mode	Miles	MPH	Kilometers	KPH	Hours	Hours	Days
2	of Travel					per Day		
3	Covered Wagon	2000	1.1	3200	1.76	12	1818	152
4	Bicycle	1750	6	2800	9.6	8	292	36
5	Automobile	1750	50	2800	80	10	35	4
6	Airplane	1200	300	1920	480	4	4	1

Suggested Use: Capitalizing on student intereset in the Oregon Trail topic, English to metric relationships can be explored as well as the relationship of speed and time. As illustrated above, the comparisons can be dramatic. A student can play "what if" by changing the speed or the hours traveled during a day or both variables and immediately see the impact of those decisions. Students could be asked to justify both the speed they selected and the length of the travel day.

An area of the spreadsheet at the top was selected and, invoking the New command, the chart at the bottom was generated by the spreadsheet. Since a feeling of continuity was not important but, rather, a discrete comparison was indicated, a column graph was selected to show direct comparisons in time among the various modes of transportation used in the spreadsheet.

The following formulas would yield the necessary calculations in this spreadsheet:

D2 = B2 * 1.6 [1.6 kilometers in a mile]
E2 = C2 * 1.6
G2 = B2/C2
H2 = G2/F2

Figure 8–21

English to metric conversions, then generating a column graph demonstrating the impact of scale

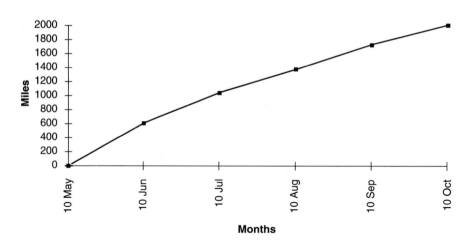

Figure 8–22

Portraying visually progress shown by numbers in the previous figure

The ability to generate graphs from the numerical data entered is a powerful feature of spreadsheets. The graph shown in Figure 8–22 comes from a slight manipulation of the data displayed in Figure 8–20, previously examined. Data were taken from that figure and entered into a new spreadsheet, a calculation was done to establish one-month intervals, and an area of the spreadsheet was selected. Invoking the New command and specifying a chart, the spreadsheet then produced a graph. A line graph was selected as being the best way to display this particular information. Looking at a progression over time, it demonstrates at a glance that better progress was made at the start of the trip. The going got slower as the wagon train encountered the formidable mountains of the West and sickness and fatigue set in.

CHARTS AND GRAPHS

Abstract numerical data can be presented in a concrete, clear, and interesting manner by line or bar graphs, pie charts, and other pictorial means. Prompted in part by the significant increase in graphs in the popular media (newspapers, magazines, and television news), graphing is now being introduced to students at a much earlier age. Graphs can display relationships that would be more difficult to convey in a text or verbal mode. As visuals, they capture attention and promote greater retention of information.

Although graphs can certainly be informative, they have the potential of expressing a bias by the manipulation of scale. Thus, the analysis and interpretation of graphs has become an important subject in the K–12 curriculum. Students can be presented data and led through exercises designed to promote an understanding of those data. They can then be asked to select the most informative and accurate presentation of the data. They may discover that, depending on the data, numeric tables show the most accurate but also the most abstract and difficult to understand relationships.

Line graphs, as shown in the upper left section of Figure 8–23, are ideal for displaying a continuous event or trends over time (e.g., growth or decline over time). Notice the steady increase in sales over the first four weeks portrayed on this graph.

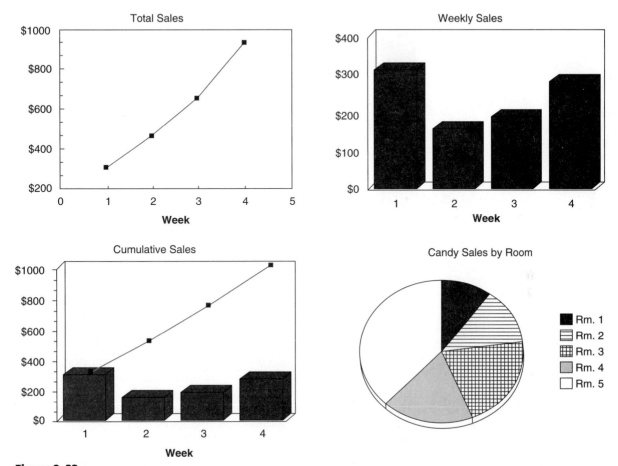

Figure 8–23
Examples of charts and graphs

The rise and fall of the line on a graph easily portrays the fluctuations in value. Multiple trends can be compared simultaneously by plotting more than one line on the graph. *Area graphs* are variations of line graphs that are successful at depicting amount or volume. A line is plotted and the area below it is filled in with a selected pattern. Each data set creates a band, with each area being stacked on the preceding one. These graphs can be eye-catching, but, since they show cumulative results, they can, at times, be more difficult to understand.

Column graphs (vertical columns), as shown in the upper right section of Figure 8–23, and *bar graphs* (horizontal bars) present changes in a dependent variable over an independent variable and are excellent ways of comparing multiple variables with a common variable (e.g., different performances during the same time frame) but lack the feeling of continuity displayed by a line graph. Notice how the individual weeks stand out in this graph, making it easy to determine that the first and fourth weeks were the sales leaders. At times column graphs and line graphs can be com-

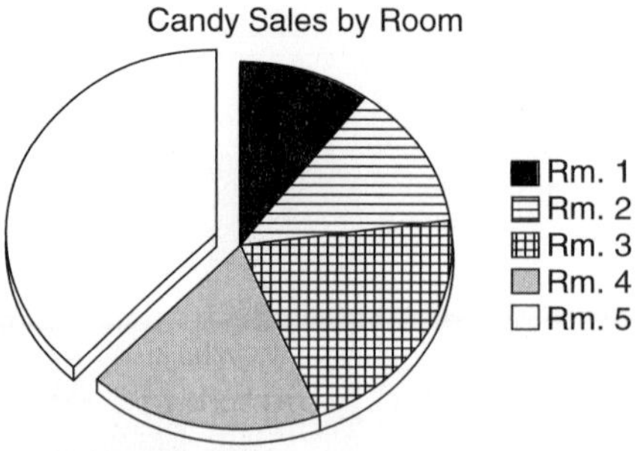

Candy Sales by Room

■ Rm. 1
▤ Rm. 2
▦ Rm. 3
▨ Rm. 4
□ Rm. 5

Figure 8–24

Pie chart in an exploded three-dimensional view

bined effectively, as shown in the lower left section of Figure 8–23, to present both discrete and incremental views of the data. More elaborate graphs adding another variable (e.g., different performances at different locations during the same time frame) can be created by stacking the columns/bars.

Pie charts are the ideal way to display part-to-the-whole relationships, or percentages, as shown in the lower right section of Figure 8–23. The size of each slice shows that segment's share of the entire pie. As shown in Figure 8–24, a segment (pie slice) may even be dragged away from the center for emphasis and the chart displayed in three dimensions. Other, more esoteric charts and graphs can be created to display central tendencies, shared variables, and relationships to a common constant.

Several integrated software packages include a built-in graphing function. A number of other computer programs exist that allow a student to enter data directly or input them from a text file, determine the appropriate scale, and select the type of graph or chart to be generated by the computer. This allows the student to examine several graphic representations of the same data and choose the most accurate and informative one.

Graph Components

Graphs are composed of certain common basic components. Note the components as they are labeled in the column graph in Figure 8–25. The *title* announces what your graph is all about and often hints at the conclusion you want your viewer to draw. In Figure 8–25 the title *Weekly Sales Are Climbing* is more suggestive of the conclusion you want drawn than would merely titling the graph *Sales*.

Data *elements* are the major components of the graph that represent the quantity of the data being portrayed. The elements in Figure 8–25 are columns. As we have seen, elements can also be bars, lines, areas, and wedges.

The *axes* are the vertical and horizontal dimensions of the graph. The horizontal axis is usually used to display the independent variable such as the *Weeks* shown in Figure 8–25.

The *scales* located along the axes indicate to the viewer how the data are measured. Scales usually begin at zero at the intersection of the x and y axes. The user can select the range, zero to the maximum amount, and the unit increments within the range. The graph in Figure 8–25 uses increments of 100.

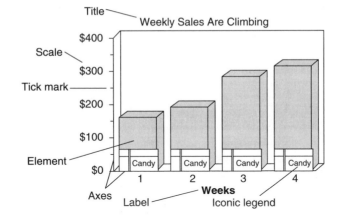

Figure 8–25

Components of a graph

Tick marks are short lines located on the axes to serve as visual reference points dividing the axes into evenly spaced units. They may be located on either side of the axis line or may cross through it. They are located at each major unit of scale and evenly distributed between them.

Labels may be applied wherever the are needed to identify other components. The word *Weeks* in Figure 8–25 designates the number of weeks along the horizontal axis.

The *legend* is usually a separate area of the graph that identifies the patterns or textures of columns, bars, or wedges and what they represent. The iconic legend may, however, be used as pictorial elements, similar to the candy boxes used in Figure 8–25, to strengthen the graph's message.

Graphs and How They Communicate

Let's explore graphs in a bit more detail. Figure 8–26 depicts population data in two different graphs, a line graph and a column graph. Both graphs use the same scale, represent data changing over time, and compare three quantities. The line graph clearly shows that population growth is leveling out in North America and in Europe, while it is increasing dramatically in Latin America. The column graph, though depicting the same data, does not show the trend as readily.

In 1950, North America and Latin America each had a population of approximately 165 million. In 1990, North America's population was 278 million and Latin America's was 447 million. Examine the line graph and area graph, shown in Figure 8–27, that portray these changes in population.

The line graph on the left of Figure 8–27 clearly demonstrates the regions' population trends. The area graph on the right effectively displays change in amount, but notice that the top sloping line represents the sum of the population in both regions, and the scale of the graph, therefore, has changed. Does it allow you to better understand the change within each region or is it more difficult to decipher? Which of the two graphs in Figure 8–27 is the most effective at communicating its information at a glance?

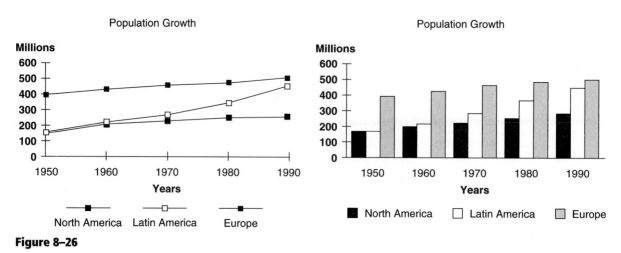

Figure 8–26

Line graph and column graph representing the same data

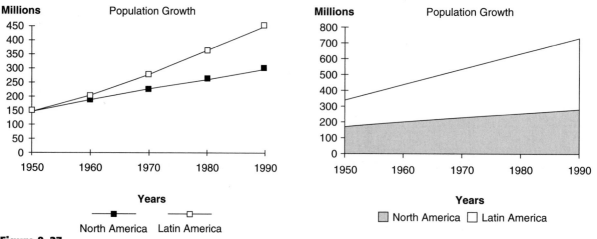

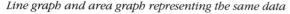

Figure 8–27

Line graph and area graph representing the same data

An inappropriate choice of scale can be very misleading. Consider the following hypothetical example. Five students received grades on an assignment; a perfect score was 10 points. Marci scored 8 out of 10, Kristin 9, Dick 7, Jerry 6, and Katie 9. The user must decide on the most accurate scale when graphing the data. Examine the two examples presented in Figure 8–28. As demonstrated in Figure 8–28, selecting the wrong scale may be misleading. Since the perfect score on the assignment was 10, a scale of 0 to 10 was chosen for the graph on the left side of Figure 8–28. When this scale is employed, the differences between the students' scores on the assignment are accurately portrayed. It is easy to see at glance that scores for Kristin and Katie were 50 percent better than Jerry's score. The graph on the right shows

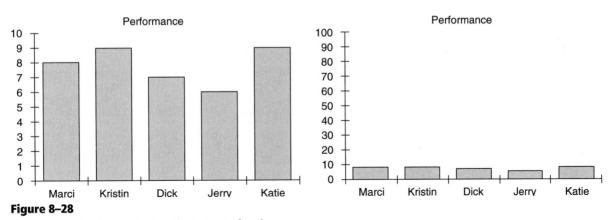

Figure 8–28

Column graphs demonstrating the impact of scale

the same data on a scale of 0 to 100. Notice how close all scores appear. The scale is too great to show clearly much differentiation and conveys the misleading impression at first glance that all scores were approximately the same.

Creating a Grade Book

Consider the creation of a computerized grade book to report student progress in your classroom. Employing the nonlinear problem-solving process reviewed earlier in this chapter and discussed in detail in Chapter 3, how might we proceed?

Given: Student names
           Student performance on a variety of measures
           Target audience of students and their parents
To Find: Complete, accurate report of student progress
Procedure: Choose software that facilitates the selected presentation format.
           Organize relevant data clearly.
           Calculate and summarize results on performance measures.

As was also pointed out in Chapter 3, a problem-solving strategy that might appeal more to a sequential learner consists of two phases, the *analysis* phase and the *synthesis* phase. In the analysis phase, we need to clearly examine the problem, define *what* must be done, and clearly identify the specific component tasks that relate to the problem. In the synthesis phase, we plan our strategy and carry out the solution to the problem. Evaluation provides feedback that could modify decisions made in both the analysis and synthesis phases.

In an effort to bring that linear problem-solving process into sharper focus, let's review the illustration in Figure 8–29 and consider once again the task of recording student progress in a computerized grade book.

Define the Problem. Develop a system to record grades given to student work and then to calculate an equitable and accurate score representative of the student's performance within the class.

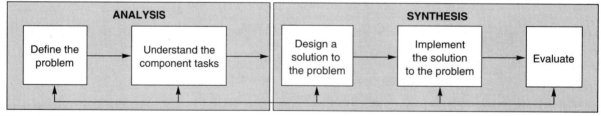

Figure 8–29
A linear approach to problem solving

Understand the Component Tasks. The following questions must be answered *before* you can sit down at the computer and begin to solve the problem:

- How will student names be entered (last name first)?
- How many different activity types will be allowed for each class (e.g., quiz, test, project, portfolio, lab)?
- How many different grades will be entered into each activity type?
- How are grades to be calculated (will they be weighted)?
- How are grades to be reported?
- What information will be calculated concerning class performance?

Design a Solution to the Problem. The primary purpose of the synthesis phase of problem solving is to help ensure that solutions designed to address the identified tasks are carried out in an effective and efficient manner and that the results are evaluated. Having defined what must be done and having identified tasks, we can now determine how each task can be carried out. The solution to this problem consists of designing labels as identifiers, creating appropriate formulas, and then entering accurate data.

Each operation must be written in a clear and effective manner.

- Student names will be entered in one column, last name first.
- Grades for two labs, one test, one midterm project, and one cumulative portfolio will be entered.
- Maximum raw scores are established for each activity as follows:
  Labs will have a maximum score of 10.
  The test will have a maximum score of 100.
  The midterm project will have a maximum score of 100.
  The cumulative portfolio will have a maximum score of 100.
- Grades will be weighted as follows:
  Labs will be equally weighted and will together account for 20 percent.
  The test will be weighted 25 percent.
  The midterm project will be weighted 25 percent.
  The cumulative portfolio will be weighted 30 percent.
- The final grade will be reported on a scale of 1–100 (a percent).
- The highest and lowest scores will be identified and an average calculated on all activities, as well as on the final grade.

Implement the Solution to the Problem. As illustrated in Figure 8–30, student names were entered in column A, last name first. They may be entered in any order and then sorted alphabetically by the spreadsheet. Grades for two labs with a maximum score of 10 each and a weighting of 10 percent each were entered in columns B and C, one test with a maximum score of 100 and a weighting of 25 percent was entered in column D, one midterm project with a maximum score of 100 and a weighting of 25 percent was entered in column E, and one cumulative portfolio with a maximum score of 100 and a weighting of 30 percent was entered in column F. The final grade will be calculated on the basis of 100 in column G. Examine the formula showing in the formula bar in Figure 8–30 that calculates this final grade. Functions named MAX, MIN, and AVERAGE were invoked in rows 11, 12, and 13 to calculate the highest and lowest scores and an average on all activities, as well as on the final grade.

The formulas that calculate the maximum, minimum, and average scores are then repeated in columns C through G. Spreadsheets will allow the user to replicate the contents of a cell (text, value, or formula) automatically to the right across a row or down a column, thus often saving appreciable time. When a formula is created that has a blank (empty) cell as a divisor, many spreadsheets will generate a #DIV/O! message, indicating that they cannot divide by zero. As soon as a value is entered in the divisor cell, the message will disappear.

Having first analyzed the problem and then designed an acceptable solution to the problem, we must now execute the tasks to solve it. We must enter grades in our computerized grade book and print reports.

Evaluate. As previously discussed, **debugging** is the process of correcting logic and construction errors. An often used debugging procedure is to give the program some test data that will produce known output over the entire range of use. Before entering your students' actual scores into your grade book, you might enter score values that you can compute easily and verify that the computer results are as expected. In Figure 8–31, zero is entered as the score in each item for the first student, and the maximum (10 or 100) is entered for the second student. If the results are other than expected, debugging allows you to verify the correctness of your formula, the appropriateness of the functions you employed, and the logic of your design. A look at column G and at rows 11, 12, and 13 verifies our expected results.

Documentation that accompanies a computer application provides valuable information for the user. The user of the grade book must clearly understand the intent of the program. Detailed written instructions about how to use the program can better ensure that the program is used effectively. The use of screen shots, such as those commonly found in software manuals, replicating what the user sees at any given point of using the program, is often helpful in illustrating the instructions. The instructions supplied with the grade book must clearly tell the user where and how to enter student names, the maximum scores allowed, where to enter the scores, how the scores will be weighted, and how the final grade will be calculated and reported.

As the classroom teacher uses the grade book/spreadsheet, it will continually calculate the students' total point accumulations and final scores and keep the statistics on each class activity. The rows may be sorted in alphabetical order by the data in column A at any time so, as new students are added, the grade book is sorted once again.

	G3		=B3+C3+(D3*0.25)+(E3*0.25)+(F3*0.3)				

Grade Book

	A	B	C	D	E	F	G
1	Name	Lab 1	Lab 2	Test	Midterm	Portfolio	Grade
2		10	10	100	100	100	100
3	Adams, Laura						0
4	Alderson, Kathy						
5	Alvarez, Manuel						
6	Drexler, Richard						
7	Kersey, Clyde						
8	Prosser, Peggy						
9	Prosser, Walt						
10	Williams, Andrea						
11	Highest Score	0					
12	Lowest Score	0					
13	Average	#DIV/0!					

The following formulas would yield the necessary calculations in this spreadsheet:

G3 = B3 + C3 + (D3 * 0.25) + (E3 * 0.25) + (F3 * 0.30) [This formula is then replicated down column G.]

B11 = MAX (B3:B10) [to calculate the highest score in rows 3–10]

B12 = MIN (B3:B10) [to calculate the lowest score in rows 3–10]

B13 = AVERAGE (B3:B10) [to calculate the average score in rows 3–10]

Figure 8–30

Creating the grade book/spreadsheet

	A	B	C	D	E	F	G
1	Name	Lab 1	Lab 2	Test	Midterm	Portfolio	Grade
2		10	10	100	100	100	100
3	Adams, Laura	0	0	0	0	0	0
4	Alderson, Kathy	10	10	100	100	100	100
5	Alvarez, Manuel						
6	Drexler, Richard						
7	Kersey, Clyde						
8	Prosser, Peggy						
9	Prosser, Walt						
10	Williams, Andrea						
11	Highest Score	10					
12	Lowest Score	0					
13	Average	5					

Figure 8–31

Debugging the grade book/spreadsheet

The grade book stores data about individual students but also reveals information about their progress and their comparative performance within the group. The results in Figure 8–32 also reveal that students had a bit more difficulty with the second lab and that grades were lower on the midterm project than on either the test or the portfolio.

The grade book **template** (blank form) can be saved after labels and formulas are created but before any names or scores are put into the grade book. By loading the template, naming it with the course name, and resaving it, the teacher may use the same grade book template for many classes.

Commercially Available Grade Books

Now that you have examined the process of building an electronic grade book on a spreadsheet program, it would be worth your while to evaluate commercially available grade book software. The fundamental question you must ask is "Is the commercial product flexible enough to meet my needs?" Can you adapt the software to meet your requirements or will you have to change your grading system? Another question to ask is "Does it provide me with information about my students' performance beyond what is available in a grade book that I would create on a spreadsheet?"

David Stanton (1994) reviewed six of the best-known grade book programs. Most are available for the Macintosh, MS-DOS, and Windows platforms. Along with publisher contact information and cost, Stanton presented information dealing with class size, grading categories and activities, linkage to other administrative systems, and the programs' ability to generate graphs, make seating charts, and track attendance. Most of the programs rated offered password protection. He found some more intuitive and easier to use than others; some were extremely rich in features but required an investment of time and effort to learn. Some were easy to customize and presented a wide variety of useful reports, with some programs printing optional reports in Spanish, French, or German.

	A	B	C	D	E	F	G
1	Name	Lab 1	Lab 2	Test	Midterm	Portfolio	Grade
2		10	10	100	100	100	100
3	Adams, Laura	9	7	78	75	80	78
4	Alderson, Kathy	10	9	98	90	95	95
5	Alvarez, Manuel	10	8	85	80	85	85
6	Drexler, Richard	9	8	80	80	90	84
7	Kersey, Clyde	6	7	75	70	80	73
8	Prosser, Peggy	10	10	98	90	95	96
9	Prosser, Walt	8	8	90	80	80	83
10	Williams, Andrea	9	9	80	85	80	83
11	Highest Score	10	10	98	90	95	96
12	Lowest Score	6	7	75	70	80	73
13	Average	8.88	8.25	85.50	81.25	85.63	85

Figure 8–32

Using the updated grade book/ spreadsheet

Whether creating your own personalized grade book or purchasing one that is commercially available, it would serve your interests well to review the analysis phase of the problem-solving process. Clearly define the requisites of your grading system, understand all of its component tasks, and proceed as your grade requirements, time, budget, and personal preferences dictate.

School Budgeting

A spreadsheet could be used in any budget matter, doing cost projections for changes in operations and investigating costs of alternate school operation plans. As an example, consider the planning of a school library media budget in which past expenditures, inflation, special curriculum needs, and per pupil expenditure are factors. Review the illustration in Figure 8–29 and, following the linear problem-solving process, apply it to your consideration of the planning of a school library media budget. Before examining Figure 8–33, which suggests an application of the spreadsheet as a budgeting tool, consider the following problem-solving process and reflect on what you know of budgeting procedures.

Define the Problem. Develop a system to record past expenditures in various budget categories and project budget needs. Past and projected student enrollment as well as inflation must be factored into the budget.

Understand the Component Tasks. The following questions must be answered *before* you can sit down at the computer and begin to solve the problem:

- How will budget categories be entered (category number first)?
- Will per pupil expenditures be calculated for each budget category?
- Will expenditures for the past two years be averaged and used for comparison purposes?
- Will two-year average per pupil expenditures be calculated?
- Will total per pupil expenditures be calculated?
- How will the impact of new or special programs be shown in the budget?
- How will changes in student population impact the budget?
- How will the budget account for inflation?

Design a Solution to the Problem. Having defined what must be done and having identified tasks, we can now determine how each task can be carried out. The solution to this problem consists of designing labels as identifiers, creating appropriate formulas, then entering accurate data.

- Actual student enrollment figures will be entered for the past two years and projected enrollment entered for the budget year.
- The current rate of inflation will be entered.
- Budget categories will be entered in one column, account number first.
  410—Supplies
  430—Library Books
  432—Reference Books

440—Periodicals
541—Equipment—New
542—Equipment—Replacement
- Expenditures in each category, both historical and projected, will be calculated on a per pupil basis.

Implement the Solution to the Problem. As illustrated in Figure 8–33, the actual and projected student enrollment is entered in B4, C4, and E4. The projected inflation rate of 3.5 percent is entered in F4 as 1.xx (1.035 in the example given). Actual expenditures are entered in the appropriate cells in columns B and C. Projected special program expenditures (e.g., curriculum changes that would have a direct impact on the library collection) are entered in column E.

In Figure 8–33, once the labels are defined and the proper formulas are created, you can project the impact on the total budget of decisions you make.

Having first analyzed the problem and then designed an acceptable solution to the problem, we must now execute the tasks to solve it. We must enter values in our computerized budget sheet and print reports.

Evaluate. In order to debug the application, test data that will produce known output will be entered. Before entering actual budget figures, you might enter values that you can compute easily and verify that the computer results are as expected. If the results are other than expected, debugging allows you to verify the correctness of your formula, the appropriateness of the functions you employed, and the logic of your design.

Document. Documentation that accompanies this application should provide guidance to another user. The user of this budget sheet must understand its intent. The instructions supplied with the budget sheet must tell the user where and how to enter enrollment figures for the past two years, the current rate of inflation, account or category names, expenditures for the past two years, and amounts requested for any new or special programs. The documentation should also explain the use of per pupil expenditures and how they are calculated, as well as how the rate of inflation affects the projected budget.

Use as Template. The budget sheet template can be saved after labels and formulas are created but before account names and values are entered. By loading the template, renaming it appropriately, and resaving it, others may use the template to assist in the preparation of other budgets.

Note that the illustration provided by Figure 8–33 is not meant to suggest that, indeed, school budgets should be prepared in this manner but, rather, it is meant to demonstrate the use of the spreadsheet as an analytical and forecasting tool. The impact of changes entered in student enrollment figures and inflation rate is revealed immediately.

Many more examples could be given. Any calculations that are done regularly are prime candidates for spreadsheet applications. The user needs only to set up a form that replicates the types of calculations that would have to be done by hand and then save the template. Whenever the calculation has to be done again, the template can be loaded and the problem addressed.

	A	B	C	D	E	F	G
1	2220 Library Media Services						
2		1997-98	1998-99		Inflation	1999-00	
3	# Students	490	545		1.035	595	
4				Average		Special	1999-00
5		Spent	Spent	Spent	Real $	Programs	Budget
6	410—Supplies	$660.87	$697.50	$679.18	$809.36		$ 809
7	$/student	$1.35	$1.28	$1.31	$1.36		
8	430—Library Books	$3,568.41	$3,967.85	$3,768.13	$4,484.11		$4,484
9	$/student	$7.28	$7.28	$7.28	$7.54		
10	432—Reference Works	$925.87	$946.50	$936.18	$1,116.56	$125.00	$1,242
11	$/student	$1.89	$1.74	$1.81	$1.88		
12	440—Periodicals	$870.25	$912.50	$891.38	$1,062.40	$42.00	$1,104
13	$/student	$1.78	$1.67	$1.73	$1.79		
14	541—Equipment, New	$1,295.00	$1,450.00	$1,372.50	$1,632.99	$600.00	$2,233
15	$/student	$2.64	$2.66	$2.65	$2.74		
16	542—Equipment, Repl.	$325.00	$650.00	$487.50	$571.46		$571
17	$/student	$0.66	$1.19	$0.93	$0.96		
18							
19	TOTAL	$7,645.40	$8,624.35		$9,676.87		$10,444
20	$. Student	$15.60	$15.82		$16.26		$17.55

The following formulas would yield the necessary calculations in this spreadsheet:

Expenditures per student in columns B and C

B7 = B6/$B$3 and C7 = C6/$C$3

Two-year average expenditures in column D

D6 = AVERAGE (B6:C6)

Average expenditure per student in column D

D7 = AVERAGE (B7:C7)

Expenditure per student adjusted for inflation in column E

E7 = D7 * $E$3

Real dollars adjusted for inflation and increased enrollment in column E

E6 = E7 * $F$3

Projected budget figures including special program needs in column G

Gn = En + Fn [n represents rows 6–16]

Budget total in cell G19

G19 = SUM (G6:G16)

Figure 8–33

Using the spreadsheet as a budgeting tool

SUMMARY

An electronic spreadsheet is a two-dimensional matrix of columns and rows. The intersection of a column and row is called a cell. The power of this software lies in the fact that cells relate one to another, allowing the contents of one cell to affect another cell. Cells may contain text, values, or formulas. Complex mathematical, statistical, and logical relationships can be described as formulas. Powerful functions are embedded in the software and can be called up by the user. Since the results of cell relationships are displayed and changing one cell immediately affects the results of the relationship, spreadsheets are often referred to as "what if" tools and are often used to make projections, or forecast results.

Reviewing a nonlinear problem-solving approach introduced in Chapter 3 and applied in this chapter allows us to appreciate this approach to problem solving, which permits divergent-thinking individuals to determine their own pattern without having a hierarchical structure imposed on them. A linear problem-solving strategy that might appeal more to a sequential learner was reviewed. It consists of two phases, the analysis phase, including defining the problem and understanding component tasks, and the synthesis phase, including designing a solution to the problem, implementing the solution, and evaluating. It was applied to the design of a grade book.

A number of examples were given in which a spreadsheet was used to predict results; to promote accuracy of the calculation of whole numbers and fractions; to calculate sums and averages; to generate graphs; to convert time and speed measurements; and, functioning as a database, to sort text.

Graphs can represent abstract numerical data in a concrete, clear, and interesting manner. They can display relationships that would be more difficult to convey in a text or verbal mode. As visuals, they capture attention and promote greater retention of information. The analysis and interpretation of graphs has become an important subject in the K–12 curriculum.

Debugging is the process of correcting logic and construction errors. The debugging procedure employed with the grade book consisted of entering the minimum and maximum scores as test data, which produced the expected results of grades of 0 and 100.

Ideally a spreadsheet would become a tool for the teacher to examine options and to forecast results. It would be taught to a student, who could use it to answer "what if" questions in any academic discipline in which the act of problem solving dealt with the examination of comparisons. Along with graphics programs, word processors, and database managers, spreadsheets are programs that truly exemplify the concept of using the computer as a tool to extend our human capabilities.

CHAPTER EXERCISES

1. Design a spreadsheet to record performances on a softball team. Calculate individual and team batting averages and on-base percentages for each game and for the season.
2. Design a spreadsheet to calculate a budget for the first Thanksgiving. From a reference source, identify the food items that were most likely present. Estimate the number of portions needed. Calculate the cost in terms of today's prices.

3. Design a spreadsheet to convert your weight in pounds to kilograms and your height in feet and inches to centimeters.

4. You are responsible for raising $2,000 in income for each home football game played. Explain your problem-solving strategy and design a spreadsheet to accomplish your goal.

5. Take a poll of your classmates to determine the five cities in which they would prefer to live. Assign a weighting of 5 for their first choice, 4 for their second choice, etc. Design a spreadsheet to record their preferences and identify an overall ranking for the cities chosen.

6. Replicate the spreadsheet shown in Figure 8–15. Change the rate of travel for the wagon train and then modify the spreadsheet to show miles traveled in a one-month interval. Generate a graph showing progress on the one-month interval.

7. Record the gender of each student in your class and the length of time he or she have lived at the current address. Rank order the data from shortest to longest occupancy for each gender. Using the graphing capability of an integrated package or a stand-alone graphing program, create a line graph showing the occupancy ranges for each gender. Describe the results to a classmate.

8. The following problem is derived from an article entitled "Can You Manage?" (Hastie, 1992). Suppose you are a biologist responsible for managing a healthy, stable deer population in a given area. You must regulate the size of the deer herd according to the habitat that supports it. In other words, you must determine an annual deer harvest so as not to exceed the carrying capacity of the habitat and ultimately destroy it.

Design a spreadsheet to manage four populations of deer. For Group One, hunters will be allowed to harvest 25 percent of the summer population; Group Two, 50 percent; Group Three, 75 percent; Group Four, 0 percent. Allow all groups to reproduce at a rate of 50 percent (new fawns equal one-half of the number of deer in the group each year).

For each group, (a) start with 20 deer the first year, (b) for year two, remove number harvested, (c) and add the yearly fawn crop. Continue this process for three more years for a total of five years.

Answer the following questions:

• Which populations decreased in size? Which increased? Which remained the same?

• Suppose you determine the winter carrying capacity of each habitat to be 20 deer. Which harvest rate would allow you to do this and still maintain a reasonably stable population?

• Could you continue to harvest at the same rate each year or would you have to adjust the harvest rate in some years? If so, what rate would you use?

GLOSSARY

active cell The cell that is selected and ready for data entry or editing.
cell The intersection of a row and a column in a spreadsheet.

debugging The process of removing all logic and construction errors.

documentation Written explanations supporting program maintenance and use.

formula bar The area at the top of the screen that displays the content of the active cell and that can be edited.

label The text descriptor related to adjacent data.

spreadsheet Software that accepts data in a matrix of columns and rows, with their intersections called cells. One cell can relate to any other cell or ranges of cells on the matrix by formula.

template A blank form in a spreadsheet or file manager program.

REFERENCES & SUGGESTED READINGS

Albrecht, B., & Firedrake, G. (1993, March). Elements of the human body. *The Computing Teacher, 20*(6), 49–51.

Beare, R. (1992, December). Software tools in science classrooms. *Journal of Computer Assisted Learning, 8*(4), 221–230.

Beaver, J. (1992, March). Using computer power to improve your teaching, part II: Spreadsheets and charting. *The Computing Teacher, 19*(6), 22–24.

Berghaus, N. (1990, April). Teach spreadsheet proficiency with personal money management projects. *The Computing Teacher, 17*(7), 54–55.

Chesebrough, D. (1993, March). Using computers: Candy calculation. *Learning, 21*(7), 40.

Crisci, G. (1992, January). Play the market: Curriculum connection. *Instructor, 101*(5), 68–69.

Harrison, D. (1990). *The spreadsheet style manual.* Homewood, IL: Dow Jones-Irwin.

Hastie, B. (1992, May-June). Can you manage? *Oregon Wildlife,* 9–10.

Kellogg, D. (1993, November). Spreadsheet circuitry. *Science Teacher, 60*(8), 12–23.

Killen, R. (1993-94, December/January). Using magic squares to teach spreadsheet fundamentals. *The Computing Teacher, 21*(4), 10–11.

Lewis, P. (1997, September). Using productivity software for beginning language learning. *Learning and Leading with Technology, 25*(1), 12–17.

North Carolina State Department of Public Instruction. (1992). *Voteline: A project for integrating computer databases, spreadsheets, and telecomputing into high school social studies instruction* (ED350243). Raleigh.

Parker, O. J. (1991). *Spreadsheet chemistry.* Englewood Cliffs, NJ: Prentice Hall.

Paul, J., & Kaiser, C. (1996, May). Do women live longer than men? Investigating graveyard data with computers. *Learning and Leading with Technology, 23*(8), 13–15.

Ramondetta, J. (1992, April-May). Using computers: Learning from lunchroom trash. *Learning, 20*(8), 59.

Reese, P., & Monroe, M. (1997, March). The great international penny toss. *Learning and Leading with Technology, 24*(6), 28–31.

Stanton, D. (1994, September). Gradebooks, the next generation. *Electronic Learning, 14*(1), 54–58.

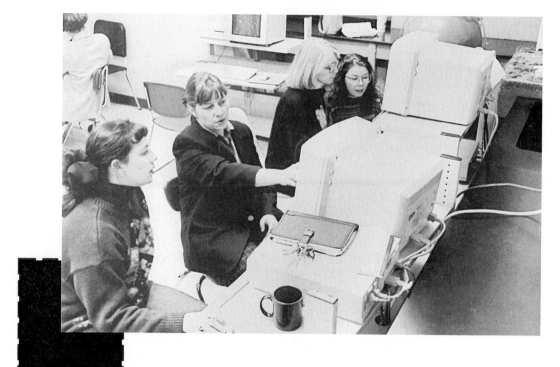

Chapter 9

Databases

ADVANCE ORGANIZER

1. What is a database?

2. What are its component parts?

3. How do you find information in a database?

4. What is a database manager and how does it work?

5. What are the important concepts related to data storage and retrieval?

6. How can you create and use files with a database manager?

7. How could the problem-solving strategies discussed in Chapter 3 be applied to designing databases?

8. Following a linear problem-solving approach, how can a community resource file be developed in a database?

9. How might you and your students use a database as a productivity tool to store, retrieve, and analyze information?

Data are everywhere. Fortunately, we are very selective in attending to them and we can ignore most of them. Our conscious and subconscious minds filter data, accepting some and rejecting the rest. We have the ability to organize the data we accept and give it meaning. Only then do data become information. Information is purposefully structured data. A database manager is software designed to structure data in order to produce information.

We commonly use databases in our everyday lives. One of the most ubiquitous is the telephone directory. It is a collection of data organized according to a clear structure. In order to derive useful information from it, we must understand its structure. It is a collection of facts organized by an individual's, a family's, or an establishment's name, residence, and phone number. The phone number is a unique identifier. Only one person, one family, one institution or business can have that phone number. When you search the phone book, you are normally looking for someone's phone number. The phone book allows you to find this information because the names are alphabetized. Searching through the alphabetical listing of names as the key, you find the name and corresponding phone number as part of the individual record. The record is composed of all of the data related to that individual entry (i.e., name, address, and phone number). Knowing only the address but not the name, it would be an extremely difficult task to find the phone number. Although the purpose of the phone directory is the listing of the telephone numbers, the name is the key to its successful use. Reverse directories organized as a numerical listing of phone numbers exist for the purpose of providing names and addresses once the phone number is known. We see that the structure of the database is the key to its usefulness.

We have defined the concept of tool as something used to facilitate the performance of a task. Chapter 3 dealt with the selection of the proper tool. A database manager is an appropriate tool in the management of information if it meets one or more of the following rubrics:

- It increases the speed of information acquisition.
- It increases the ease with which information is acquired.
- It increases the quality of the information acquired in terms of both accuracy and completeness.
- It improves the dissemination of information.

If you had an electronic version of a phone book on your computer and you were looking for Peggy Cummings' phone number, you could enter a find request by typing her name in the name field. Within moments you would see the complete record, including her name, address, and phone number displayed on the screen, instead of having to browse through pages, looking for first "C" and then "Cum," reading down a column to find "Cummings," and finally isolating the record for Peggy Cummings. This could be considered an example of effective tool use in that it meets the criteria specified in the first and second rubrics.

This chapter will deal with concepts related to understanding, creating, and using a data file. It will examine a database manager and its component parts. It will discuss Boolean logic and the searching and sorting of data to develop search strategies. Some concepts associated with database management are fairly abstract. In an effort to bring them to a more concrete level, we will use examples created with *FileMaker Pro,* published by Claris for both the Macintosh and Windows platforms.

FILE/DATABASE MANAGERS

What is a **database**? A database is an organized, structured collection of facts about a particular topic. At times these facts are grouped together in subsets called **files.** Examine the organization of data presented in Figure 9–1. Notice that true databases and files are not the same. An address file and a health file are both part of the student database in this example. A database may consist of a single file or a number of related files. Systems for file management are often called **database managers.** The term implies the capability of managing a number of files of data simultaneously or at least in a closely related manner. Programs with this capability are properly called **relational database managers.** Software designed to manage a single file is properly referred to as a file manager. Through popular usage, however, distinctions have blurred and the terms have come to be used interchangeably, with file managers now being called database managers or simply databases. Many types of soft-

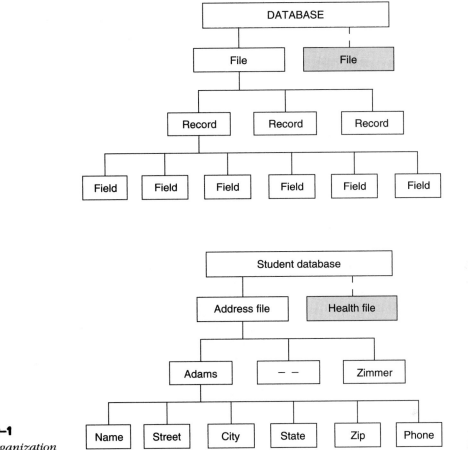

Figure 9–1

Data Organization

ware commonly used in schools are truly file managers but have come to be known as database managers. We will accede to this change of terminology so that when reference is made to *database* we will treat it synonymously with *file*.

Database Operation

What is a database manager and how does it actually work? Figure 9–2 presents the seven major functions of a database manager and indicates that database management software is designed to allow the user to create a structure for the storage, manipulation, and retrieval of data. Once data are entered into the file, the software allows the user to act on those data in a variety of ways. New data can be created through calculations based on existing data entered into the file. A good **file management** system lets you do three basic things: gather related data into a central collection, reorder those data in various ways depending on need, and retrieve the

• **File design:**	establish structure of file by creating data fields of appropriate type
• **Form design:**	create a layout of fields and where they will appear displayed on the screen or printed on paper
• **Record editing:**	allow data to be entered, altered, and deleted
• **Record finding:**	facilitate the selection of certain records while ignoring others
• **Record sorting:**	organize records according to some field order
• **Report creation:**	find specific records, sort them, and arrange them on a selected form
• **Report printing:**	display the information on paper or on the screen

Figure 9–2

Functions performed by a database manager

product of that reordering in a useful form. The products of file managers fall into two main categories: the real-time, "online" search for specific information and the ability to print reports organized in a particular fashion.

File Design. The individual data item is the most discrete element of a database and is called a data field, or simply a **field.** In the case of the telephone directory, a phone number is an individual field, as are address and name. Fields can contain text, numeric values, dates, and even pictures or sounds. Fields can contain calculations that perform mathematical operations on other numeric fields within the record and store the resulting values (e.g., multiplying the contents of two other fields). Fields can also contain summaries of data across a number of records and display the result (calculate the total or the average of specific field values for a group of

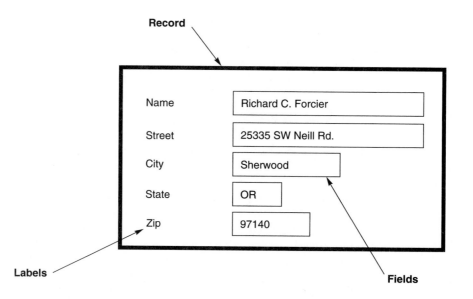

Figure 9–3

A record showing fields and their labels

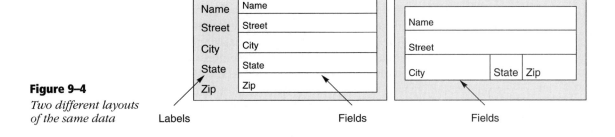

Figure 9–4

Two different layouts of the same data

records). In order to assist recognition of fields on the screen or in reports, field **labels** are created. Figure 9–3 illustrates fields and their labels. Keep in mind that labels simply identify or describe the fields where the data are actually stored.

The data record, or simply **record,** is the building block of the file. A record is composed of all the related fields. An individual record in the phone book contains all the data related to that entry (i.e., name, address, phone number). A file is the aggregation of all the records. The phone book file is the collection of all the records for that city, town, or region. A file, then, is composed of individual records that are themselves composed of individual fields. Review Figure 9–1 and notice that a *field* is the most specific and discrete piece of information. A *record* is composed of a group of related fields. Records accumulate into a *file*. A *database* may be made up of several files.

Form Design. As fields are defined, labels are created and grouped together, creating a **form,** or **layout,** which appears on the screen with blank spaces where data are to be entered. It is common to create several layouts for a file. Once data are entered, the layout that is selected or created can be thought of as a window through which to examine data in selected fields. Some file managers allow you a good deal of freedom in custom-designing a layout, while others are much more limited. Figure 9–4 shows a layout on the left, where fields and their labels are included to facilitate data entry, for example, and a second layout on the right, containing only the fields, perhaps to be used as a mailing label. Layouts are created based on the information required by the user. Fields are individually chosen to appear in a layout and their most appropriate position determined.

Data Entry and Editing in a Record. After each field has been defined, this information will be saved as the file structure (how the data in each record are to be stored). During data entry, the file manager displays the field labels on the screen, places the cursor at the first position in the first field, and facilitates the entry of data (e.g., letters, numbers, pictures, or sounds). The user is free to alter or change the data in any field in any of the records at any time. To edit records, you place the cursor in the appropriate field and type the change.

Record Finding and Sorting. The software allows the user to perform a **logical search,** sometimes called a **query,** to select records based on a wide range of criteria. An exact match of a value in a field can be requested (e.g., find field value equaling "Francis" = *Francis*). A match containing a value in a field can be requested (e.g., find field value containing "Francis" = *Francis,* San *Francis*co, etc.). Many other searches can be performed, including those greater than, less than, or not equal to a value. Searches can be performed on ranges of data by specifying the extremes of the range (e.g., minimum and maximum values). Searches can find all the records except those indicated to be omitted. Compound searches can be constructed to examine data in multiple fields using the Boolean connectors illustrated in Figure 9–5. The use of the AND connector restricts the search and makes it more specific. The use of the OR connector expands the search, making it less specific. The NOT connector removes those records having the second search criterion from the set of records otherwise found.

For example, as illustrated in Figure 9–6, one could search a student file by gender and address for all records of girls who live in Springfield, a specific town in the attendance area. The search would be "girls" AND "Springfield." Both criteria would have to be present in the same record in order to select that record. On the other hand, one could search the file for records of girls or records of all students (boys or girls) who live in Springfield. The search would be "girls" OR "Springfield." Either criterion would have to be present in a record in order to select that record. All records of girls plus all records of the specified town (both boys and girls) would be selected. A popular way of distinguishing between the two selection connectors is to remember that "OR is more." The NOT connector would be used to find all girls who are not living in Springfield.

Data can be sorted or arranged in a prescribed alphabetic, numeric, or chronological order in either ascending (e.g., A–Z, 1–99, 1941–2000) or descending (e.g., Z–A, 99–1, 2000–1941) fashion. This organization of records within the file can be based on any individual field. Most software also allows nested, or multilevel, sorts. For example, one could sort a grade book in ascending alphabetical order by last name and then as a second level, by first name. This would create an alphabetic list of students by last name and then, if any students shared the same last name, the sort would alphabetize those students by first name.

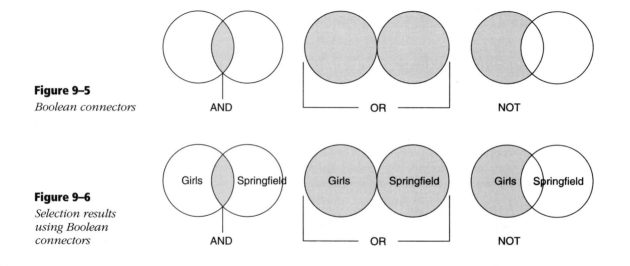

Figure 9–5
Boolean connectors

Figure 9–6
Selection results using Boolean connectors

Report Creation and Printing. To develop a report for printing information from the file, the user first selects the appropriate layout, then selects the records to be included in the report (find the records indicated by the search criteria), and, finally, designates their order (sort the records found in ascending or descending order in a particular field). For example, to print a report consisting of students' first name, last name, and birth date, the user would

- Designate the size of the printed page and create column titles that would serve as labels:
    First Name, Last Name, Birth Date
- Choose the records to be printed:
    All records?
    Only those after a certain birth date?
- Define the order:
    Alphabetic by last name?
    Birth date order?

In this example, the report might be sorted by birth date, and, if two or more students had the same birth date, these names would be sorted alphabetically, by last name. This technique is referred to as a **nested sort, or multilevel sort.**

Many different reports can be produced from the same file. In our example, another useful report would print mailing labels on continuous-form label stock. Both the mailing labels and the student lists constitute reports. By adding fields for grade level and teacher's name, reports could be generated, presenting a list of students by grade or teacher, thereby increasing the usefulness of the file.

The power of database managers is that the information can be entered once, and many reports can be generated simply by instructing the computer program how to organize the data. You do not have to rework the collected information by hand. All of your time and energy goes into data entry and maintenance. Very little time is spent generating reports.

Using a Database Manager

To make the best use of a file management system, the user must be able to meet the following four requirements:

1. *Understand your information needs.* Know the information you want your system to manage. Analyze what you are doing, what information is used, and how it is being used. How could the processing of that information be improved?
2. *Specify your output needs.* Although you cannot predict everything you will need from your file, you know the reports that are commonly needed and the information that is frequently accessed. Design those report formats.
3. *Specify your input needs.* Once you have determined output needs, input needs become obvious. Take advantage of the features of your file manager that will simplify and expedite data entry.
4. *Determine the file organization.* Consider the file input and output requirements in completing the record design.

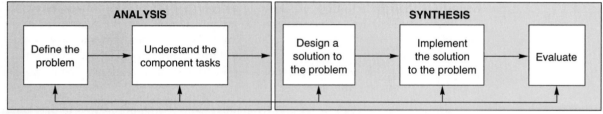

Figure 9–7
A sequential approach to problem solving

When contemplating the use of a file manager, analyze what you are doing and determine what you would like to do. If you cannot design a way to perform a task by paper and pencil, a file manager probably can't help you.

PROBLEM SOLVING WITH DATABASES

Consider the process of problem solving discussed in Chapter 3 that might be approached by an individual with a sequential learning style. Let us review the linear method and the illustration that was presented. Figure 9–7 illustrates the two phases, the analysis phase and the synthesis phase. In the analysis phase, we are developing a clear definition and understanding of the problem and of the component tasks that relate to the problem. In the synthesis phase, we plan our strategy and carry out the solution to the problem. Evaluation provides feedback that could modify decisions made in both the analysis and synthesis phases.

Analysis

Remember that *analysis* is defined as the separation of a whole into its component parts for the purpose of examination and interpretation. The need is to clearly define the problem and clearly identify the specific tasks that must be accomplished. In defining the problem you will establish a need.

Problem Statement
A teacher wishes to make the best use of the local resources in the community.

In an effort to bring the problem-solving process into sharper focus and to understand component tasks, let's consider the management of some resources external to the classroom. Apply the problem-solving process just reviewed and illustrated in Figure 9–7 to accomplish the stated task. Begin by analyzing the required output and formulating questions, such as those that follow, to help determine what is necessary to produce this result.

Understanding Components

What are the resources?

How do they align with the curriculum?

How might they be accessed by teachers and students?

These items could certainly be further expanded, refined, and organized in an outline fashion. Chapter 3 presented the written algorithm and the flowchart as effective outlining tools particularly adaptable to sequential operations. An outlining strategy is often helpful in reaching a better understanding of the components. The top-down outlining approach illustrated in Figure 9–8 is one that proceeds from global to specific concerns and facilitates systematic analysis.

As you attack the problem of managing external resources, you must make sure that you understand what is required of the software *before* you attempt to solve the problem. Otherwise, you might select the wrong software or spend a lot of time and effort producing something that will not meet your expectations.

The outline presented in Figure 9–8 identifies Type, Curriculum Areas, and Access as the major headings in response to the questions above. It refines each heading by more specific subheadings and, in some instances, even more specific third- and fourth-level subheadings.

These fifth graders are collaborating on a project. They are discussing how to design a database so that the resulting information is useful to their report on weather patterns

```
┌─────────────────────────────────────────┐
│ Resources                               │
│ Type                                     │
│    Industrial corporations               │
│    Retail commercial ventures            │
│        Goods                             │
│        Services                          │
│    Government agencies                    │
│    Nonprofit corporations                │
│    Individuals                           │
│ Curriculum Areas                         │
│    Occupations                           │
│    Social studies/language arts          │
│    Science/mathematics                   │
│    Performing arts                       │
│    Health/physical education             │
│ Access                                   │
│    Contact                               │
│        Name, address, phone number       │
│    When available                        │
│    Come to the school                    │
│        To the classroom                  │
│            Speakers/demonstrations       │
│            Film/video                    │
│        To an assembly                    │
│    Host on their site                    │
│        Group size                        │
│        Safety issues                     │
└─────────────────────────────────────────┘
```

Figure 9–8

Outlining components

Synthesis

Synthesis is defined as combining elements to form a coherent whole. The primary purpose of the synthesis phase of problem solving is to help ensure that solutions designed to address the identified tasks are carried out in an effective and efficient manner and that the results are evaluated.

Field Definition. The solution to the information management problem just outlined involves designing a database to store relevant data and to allow easy retrieval of useful information. Referring to the outline developed in Figure 9–8, a Resources file can be developed by defining appropriate fields.

Figure 9–9 presents the fields derived from the outline presented in Figure 9–8. Notice that a field to store the record entry date is also included so that the information can be examined on a periodic basis to determine its validity or usefulness.

Error Trapping. There is an old saying in computer circles, *Garbage In, Garbage Out* (GIGO). Accurate data entry is essential to the production of meaningful information from a database. Error trapping is a process of designing safeguards into your solution. In error trapping, a designer makes sure that entry of incorrect data is not ac-

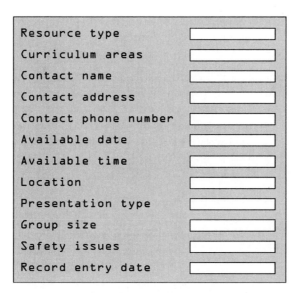

Figure 9–9

Fields defined for the Resources file

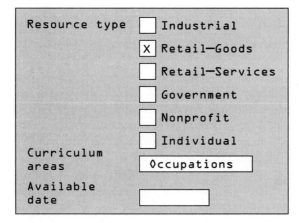

Figure 9–10

Checkboxes to control data entry

cepted by the program. If certain values must be excluded when entering data into the file, then a technique must be employed to ensure that the unwanted data cannot be entered, thereby preventing potential errors that could cause the program to yield faulty information. Depending on the capability and sophistication of the software being used, the *Resource type* field in the Resources file example could present checkboxes on the screen, as shown in Figure 9–10, representing the available entries rather than depending on input typed from the keyboard. The *Curriculum areas* field might present the user a list from which to select. The *Available date* field might be restricted to accept values that fall between 9/1/98 and 6/15/99, for example, to make sure that the date falls in the correct school year.

An example of error trapping data entry in a student records database is to designate a range of values from 0 to 4.0 in a field designed to store a numerical equivalent of an *F* to *A* course grade. Limiting data entry to this range would catch typing errors, such as a double key press, that might attempt to enter a nonsensical value of 33, for example.

Debugging. Debugging is the process of correcting logic and construction errors. In designing a database, it is especially important to verify calculation and summary fields. An often-used debugging procedure is to give the program some test data that will produce known output. If the results are other than expected, debugging allows you to verify the correctness of your data entry and calculations, the appropriateness of the functions you employed, and the logic of your design.

> "Information skills are taught using the computer to access research tools. Kids who might neglect or not get too excited about using hardbound reference books will stand in line to use those on CD-ROM. The color, graphics, movement, and sound are very attractive to them."
>
> *Lisa Hearn, Library Media Specialist*
> *Canongate Elementary School, Sharpsburg, GA*

CURRICULUM APPLICATIONS OF DATABASES

Teachers want help in alleviating the paperwork demands made on them. They want help in accomplishing activities that do not involve students directly and are quite often done outside of actual class time. If the time required to perform these tasks could be decreased, the teacher would have more time to devote to working with students.

Students need access to increasing amounts of information if they are to construct their own knowledge. The teaching of information organization and retrieval skills can be taught through the use of databases. The database is an ideal tool for students to gather and arrange data, examine trends and relationships, and test theories.

We have described the file, a term that has become interchangeable with database, as an organized, structured collection of facts and have examined its operation. We understand that it can handle text and values, that it is founded on the ability to group data fields into records that can be selected and ordered. We recognize that database managers have powerful built-in formulas. We are also beginning to explore some of the functional uses of databases to record data, organize it according to specific criteria, calculate values, sort data, and print reports.

A number of activities are presented to illustrate how a database might be used as a tool by the student or the teacher. The examples present a number of database applications in a variety of subject areas and grade levels and could be easily modified and adapted to individual lessons or units of instruction. If students are to capitalize on the power of the database manager as a tool and use it with confidence, they must develop an understanding of its application and a reasonably high level of skill in its use. Table 9–1 lists the possible curriculum areas of the examples given. The Presidents File shown in Figure 9–11 gathers data relevant to each U.S. presi-

Figure	Curriculum
9–11	Social studies
9–12	Social studies
9–13	Language arts
9–14	Management
9–15	Health/nutrition
9–16	Health/nutrition

Table 9–1

Sample Database Curriculum Choices

dent's term of office and provides opportunity to generate interesting information. The database suggested in Figure 9–12 might be set up for all countries of the world or only for countries in a specific geographic region. The process of entering data will require the students to conduct some research to gather the relevant facts. As information about the countries is studied, students could be encouraged to suggest additional fields for the database.

Specific inquiries might be made such as "Which country has the largest land mass? Which country has the highest population density? What countries have significant rivers and/or mountains? Which countries are Spanish–speaking? What countries have the same ethnic groups?" Once information is generated, relationships can be explored. Does the area of the country relate directly to its population density? Is climate related to population density? Referring to a map of the region, do any of the physical features (rivers, mountains, etc.) form political boundaries? Examining countries whose citizens speak the same language, do they share something else in common? Were they part of a political union or an empire? A number of other relationships can be explored based on the students' interest and need for information and the teacher's direction.

A travel agency classroom simulation could be designed to explore existing countries in the database and to determine interests of students. Students could ask to go mountain climbing, to spend time in the sun, or to go where they could practice a foreign language they are learning. As students reveal a variety of interests, additional fields could be added to the database on that basis.

As a departure from the example illustrated in Figure 9–12, a database could be designed and data entered by students using the program *Where in the World Is Carmen Sandiego?™* The following fields could be defined: *Country, City, Currency, Language, Chief Products, Points of Interest, Bodies of Water, Mountains, Deserts,* and *Miscellaneous.* As students encounter clues, they could search the database and, if results were not achieved, they could research the relevant information and create a new record in the database. The database would grow more powerful as more clues are encountered, and students would be refining their information-gathering skills.

The database suggested in Figure 9–13 would be created by and for students. Unlike the previous examples, it would be used mainly for on-line searching. It is not intended to replace a library automation system's public access catalog but, rather, to be a file of student opinion regarding books in the school library.

Last Name	
First Name	
Party	
Prior employment	
Vice President	
Term of office	
Rank	
Home state	
Event 1.	
Event 2.	
Event 3.	

Suggested Use: The process of entering data into the fields will require the students to conduct some research to gather the relevant facts. Students will be able to print out the following informational tables:

a. Chronological list of presidents

b. Alphabetical list by last name of presidents to find information pertinent to a specific president

c. List of presidents sorted by party to examine voting patterns

d. List of presidents sorted by home state to examine any geographical patterns

e. List of presidents and events to examine possible expressions of party philosophy at the time

f. Alphabetical list of the prior employment of presidents or a selection of only one employment such as attorney

The following printouts could serve as games, as contests, and for drill and practice.

1. Leave a blank column for the president's name and print a column of events for a selected date range based on the term of office field. Students must indicate the president who was in office when each event occurred. 2. Print two lists in alphabetical order, one of the presidents and the other of events, with the objective being to match presidents and events. 3. Print any of the reports below, with a blank column requiring information to be entered.

POSSIBLE REPORTS

a. Rank	Term Dates	First/Last Name	Party	Vice President
b. Last/First Name	Rank	Term Dates	Party	Vice President
c. Party	First/Last Name	Rank	Term Dates	
d. Home State	First/Last Name	Term Dates		
e. Last Name	Party	Event 1_ _ _ _ _ _		
		Event 2_ _ _ _ _ _		
		Event 3_ _ _ _ _ _		
f. Prior Employment	President	Term Dates		

Figure 9–11
Presidents File

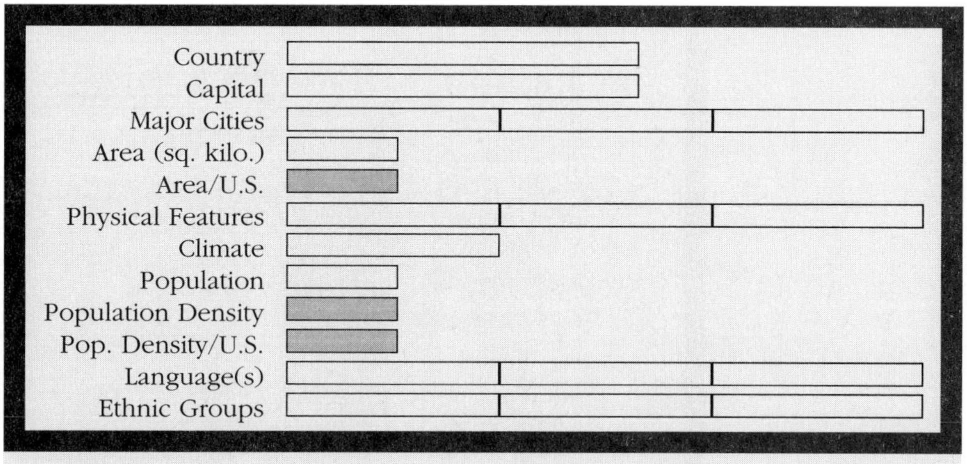

Suggested Use: The database contains three calculation fields: Area/U.S. field (Area field/area of the United States expressed as a ratio); Population Density field (Population field/Area field expressed as a ratio); and Pop. Density/U.S. field (value calculated in the Population Density field/population density of the United States expressed as a ratio). Four fields (Major Cities, Physical Features, Language(s), and Ethnic Groups) are defined to be able to store up to three different values. Students can print out the following informational tables:

a. List by country to find information about cities in a specific country
b. List by country to find land mass, population, and comparison with U.S.
c. List by country to find climate and physical features of a specific country
d. List by country to find ethnic groups and languages in a specific country
e. List by ethnic group to determine countries
f. List by population density to view rank order of countries

POSSIBLE REPORTS

a. Country		Capital	Major Cities		
b. Country	Area	Area/U.S.	Population	Pop. Density	Pop. Density/U.S.
c. Country		Climate	Physical Features		
d. Country		Ethnic Group(s)		Language(s)	
e. Ethnic Group		Country			
f. Pop. Density		Country			

Figure 9–12
Geography File

Title	
Author(s)	
Subject/Genre	
Call Number	
Copyright Date	
Grade Level(s)	
Awards	
Brief Description	
Review	
Reviewer	
Rating Scale	

Suggested Use: This file created by and for students would be used mainly for on-line searching of student opinions regarding books in the school library. Data could be gathered as part of a school library's reading promotion effort. The data entry itself might be restricted to a few students in order to control the integrity of the file. An authority list (approved headings) might be used for the Subject/Genre field to facilitate accurate retrieval of information. A high to low numeric rating scale would be devised (e.g., 4–1). The file could be designed to hold multiple reviews of the same title and reviewers' names. In addition to the online use, the following tables could be printed:

a. List of most popular books
b. Descriptions and reviews
c. List by copyright date and rating
d. List of award-winning books

POSSIBLE REPORTS

a. Subject/Genre		Title	Grade Level	Rating
b. Call #	Title	Reviewer		
	Description			
	Review			
c. Author		Title	Copyright	Rating
d. Title		Award	Rating	Reviewer

Figure 9–13

Recommended Books File

Data would be gathered by students and, for some, might serve as a motivation to read. The data could be gathered as part of a school library's reading promotion effort. The data entry itself might be restricted to a few students in order to control the integrity of the file. An **authority list** (approved headings) might be used for the *Subject/Genre* field to facilitate accurate retrieval of information. A high-to-low numeric rating scale would be devised (e.g., 4–1). The file could be designed to hold multiple reviews and reviewers' names.

Students might query the database by a specific subject/genre, asking for a list of titles at a particular grade level, and then sorted in descending order by rating scale. They would then be able to find the most popular books in their area of interest.

Once having selected a group of records to examine, students could change to a layout that would let them read the brief description, review, and reviewer name in order to choose a book that appealed to them. The addition of the call number in the layout would let students find the book on the library shelf. A student could search for a favorite author and get a list by title, copyright date, and rating scale to find the most recent and popular work by that author.

A layout that listed the awards (e.g., Caldecott, Newbery, Young Reader's Choice), the rating scale, and the reviewer name for each title would allow students to form their own opinion of a reviewer's judgment when compared against a broader measure.

Test Items File

1. Exams have been prepared by typewriter for many years and, more recently, by word processor. The database suggested in Figure 9–14 would allow a teacher the highest degree of flexibility in test construction for a paper-and-pencil objective exam. Though the example shows only true-false and multiple choice questions, other forms such as matching, fill-in, and short answer are also feasible in a database format.

2. A data entry layout would include a *Question* field; an *Answer Key* field to store the correct response; a *Topic* field or, for concept identification, a *Chapter* field correlated to a text; and an *Exam* field that could be used to note different exams or different forms of the same test. The layout might resemble the following:

```
        Question   It is always wise to check your spreadsheet work by
                   testing it with a problem that produces known value


        Answer Key  T  Topic  spreadsheet  Chapter  6  Exam  midterm
```

3. A layout could be designed for the purpose of selecting questions to include in the exam. This layout might closely resemble the previous one, with the addition of a *Select? (Y/N) field*. The exam is composed by choosing the

CSE 410 Computers in Education   **Midterm Exam**

Please respond on the answer sheet provided. Mark the first column (a) if the answer is TRUE or the second column (b) if the answer is FALSE.

7. It is always wise to check your spreadsheet work by testing it with a problem that produces known values.

CSE 410 Computers in Education   **Midterm Exam**

Multiple Choice

Please respond on the answer sheet provided. Select the best answer for each questions

17. The process of correcting application program design errors is referred to as
    a. error trapping
    b. programming
    c. documenting
    d. debugging

Suggested Use: This file created by the teacher could be used to prepare and print an exam master for duplication, but it could also be used for on-line testing of students. A database of test items affords the teacher the greatest flexibility in preparing objective exams. The file can be added to and easily modified over time. Each exam can be tailored to the instruction given to a particular group of students. It can be used for grading purposes or as a self-test for review.

This example illustrates a True-False and a Multiple Choice format. The following layouts could be constructed:
a. Data entry
b. Question selector
c. True-false form
d. Multiple choice form
e. Fill in the blanks form
f. Short answer form

Figure 9–14

Test Items File

questions marked for selection. If the teacher wishes to randomize the topics or the correct responses, the selected records could then be sorted by question. When preparing a final exam at a later date, observing whether or not a question was used in the midterm might influence its selection.

> Question | It is always wise to check your spreadsheet work by
> testing it with a problem that produces known value
>
> Answer Key [T] Topic [spreadsheet] Chapter [6] Exam [midterm]
> Select?(Y/N) [Y]

4. A layout in a multiple choice format might resemble the following:

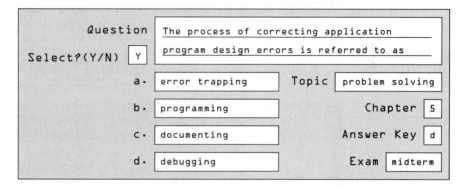

> Question | The process of correcting application
> Select?(Y/N) [Y] | program design errors is referred to as
>
> a. error trapping   Topic [problem solving]
> b. programming   Chapter [5]
> c. documenting   Answer Key [d]
> d. debugging   Exam [midterm]

5. After carefully choosing the questions and sorting them, by selecting the proper layouts, a teacher could print a master copy of the exam for duplication and a copy to serve as the answer key.

6. A **template,** or empty copy of the file with all the fields defined and all the layouts built, could be shared among a group of teachers. They could tailor it to their own needs and then share the modified version.

This last example is more complex than the previous ones. It is composed of two related files and could be designed on any relational database. It can also be built on *File-Maker Pro™,* a file manager that has a lookup capability from one file to another. The main file, named Menu Planner, as shown in Figure 9–15, is designed to allow the user to create a menu for a number of meals in a given week by choosing items from the four main food groups. The secondary, or lookup, file named Nutritional Values (Figure 9–16) contains nutritional information on a large number of food items. A record in this file would contain the name of a meat, dairy, vegetable/fruit, or cereal/bread item and its corresponding values of calories, fat, cholesterol, and percentage of average daily requirements in vitamins. As a user enters food items in the Menu Planner file, corresponding nutritional data are transferred from the lookup file. An entire week's menus could be planned and, using the summary capability of the database software, the total nutritional value of the week's menus could be analyzed, as shown in Figure 9–17. By changing various food items, a healthier menu might be achieved.

Menu Planner

Day	o Sun o Mon o Tue o Wed o Thu o Fri o Sat
Meal	o Breakfast o Lunch o Dinner
Meat	
Dairy	
Vegetable/Fruit	
Cereal/Bread	

Figure 9–15

A menu planning file

Nutritional Values

Meat	
Dairy	
Vegetable/Fruit	
Cereal/Bread	
Calories	
Grams of Fat	
Cholesterol	

% ADR Vitamins:

A	
B	
C	
D	
E	

Figure 9–16

A nutritional analysis file

Day	Meal	Food	Cal	Fat	Cholest	VitA	VitB	VitC	VitD	VitE
——		meat	————	——	——	——	——	——	——	——
		dairy	————	——	——	——	——	——	——	——
		veg/frt	————	——	——	——	——	——	——	——
		cer/brd	————	——	——	——	——	——	——	——
——		meat	————	——	——	——	——	——	——	——
		dairy	————	——	——	——	——	——	——	——
		veg/frt	————	——	——	——	——	——	——	——
		cer/brd	————	——	——	——	——	——	——	——
		TOTAL:	————	——		——	——	——	——	——

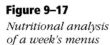

Figure 9–17

Nutritional analysis of a week's menus

Databases as Managers of Electronic Portfolios

As teachers have become increasingly interested in authentic assessment measures and techniques, the portfolio has surfaced as an interesting alternative. Typically the portfolio is seen as an attempt to gather evidence of a student's performance. This evidence can take the form of tests, written assignments, and exercises completed by the student. By comparing like measures over time, growth can be observed in the individual's performance. The measures just mentioned can be effective in the areas of mathematics, composition, and writing and may provide one perspective of an individual's cognitive development. A complete assessment calls for additional measures that deal with the individual's speech, visual and spatial capabilities, and kinesthetic performance. This calls for the addition of audio, photographic, and video measures.

Manual portfolios are difficult to manage and cumbersome to store. As more and more performance evidence is gathered, portfolio management and the analysis of like measures become more and more difficult. The shear size of the container for the documentary evidence grows to the point that storage becomes an issue for the teacher and for the school administrator.

Electronic portfolios appear to present an answer to the problems created by manual versions. Written documents and photographs can be scanned into electronic files. Digital pictures can be recorded. Videotaped sequences can be converted to electronic formats. A database manager such as *FileMaker Pro™* can provide the management needed to organize the various artifacts collected and can provide efficient analysis of like measures over time. Each student's electronic portfolio can be stored on a removable magnetic medium such as a Jaz cartridge or on a recordable CD-ROM.

Commercially Available Databases Related to Curriculum

A number of commercial databases are being marketed to address specific content areas. Databases of scientific facts (e.g., periodic table, scientists, inventions), historical

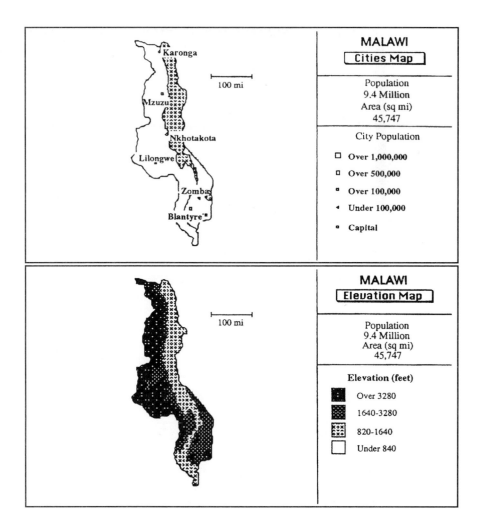

Figure 9–18

Map screens from MacGlobe (Courtesy of Broderbund Software, Inc.)

facts (e.g., famous people, events, timelines), and geographic facts (e.g., map locations, climates, migration) are becoming readily available from various publishers of educational software.

The examples that follow as Figures 9–18 through 9–20 are taken from an award-winning program called *MacGlobe™* (also available as *PC Globe™* for Windows machines), a rich database of geographical facts covering every country in the world. It begins with a world map and lets the user choose from regional maps (e.g., continents, political and economic alliances), country maps (e.g., political divisions and elevation), and thematic maps (e.g., population, natural resources, agricultural production, education). The user can paint selected countries or regions in a chosen pattern and return to the world map to observe the results. The program can also display the flag of any country and can display distances, currency conversions, and a number of charts revealing information about each country.

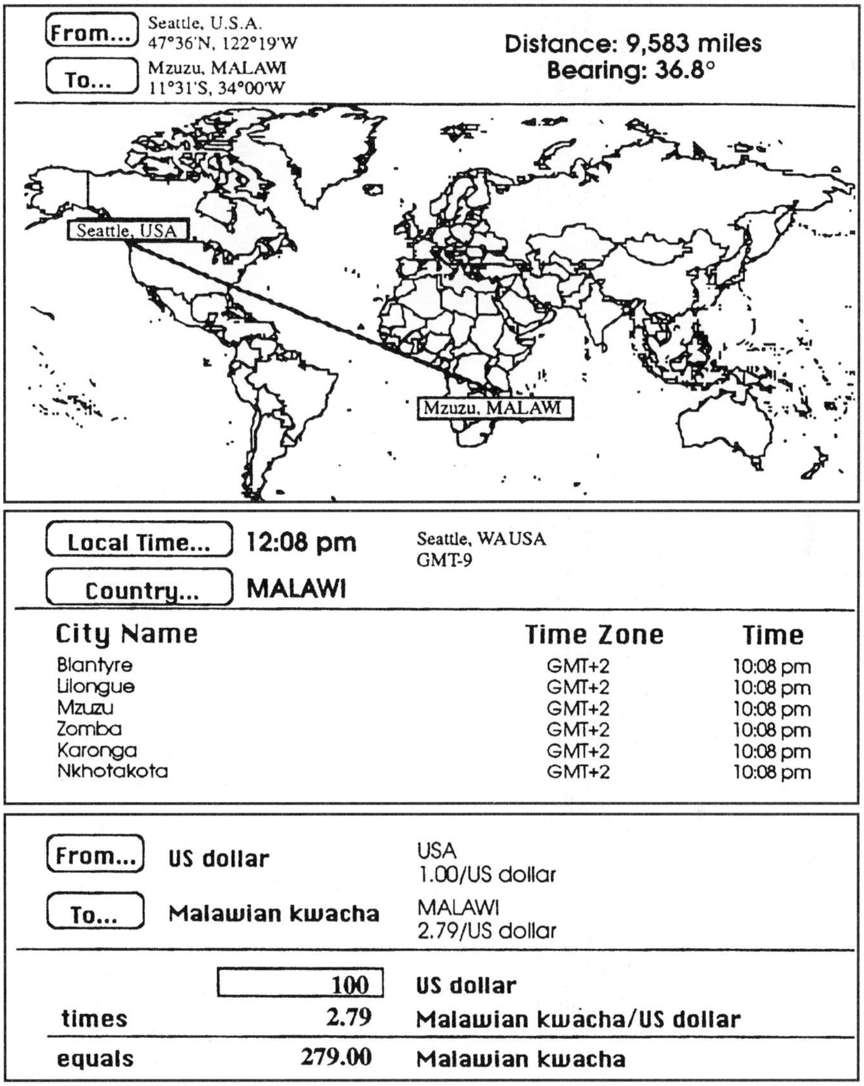

Figure 9–19

Map screens from MacGlobe™ (Courtesy of Broderbund Software, Inc.)

Programs such as this one present the student with a valuable resource of information with which to make comparisons, draw inferences, and construct knowledge. After examining Figures 9–18 through 9–20, what would you say in describing Malawi to another student? How is it similar to and how is it different from the United States? What else do you want to know about that country?

The top screen in Figure 9–18 shows the location and population of the major cities of the African country of Malawi. The bottom screen shows the elevation of the different regions in the country. Figure 9–19 explores differences. The top screen gives the user a sense of the distance from the West Coast of the United States to the African country of Malawi (distance can be calculated between any two points on

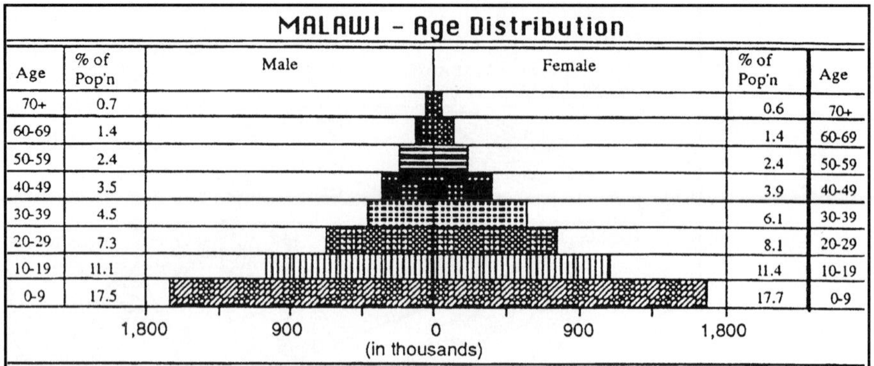

Total Population: 9,438,000
Total Male Population: 4,568,000
Total Female Population: 4,870,000

Life Expectancy (Male): 48 years
Life Expectancy (Female): 51 years

Health Statistics

Life Expectancy (Male):	48 yrs
Life Expectancy (Female):	51 yrs
Crude Birth Rate:	52 / 1000
Crude Death Rate:	18 / 1000
Infant Mortality:	136 / 1000

	Number	Pop'n per
Hospitals	395	23,894
Hospital Beds	12,617	748
Physicians	262	36,023
Dentists	12	786,500
Pharmacists	12	786,500
Nurses	2,002	4,714

Education Statistics

	Schools	Teachers	Students	Students per Teacher
Primary	2,660	16,885	1,066,642	63
Secondary	91	1,492	30,030	20
Third Level	4	306	2,330	8

GNP for Education	3.3 %
Literacy Rate	22 %

Figure 9–20
Map screens from MacGlobe™ (Courtesy of Broderbund Software, Inc.)

the globe). The middle screen reveals time differences between the local point and the distant country. The bottom screen converts currency between the two countries. The three screens in Figure 9–20 reveal statistics about the age, health, and education of the Malawi population.

A new multimedia, CD-ROM–based literature database called *Find It! Science™*, published by Follett Software Company, makes it possible for students to search by topic, to view a science book's cover in full color, to see a content summary, and to search for related titles among more than 3,000 award-winning science books. *Find It! Science™* can produce bibliographies on a range of topics, selected by type (fiction, biography, reference), author, awards won, and other criteria. See Figure 9–21.

Figure 9–21

Find It! Science™ database

Advantages of Developing and Using Databases

In developing a database, students are engaged in activities that contribute to the development of organizational skills and higher-order thinking skills. They refine a specific vocabulary. They research information on a given topic. They verify the accuracy of data, note the similarities and differences among data examined, and explore relationships. They classify information discovered. They consider how information might be communicated effectively to others.

In searching for information in a database, students develop and refine information retrieval skills. They improve their ability to recognize patterns, trends, and other relationships. They are encouraged to think critically by interpreting data and testing hypotheses. All of these skills have real-world applications and contribute to preparing students to take their place as productive members of society.

SUMMARY

Information is purposefully structured and organized data to which we give meaning. A database manager is software designed to structure data to produce information. It is an information management tool with the potential to increase the speed of information acquisition, the ease with which information is acquired, and the quality of the information acquired in terms of both accuracy and completeness.

A database is an organized, structured collection of facts about a particular topic. A database may consist of a single file or a number of related files. Database management software is designed to allow the user to create a structure for the storage, manipulation, and retrieval of data. The products of file managers fall into two main categories: the real-time, "on-line" searching for specific information and the ability to print reports organized in a particular fashion.

The individual data item is the most discrete element of a database and is called a field. Fields can contain text, numeric values, dates, pictures, sounds, and calculations that perform mathematical operations on other numeric fields within the record and can store the resulting values. Fields can also contain summaries of data across a number of records and can display the result. Field labels are created that identify or describe the fields where the data are actually stored.

The record is the building block of the file and is composed of all the related fields. A file is the aggregation of all the records. As fields are defined, labels are created and grouped together, creating a layout that appears on the screen. Once data are entered, the layout that is selected or created can be thought of as a window through which to examine data in selected fields.

The database manager software allows the user to search for and select records based on a wide range of criteria. Compound searches can be constructed to examine data in multiple fields using the Boolean connectors AND, OR, and NOT. Data can then be sorted or arranged in a prescribed alphabetic, numeric, or chronological order in either ascending or descending fashion based on any individual field. Most software also allows nested, or multilevel, sorts.

To develop a report for printing information from the file, the user first selects the appropriate layout, then selects the records to be included in the report, and, finally, designates their order. Information can be entered once, and many reports can be generated simply by instructing the computer program how to organize the data.

To make the best use of a file management system, you must be able to meet the following four requirements: (1) understand your information needs, (2) specify your output needs, (3) specify your input needs, (4) determine the file organization.

Teachers want help in alleviating the paperwork demands made on them. They want help in accomplishing activities that do not involve students directly and are often done outside of actual class time. Students need access to increasing amounts of information if they are to construct their own knowledge. The teaching of information organization and retrieval skills can be taught through the use of databases.

Electronic portfolios provide for the storage of written documents, images, and video. A database manager can organize the various artifacts collected and can provide efficient analysis over time. Portfolios can be stored on a removable magnetic medium or on a recordable CD-ROM.

A number of commercial databases are available in a variety of content areas from several publishers of educational software. Many of these databases are distributed on CD-ROM.

CHAPTER EXERCISES

1. List at least three database management applications for each of the following and explain how the database addresses a particular productivity need.
   a. Classroom teacher
   b. Library/media specialist
   c. Student
2. Look at your personal records. To what areas might you apply a file manager? Do you have records in a paper format that could be stored and manipulated electronically? What would be the advantages and disadvantages of doing this? Would it make you more productive?
3. Develop the field definition for a file that would include all the information you would need on the students in a given class.
4. Determine the kinds of reports you would need if the entire student population of your school were put on a database. What kind of information would have to be placed in the database and how often would this information have to be updated?
5. Select one of the database examples illustrated in Figures 9–11 through 9–15 and create it, using the database software available to you. Add, delete, or change the fields suggested in order to modify the database to suit your particular needs. Enter sample data and prepare a user's guide so that a classmate can run some reports.
6. Design a database application for a model electronic portfolio. In addition to identification and date fields, include all fields necessary to capture required documentation in text, audio, picture, and video formats. Develop two sample reports that would support comparison of like measures.
7. After examining Figures 9–18 through 9–20 as products of the software *MacGlobe™,* write a brief description of Malawi. Be sure to point out similarities to and differences from the United States. Indicate what else you would like to know about Malawi.

GLOSSARY

authority list A list of approved headings, names, terms, and so on designed to control what is entered into a field.

database The collection of related data records stored and accessed electronically by computer. By popular use, now used interchangeably with the term *file.*

database manager Software that is designed to manage electronic files. The term is often used interchangeably with file manager.

field The group of related characters treated as a unit within a record—for example, the last name of a student. The smallest, most discrete element of a file. A group of fields constitutes a record.

file A collection of related records treated as a unit.

file management A systematic approach to the storage, manipulation, and retrieval of information stored as data items in the form of records in a file.

form See *layout.*

label The descriptor related to a data field.

layout The selection and positioning of fields and their labels for screen or printed use.

logical search The ability to apply logical operators to a search—for example, "Find all words that contain 'th' " or "Find all values greater than 100."

multilevel sort A series of second, third, and so on levels of sorts performed after a primary one has been performed—for example, sorting a group of students by first name after they were first sorted by last name.

nested sort See *multilevel sort.*

query See *logical search.*

record A group of related fields treated as a unit. For example, in a student file, a record might be all the information stored relating to a given student. A group of records constitutes a file.

relational database manager Software designed to manage a collection of related electronic data files.

template A blank form in a file manager containing labels and perhaps report formats but no data.

REFERENCES & SUGGESTED READINGS

Beare, R. (1992, December). Software tools in science classrooms. *Journal of Computer Assisted Learning, 8*(4), 221–230.

Benjamin, L. (1993, April). Motivational meteorology. *Science Teacher, 60*(4), 20–25.

Browning, C. A. (1992, December). A "handy" database activity for the middle school classroom. *Arithmetic Teacher, 40*(4), 235–238.

Cox, A. C. (1991, July–August). Western Europe—A trading game. *Journal of Geography, 90*(4), 168–173.

Davey, C., & Jarvis, A. (1990). Microcomputers for microhistory: A database approach to the reconstitution of small English populations. *History and Computing, 2*(3), 187.

Dean, B. R. (1992, May-June). Curriculum connection: Take technology outdoors. *Instructor, 101*(9), 66–68.

Ennis, D. L. (1993). A transfer of database skills from the classroom to the real world. *Computers in the Schools, 9*(2–3), 55–63.

Gettys, D. (1994, October). Journaling with a database. *The Computing Teacher, 22*(2), 37–40, 48.

Hauserman, C. (1992, November). Discipline tracking with databases. *The Computing Teacher, 20*(3), 20.

Jankowski, L. (1993–94, December/January). Getting started with databases. *The Computing Teacher, 21*(4), 8–9.

Kawasaki, G. (1991). *Database 101: A database primer for the rest of us.* Berkeley, CA: Peachpit Press.

Lewis, P. (1997, September). Using productivity software for beginning language learning. *Learning and Leading with Technology, 25*(1), 12–17.

Mernit, S. (1991, February). Black history month—Let your database set the stage. *Instructor, 100*(6), 109–110.

North Carolina State Department of Public Instruction. (1992). *Voteline: A project for integrating computer databases, spreadsheets, and telecomputing into high school social studies instruction* (ED350243). Raleigh.

Rae, J. (1990). Getting to grips with database design: A step by step approach. *Computers and Education, 14*(6), 281.

Smith, C. B. (1991, February). The role of different literary genres. *Reading Teacher, 44*(6), 440–441.

Thomas, R. (1993, March). Envisioning data: Tables, scatter plots, choropleth maps, and correlation. *The Computing Teacher, 20*(6), 37–40.

Chapter 10

Networking and Telecommunications

ADVANCE ORGANIZER

1. What are the advantages of creating networks of interconnected computers?

2. How are physical connections among computers accomplished?

3. How are networks configured?

4. How should networked computer labs be designed?

5. How do digital and analog signals differ?

6. How does hardware serve as a communication tool?

7. What software is necessary to use a computer as a communication tool?

8. What are the most common applications of telecommunications?

Telecommunications is defined as the sharing of information over distance. In its simplest form, one computer connected to another could be sharing information over distance. Telecommunications allows users to exchange messages, view files on remote computers, and transfer files. A cluster of interconnected computers sharing information is called a **network**. It seems appropriate, therefore, to discuss physical networks and the virtual networks of long-distance telecommunications together.

Networks are constructed in order to maximize the use of software and the exchange of information. Software made available on a network can be accessed by a number of different machines, providing that the appropriate license fee has been paid to the software publisher. **Electronic mail**, commonly referred to as **e-mail**, allows messages to be exchanged between users. Electronic bulletin boards allow documents to be read simultaneously by a number of networked users.

Networks, though they are sometimes thought of as local facilities, in reality span the globe. Effective long-distance communications are in fact moving us toward the promised *global village*. Over a decade ago, Naisbitt (1984) identified the trend toward the shrinking *information float,* or the time lag between the occurrence of an event and widespread knowledge of its occurrence. For all practical purposes, the information float no longer exists.

As teachers are becoming more comfortable with telecommunications, they are exploring the concept of *global classrooms*. These are composed of computers in classrooms around the world interconnected for the purpose of sharing information, ideas, interests, collaborative projects, and questions. Children and young adults in global classrooms are indeed in the process of becoming citizens of the world.

NETWORKING

Networking is the interconnecting of computer stations with each other, as well as with selected input and output peripheral devices. It offers several important advantages to schools. A network permits resource sharing—that is, the sharing of software and peripheral equipment. Buying network licenses is considerably less expensive than purchasing multiple copies of individual software packages. Without a network, one peripheral device (such as a printer) can serve only one computer. A network allows many computers to access connected peripheral devices regardless of where they are physically located.

A network also promotes resource management. Individual users do not have to have every program or file on a disk because those resources can reside on a central network server. Many school networks employ student data management software that provides security and record-keeping functions. Finally, and most important, a network facilitates information exchange and student collaboration. Students can read files created by a teacher, exchange files among themselves, communicate with others by e-mail, or, with the proper software, work simultaneously and interactively on a project.

When the network is composed of devices that are housed in close proximity to one another such as in one building or on a campus, the network is referred to as a **local area network,** or **LAN**. A network that spans great distances or covers a wide geographical area is called a **wide area network,** or **WAN**. LANs may be classified by the type of interconnection and by the topology or configuration, which facilitates either a peer-to-peer relationship, in which computer stations can exchange files between each other, or a client/server relationship, in which computer stations exchange files between themselves and a central computer.

Network Cabling

Cabling, as illustrated in Figure 10–1, is most often twisted pair wiring that has been used in the telephone system. This older, twisted-pair wiring is being gradually replaced by optical fiber or coaxial cable often used in a closed-circuit television system. The most recent mode of interconnection is wireless connectivity, which employs either infrared or radio wave transmission and reception. Infrared communication, the kind of signaling used by a TV remote control, is limited because it cannot penetrate solid objects and is, therefore, restricted to close ranges such as a single room. Radio wave communication does not have these restrictions and exhibits properties similar to cable networks, without the limitations of being *hard wired.* In July 1992, the FCC designated a band of radio waves for User-PC products. Melanie McMullen, a specialist in mobile computing and networking, predicts that "by the year 2000, wireless LANs will account for 10 percent of all nodes" (McMullen, 1993).

Twisted pair is the least expensive copper cabling, often used for wiring phone systems, and is suitable for short distances. Single pairs of wires are used in a circuit, but many pairs are often wrapped in a bundle, surrounded by an outer sheath. An

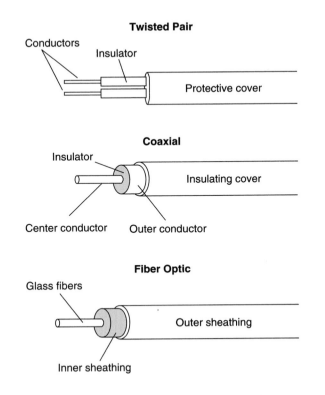

Figure 10–1

Types of cabling

unused pair of wires in a building's existing phone system can often be used to network computers. If unshielded twisted pair wiring is used, the network may be susceptible to electromagnetic or radio frequency interference. **Coaxial cable**, composed of a central core conductor surrounded by insulation and then by a second conductor, is more expensive and more difficult to install. It has the advantage, however, of transmitting a much greater quantity of data at a much higher speed. It is also resistant to most interference. The 75 ohm, or broad-band, cable capable of supporting up to 32 simultaneous channels is usually used. In new or remodeled construction, **optical fiber** is often installed. Although it is the most expensive cabling, it has the greatest bandwidth, allowing up to 600 voice-grade channels to be used simultaneously. It is capable of the highest-speed transmission and is virtually impervious to unauthorized access.

Network Protocols and Topologies

Network software **protocols,** or standardized rules, allow many devices to share network cabling without interfering with one another. The most popular protocol is Ethernet. It can be added to a computer by purchasing an interface card and connecting cable. Many newer computers come ready to connect to Ethernet.

The linear **bus topology,** shown in Figure 10–2, is the most common configuration for small networks designed primarily to share peripherals, or to share information

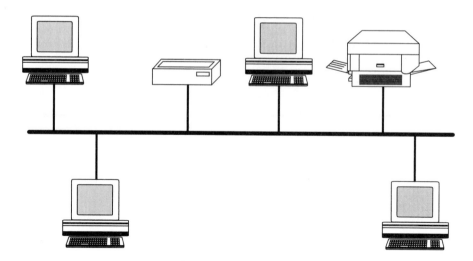

Figure 10–2

*Bus network
configuration*

housed on an individual computer's hard drive with other computers on the network. In a peer-to-peer relationship, one computer interacting directly with another computer on the network, the failure of any one computer does not disable the entire network. It is also possible to dedicate one or more computers in this configuration as a **network server,** or **host**, a device that all other **client** computers access for programs and files. In this case, the failure of the host computer disables the network.

In a linear bus topology, the main wiring, sometimes referred to in this configuration as the "backbone," may be twisted pair, coaxial cable, or optical fiber with connectors for each node, or piece of equipment, attached to the network. An advantage of this topology is the ease of network expansion. However, this capability is also one of its drawbacks: as the network expands in length and in number of nodes, the system slows down because messages collide more frequently and must be re-sent. The user notices the degradation of performance as operations such as accessing a remote computer, opening files, and saving files become slower. Also, if the host server is "down" (i.e., not functioning), access to files stored on the server is denied to the clients. To prevent this scenario, alternative systems should be provided to avoid the loss of instructional time. A possible remedy is the installation of a backup server containing duplicate files that would be available to the clients.

The **star topology,** shown in Figure 10–3, is also a popular network configuration. In this arrangement, one computer is dedicated as a network server. However, if it fails, the entire network ceases to operate. The other computers connected on this network are considered clients to the host network server. Communication between any two client computers must go through the host. A common application for computers arranged in a star topology is the storage of a database meant to be accessed by several computers. An electronic mail service is easy to implement in this set-up. Each client computer has a mailbox on the network server, and messages are easily routed and stored and responses sent. Network operating system software such as *Novell Netware™* and *AppleShare™* is located on the server and controls access and security on the network.

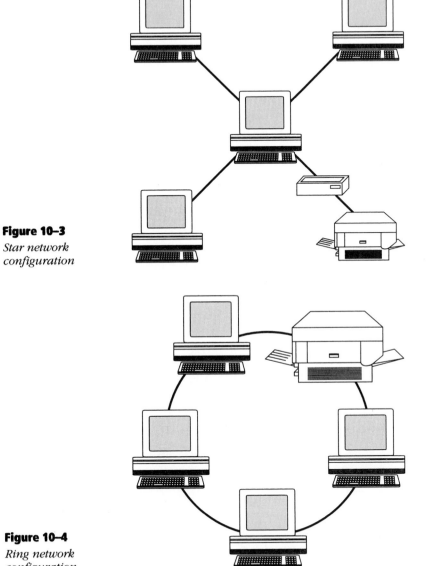

Figure 10–3

Star network configuration

Figure 10–4

Ring network configuration

The **ring topology,** illustrated in Figure 10–4, is the one used least often. Although a ring network may provide multiple access, it usually employs a special coded message, called a token, that the operating software passes in sequence to each computer on the network. This type of configuration, as implemented by IBM, is referred to as a token ring network. The ring topology has advantages and drawbacks similar to those of the bus configuration.

Once again, there are several advantages to all three types of local area networks. Costly peripherals are shared instead of duplicated; programs and files also can be shared between computers on the network; electronic mail can travel over the network, facilitating a timely exchange of information; a network can facilitate computer use by minimizing the number of floppy disks needed.

Computer Labs/Classrooms

Although networks can exist throughout a school building, they are most often installed in a networked computer lab. There, computers are interconnected to a file server (often located in another room) and to one or more printers. The file server may store programs as well as files meant to be accessed by all the computer stations.

The design of the physical space of the computer lab will be affected by several factors: the number of computer stations; the number of peripheral devices such as printers, scanners, and **MIDI** keyboards (musical synthesizers); and, most important, the style of teaching that will predominate in that room. Figures 10–5 through 10–7 suggest designs to accommodate various teaching styles and student learning environments. Computer labs often also serve as computer-equipped classrooms. When teaching in such a room, a common challenge for the instructor is competing with the computer for the students' attention. When the instructor requires the students' attention, one effective strategy is for the instructor to call "mouse up," meaning that the students are directed to turn the mouse on its back, thereby minimizing the temptation to continue working on the computer.

Figure 10–5 illustrates a design of one student per computer station. All student stations face toward the front of the room to attend to the instructor as a lecture or demonstration is conducted. This configuration is really a teacher-centered classroom design rather than a laboratory. All stations have an unobstructed view of the

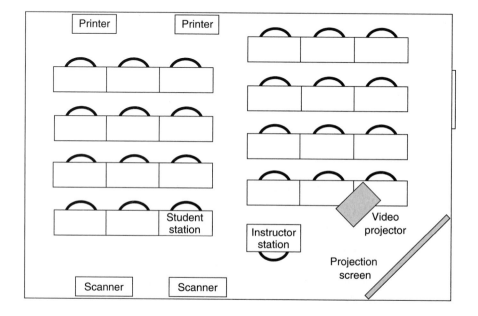

Figure 10–5

A 24-station, instructor-centered lab design

projection screen, since the video projector is suspended from the ceiling. Students can easily replicate at their stations whatever is being projected on the screen, and instruction can progress, with the whole class progressing at approximately the same pace. This lab design can be especially useful in demonstrating software operation.

The design illustrated in Figure 10–6 has stations with large desktop surfaces so that students can gather around a computer and monitor. Given a large enough room, the large surface also allows space for students to work in pairs at one station in order to facilitate collaborative learning techniques and to maximize the investment in equipment. All stations face outward to facilitate the instructor's and students' mobility and ability to view other stations' monitors. Some movement would be required when students are called on to view an image projected on the screen in this configuration.

Software and hardware also exist to allow the image from one monitor to be displayed on all others simultaneously. One video switching system manufactured by Robotel™ Electronique Inc., illustrated in Figure 10–7, places an interface at each station, linked to junction boxes that connect to a master controller at the instructor's station. This system allows the instructor to choose from five different operating modes: (1) *Group Work* allows the instructor to select the screen from any station and display it on all monitors, with the provision that the instructor can take over keyboard and mouse control of the remote station; (2) *Subgroup Work* allows the instructor to make presentations to selected stations while the rest of the class works independently; (3) *Individual Work* allows the instructor to supervise and help individual students by monitoring their displays; (4) *Team Work* allows the instructor to divide the class into groups whose members share monitors, keyboards, and mice; and (5) *Evaluation Mode* allows the instructor using Smartclass™ software to display

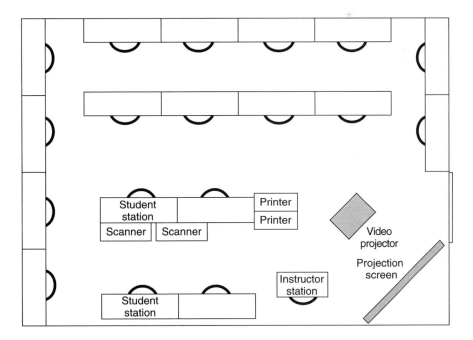

Figure 10–6

An 18- to 36-station, student-centered lab design

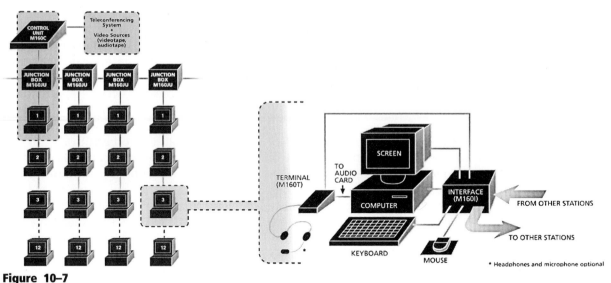

Figure 10–7

A video switching system (Courtesy of Robotel™ Électronique Inc.)

prepared questions on students' stations so that students can answer them via their terminals. The system compiles results and generates a printed report on request. An interesting advantage of this system is that it is easy to modify into an interactive videoconferencing environment, turning a computer classroom into a distance learning facility. The advent of inexpensive video cameras attached directly to a computer and user-friendly software such as the freeware *CU-See-Me* have made videoconferencing, or desktop conferencing, an important and affordable reality in some schools.

The design illustrated in Figure 10–8 has smaller desktop surfaces in order to accommodate more stations in a restricted space. Once again, all stations are facing outward to facilitate the instructor's and students' moving around and viewing other stations' monitors. Worktables are provided to encourage off-computer work by individual students and collaborative groups. Some movement would also be required in this arrangement, when students are called on to view an image on the projection screen. Scanners and printers are provided as necessary peripheral devices to many activities conducted in a computer lab.

A lab should accommodate large groups, small groups, and individual work. In planning a computer lab, ask "Will this room truly function as a laboratory where students will use the computers as tools in their exploration of concepts, or is this room primarily intended to be a computer classroom?" It is difficult, though not impossible, for one room to optimally serve both functions.

Collaborative Learning and the Computer Lab

Since "one computer per student" is not yet reality, teachers have turned toward grouping two or more students around a computer as a preferred strategy. Collabo-

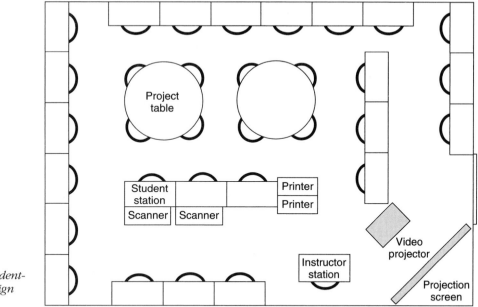

Figure 10–8

A 24-station, student-centered lab design with worktables

rative learning—or cooperative learning as it is sometimes called—has been widely implemented in many classroom situations. Computers are usually designed with the individual in mind; thus, true collaboration does not mean simply clustering students around a computer monitor, nor does it mean simply letting them take turns at the keyboard.

A productive environment must be created by carefully grouping students and monitoring the behavior of groups to prevent students from "slacking off" and riding the coattails of more able partners and to prevent higher-ability students from lowering their own effort and achievement because of a feeling of being used by others. True collaboration must provide for structured sharing in creation and decision making, resulting in a negotiated product. Teachers must prepare students for collaborative computer activities by issuing specific directions relating to each group member's role and expected interaction with others and the computer. Individual and group assessment must be considered. Individual student journals or portfolios may be used, along with an evaluation of the product produced by the group. Individual assessment tends to keep the individual student on task, while product assessment fosters peer tutoring and a feeling of responsibility to the group.

Collaborative learning prepares the student for the world of work, where some measure of collaboration is found in nearly every job situation. Research indicates that collaborative learning supports task-oriented behavior and improved peer relations. It provides social skill benefits, with achievement benefits for low-achievers and no penalty on high-achievers (Schlechter, 1990). Thus, collaborative learning, correctly implemented, is one way teachers can effectively stretch scarce computer resources.

TELECOMMUNICATIONS

Telecommunications involves taking the concepts present in a local network and extending them to buildings within a school district, to the community at large, to the state, to the nation, and even to the entire world. Through advances in technology and with federal and state government support, telecommunications is becoming far easier, less costly, and much more prevalent as teachers and students receive a modest amount of training and observe enough instructional applications to validate its use.

Fundamental Concepts

As was discussed briefly in Chapter 5, computers are composed mainly of digital circuits. They process information as voltage in a digital, or **binary,** code of 1s and 0s.

Consider the illustration in Figure 10–9. **Digital** signals are high or low, with no smooth, gradual transition. **Analog** signals, on the other hand, are continuous signals, varying in amplitude and frequency, that flow from high to low, with varying intervals between peaks. One way of understanding the difference might be to think of a clock. Its ticking is like a digital signal. It makes a ticking sound and then there is silence; in other words, a binary state exists—a tick or silence. Most clock faces, however, are analog in the sense that hands sweep through a continuous, unbroken circle.

Until very recently, telephone lines were designed to carry only analog signals. A hardware device called a **modem** (MOdulator-DEModulator) was created to translate digital and analog signals. Figure 10–10 illustrates the connection of computers by phone lines. Notice that a modem connected to a computer must be present at both sites.

Communications Hardware

A connector, or port, on a computer allows data to flow between the computer and the outside world. Interface ports allow the user to use a cable to link the computer

Figure 10–9

Digital and analog signals

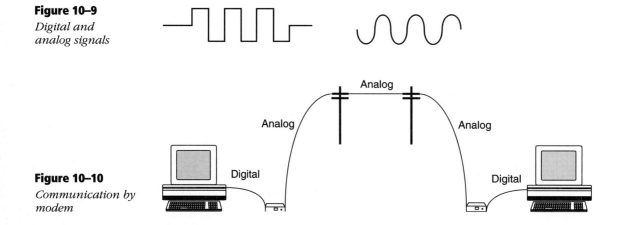

Figure 10–10

Communication by modem

and a peripheral device. Most ports supply data in a serial fashion. The RS-232 is the most common serial port. It is so named for Recommended Standard No. 232 of the Electrical Institute of America.

A modem is connected to the serial port in order to convert the digital data into analog form to transmit over the phone lines. A modem connected to the serial port of a receiving computer translates the analog data back to digital form. Modems were identified by the term **baud rate**, a measure of signaling speed. The higher the baud rate, the faster the modem could transmit data. Common rates in the early days of telecommunications were 300 and 1,200 baud. The advent of the 2,400 baud modem created quite a bit of excitement. It was deemed so efficient that commercial information services at one time increased the connection charges to users of 2,400 baud and faster modems.

The measures *bits per second* (**bps**) and *kilobits per second* (**Kbps**) have now replaced baud rate as the indicator of data transfer. Remember that a bit (a contraction of *bi*nary digi*t*) is the smallest data unit in a digital system and that the prefix *kilo* represents 1,000. Bps and Kbps are more accurate units of measure at higher speeds, since modems are now designed to encode more than one bit in a signal element; 28,800 bps modems (28.8 Kbps) are now common, with even faster ones at 33.6 Kbps now entering the marketplace. 56 Kbps modems have been introduced but are limited, however, to digital telephone lines. Faster modems mean lower long-distance phone charges and perhaps lower connection fees from services that assess time charges. Ordinary telephone line quality is now placing a practical limit, however, on the transfer rate.

Telecommunications experts have turned both to high-capacity Integrated Services Data Network (**ISDN**) telephone lines designed to carry digital signals and to cable networks as a means of achieving a far more rapid data transfer. Cable modems finding their way into schools operate at a transfer rate of 10 to 30 megabits per second (**Mbps**). The significance of this dramatic speed increase becomes apparent when you consider that a 10-megabyte file that takes 46 minutes to download when using a 28.8 Kbps modem would take only eight seconds when using a cable modem (Shearer, 1997). For a number of years, telecomputing dealt primarily with the exchange of moderate-sized text files. With the explosion of multimedia resources now available, users are downloading files containing complex graphics, movies, and sound. These files are many times larger than text files and are often measured in megabytes. The only solution is for the telecommunications industry to continue to develop higher-speed methods of transferring data.

A modem contains instructions that interpret and respond to commands typed at the computer keyboard. The command mode, illustrated in Figure 10–11, controls the action of the modem. In addition to the *dial-a-number* and *disconnect-the-call* commands, a user can directly address the modem in command mode to set the baud rate, number of bits per character, and error-checking conventions. Most of these commands, however, are taken over and simplified by the communications software.

The industry standard command set is the AT set developed by the Hayes Corporation. Employing this set, a user could type AT DT followed by a phone number. The Hayes-compatible modem recognizes that AT signifies a modem command, and the following DT signals that it is to dial a touch-tone call. (DP would signify the

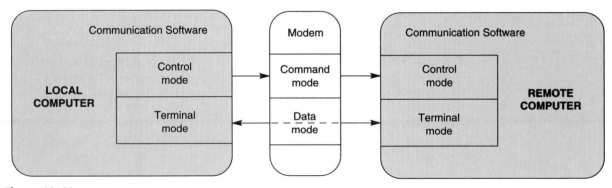

Figure 10–11

Modems communicate through a command and a data mode

older, pulse dialing convention.) Once an answering signal is heard, the modems maintain this carrier signal and switch to data transfer mode.

Communications Software

As illustrated in Figure 10–12, telecommunications software has both a control mode and a terminal emulation mode. The **control mode** regulates the performance of the modem to match the remote computer and modem. In control mode, the user sets the speed of the data transfer and determines the number of bits per character and parity. The number of bits per character is usually set at eight bits to allow for the transmission of text and graphics symbols. Eight bits also closely matches the format used by computer programs and is, therefore, commonly used in personal computer communications. **Parity** is a simple form of error checking that the user usually sets to even, odd, or none. *Even* parity would turn a bit on or off to ascertain that the number of binary 1s in a character is always an even number. *Odd* parity

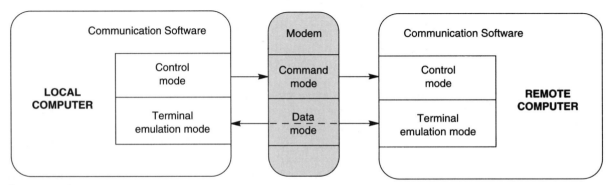

Figure 10–12

Computers communicate through a control and a terminal emulation mode

would turn a bit on or off to ascertain that the number of binary 1s in a character is always an odd number. *None* has become the most common setting today. The control mode also governs file access and storage, as well as printer operation.

Terminal emulation mode primarily governs screen display format. The VT-100 is the name of a computer terminal developed by Digital Equipment Corporation, and the VT-100 terminal emulation mode has become an industry standard. When the user selects VT-100 emulation, the computer screen display (line length and spacing, carriage returns, line feeds, and cursor movement) resembles that of a VT-100 terminal. This mode is particularly useful when establishing a connection to a remote host computer housing, for example, a library's electronic catalog.

Curriculum Applications of Telecommunications

In the early stages of the use of telecommunications in the classroom, Margaret Honey and Andrés Henríquez (1993) surveyed teachers who used telecommunications in their classrooms. The respondents were highly self-motivated and generally self-taught—the pioneers of an emerging movement. Fred D'Ignazio (1990) describes the paradigm shift teachers will need to make before networking and telecommunications become widespread in the classroom:

> Most teachers see the computer as a kind of electronic Cuisinart. You pour information into the computer and—it slices. It dices. It blends. It whips. It purees. And then it disgorges . . . .
>
> A new paradigm for "computer" is suddenly emerging. Associated with this paradigm are the concepts: network, communication, connectivity, multimedia, and vehicle.
>
> We are overnight crossing the threshold from personal computing to interpersonal computing. In tomorrow's workplace, we will all be using workstations instead of mere computers. The word "workstation" implies communication. The workstation must talk with the other people and the other machines. . . .
>
> If we couple this concept of a communicating workstation with multimedia, we can see how the computer is no longer a stationary device, but a vehicle. . . . Students and teachers can ride that vehicle to the furthest reaches of human knowledge and imagination.

Among the applications of telecommunications that allow the computer to become a vehicle to transport students and teachers along the information highways are e-mail, electronic conferencing, commercial information services, and educational networks.

E-Mail. E-mail allows users to exchange messages within a local area network or with users in faraway places. E-mail has phenomenal holding power. Students eagerly spend time each day reading and writing at the computer. What an opportunity for a teacher to develop language arts skills! Once the novelty and electronic pen-pal syndrome wear off, students might see e-mail as a means of accessing information on specific topics and learning about different cultures. A study of college students (Deal, 1995) suggests that an e-mail journal helps students to increase self-assessment skills and synthesize their learning better than traditional journaling.

E-mail is a great equalizer. A librarian at the Seattle Public Library was discussing e-mail with a homeless person who was sitting at one of the library terminals connected to the Internet. The person indicated that he was contacting other users, hoping to find a job or perhaps job training. He commented that it didn't matter if he was black, Hispanic, or physically impaired; the other users simply reacted to him as an electronic contact. Students building relationships with each other on e-mail might help to dissolve old prejudices.

A simple, cost-effective way of preparing students to use e-mail is to allow them access to a local e-mail program mounted on the teacher's computer lab host server. Practice sessions provide the opportunity to stress proper communication rules and mitigate what some believe to be e-mail's negative effect on writing habits and skills because of its informal nature.

Bulletin Board Systems. As its name suggests, an electronic **bulletin board system (BBS)** organizes groups of messages by topic. It is the telecommunications equivalent of the multicolored notices tacked up in a college's Student Union to announce meetings, roommates wanted, and items for sale. Subject areas may be referred to as conferences, forums, or echoes; they span the broad range of human interests from astrology to zoology. Whereas e-mail allows an individual to correspond with another individual or small groups of individuals via distribution lists, an electronic bulletin board permits an individual to publish messages to a multitude of readers located anywhere in the world.

Using skills and techniques acquired in the design and creation of databases, teachers can develop a simple, cost-effective way to prepare students to use bulletin boards. The teacher can set up a computer in a common area such as the school library or a computer lab to resemble a message area of a bulletin board. Figure 10–13 suggests some fields that might be used. Next, the teacher can choose series of topics, ranging from local to national issues, and encourage students to leave specific messages on one or more of the topics. The teacher can also encourage them to use the computer to search for responses to questions they might have on any of the topics.

Once this has proven successful, the teacher can follow-up the simulation by establishing an in-school bulletin board. Software to establish a local bulletin board system is freely available on many existing BBSs.

Commercial Information Services. A number of companies market services such as e-mail, conferencing, and database access for a monthly membership fee and possibly

NAME	Test
DATE	Auto enter today
SUBJECT	Text
TO	Text
FROM	Text
MESSAGE	Text

Figure 10–13

Message database

connect-time charges. This industry has been in a state of flux. More and more people are becoming comfortable with telecommunications and are demanding more and faster services. Established companies have gone bankrupt or have merged or been bought out by others. It is even possible that one of the two commercial vendors discussed as examples in this section may no longer exist.

America Online. America Online (AOL) is the largest commercial service and provides live, interactive conferencing; databases of games, graphics, and computer applications, including educational programs and lesson plans for teachers; electronic versions of popular magazines; e-mail; and a gateway to the Internet, along with a World Wide Web browser—all this for a modest monthly subscription fee. Over 250 hardware and software producers maintain bulletin boards to offer assistance with their products. The latest news, weather, sports, and stock market information is available. Thousands of public domain software programs are available. A reservation system allows the user to make airline and major hotel reservations.

CompuServe. CompuServe, a long-time service provider in its own right, is a subsidiary of AOL. It also provides electronic conferencing; games, graphics, and computer applications; electronic versions of popular magazines; e-mail; and a gateway to the Internet. The basic monthly subscription is quite modest, with surcharges applied for access to some service areas. Check the latest news on the *Associated Press Online* hourly summaries, read the current issue of *U.S. News & World Report*, search for the treasure in *CastleQuest*, or "shop 'til you drop" in the *Electronic Mall*®.

Educational Networks. A number of networks aimed primarily at K–12 education have developed during the past few years. The names, addresses, and phone numbers of the five major educational networks are listed in Appendix K.

AT&T Learning Network. This network is designed to connect students and teachers in seven to nine classrooms in different locations into a Learning Circle. The Learning Circles form according to specific themes and for a specific duration. Students investigate a topic, share ideas, and collaborate in producing a final publication.

FrEdMail. Free Educational Electronic Mail Network (FrEdMail) is a loosely organized international network of more than 150 school-based electronic bulletin boards. Messages are exchanged between sites during off-peak hours. Users issue calls for collaboration on specific project ideas. FrEdMail also publishes a newsletter including project ideas, most of which are designed to promote writing activities.

In 1991, more than 5,000 classrooms around the country participated in such projects as "Acid Rain," in which students collected rain samples, plotted the resulting data, and shared conclusions on the causes and effects of acid rain. Since a single individual is not in charge of a project and has no authority to require participation, some projects are never completed. This can lead to some frustration among participants.

K12 Net. K12 Net is a collection of **electronic conferences** specifically designed for use in schools. There are more than three dozen of these forums devoted to curriculum (e.g., art, music, science, and math); language exchanges with native speakers in French, German, Japanese, Russian, and Spanish; and classroom-to-classroom projects designed by teachers and listed each week in the "projects" conference.

There are also four informal chat areas for elementary, middle, and high school students, as well as teachers. The conferences are privately distributed as a group to more than 600 participating bulletin board systems on six continents and to the Internet as Usenet newsgroups in the k12.* hierarchy. Participants are located all over the world; every message in every conference can be read by students and teachers on every system, so any inquiry may receive a reply from Taiwan or South Africa, as well as from the United States or Canada.

K12 Net is supported by the system operators of the bulletin boards that participate, so it is free to users who can connect with a local phone call. The messages are compressed and exchanged late at night, when phone rates are cheapest. K–12 educators and students who do not have access to the Internet have found K12 Net to be an exciting "network with training wheels" to learn and teach about telecommunications.

National Geographic Kids Network. This is a highly structured international network that allows middle-grade students to participate in science and geography projects developed by curriculum specialists under the joint funding of the National Geographic Society and the National Science Foundation. Activities on the network are based on the belief that children learn by doing. Students use instruments in hands-on experiments and record changes over time. They conduct surveys, read maps, and create graphs. Students analyze data they collect locally and share with others on the network. They form and test hypotheses, they make comparisons and look for patterns, and they draw conclusions and discuss the implications. The information is also analyzed by experts, and summaries of their findings are sent back to the students. In the past, topics have included acid rain, water pollution, weather, recycling, solar energy, and nutrition. In this top-down curriculum model, participants receive a teacher's guide, handbooks, and activity sheets.

SpecialNet® (GTE Education NetServices). SpecialNet® is a commercial network in operation since 1981 and aimed specifically at education, serving the United States and Canada. It provides e-mail, databases, and a variety of conferences on education-related topics. These include federal legislation, employment opportunities, promising practices, new products and publications, computer applications and software, and a wide variety of special education topics.

Importance of Telecommunications to Education

Telecommunication offers significant advantages to classroom teachers and other educators because it allows them to transcend the isolation that typifies their profession. Library media specialists and teachers of art, music, and other subjects, who are frequently one of a kind in their buildings, can share teaching strategies and curriculum ideas with their peers in a daily electronic "convention."

Information is broadcast across electronic networks sooner and in greater quantity than in any other publication medium. Many newspapers, government documents, and periodical indexes are published electronically, as well as in print. For teachers of health and social studies, timely access to current resources is a major incentive to use telecommunications in their curriculum.

Social studies and foreign language teachers are also enthusiastic about wide-area computer networking because it facilitates significant cultural exchanges. Science teachers can expand the scope of their data collection far beyond their local environment by collaborating with classrooms across the country or, indeed, the world. Finally, because students are evaluated by the clarity of their written expression with immediate feedback from their peers, they are highly motivated to improve their writing skills.

Telecommunications supports the reform movement in education by facilitating cooperative and interactive learning. Since personal appearance, physical disabilities, and special needs are invisible on the network, students who are set apart from their classmates can participate as equals. Many who are reluctant participants in the classroom become eager contributors when they can compose their inquiries and responses on their own time.

Keep in mind the paradigm shifts explored in Chapter 1 and the dramatic changes in schooling. Telecommunications allows educators to create a virtual classroom without walls, bringing global resources and experiences to their students. Students have access to information resources as never before as they develop their problem-solving skills and construct their own knowledge.

SUMMARY

Networking is the interconnecting of computer stations with input and output devices to facilitate sharing of information and equipment and to reduce the number and cost of peripherals. When the network is composed of devices that are housed in close proximity to one another, the network is referred to as a local area network, or LAN. A network that spans great distances or covers a wide geographical area is called a wide area network, or WAN. Network cabling is most often inexpensive twisted pair wiring used in the telephone system or high-speed, broad-band coaxial cable used in a closed-circuit television system. Optical fiber has the greatest bandwidth, thereby allowing the greatest number of channels to be used simultaneously.

Network software protocols allow many devices to share networked resources without interfering with one another. The bus topology is the most common configuration for small networks mainly designed to share peripherals. The star topology is a popular one, with one computer dedicated as a network server. The ring topology usually employs a special coded message, called a token, that is passed in sequence to each computer on the network. Local area networks allow costly peripherals, programs, and files to be shared. Electronic mail can travel over the network, facilitating a timely exchange of information.

The design of the physical space of the computer lab will be affected by the number of computer stations; the number of peripheral devices such as printers, scanners, and MIDI-keyboards; and, most important, by the style of teaching that will predominate in that room. It is difficult for one room to function both as a laboratory for students and as a teaching station or demonstration classroom.

Telecommunications involves taking the concepts present in a local network and extending them to buildings within a school district, to the community at large, to the state, to the nation, and even to the entire world.

The computer processes digital signals as voltage in a binary code of 1s and 0s. Digital signals are high or low, with no smooth, gradual transition. Analog signals are continuous signals, varying in amplitude and frequency, that flow from high to low, with varying intervals between peaks. A modem is connected to the computer's serial port to convert the digital data into analog form to transmit over the phone lines. A modem connected to the serial port of a receiving computer will translate the analog data back to digital form. The measure bits per second (bps) has gradually replaced baud rate as the indicator of data transfer rate; 28,800 bps modems are often used and faster ones are becoming common.

Telecommunications software has both a control mode and a terminal emulation mode. The control mode regulates the performance of the modem to match the remote computer and modem. Terminal emulation mode primarily governs screen display format.

In order to take advantage of telecommunications, teachers must move from seeing the computer as a static piece of equipment they use to process data to seeing the computer as a vehicle capable of transporting them and their students along a myriad of information highways. Among the applications of telecommunications that allow the computer to become this vehicle are e-mail, electronic conferencing, commercial information services, and educational networks.

CHAPTER EXERCISES

1. Using an electronic encyclopedia on CD-ROM to find the necessary information, explain the basic difference between analog and digital circuits.

2. Locate a modem. Write down its manufacturer's name, the model, and its data transmission rate.

3. Locate the communications software and manual intended for use on the modem mentioned in exercise 2. Determine how to set up the software for that modem. Set the terminal emulation mode.

4. Call a local computer store or your public library and get the phone number of the local node of K12 Net or FidoNet. Using a modem connected to your computer, dial that number and follow the instructions presented to you. Describe the process and the result.

5. Using the fields suggested in Figure 10–13, develop a database to resemble a message area of a bulletin board. Select topics dealing with national issues and encourage your colleagues to leave messages on one or more of the topics. Encourage them to search for responses to questions they might have on any of the topics.

6. Referring to Appendix K, contact educational network providers, requesting materials describing their services.

7. Interview the director of your library or the director of academic computing on your campus and determine (a) how students are permitted to establish e-mail accounts, (b) what regulations govern the use of the accounts, and (c) how many students have current accounts. Inquire about available training.

8. Look up this textbook's author's e-mail address in the text. Send a brief message, stating your opinion of this textbook. You might suggest improvements you would like to see or ask questions about some of the newer technology. Share some ideas, some triumphs, some concerns. Describe to the author how you are using the computer as a productivity tool.

GLOSSARY

analog Signals of continuous nature that vary in frequency and amplitude. Analog signals can be transmitted over telephone lines.

baud rate A rate of data transmission term that has been replaced by bps.

binary Consisting of two parts; limited to two conditions or states of being. Computer memory is designed to store binary digits, symbolized by 0s and 1s in a code. The computer circuitry is designed to manipulate information in an on/off state.

bps A measure of a modem's data transmission speed between computers in bits per second. Common rates are 28,800 bps and faster.

bulletin board system (BBS) A dial-up accessible telecommunications system that usually features e-mail, topic-oriented electronic conferences, and files available for downloading.

bus topology A network configuration consisting of a major wiring circuit to which nodes are connected.

client A computer that is connected to a host computer on a network and that is using some of its files.

coaxial cable A cable composed of a central conductor surrounded by insulation and then by a second conductor; used for television distribution and for high-speed computer networks.

control mode Settings that regulate the performance of the modem to match a remote computer and modem. In the control mode, the user sets the speed of the data transfer and determines the number of bits per character and parity.

digital Signals of a discrete high or low state represented by the digit 0 or 1.

electronic conferences Electronic forums usually organized around specific topics designed to allow the exchange of information by a number of simultaneous users.

electronic mail Software that allows messages to be exchanged between users.

e-mail See *electronic mail.*

host See *network server.*

ISDN (Integrated Services Data Network) High-capacity (128 Kbps) telephone lines.

Kbps A measure of a modem's data transmission speed between computers in thousands of bits per second. Common rates are 28.8 Kbps and faster.

local area network (LAN) A network composed of devices located in close proximity to one another.

Mbps A measure of a modem's data transmission speed between computers in millions of bits per second. Cable modem rates are 10 Mbps and faster.

MIDI Musical Instrument Digital Interface is a standard, agreed upon by manufacturers of musical synthesizers, that allows the communications of musical signals. MIDI interface and software allow the computer to control musical instruments.

modem (MOdulator-DEModulator) A device that translates digital computer information into analog signals, which can be transmitted over telephone lines, and analog signals into a digital form, which can be processed by a computer.

network The interconnection of computers to allow multiple users to access software and to exchange information.

network server A computer dedicated to the operation of a network and providing file storage.

optical fiber The most expensive cabling, with the greatest bandwidth, allowing up to 600 voice grade channels to be used simultaneously. It is capable of the highest-speed transmission and is virtually impervious to unauthorized access.

parity A simple form of error checking that the user usually sets to even, odd, or none. Even parity would turn a bit on or off to ascertain that the number of binary 1s in a character is always an even number. Odd parity would turn a bit on or off to ascertain that the number of binary 1s in a character is always an odd number.

protocol Software standards governing information exchange between computers.

ring topology A network configuration in which all data flow in a single direction from one device to the next one in the circuit.

star topology A network configuration that employs a computer dedicated as a network server, through which all communications pass.

telecommunications The sharing of information over distance.

terminal emulation mode Settings that govern screen display format. In the terminal emulation mode, the user determines screen line length and spacing, carriage returns, line feeds, regular and inverse video, and cursor shape and movement.

twisted pair The least expensive copper cabling, often used for wiring phone systems and suitable for short distances. Pairs of wires are used in a circuit, but many pairs are often wrapped in a bundle surrounded by an outer sheath.

wide area network (WAN) A network that spans great distances or covers a wide geographic area. Wide area networks often interconnect LANs. The Internet is an example of a wide area network.

REFERENCES & SUGGESTED READINGS

Axelson, M. (1996, September). Networking 101. *Electronic Learning, 16*(1), 52–55.

Bingham, M. H. (1992, November). Results of two studies on the benefits and pitfalls of technology-based information accessing. *T.H.E. Journal, 20*(4), 88–92.

Cahall, L. (1994, February). The urban child and the AT&T Learning Network. *The Computing Teacher, 21*(5), 19–20.

Cowan, H. (1997, May-June). Lesson sites just for teachers. *Electronic Learning, 16*(6), 24.

Cowan, H. (1997, May-June). School-made sites worth visiting. *Electronic Learning, 16*(6), 26.

Daly, K. (1994, September). A planning guide for instructional networks. *The Computing Teacher, 22*(1), 11–15.

Deal, N. (1995). Is the medium the message? Comparing student perceptions of teacher responses via written and e-mail forms. Research report in *Emerging Technologies,* Lifelong Learning, NECC '95.

D'Ignazio, F. (1990, May). Electronic highways and the classroom of the future. *The Computing Teacher, 17*(8), 20–24.

Fraundorf, M. C. (1997, April). Distributed computers and labs: the best of both worlds. *Learning and Leading with Technology, 24*(7), 50–53.

Herndon, J., & Yarrow, J. (1996, January). Guidelines for creating a network: A case study. *Learning and Leading with Technology, 23*(5), 31–33.

Honey, M., & Henríquez, A. (1993, June). *Telecommunications and K–12 educators: Findings from a national study.* New York: Center for Technology in Education.

Kay, A. (1991). Computers, networks, and education. *Scientific American, 262*(3), 138–148.

Marshall, G., & Taylor, H. (1995, December). The success stories project: An international collaboration. *Learning and Leading with Technology, 23*(4), 28–29.

McMullen, M. (1993, December). Toys of the trade. *LAN, 8*(13), 40–48.

Mintz, D. (1993–94, December/January). Networks in classrooms. *The Computing Teacher, 21*(4), 27–29.

Murray, J. (1993, August). K12 Network: Global education through telecommunications. *Communications of the ACM,* 36–41.

Naisbitt, J. (1984). *Megatrends: Ten new directions transforming our lives.* New York: Warner Books.

Peha, J. (1995, October). How K–12 teachers are using networks. *Educational Leadership, 53*(2), 18–25.

Schlechter, T. (1990, November). Relative instructional efficiency of small group computer-based telecommunications for instruction. *Journal of Computer Based Instructions, 6*(3), 329–341.

Shearer, R. (1997, March). The Internet: How fast can you download? *Techtrends, 42*(2), 47–49.

Chapter 11

Telecomputing:
The Internet

1. What is the Internet and how did it develop?

2. What kinds of resources are available on the Internet?

3. What are some tools that increase the user's productivity when using the Internet?

4. What is the World Wide Web and how does it relate to the Internet?

5. How can a user maximize the World Wide Web's potential as an information source?

6. How does one publish on the World Wide Web?

7. How can students evaluate the accuracy of information available on the World Wide Web?

8. How can teachers incorporate both directed and exploratory learning styles utilizing the World Wide Web?

9. What are some styles for citing references to information obtained on the World Wide Web?

10. What are some copyright and ownership concerns regarding information, either textual or graphical, obtained from the Internet?

It would be impossible, within a single chapter of this text, to thoroughly describe all of the features of a topic so far-reaching and as constantly changing as the world-wide collection of computer networks known as the Internet. This wonderfully dynamic medium can help create a rich environment that extends the curriculum and enhances student learning. The emphasis of this chapter will be to introduce the reader to many of the exciting ways in which the Internet can be utilized by educators to bring the resources of the global community into the classroom. There are several references in the References & Suggested Readings section at the end of this chapter that the reader may find useful for more in-depth coverage.

ORIGINS OF THE INTERNET

The **Internet** is without a doubt the best-known network today. In reality, though, it is a network of networks. The creation of this supernetwork was a Cold War attempt by the U.S. Department of Defense to develop a nonlinear method of linking government installations in the hope that such a diffuse network would survive a nuclear attack on the United States. How did this supernetwork begin? First, there needed to be an agreement on the manner in which data was to be formatted for transfer among various computers in widely separated locations. A technique called "packet-switching," a data transmission method that divides a message into numerous components, or packets, each framed by synchronizing signals in a header and a trailer, was developed. The header signals the start of the frame and identifies the sender, receiver, and amount of data contained in the packet. The trailer signals the end of the frame and contains information used by the receiving computer to check for transmission errors. This packet-switching method transmits individual packets from point A to point B over potentially a number of different routes. If one route (such as a telephone line) is busy or is destroyed, packets are simply transmitted over other routes and still arrive at their destination, where they are reassembled into the message. A set of standards, called **Transmission Control Protocol/Internet Protocol (TCP/IP),** was developed to allow different networks to interconnect. Campuswide networks at the major U.S. universities, as well as large regional networks, were linked together in what is now known as the Internet, an interconnection of thousands of networks that spans the globe and serves millions of users. Interestingly, the original, decentralized design of the Internet with no one central hub and no centralized control has current consequences. Growing out of a tradition of the free exchange of ideas in an academic context, its users resist most forms of regulation or censorship, including governmental.

Figure 11–1 illustrates one small portion of the Internet, the Oregon State System of Higher Education's OSSHE Net, a statewide network connecting the public institutions of higher education in the state of Oregon. It links to NorthWest Net, a regional network service provider headquartered in Seattle, Washington, and through that network to the Internet.

It was not, however, until the advent of the World Wide Web, with its graphic user interface, that the rapid growth in size and popularity of the Internet began. The Internet has expanded from its original national defense and academic functions to a role as a medium for sharing information among educational institutions at all levels, businesses large and small, governmental and private agencies, and individual users. For most, it is seen as an enormous and immediate source of information. Others see it as an expansive channel for profitable sales of goods and services, while, to some, it is the source of concern about portions of its content or the social inequities of access to its potential.

For educators, the Internet offers many opportunities to access an ever-increasing base of knowledge on a global scale. Students may search extensively for information relevant to their lives and aspirations, may increase or refine their communication skills, and may practice critical evaluation of the information available to them. In addition, the Internet provides a rich environment for students to display, transmit, and discuss the knowledge they have constructed with others outside of their immediate community. Regardless of the diversity of opinion about its uses, the Internet is rapidly expanding as a dynamic repository for human knowledge and experience, and it will continue to have a profound influence on both the form and the content of human communications.

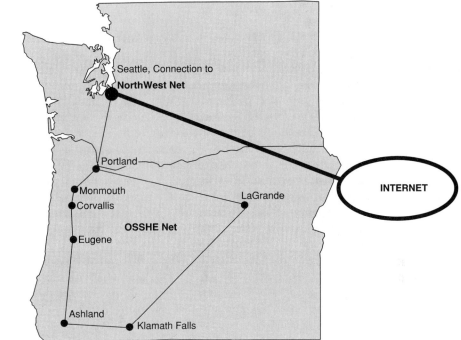

Figure 11–1

OSSHE Net connected through NorthWest Net to the Internet

RESOURCES ON THE INTERNET

As one would expect in this interconnection of networks, various resources are available. Among the primary ones are e-mail, electronic conferencing, databases, and LIST-SERVs. As software has become increasingly user-friendly, it is no longer necessary to learn the intricate UNIX commands that typified early Internet connections. It is more likely that the software will be relatively transparent to the user, with hypertext features seamlessly embedded within documents. Many functions will be done automatically for the user through a series of predefined instructions or from a "point and click" (or even voice activated) menu of commands. It should be remembered, though, that the old computer axiom addressed previously, GIGO (i.e., Garbage In, Garbage Out), applies to this medium as well. Information posted on or transmitted through the Internet must be subject to the same critical evaluation for accuracy and reliability that we might give to any other media. Educators need to incorporate training and practice in these skills within any classroom activity that involves use of the Internet.

E-Mail

As discussed in the previous chapter, e-mail allows users to exchange messages with others, even in faraway places. An individual anywhere in the world, using an e-mail system with an Internet connection, can exchange messages with any other user on a connected e-mail system, providing the e-mail address is known.

This textbook's author's home e-mail address is forcier@gte.net. It is composed of several parts called a *domain* and *subdomains.*

Figure 11–2 identifies the parts of that Internet e-mail address. Reading from right to left, .net represents one of the major domains on the Internet and identifies the site as a network. Some other domains are education (.edu), government agencies (.gov), commercial vendors (.com), and organizations (.org). International sites are frequently identified geographically by two characters representing the country in which they are located—for example, Canada (.ca), United Kingdom (.uk), and Australia (.au). Because of the phenomenal volume of new users joining the Internet, the convention of using geographic identifiers within the United States is supplementing the use of .edu and similar domain names. Each part of an address is separated by a dot (period). Again, reading from right, the next part of the address, gte, identifies the subdomain name of the network subscribed to. The symbol @ separates the leftmost part of the address, which is the user ID, forcier (*user ID*@network provider.a network). Now that you know my addresses, I hope to hear from you with your comments and suggestions related to this book.

If students are using e-mail to communicate with other students or with content experts, they might best compose their communication off-line on a text processor, following guidelines for grammar and spelling, then copy and paste their message into the message box of the e-mail program. Figure 11–3 reviews some guidelines users should adhere to when using e-mail.

forcier@gte.net

User ID	Service provider	Domain (internet)

Figure 11–2

Parts of an Internet e-mail address

- Compose all but brief messages off-line to minimize network traffic.
- Limit each message to one topic and keep it succinct.
- Use subject headings that are very descriptive.
- Reply promptly to messages received.
- When replying restate enough of the message to clearly identify context.
- Delete messages once you have read them.
- Don't be vulgar or offensive.
- Don't attempt to represent yourself as someone you are not.
- Don't criticize ("flame") others on the network.
- Supply clues if you are intending to write humor, irony, sarcasm, or emotion. Your intent may not be obvious to the reader. Using all uppercase in a word or phrase SHOUTS. Try :-) for a sideways smile or ;-) for a wink.
- Use a signature footer that includes your name, school, and e-mail address.
- Practice safe communications. Don't spread viruses! Check downloaded executable files.
- Consider yourself a guest on the system and behave accordingly.

Figure 11–3

E-mail netiquette: network communication etiquette

Electronic Conferencing

Electronic conferencing allows users with similar interests to exchange information and opinions. Usenet newsgroups are the most widely used topic-oriented conferences on the Internet. Newsgroups are organized hierarchically into groups with identifiers such as news, info (information), comp (computers), alt (alternative), misc (miscellaneous), soc (social), and k12 (K–12 education).

Messages posted to newsgroups may be seen by thousands of readers all over the world. Messages should be kept brief and purposeful. When responding to a message, a user should consider sending e-mail to the individual if the message would not be appropriate to the broader readership. Users should quote enough of the message in the reply to give a clear context to the response. Teachers should consider discouraging students from including personal information such as full names or addresses in messages, in order to protect their privacy.

Teachers should educate their students in appropriate use of the network (netiquette) and monitor their usage because some newsgroups contain material not suitable for minors. Many school districts and regional networks have developed **acceptable use policies (AUPs)** and require permission forms to be signed by both parents and students before allowing students access to the Internet (Appendix J). An acceptable use policy for an instructional setting might be thought of as similar to the laboratory safety contract that a science teacher might require. It would include a statement of the responsible behaviors expected of students, with particular attention to potentially unsafe or inappropriate actions, and a set of measured consequences. Parental notification demonstrates that the parents are aware of the instructor's intent and reasonable supervision in order to ensure the educationally productive use of classroom resources.

LISTSERVs

LISTSERVs may be thought of as e-mail by subscription. Groups of users develop around common topics or interests. Once a user joins, or subscribes to, a LISTSERV any message sent by that user will be distributed to all participants of the LISTSERV. That user will also receive all messages. It becomes important to delete read or unwanted messages in order to effectively manage your mailbox.

A word of caution: LISTSERVs can easily generate 40 or 50 messages a day that have to be read, saved to disk, or deleted. You can imagine how many messages might be waiting for you after summer vacation if you don't know how to turn off a LISTSERV before vacation. Don't oversubscribe to LISTSERVs. You will find that they require considerable time every day to deal with messages.

Databases

The Internet provides access to many types of databases, some accessible at no charge and others that charge an access fee. Some no-fee databases are campus directories, lists of people with Internet accounts and their addresses, library public access catalogs, and government databases.

It's fascinating to search the library catalogs at Harvard, UCLA, and Oxford. Once a resource is identified, even in a faraway library, it may be possible to borrow it with the assistance of the interlibrary loan department of your local library. You may even be surprised to discover that the same resource is available closer to home!

One Internet database useful to educators is The Eisenhower National Clearinghouse (ENC) for Mathematics and Science located at Ohio State University and funded by the U.S. Department of Education. Its purpose is to improve access to the most current materials in math and science resources in the nation. Descriptions and evaluations are available. ENC can be reached electronically at galileo.enc.org.

The Educational Resources Information Center (ERIC) provides access to its extensive collection of education-related literature, archives of LISTSERVs, and electronic library listings through a gopher server and e-mail inquiries directed to AskERIC@ericir.syr.edu.

Another government database, the Science and Technology Information System (STIS), contains announcements and reports of National Science Foundation activities, including grant-related information.

INTERNET NAVIGATION AND RETRIEVAL TOOLS

As you contemplate tens of thousands of networks serving millions of users around the world, you may think, "How can I possibly find my way through this maze?" There are a multitude of recently published books designed to guide users' explorations of the Internet available at your local library or bookstore. Several such references are listed at the end of this chapter, and many have been written by teachers based on their own classroom experiences. Evaluate their usefulness by realistically assessing your own level of expertise and skimming several sections to find one with a writing style and level of technical detail appropriate for you.

Because the Internet is a rapidly changing environment, the best and most current resources are always available online rather than in print. This places new users in the rather uncomfortable position of first needing to be online in order to gain access to the information necessary to effectively maximize their Internet use. However, there are several navigation and information retrieval tools that can be of great help. Those relying less on a graphic user interface are more efficient at slower modem speeds but are slowly fading from favor.

FTP

File Transfer Protocol (FTP) is used to transfer files between two remote computers. A user can **download** (copy) a file by using software designed for that purpose, providing the address for the remote site is known. Typically, a user must also have a valid user ID and sometimes a password. Many FTP sites allow the use of "anonymous" as a log-in or user ID and your e-mail address as the password. The same software and three pieces of information will be required on the rare occurrence when a user wishes to **upload** (send) a file to an FTP site. FTP remains an important process for educators to both send and receive files, especially for downloading educational software or for uploading a teacher- (or student-) designed web page to the file server that will be posting it. Fetch™ is a Macintosh FTP utility program developed at Dartmouth to provide "point and click" facilitation of this transfer process, and WS_FTP™ is a Microsoft Windows equivalent. Each is available to educational institutions without a licensing fee.

Gopher

The easiest way to understand a **gopher** is to think of it as a local menu of available files. It was originally created at the University of Minnesota and was named after its athletic teams' mascot (the Golden Gophers). It has since spread to Internet sites around the world. Client software in Macintosh or PC format on the user machine interfaces with server software on the remote site's computer. Before the advent of the World Wide Web, this text-based navigation tool was one of the most popular.

Archie

Archie is a service provided by McGill University in Montreal, Canada. It is an updated, integrated list of directories from participating anonymous FTP sites of the many host computers connected to the Internet. Using Archie greatly facilitates the search for information.

Veronica

Examining the names of the Internet tools mentioned so far, you've discovered that Internet users have a sense of humor: a burrowing rodent and names from comic strip characters of the past! There is a suspicion that the name **Veronica** was chosen to accompany Archie and then an acronym was later fabricated (*Very Easy Rodent-Oriented Netwide Index to Computerized Archives*). A user must go through a gopher in order to reach Veronica. It is a collection of gopher menus. In other words, Veronica is to Archie as Archie is to gophers.

It is evident that Veronica, Archie, and gopher are tools designed to support broadcast rather than serial searches for information. Rather than requiring the user to search a multitude of individual directories, those tools provide an umbrella that can be searched, ending up in one particular directory or file. The relationship among Veronica, Archie, and gopher menus is illustrated in Figure 11–4.

World Wide Web

World Wide Web (WWW) is an Internet navigation system developed at the European Centre of Particle Physics in Switzerland. Information is stored in a format that has addresses of other sites with similar information embedded in it. This is accom-

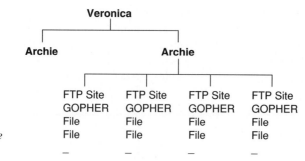

Figure 11–4

*Relationship of some
Internet tools*

plished through the use of **HTML** (HyperText Markup Language), which provides the means to display both text and graphics along with dynamic links both within the document and to other external Internet sites and **HTTP** (HyperText Transfer Protocol), the format by which World Wide Web documents are transferred over the Internet.

Web Browsers. A **web browser** is software that runs on the user's machine and translates HTML code delivered from a web server running on the remote site's computer. The World Wide Web is comprised of many **web sites,** each having a unique address. Each web site has at least one display referred to as a **web page.** The server software makes sets of web pages available for viewing with a web browser. One site may have a number of pages, each capable of displaying text, graphics, and dynamic links to other pages or sites. The main page of a web site is the one usually accessed first and is called its **home page**.

Mosaic™ for Macintosh, Windows, and other platforms was the first popular graphic user interface client software for information searching and retrieval. *Netscape Navigator*™ has since become one of the most popular browsers for the World Wide Web. Figure 11–5 is an example of a web page viewed by *Navigator*™. It is available as a stand-alone program or as part of a package, called *Netscape Communicator*™, that includes some sophisticated utilities that extend *Navigator's* functionality. It is one of the easiest tools to use, since it has all of the linking and graphics capability of *Mosaic*™, and it facilitates leaving a trail of sites browsed in order to determine your current location on the Internet. *Navigator*™ allows you to create **bookmarks** to identify sites so you can return to them easily. Your bookmarks, in fact, become your personalized directory of your favorite web pages. A bookmark may also be saved as an individual file that can be transferred electronically to another machine and then used to call up the web site. In addition, the entire set of bookmarks for a given computer can be saved as an HTML file that can be opened and viewed as a document in another computer's browser, complete with the individual bookmarks linked to their URLs. Educators can utilize these capabilities to provide for Internet-based lessons, with students directed to specific web locations in the order desired by the instructor. A recent version of *Netscape Navigator*™ has included an HTML editor to assist the user in creating or modifying web pages, as well as providing annotations for a bookmarks page. The most recent versions of

Figure 11-5

Netscape is a user-friendly graphic interface to the World Wide Web

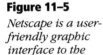

Navigator™ and *Communicator*™ may be downloaded at no cost by educational institutions from the Netscape site (http://www.netscape.com).

Microsoft Internet Explorer™ is a third graphical navigation tool, with some functional similarities to *Netscape Navigator*™. A version of this browser is used as the web browsing tool on America Online. It also allows the user to bookmark favorite sites and trace the user's path of Internet use. Versions of the *Netscape*™ and *Explorer*™ browsers are available for both the Macintosh and Windows platforms, and most are provided with free licenses for educational institutions.

Features common to most web browsers include the ability to print out the web page, giving students the means to capture information from the web. This print capability is important in a classroom or media center setting, where there are many students yet fewer computers with Internet connections, because it allows students to progressively get online, download some information, then free up the computer for another student. An even more efficient feature is the ability of most browsers to copy both text and images to temporary memory and save to disk. This is usually accomplished by highlighting the text desired and then using the Edit...Copy command to place the text in temporary (RAM) memory, and then using the Edit...Paste command to place the text into, for instance, a word processing document. Images can also be copied into memory or saved to disk by simply pressing down the mouse button while pointing at the image (the right mouse button in the case of Windows versions). Students should always properly cite their web sources, using the appropriate electronic citation style. These styles usually include the name of the web site, the address of the site, the author(s), the date of posting or revision, and the date the site was accessed by the student.

Uniform Resource Locator. The World Wide Web is often described as a system, but some may prefer to think of it as an index. Each site accessible by a browsing tool such as *Netscape™* or *Internet Explorer™* has a web page. Each site also has its own address, or **Uniform Resource Locator (URL)**. Typing a URL in the browsing tool connects the user with a computer at that particular location. The parts of a URL are explained in Figure 11–6. The user must type in the URL exactly, noting the use of either upper or lower case letters, along with the use and placement of characters such as the colon, slash, period, tilde, and underscore. Figure 11–7 shows four examples of URLs, addressing different communication methods on the Internet.

Search Engines. **Search engines** are commonly employed within many Internet applications, particularly through browsers, and usually as web sites of their own, to assist the user with the seemingly overwhelming task of finding specific information on the Internet. They are often considered as being in one of two categories: (1) directories or catalogs organized by subject areas and (2) true search engines that index the content of web sites. The process of searching is fundamentally similar to

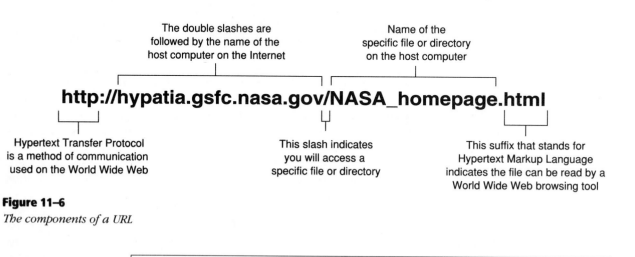

Figure 11–6

The components of a URL

Figure 11–7

Four types of Uniform Resource Locators (URLs)

- FTP file: ftp://quake.think.com/pub/etext/1992/zen10.txt
- Gopher site: gopher://gopher.nwnet.net:3333
- Telnet site: telnet//uwin.u.washington.edu
- Web page: http://www.wou.edu/research/library/refguide/citing.htm

that used to search through databases or in online library catalogs (which often can be accessed through **Telnet** on the Internet). That is, the user enters a search term, and then the directory or search engine looks through its database of Internet sites for the best matches. Some directories such as Yahoo™ (http://www.yahoo.com) provide additional categories and subcategories of information to assist in narrowing down the search. Search engines such as AltaVista™ (http://www.altavista.digital.com) search web pages for a match with any of the words posted on these pages and rely on Boolean connectors such as AND, OR, and NOT, as well as other qualifiers to narrow the search. Acknowledging its own limitations, Yahoo™ provides a link to AltaVista for its users who need to perform more sophisticated searches. Figure 11–8 compares the availability of some features found in a few popular directories and search engines.

There is even a search engine of search engines, MetaCrawler™ (http://www.metacrawler.cs.washington.edu), which checks each of several other search engines for the best match with the given search terms (see Figure 11–9). Teaching search strategies to students will pay off in a more efficient use of their time while online and will give them experience in the logical cognitive process of defining and narrowing a search for information.

Citations. Once information is found on the Internet, it should be cited appropriately. Users of the American Psychological Association (APA) style can find current general information in the APA Publication Manual Crib Sheet at http://www.gasou.edu/psychweb/tipsheet/apacrib.htm. The citation form varies for information retrieved from the World Wide Web, on-line chats, LISTSERVs, e-mail, on-line databases, and online encyclopedias. The basic form of the citation for the World Wide Web is as follows: author's name, (date of publication or last revision), document title, in title of complete work, [type of document], URL, (date visited Year, Month, Day). Users of the Modern Language Association (MLA) style can find current general information in the MLA Style Citations of Electronic Sources at http://www.cas.usf.edu/english/walker/mla.html. The basic form of the citation for the World Wide Web is as follows: author's name, document title, in title of complete work, date of publication or last revision, < URL >, (date visited Day, Month, Year).

	Alta Vista	Excite	InfoSeek	Lycos	Yahoo
Boolean operators allowed	√	√			
Case sensitive	√		√		
Required term qualifier	√	√	√		
Prohibited term qualifier	√	√	√		
Wildcard	√			√	
Confidence ranking	√	√	√	√	
Refine search based on first one		√			

Figure 11–8

Five search tools compared

MetaCrawler works by sending your queries to a number of existing free search engines, including Lycos, WebCrawler, Excite, AltaVista, Yahoo, HotBot, and Galaxy, organizes the results into a uniform format, and displays them.

MetaCrawler has many useful features, including
- **Complete Coverage**
  Each search service tends to produce a fairly unique set of references. Using the MetaCrawler, you're able to see one page that contains all of the references from each service.
- **Advanced Searching Syntax**
  MetaCrawler offers a powerful search syntax. In addition to any basic words, all words, and phrase options, MetaCrawler recognizes a special search syntax that allows you to describe your desired results very accurately.
- **Service Vote Rankings**
  MetaCrawler combines the confidence scores given to each reference by the services that return it. Thus, when MetaCrawler returns a reference, it sums the scores given by each service and presents them in a "voted" ordering.

One method for refining, MetaCrawler searches is to use MetaCrawler's advanced search syntax: when you create a search, specify groups of words by surrounding them in quotes. Also, specify words or phrases that must appear in documents by prefixing them with a plus sign, and prefix words or phrases that must not appear by prefixing them with a minus sign.

Some advanced search syntax examples:
- "George Washington" −president
- +"Incan civilization" Peru
- +football −Americano
- "PC operating systems" −windows −microsoft −"Bill Gates"

Please note that not all sources queried support these features. They are, therefore, only suggestions that MetaCrawler will use when tailoring each source's query.

webmaster@metacrawler.com

Figure 11–9

MetaCrawler, a search engine of search engines

Web Page Design. Web page design, either through programming in HTML on a text editor or through the use of **HTML editor** programs such as *PageMill™, Microsoft Front Page™,* and *Claris HomePage™,* is an excellent way to have either the teacher or the students present information on the web. Web pages can vary greatly in layout and content, but most include some standard HTML commands. These commands are always enclosed in brackets,<...>, and are usually "nested" so that one command at the beginning of a passage turns on a given function, and another command (usually denoted by a forward slash /) turns off that feature. Figure 11–10 is an example of a set of commands for a simple HTML document that would include a graphic, some formatted text, and a link to another web address. Examine its representation as a web page at the bottom of Figure 11–10.

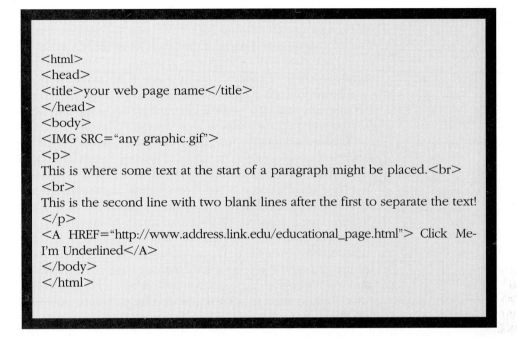

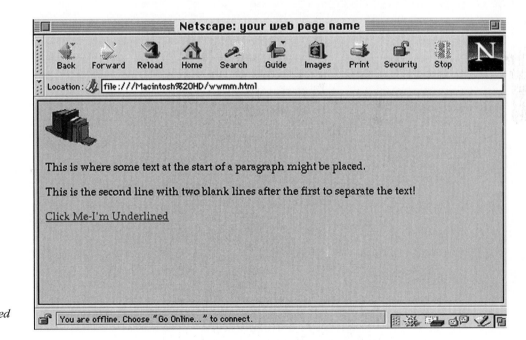

Figure 11–10

*Web page generated
by preceding text*

Figure 11–10 is just a preliminary design, but the reader will notice that most of the terms are paired, and that <IMG SRC> refers to a graphic image source that would appear near the top of the page, while the <A HREF=...> is a link to another web page, using its URL address. One approach to teaching web page design is to send students, via either e-mail or a text editing document, this set of commands as a boilerplate upon which to build their own page. Of course, there are many other refinements that may be added, and there are some excellent online HTML tutorials on the web, but the framework shown in Figure 11–10 is a possible start.

The fundamental approach is to begin publishing for the web using a simple page and then to elaborate as the skills or content needs develop. Publishing on the web is far more than just another mode of expression; it provides opportunities for interaction among individuals. A few words of caution: since publishing on the web is much like publishing in any other medium, the person or student group posting a web page is responsible for the accuracy of the content, which should be free of bias or at least with any biases clearly stated, and should have sources of information such as text and graphics accurately cited. It is also very helpful to the viewer of the page to be able to see the name of the person who developed the page, the date on which the page was posted or last revised, and an e-mail address so that the user could contact the developer directly. Students, however, should not post their photographs and complete names and addresses.

> "With the gigantic scope of the Internet, we realize that students could place themselves in jeopardy. We set some very simple rules for students to access the Internet in our lab:
>
> 1.   Ask a teacher for permission.
> 2.   A teacher must be present in the lab.
> 3.   Use good judgment in choosing sites.
>
> If any of the rules are broken, we follow these steps: 1) talk to students and make sure they understand the rules, 2) remove the student from the computer lab for the remainder of that class period, 3) contact the principal with a referral or a call home to parents to possibly set up a conference with the parents and student.
> We've not yet had to go beyond the second step."
>
> *Sandy Cummings, Teacher, Information Center*
> *West Valley/Hutchison Career Center, Fairbanks, AK*

CONTROLLING ACCESS TO THE INTERNET

One of the concerns frequently expressed by many teachers, school administrators, school boards, and parents is that of the potential for students to access Internet materials that are inappropriate for minors. These materials might be either intentionally or inadvertently located via one of the gophers or search engines and may include expressions or descriptions of violence, ethnic hatred, or pornography. As stated previously, it is advisable for the classroom teacher, school building, and school district to have workable acceptable use policies (AUPs) agreed to in writing prior to student use of the Internet. However, even with these in place, many educators are looking to a web **filter,** or blocking program (e.g. *Net Nanny™* or *Cyber Patrol™*), to screen out undesirable content. These are often effective in looking for key descriptive terms that may reside at Internet locations and thus block student access. However, they may also block an educationally valid search term that possesses meanings other than those appropriate for students of a specific age or ability. Perhaps the best policy, as with most educational functions, is to provide consistent expectations for student behavior, combined with diligent teacher supervision of student activities during the course of the Internet-based activity.

"We require a student and parental signature on the district form for e-mail accounts; we keep a copy and send the original to the system administrator, who sets up the accounts.

We do NOT require 'licenses' or signed permissions to use the world wide web 1) because students come as classes, and separating them into licensed users and those who are not would impair the instructional opportunity; 2) because it would be a paper trail nightmare.

We have 'rules of the road' on the information superhighway which I have distributed at several meetings. Essentially, I view the Internet as an instructional resource (like the reference books). Students are not to play games, 'chat', download without permission, subscribe to any on-line 'offers', or use bulletin board systems. Portland Public Schools has an acceptable use policy which applies to all computers on the PPS Network; therefore, I also prohibit subscribing to free e-mail services like 'HotMail' because students are not required to use their real names and be accountable for their communications. Students can telnet to other e-mail servers where they have accounts.

Audio files are distracting to other users.

We have a security system which allows you to set permissions for individual applications and deny access to the System Folder. I also lock the Netscape preferences and we do not use Netscape for e-mail.

We load the 'local' home page on each hard drive so as not to overload or be dependent on any one server. This is a major pain whenever you change the local home page because you have to reload the file on each machine, but it's proven its worth more than once. We manually empty the cache twice a day and rebuild the desktops regularly."

Janet Murray, Librarian
Wilson High School
Portland, OR

CURRICULUM APPLICATIONS OF THE INTERNET

A number of Internet activities have already been mentioned. Student and teacher use of e-mail to communicate with peers or with experts in a given field extends the classroom experience to begin the realization of what is rapidly becoming a "global schoolhouse." Databases and search engines assist both students and teachers in utilizing the encyclopedic quality of the vast array of content available on the Internet. However, just as it is a myth that merely placing a student in front of a computer will result in substantive learning, it is equally a myth that merely having access to the Internet will result in productive student acquisition and use of information. The immediacy of access, the sheer volume, and the dynamic quality of the information available is very different from that of previous media for storing and displaying knowledge. For instance, on July 4, 1997, the Pathfinder mission successfully landed the Sojourner rover on Mars. For the next week, 40 million to 45 million people around the world visited the NASA web site to view color images, similar to those in Figure 11–11, being transmitted from the Martian surface. Students and teachers need training in effective information retrieval strategies, methods of repurposing and incorporating properly cited information into student displays of learning, and evaluation of the currency and accuracy of information posted on the Internet. The following are just a few of the considerations and techniques teachers should be aware of when using the Internet.

Figure 11–11

Sojourner on the Martian surface

The rover has a panoramic view from the landing area   (NASA)

Classroom or media center access is usually through the channel of modem-based communications or via a "hard-wired" cable in a local-area network. The main differences are the provider costs to the school district, long-distance fees if by modem connection, the speed of information transfer, and the number of connected computers in any given setting. Speed of transfer is often crucial (this is where networked cable communications have the advantage), especially where the number of computers or the time available for student online access is limited. Teachers need to plan the time allotted to Internet access, as well as the placement of connected computers within a classroom. If there is a single computer, then the logistics of providing equity of access to all students or a display that can be viewed by the entire class become very important. Equality of access means that students are not limited by such features as age, gender, socioeconomic background, and experience in working with computers.

Teachers should plan the use of the Internet as they would any other media, with a clear set of objectives, appropriate preparation and integration into the unit of study, and methods of assessing and reporting student performance.

Generalized searches of the Internet are often useful for determining just what is available. Teachers should assist the students beforehand in the ways of stating terms that narrow and define their search if they are to avoid "information overload." Additionally, students need to understand the appropriate methods of citing electronic information, paying special attention to the person or organization posting that information, and when then information was posted or last revised.

More specific searches can be accomplished by several strategies. One such strategy is the "scavenger hunt." In this strategy, the students are given a list of terms or concepts to search for that perhaps all relate to the same topic or theme. The students are asked to report back on specific information, along with the URL they located it at. For example, when asked to find the number of airports in Burkina Faso, students must determine what Burkina Faso is, where it is, and the search tool that would most likely yield the answer. Though such a question might relate to a geography lesson, its primary purpose may be to refine search skills and acquaint the students with new information resources. A second strategy is to give students a specific set of bookmarks that they are to locate and then to provide specific questions or responses that the students need to respond to. Many Internet sites are particularly targeted to students and can provide interactive lessons of their own. Bookmarks can be distributed as simply as having the URLs typed on a handout, or more efficiently in a HTML document that could provide a given order for access along with some teacher annotations. Web pages can even be "whacked"— that is, copied—while online to have their images stored in a data-storage device (e.g., a hard-drive) for later instructional use by students viewing specifically saved sites. An interesting collaborative strategy is to give individual students, or teams of students, specific portions of an overall task and then to have them e-mail each other to share and combine what they have found. This furthers the concept of knowledge as a shared process of interaction that combines multiple sources and interpretations of information.

Once information has been located, students should have the opportunity to develop skills in evaluating the accuracy of the information, as well as the way it is displayed on the Internet site in order to become critical readers of web pages. Media literacy applies as much to the Internet as to any other medium such as television or print. A teacher-generated checklist or survey document can assist the students in making their evaluation. Figure 11–12 is a brief look at a few simple criteria that students might use in evaluating a web site.

In Figure 11–13, Don Descy (1996) has developed a thorough and sophisticated set of guidelines to evaluate on-line resources.

Several excellent sites exist on the Internet to provide examples of evaluation devices and strategies. Figure 11–14 identifies and links to a number of sites that contain useful evaluation guidelines. If you choose to look at this site, you will find more current links than contained in this illustration.

Students might wish to download and save some of the text or graphics and then integrate that information into a report or a web page. This raises the issue of copyright of electronic information. Usually, properly cited text or graphics, which are utilized for educational purposes and not redistributed for profit, fall within the "fair use" guidelines of copyright law. Students need to understand that information car-

---

Evaluating Web Sites

URL of the web page: http://_____

Does the page load quickly into your computer?	YES___	NO___
Do the pictures contribute useful information?	YES___	NO___
Do headings divide the page?	YES___	NO___
If so, are the headings helpful?	YES___	NO___
Does the page contain the author's name?	YES___	NO___
Does it have the author's e-mail address?	YES___	NO___
Is the information current?	YES___	NO___
Do you detect a particular bias in the information?	YES___	NO___
Was the information useful to you?	YES___	NO___

When was the page created? _____
When was it last updated? _____

Comments: Describe how you feel about this site. Was it valuable to you? Discuss its appearance and the quality of the information.

_____
_____
_____
_____
_____
_____

Figure 11–12

Simple criteria for evaluating web sites

Author: Who are the authors of the field? Does this author list any affiliations? Is there a "mail-to" or an e-mail address included? Have you tried to find other information about this author by a search of *Who's Who in Education, ERIC, Journals in Education (JIE),* or *Current Index to Journals in Education (CIJE)?* Is the author the creator of the information or a compiler of other information resources? Can you find a personal home page or a campus listing for this author?

Producer: Is the producer/affiliation of the page clearly noted? Was this produced by an organization? Is it a well-know professional organization or is it a relative unknown? Are the members professionals, advocates, or consumers? Does this organization have an inherent bias? Is there a way to contact the producer?

Site: Is the URL clearly noted? What is the ending suffix (.edu, .com, .org, .net, etc.)? Can you find out where it is located. Does it seem to make sense that a producer like this one would reside on a site like this?

Publication: Is this a single page or part of a series? Is the remainder of the series by the same author, a collection of authors, or an organization? Is this an abstract or the full text of an article or a presentation? Where was the article published or presentation given? Was it published by or presented at a nationally known organization or conference?

Purpose: What is the purpose of the document? Was it designed to inform others of new research, summarize existing research, advocate a position, or stimulate discussion?

Date of publication: When was the page placed on the Internet? When was it updated?

Arrangement: How difficult was it to find information related to the six guidelines presented above? Was the information clearly presented in a conspicuous place or was it missing altogether?

Intended audience: Who is the intended audience of this page (professionals, advocates, consumers, etc.)? Would the intended audience change the scope or slant of the information?

Coverage: Does the page cover the information that you need? Does the page include links to other references or backup information? Does the page itself contain substantive information or is it just a collection of links to other sources?

Writing style/reasoning: Is the information presented in a thoughtful, orderly, well-reasoned manner? Does the information appear to be well researched? Are assumptions and conclusions well documented? Is the information presented as fact or opinion? Can you detect any bias? Do the words tend to evoke strong emotions?

References: Is the page well documented? Are there links to any primary sources? Is the page referenced to information on the same server or to servers at different sites? How current or relevant are the references?

Figure 11–13

Guidelines for evaluating Internet resources (Adapted from Descy, [1996, February], Tech Trends copyright 1996 by the Association for Educational Communications and Technology. Reprinted with permission.)

WLMA ONLINE: Evaluating Web Sites
http://www.wlma.org/libint/evalweb.htm

Evaluation of Information Sources

This page by Alistair Smith contains pointers to criteria for evaluating information resources particularly useful to those selecting sites to include in an information resources guide.

Kathy Schrock's Web Evaluation Surveys

An excellent site that gives information to evaluate web sites and think critically about them.

Web Evaluation Form, by Dr. Nancy Everhart

A form that provides evaluation activities for examining web sites. It presents a rating scale for currency, content, authority, ease of navigation, experience, graphics, sound and video, treatment, and access.

Comparing and Evaluating Web Information Sources

Wise information users will give thought to the criteria suggested in this page by Jamie McKenzie.

Teaching Critical Evaluation Skills for World Wide Web Resources

A set of web pages that provides materials to assist in teaching how to evaluate the informational content of web resources. It focuses on teaching how to develop critical thinking skills, which can be applied to evaluating information found on web pages. Includes a great *PowerPoint™* presentation.

Thinking Critically About World Wide Web Resources

Points to consider regarding a source's value and reliability, written by Esther Grassian.

Figure 11–14

Adapted from Evaluating web sites on the Washington Library Media Association web site

ries the ownership of the individual or group of persons that originated it, even when it is posted on the Internet. Citation styles have been previously discussed, but it is especially important to note the URL where the information was obtained, along with the author's name if available.

The Internet is not just for student retrieval of information. There are many opportunities for educators to grow as professionals. E-mail communication with other teachers provides for sharing of lesson plans or the solutions to specific classroom problems and issues. Also, teachers in many different parts of the world can have their classes collaborate and share such things as environmental data, poetry and artwork, and discussions of various cultural points of view. Many professional organizations for educators have web pages posted, and many educational journals and sources of research information (e.g., ERIC) can be obtained on-line. Specialized sources of data provide the raw material for building curriculum and assessment and keep the educator up-to-date with local, state, and national standards in their particular content area.

Figure 11–15 is an example of a web site dedicated to archiving and sharing lesson plans in various curriculum areas. Its URL is http://faldo.atmos.uiuc.edu/CLA.

Collaborative Lesson Archive

The Collaborative Lesson Archive consists of an archive of lessons for grades preschool through high school. After choosing the appropriate grade level, the user is shown a hyperlinked list of subject areas available for that grade. By clicking on these hyperlinks, the user views the lessons available for that subject area. At every level of exploration, the user can print the information displayed to a local printer.

Contributions to the Collaborative Lesson Archive are made by the public. Contributors submit their noncopyrighted material and ideas and they will be installed in the archive, making them accessible to the public. Through this electronic forum, teachers from across the nation can collaborate asynchronously on ideas for lesson content, creating an archive that evolves and grows with time.

To submit your lessons or ideas to the archive, send electronically to chapman@uiatma.atmos.uiuc.edu or through U.S. mail to

William L. Chapman
Dept. of Atmospheric Sciences
University of Illinois at Urbana/Champaign
105 S. Gregory Ave.
Urbana, IL 61801
phone: (217) 333-6881
fax: (217) 244-4393

In the future, friendly user interfaces will be available so that contributors can automatically install their own lessons and units.

Figure 11–15

Collaborative Lesson Archive overview

Figures 11-18 through Figure 11–22 illustrate a few of the many web sites that are of particular interest to educators. The danger in identifying specific references on the Internet is that this dynamic structure is in a constant state of flux. New sites are added and existing sites are withdrawn. Hopefully, the sites represented in these illustrations possess a fair degree of longevity.

KidPub (Figure 11–18) at http://www.kidpub.org/kidpub contains thousands of stories written by children from all over the world. By accepting stories submitted by children in your classroom, it might motivate your students to write. It encourages reading and presents an opportunity for a look at different cultures.

The Children's Literature Web Guide (Figure 11–19) at http://www.ucalgary.ca/~dkbrown/ is a valuable resource of children's stories, authors, and book reviews. It contains excellent links to children's authors, stories, awards, movies, and television, as well as children's literature organizations.

A *21st Century Schoolhouse* (Figure 11–20) at http://www.viser.net/gs21/twensch.htm is an ambitious project begun in 1996 by two teachers, Molly Kellar and Andrew Goldstein, at South Salem High School in Salem, Oregon. They connected their students with high school students in Australia, South Africa, Israel, Brazil, and Japan to study the environment's sustainability for future generations. After working collaboratively for more than a year over the Internet, they brought 120 students from

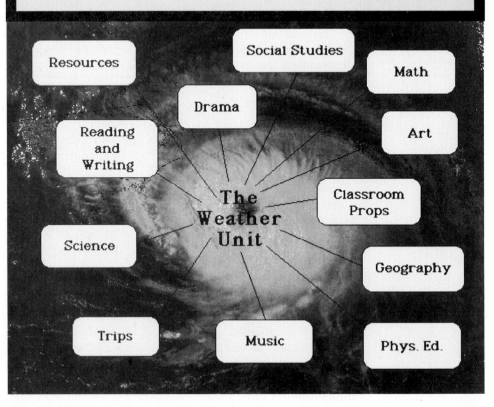

Welcome to the Collaborative Lesson Archive. Further information on how to use, submit to, or comment on this archive is available.

Lessons from this lesson database are intended for distribution to other educators on a nonprofit basis. If you should distribute, please cite the source.

Grade Levels

Preschool	Grade 6
Kindergarten	Grade 7
Grade 1	Grade 8
Grade 2	Grade 9
Grade 3	Grade 10
Grade 4	Grade 11
Grade 5	Grade 12

Other Internet Resources for Educators
Post Comments About the Archive
Read Comments About the Archive
Read Usage Reports

Figure 11–16

Collaborative Lesson Archive: Weather Unit

Weather Unit: Science Applications

Current Lessons Available

*Hey, You Stole My Rain!
*Precipitation
*Condensation
*Reflectivity and Absorption
*Evaporation
*The Seasons
*Light and Heat
*The Water Cycle
*Day and Night
*Direct and Diffuse
*Our Town
*The Rain Game
*Night Creatures
*Country Climates

Return to Weather Unit Home Page

Lesson: The Water Cycle

Prerequisites
*Evaporation   *Condensation   *Precipitation

Objectives
1.   Prepare terrariums for initial observations.
2.   Use terrariums to connect concepts of precipitation, condensation, and evaporation into a unified water cycle concept.

Materials
*Have each student supply his or her own plastic salad container from a fast-food restaurant or a similar clear plastic container. (A ziplock baggie will work if there are not enough salad containers available.)
*soil
*water
*spray bottle
*large, sunny window or grow light
*quickly and reliably germinating seeds (marigolds, herbs, lima beans, etc.)

Introduction
Ask: "What are clouds? What are they made of? What is rain? What does the sky look like when it rains? Why does it rain? Where does the rain go after it falls? What happens to puddles after it rains?" Get a discussion going about the different parts of the water cycle: evaporation, precipitation, and condensation. Use as many questions as possible to determine which concepts the students understand and where any misconceptions may be.

Figure 11–17

Collaborative Lesson Archive: Weather Unit/The Water Cycle

Body

1. Assemble the terrariums: have each student build his or her own terrarium by putting about an inch of soil in the bottom of the plastic container, planting a seed according to the package instructions, and giving a thorough soaking of water. The initial watering should be all that is necessary, since the plastic container will create a closed environment, which will not allow the water to escape into the atmosphere. Label the terrariums and put them in a sunny window or under a grow light.

2. Observe the terrariums: have the students make observations about their terrariums each day and record their observations in their weather journals. Try to do the observations at different times each day. Have the students record what they see in writing and/or in pictures. Discuss as a class anything the students observe. Continue this throughout the lessons on the water cycle (evaporation, condensation, precipitation).

3. Proceed through the following lessons in this order: evaporation, condensation, precipitation.

Conclusion

Possible questions to ask the students: "We only watered the soil in our terrariums once; how did the water get on the lid? Take your lid off the terrarium and feel the soil; why is the soil still wet? Do you think that any water has evaporated from the soil? Why? If water evaporated, where did the evaporated water go? Did it ever rain in your terrarium? How do you know? Where did the rain come from? Is there anything in your terrarium that reminds you of a cloud or cloud drops?

The teacher may want to make a connection between the water cycle in the terrarium and in the real world, with a discussion using the following: "if the terrarium is a model of the real world, what do you see outside that reminds you of the plant in your terrarium? reminds you of the soil in your terrarium? reminds you of the small water droplets on the lid? The soil in your terrarium stays moist; the ground outside never dries out completely. Why? What keeps it moist? What collects on the lid of the terrarium; water also collects in the sky as clouds; where does the water in the clouds come from?

Evaluation

1. Have the students make a picture model in their weather journal that represents their terrariums. Have the students include all the parts of the terrarium such as container, soil, water, lid, and plants. Also, have them draw and label the process (evaporation, condensation, precipitation) they see happening and their locations in the terrarium.

2. Have the students complete the water cycle page in their weather journal by labeling the evaporation, condensation, and precipitation processes.

Follow-Up Lessons
*Willy the Water Molecule
*Debate: Hey, You Stole My Rain!

About the Authors
Post Comments About the Unit
Read Comments About the Unit
Return to Weather Unit Home Page

Figure 11–17
(Continued)

Figure 11–18

KidPub (Courtesy of KidPub Worldwide Publishing.)

the six high schools together to join with prominent scientists and political leaders in an environmental conference in the United States, thanks to a grant they received.

C.I.A. Publications (Figure 11–21) at http://www.odci.gov/cia/publications/pubs.html, maintained by the Central Intelligence Agency, is an excellent resource for any geography or current events class. The high-quality maps are current and may be downloaded. The World Factbook alone is worth a visit to this site.

Louisiana Lessons (Figure 11–22) at http://www.challenge.state.la.us/k12act/index.html, funded by the Louisiana Challenge Grant, is not only a phenomenal resource for teachers in the state of Louisiana but also a valuable source of ideas for lesson plans, collaborative projects, and multidisciplinary units at a variety of grade levels for teachers everywhere.

A growing trend in distance education is to encourage instructors to present either their entire course, or its supporting materials, by means of a web page. Students access these pages in order to read instructional materials, download or submit assignments, and communicate with both the instructor and other students via

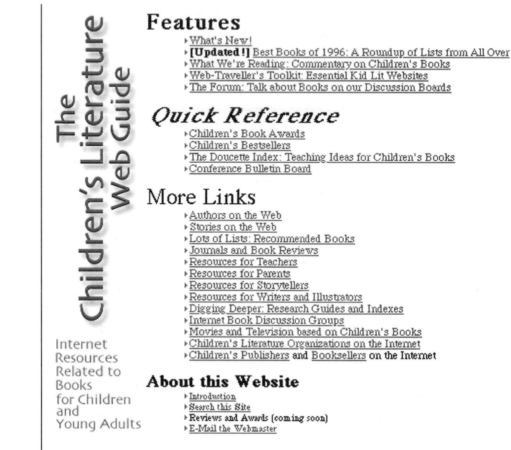

Figure 11–19

The Children's Literature Web Guide

e-mail. This method of delivery opens many opportunities for instruction of students whose access to education is limited by either distance or physical impairment. Perhaps most important, the Internet offers the means for the teacher to connect to a global educational system and to transition from being the source of any and all information in the classroom to being a facilitator of student skills in locating, retrieving, evaluating, assimilating, repurposing, and displaying the ever-increasing amount of information available on the Internet.

SUMMARY

The Internet is a network of networks that spans the globe, serving millions of users. The primary resources available are e-mail, electronic bulletin boards, databases, LISTSERVs, and information posted on World Wide Web pages. Tools such as gopher, Archie, Veronica, FTP, and the graphical web browsers are available to navigate this labyrinthine packet-switched network.

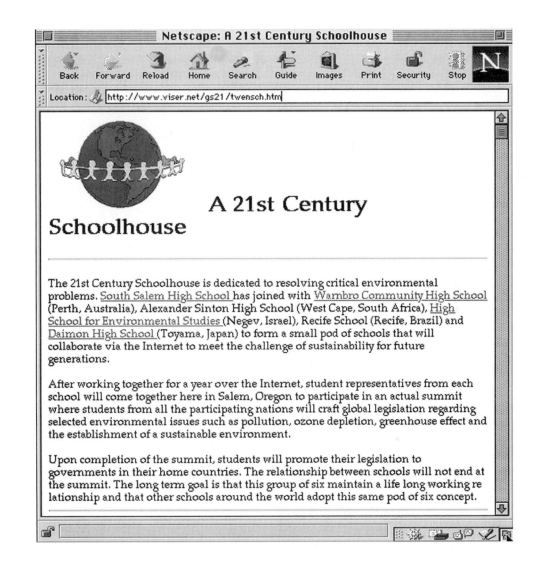

Figure 11–20

A 21st Century Schoolhouse

The World Wide Web is an Internet navigation system in which information is stored in a format that has addresses of other sites with similar information embedded in it. This navigation is accomplished through the use of HyperText Markup Language (HTML), which provides the means to display both text and graphics, along with dynamic links both within the document and to other, external Internet sites. Each site also has its own Uniform Resource Locator (URL), or address.

Web browser software on the user's machine translates HTML and interfaces with server software on the remote computer's web site. Each web site has at least one display, referred to as a web page. The main page of a web site is the one usually accessed first and is called its home page.

Search engines are commonly employed to assist the user with the task of finding specific information on the Internet. The user enters a search term or terms, along

Keyword Search C.I.A. Publications

* The World Factbook 1996

* 1995 Factbook on Intelligence

* Chiefs of State and Cabinet Members of Foreign Governments Updated: May12, 1997

* Handbook of International Economic Statistics, 1996

* Persian Gulf War Task Force

* Intelligence in the War of Independence

* 1997 CIA Maps and Publications Updated: June 19, 1997 -- PDF Version

* The Balkans Regional Atlas

* DCI and DDCIs of Central Intelligence

* Intelligence Literature: Suggested Reading List

* Search our GILS records! -- Hosted by the Government Printing Office (GPO)

* Keyword Search These Publications

http://www.odci.gov/cia/publications/pubs.html

Figure 11–21

C.I.A. Documents

with qualifying terms or connectors such as AND, OR, and NOT, and then the search engine looks through its database of Internet sites for the best matches.

Publishing on the World Wide Web begins with a simple page and then elaborates as the user's skills or content needs develop. Publishing on the web provides opportunities for interaction among individuals. The person or group posting a web page is responsible for using accurate content, free of bias, or at least with any biases clearly stated, and with sources of information such as text or graphics accurately cited.

Telecommunications offers significant advantages to the educator who wishes to collaborate with colleagues, access current information, and expose students to a

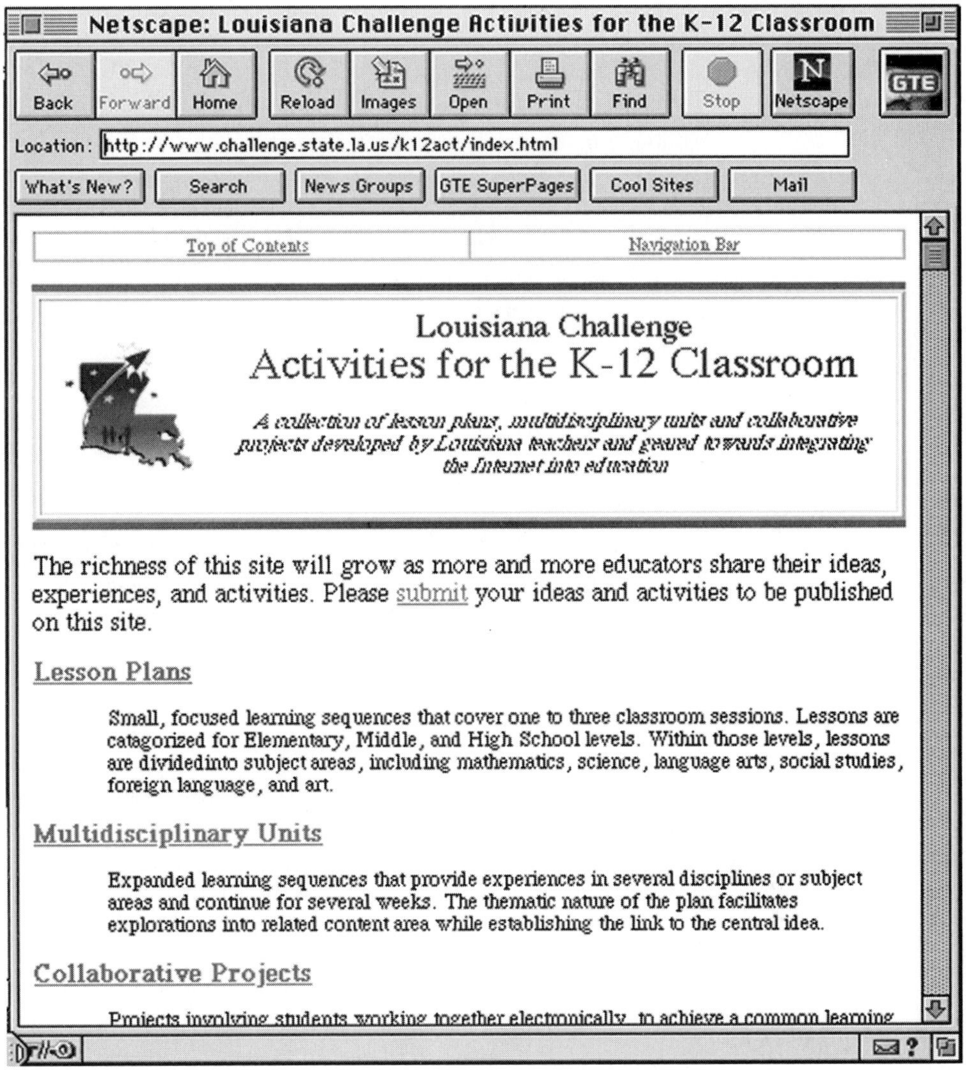

Figure 11–22

A lesson plan project (Courtesy of the Louisiana Challenge Grant.)

broad range of cultures and curricular resources. Electronic networks overcome traditional barriers of social and geographic isolation, facilitate interactive and cooperative learning, and serve as highly effective motivators to reluctant writers. In particular, the Internet allows students to construct their own knowledge; promotes the use of technology as a powerful resource tool; enables collaboration between and among students through various projects and thematic units; provides a global perspective and interchange of ideas; allows teachers to individualize student instruction; and encourages the use of technology as a tool and enabler.

Netscape: Louisiana Challenge Activities for the K-12 Classroom

Back | Forward | Home | Reload | Images | Open | Print | Find | Stop | Netscape | GTE

Location: http://www.challenge.state.la.us/k12act/index.html

What's New? | Search | News Groups | GTE SuperPages | Cool Sites | Mail

Small, focused learning sequences that cover one to three classroom sessions. Lessons are categorized for Elementary, Middle, and High School levels. Within those levels, lessons are divided into subject areas, including mathematics, science, language arts, social studies, foreign language, and art.

Multidisciplinary Units

Expanded learning sequences that provide experiences in several disciplines or subject areas and continue for several weeks. The thematic nature of the plan facilitates explorations into related content area while establishing the link to the central idea.

Collaborative Projects

Projects involving students working together electronically, to achieve a common learning goal. These collaborative projects are designed to integrate Internet technology into the curricula and to foster communication and cooperation across previously untraveled avenues. Join a project or post a call for collaboration.

Louisiana Lessons

Read about a special feature of some of the lessons, units, and projects (denoted by) in our classroom activities library. Learn how you can submit your classroom activity and become published on the World Wide Web.

| Top of Page | Top of Page Content |

| Challenge Resource Hotlist | Activities for the K-12 Classroom | Teacher Education |

| Educational Resources | Louisiana Challenge Homepage |

14744 hits since Jul 23 '97 | Guide | Feedback | Guestbook | Disclaimer | Revision Information |

Figure 11–22
(Continued)

CHAPTER EXERCISES

1. Using the Acceptable Use Policy from your campus and/or those shown in Appendix J of this text as guides, design an AUP that might fit the requirements of an individual classroom in which you are or might be teaching. Try to incorporate parental notification and involvement in reinforcing responsible Internet use by students.

2. Put together an Internet scavenger hunt for a particular theme or content area. This should include descriptions of the relevant information to be found, a

space for the answer, and another space for the recording of the URL. This activity may need to include instructions on appropriate search strategies.

3. Put together a set of bookmarks for the Internet browser program you are using. These should be organized into "folders" according to the nature or purpose of the Internet sites, using, for instance, the Window...Bookmarks feature of the *Netscape™* browser. The site titles could also be annotated with your own descriptive text, placed in any order you choose, and then saved as a separate bookmarks file for distribution to students.

4. Do an Internet search for information on the copyright requirements for electronic media. How does the "fair use" provision apply to information (text or graphics) downloaded from the Internet?

5. Put together a simplified style manual for citing Internet sources that would be useful to a specific group of K–12 students. For guidelines, do an Internet search for on-line style manuals such as those for the MLA and the APA.

6. Design a form for students to use in evaluating Internet sites for content accuracy or completeness, currency of information, purpose of the site, authorship, date of posting or most recent revision, degree of interactivity, appropriate use of graphics, and useful links to related sites.

7. Using HyperText Markup Language (HTML) and the suggested template from this chapter, design your own World Wide Web page to include a title, some text, a graphic (image source), and a link to another page (H REF). For additional help, do a search for some of the several online HTML tutorials that are available.

8. Pick out a topic or theme that you wish to explore, and then compare several Internet search engines for their ease of use, cataloging of sites, speed of finding information, and use of logical terms to help narrow your search.

9. Design a classroom lesson plan that in some way incorporates the use of the Internet by students. This use could involve free exploration, guided searching, accessing specific sites, or e-mail communications with other individuals but should definitely include the prerequisite skills, on-line activities, educational objectives (desired outcomes), and assessment criteria for student performance.

10. Communicate via e-mail with the author (or webmaster) of a World Wide Web site, perhaps conveying such things as what you thought about the design of his or her site, its accuracy or completeness, its instructional usefulness, a question for clarification or further information, or related sites you have found.

11. Using a search engine, locate some web sites for education-related or content area professional organizations. Compare what these sites have to offer in terms of useful professional information, communication of the dates and session topics for upcoming or past conferences, or benefits for organization members. If possible, look for ways in which you can communicate with other individuals interested in your field. There may be a sign-up form for you to join a particular LISTSERV in order to receive more information.

12. Investigate the sites for Internet filtering programs. See if there are demonstration versions of these programs available. Compare their claims as to ease of operation, methods of filtering (e.g., keyword), appropriate settings for use, and the relative completeness of filtering inappropriate sites.

GLOSSARY

Acceptable Use Policies (AUP) Statements of access privileges, legitimate uses of online materials, and the behaviors expected of individuals while using on-line resources.

Archie An updated, integrated list of directories from participating anonymous FTP sites of the one million-plus host computers connected to the Internet.

bookmarks A feature of World Wide Web browser programs that allows the user to save and organize the URLs of desired Internet sites.

download To transfer a file from a remote computer to a local one.

filter An Internet tool that monitors specific site contents in order to screen out that which might be considered inappropriate in certain context (such as within an educational setting).

FTP (file transfer protocol) A set of standards facilitating the transfer of files between two computers over a network.

gopher A local menu of files available to users at remote sites on the Internet. Client software on the user machine interfaces with server software on the remote site's computer.

home page Usually the first web page accessed at a web site, it often includes links to other web pages within that site or at other web sites. This term is also given to the web page that may be specified to be accessed by a web browsing program when that program is first opened or when the "home button" is selected within the program.

HTML (HyperText Markup Language) A programming language that allows the user to post a World Wide Web document with text, graphics, and dynamic links to other web sites.

HTML editor A program designed to streamline the process of building a web page through the automation of adding certain HTML language code. Many editors provide the ability to visualize what the web page will look like when opened in a web browser.

HTTP (HyperText Transfer Protocol) The format by which World Wide Web documents are transferred over the Internet (every WWW address begins with "http://. . .").

Internet The Internet is a worldwide network of networks based on the TCP/IP protocol.

LISTSERV E-mail available by subscription to user groups that develop around common topics or interests. A message sent by a subscriber will be distributed to all participants of the LISTSERV. That subscriber will also receive all messages.

Microsoft Internet Explorer™ A popular web browser available for both Macintosh and Windows platforms.

Mosaic™ One of the original graphical browsers used to access information on the web. It has continued to evolve but has been replaced in popularity by other browsers.

Netscape Navigator™ A popular web browser available for Macintosh, Windows, and other platforms.

search engines Web tools that allow the user to search for desired web sites based on a set of search criteria, including keywords and logical connectors (e.g., AND, OR, NOT)

Telnet A remote login function that allows a user to log onto another computer connected to the Internet and thus utilize the resources of that computer.

Transmission Control Protocol/Internet Protocol (TCP/IP) A set of standards developed to allow different networks to interconnect electronically.

Uniform Resource Locator (URL) The address of any site on the Internet, including gopher and the World Wide Web sites.

upload To transfer a file from a local computer to a remote one.

Veronica A collection of gopher menus that must be accessed through a gopher.

web browser A graphic user interface program used to display text, graphics, and dynamic links on a web page. It also contains functions that facilitate the downloading of files and maintenance of bookmarks referencing favorite web sites.

web page A document written in HTML that is displayed by a web browser. It can contain text, graphics, and links to other pages.

web sites Locations within the World Wide Web that reside on a web server computer and is identified by a URL.

World Wide Web An Internet navigation system that allows users, through a graphic browser interface, to access information organized on hypertext-linked screens called pages.

REFERENCES & SUGGESTED READINGS

Barron, A., Ivers, K., & Sherry, L. (1994-95, December/January). Telnet activities on the Internet. *The Computing Teacher, 22*(4), 12–15.

Brandt, D. S. (1996). Evaluating information on the Internet. *Computers in Libraries, 16*(5), 44–46.

Campbell, D., & Campbell, M. (1995). *The student's guide to doing research on the Internet*. Reading, MA: Addison-Wesley.

Cowan, H. (1996, September). The net—And how to use it. *Electronic Learning, 16*(1), 21.

Descy, D. E. (1994, September). World Wide Web: Adding multimedia to cyberspace. *Tech Trends, 39*(4), 15–16.

Descy, D. E. (1996, September). Evaluating Internet resources. *Tech Trends, 41*(4), 3–5.

Dickinson, K. (1997, March). Distance learning on the Internet: Testing students using web forms and the computer gateway interface. *Tech Trends, 42*(2), 43–46.

Forcht, K. A., & Fore, R. E. III. (1995). Security issues and concerns with the Internet. *Internet Research: Electronic Networking Applications and Policy, 5*(3), 23–31.

Goodrich, T. (1994, November/December). Mining the Internet: Tools for access and navigation. *Syllabus, 8*(3), 16–22.

Grassian, E. (1995). *Thinking critically about World Wide Web resources.* (http://www.library.ucla.edu/libraries/college/instruct/critical.htm)

Gray, T. (1997, September). No crazy gods. *Learning and Leading with Technology, 25*(1), 40–45.

Harris, J. (1994, February). People-to-people projects on the Internet. *The Computing Teacher, 21*(5), 48–52.

Harris, J. (1994, April). *Opportunity in work clothes: Online problem solving project structures.* (http://www.ed.uiuc.edu/Mining/April94-TCT.html)

Heide, A., & Stillborn, L. (1996). *The teacher's complete & easy guide to the Internet.* Trifolium Books.

Lamb, A., Smith, N., & Johnson, L. (1997, April). Wondering, wiggling, and weaving: A new model for project- and community-based learning on the web. *Learning and Leading with Technology, 24*(7), 6–13.

McKeon, J. (1993, October). Building vehicles for the information highway. *Communications Industry Report, 1*, 6.

Milheim, W. (1997, March). Instructional utilization of the Internet in public school settings. *Tech Trends, 42*(2), 19–23.

Roberts, L. (1997, May). Web searching made easy. *Learning and Leading with Technology, 24*(8), 60–62.

Roblyer, M. D. (1997, September). Predictions and realities: The impact of the Internet on K–12 education. *Learning and Leading with Technology, 25*(1), 54–56.

Ryder, R. J., & Hughes, T. (1997). *Internet for educators.* Englewood Cliffs, NJ: Merrill.

Scholz, A. (1996). *Evaluating World Wide Web information.* (http://thorplus.lib.purdue.edu/research/classes/gs175/3gs175/evaluation.html)

Sellers, J. (1994, February). *Answers to commonly asked "primary and secondary school Internet user" questions.* IETF School Networking Group, Internet FYI RFC1578.

Sugrue, B., & Kobus, R. (1997, March). Beyond information: Increasing the range of instructional resources on the World Wide Web. *Tech Trends, 42*(2), 38–42.

Valenza, J. (1997, February). Handling citations, cyber-style. *Electronic Learning, 16*(4), 60–61.

Williams, B. (1996). *The World Wide Web for teachers.* San Mateo, CA: IDG Books.

Wresch, W. (1997). *A teacher's guide to the information highway.* Englewood Cliffs, NJ: Merrill.

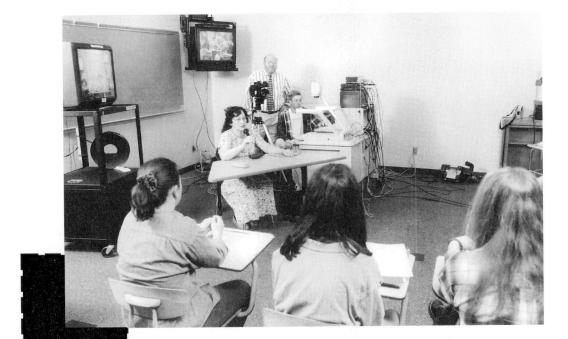

Chapter 12

Multimedia

ADVANCE ORGANIZER

1. What is multimedia?

2. What are some multimedia authoring tools?

3. What hardware is often associated with multimedia?

4. What are desktop presentation programs and how do they relate to multimedia?

5. How might you use desktop presentations?

6. What is virtual reality and why is it being called the ultimate multimedia experience?

7. How does communication in virtual reality differ from communication in other modes of learning?

8. What promise does virtual reality hold for education?

Many years ago, Edgar Dale (1969) developed a model for learning that became known as the "Cone of Experience." This model, as shown in Figure 12–1, illustrates a continuum from direct, purposeful experiences directly involving the learner, located at the base of the cone, to abstract symbols that learners passively observe at the top of the cone. *Multimedia* was missing when Dale constructed this model in 1946, but it fits neatly in the mid section of the cone. The terms *multimedia* and *cross-media* surfaced several years later in the 1950s as educators combined various media in support of each other to heighten the effect on learning.

For more than 50 years, educational researchers have been telling us that people learn better when they are involved in their learning, and that involvement increases as more senses are used by the learner to acquire information. Thus, multimedia technologies, which can provide stimulating and interactive, multisensory experiences to learners, can help teachers improve the quality and the appeal of their instruction.

Members of the Association for Educational Communications and Technology (AECT), as professional educators, have led the way in showing the power of various instructional media (sounds and projected and nonprojected images, for example) on learning. Multimedia is certainly multidimensional and multisensory and has great potential for involving the user. We've known about the benefits of multimedia for a while now, so what's all the recent hype about? Multimedia has gone digital! The familiar "low-tech" slide series accompanied by synchronized audiotapes with perhaps film clips thrown in have given way to personalized "high-tech" expe-

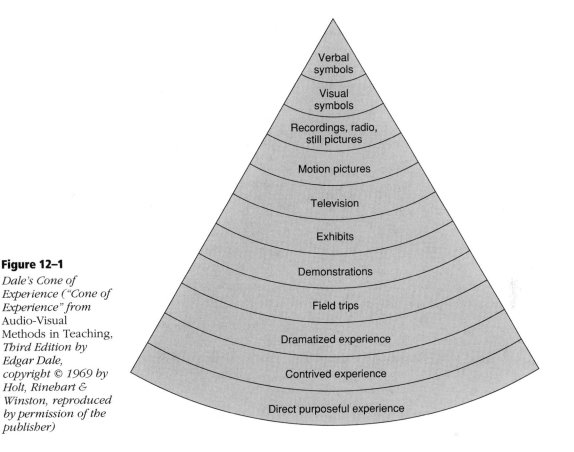

Figure 12–1

Dale's Cone of Experience ("Cone of Experience" from Audio-Visual Methods in Teaching, *Third Edition by Edgar Dale, copyright © 1969 by Holt, Rinehart & Winston, reproduced by permission of the publisher)*

riences of sounds, images, animation, and movies presented to the user on a computer screen. The impact of digital technology on multimedia is impressive. Digital multimedia has made it possible for the learner to navigate through combinations of sights and sounds as never before. For educators, the opportunity to involve students so directly in learning and problem solving is one of multimedia's most appealing qualities.

MULTIMEDIA: HYPERTEXT AND HYPERMEDIA

Digital **multimedia** is a relatively recent development that allows a computer user to combine and control a number of instructional resources in order to present information. Its power lies in its ability to network information resources and to provide ready access to the learner. As suggested by Figure 12–2, some multimedia computer programs may be used to control the presentation of video information from external sources such as videotape or videodisc, as well as graphic, audio, and textual information from CD-ROM. This audio and video information is presented

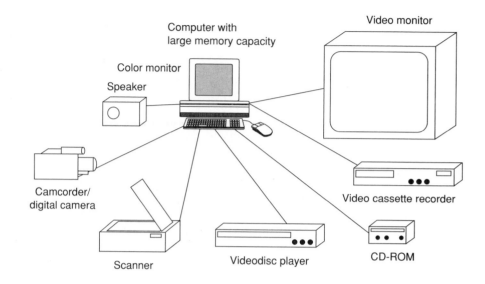

Figure 12–2

Equipment supporting multimedia

to the user under the control of the computer. Other programs may be totally self-contained, with all data stored on an optical disk and the information presented to the user through the computer's monitor and speaker.

Multimedia presentations can create multisensory learning experiences for students. As a teaching tool, for example, commercially prepared or teacher-designed multimedia programs might include the use of textual, graphic, audio, and video materials to convey information to the user, who would interact with it by reading, listening, observing still and moving images, and navigating through options presented on the screen. As a learning tool, not only can students navigate through this rich medium as they search for information from which to construct knowledge, but they can also express themselves in a number of ways as they author multimedia reports. Features that underlie the power of multimedia as a teaching and learning tool are listed in Figure 12–3.

Multimedia allows students to create their own visuals and incorporate them into their products and to navigate in original and customized ways through existing resources. It gives the student control of powerful tools in the exploration and creation of information. A camcorder, digital camera, optical scanner, CD-ROM drive, videodisc player, and video cassette recorder all become potential information-gathering tools. Multimedia tools allow a student to create a complex statement that might include computer-generated sound, graphics, and animation, along with sound and visual forms stored in another medium such as videodisc, videotape, or CD-ROM.

While normal text written on a page is designed to be read in a linear fashion from beginning to end, hypertext is a nonlinear way of representing text. Because the meaning of the text in this medium doesn't depend on sequential ordering, readers can access information according to their own interests and needs, thus giving them much more control in the reading process.

• **Text**	Text can be presented in an attention-getting manner. Text may be selected and made into a *button* or *link*.
• **Graphics**	Graphics can be created or imported. Photographs, video still frames, and scanned images can be imported as well.
• **Animation**	Graphics and text can be animated to illustrate concepts.
• **Sound**	Digitized sounds can be captured from a microphone, audio recorder, or CD-audio disk. Sounds can be used for an attention-getting effect or to clarify a concept.
• **Video**	Digitized video, a powerful instructional medium, can be captured from a camcorder, VCR, CD-ROM, and other sources.
• **Data storage**	Database capabilities allow the student to search for information or can be used by the teacher to record and analyze a student's performance.
• **Integration**	Integration with audio and video storage devices and with the Internet facilitates direct access to information by the user.
• **Navigation**	The user controls the pace and usually the level of difficulty of the material covered by a response ranging from a simple keystroke or mouse click to text entry and evaluation. Links can be established to internal information or external devices, giving the user a good deal of control in moving from one concept to another.

Figure 12–3

Features found in multimedia programs

To understand how hypertext works, think of the analogy of a Rolodex. Each information screen is seen as a card. Cards can be arranged in any order and a user can navigate among the cards in a nonlinear manner. Cards are grouped into logical units, or stacks, and a user can navigate between stacks in a seamless fashion. Navigation, in most instances, is accomplished by clicking buttons. **Buttons** can be visible objects or invisible areas of the screen, often covering images or text. Buttons can be programmed using a scripting language to perform certain actions such as linking to another card or controlling another device.

Hypermedia embeds hypertext elements into multimedia. The cards in a hypermedia stack might contain text, but they also might provide users with information in other forms. Hypermedia programs can contain text, graphics, and sounds on their cards, and they can play animation sequences or compressed video clips. They can even reach into cyberspace by sending a URL to a web browser such as *Netscape Navigator*™. The term *hypermedia* has largely given way to *multimedia*. It is now expected that digital multimedia programs contain the navigation control elements of hypermedia.

To illustrate this concept, imagine that you are using a multimedia geography program and that you are looking at a screen of information about a country. Buttons on that screen may lead you to additional text-based information about that country such as lists of products exported, population statistics, or climate conditions. Other buttons could also lead you to graphical information in the form of topographical or political maps, to an audio clip playing a traditional song, or to a digitized film clip on the World Wide Web recorded from yesterday's evening newscast of the country's president delivering a speech to the United Nations Assembly.

MULTIMEDIA HARDWARE

Now that you understand what multimedia and hypermedia are, you are probably wondering about the hardware that supports these multisensory products and presentations. The trend in multimedia hardware development is in line with the paradigm shifts identified in Chapter 1: equipment is becoming smaller, more portable, less costly, and more user-friendly. The most noteworthy developments in multimedia hardware are in the categories of display devices and optical storage devices.

Display Devices

Most multimedia formats are designed for small groups and individual users. A high-resolution color monitor with a pair of high-quality stereo speakers or headphones are the only pieces of display equipment required.

Display devices for multimedia desktop presentations must be appropriate for the size of the audience. A 25-inch color monitor may be adequate for viewing by a small group of a dozen or fewer viewers. Larger group sizes call for devices such as video projectors or overhead display panels capable of displaying larger images.

Video projectors capable of handling data transmitted from computers range from large, expensive devices usually permanently mounted to the ceiling to small, portable, fairly inexpensive ones often fastened for the sake of security to a rolling equipment cart. In a school setting, these are often housed in a library media center and circulated from there. Just as printers are configured to accept parallel or serial transmissions (or both), video display devices accept a certain signal transmission. Most video projectors are capable of accepting an RGB signal and an NTSC composite signal, which are common standards.

Overhead display panels, often called LCD panels, have become somewhat popular as large image display devices. They are moderately priced and are capable of displaying high resolution, color, and full motion. They are placed on the stage of the overhead projector. They require a considerably stronger light source than the typical overhead transparency and, in fact, may require the dimming of room lights for the projected image to be fully appreciated. Video projectors, with their considerably higher light output, have an advantage in situations where room light control is an issue.

Optical Storage Devices

Technological developments in laser disk optical storage have greatly facilitated the development of multimedia. Due to the vast amount of information present in multimedia programs, this technology has demanded a great deal of external memory

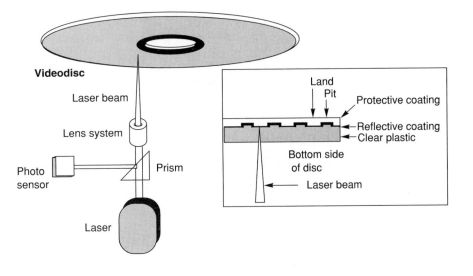

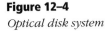

Figure 12–4

Optical disk system

storage. Traditional floppy disks and even hard disks were inadequate. Optical disk technology with storage capacity measured in Gigabytes provided the answer.

As shown in Figure 12–4, a laser beam reads a precise series of tiny depressions (or pits) and smooth reflective areas (called lands) on the bottom surface of an optical disk. The lands reflect the laser beam to a photo sensor and the pits diffract the light beam. The recorded tracks composed of these pits are either spiral or concentric circles that can contain information in either analog or digital form. The length of each pit and the distances between them determine the data in the videodisc format, and the videodisc player translates them to analog video while reading an index code and audio in a digital manner. The data in a CD-ROM, however, are represented in terms of the transition between pit and land in a digital manner. Present systems are read-only memory (ROM), produced by a publisher; write once, read many (WORM), created by the user; or erasable systems. The optical disk reader or player employs a laser beam to detect the pits and then decodes the data into the original information to be displayed on a video screen or printed as hard copy.

Figure 12–5 shows a photograph taken by a scanning electron microscope of pits and lands on a CD-ROM surface. The photograph is a magnification of 2,000x.

Videodisc. The first of the optical technologies, **videodisc,** was commercially introduced in 1978 and has been aimed primarily at the education/training, sales/promotion, and consumer recreation markets. A 12-inch disc can contain up to 54,000 different images per side and two continuous audio tracks. (Imagine a carousel slide tray containing 54,000 color slides!) The information may be displayed as still pictures, drawings, or up to 120 minutes of live video and audio.

Videodiscs are classified as either **CLV** (constant linear velocity), in which a single track is recorded as a spiral divided into data sectors of equal length, or **CAV** (constant angular velocity), whose tracks are recorded as concentric circles with radial data sectors. CLV discs allow for extended play time but are not frame-addressable, meaning that a search of a CLV disc is limited to playing time or to an arbitrary break called

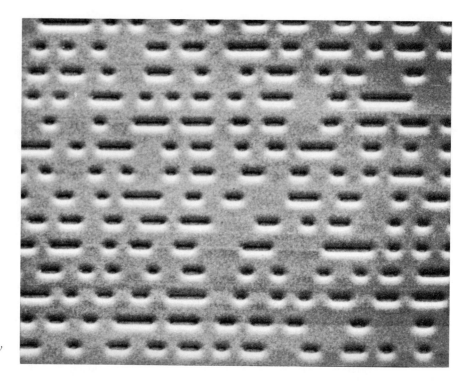

Figure 12–5

A magnified view of pits and lands (Photograph courtesy of 3-M.)

a chapter rather than to a specific frame. A CLV disc rotates at a variable rate of speed from 1,800 rpm at the start (innermost point on the disc) and gradually slows to 600 rpm as the laser approaches the outer edge of the disc. Since each image frame occupies the same length of track, three times the amount of data is stored on the track located at the outer edge of the disc than on the innermost track. CAV discs rotate at a constant 1,800 rpm (30 revolutions per second, which corresponds to the rate of standard video imaging in the United States.) Each revolution of a CAV videodisc corresponds to one frame of information, allowing each frame to be indexed and addressed individually. The maximum search time for any given frame on a CAV disc is three seconds. Minimum predicted life expectancy of optical disks is in the vicinity of 25 years.

Videodisc players are classified into three levels according to how they can be controlled. **Level I** players are sometimes thought of as consumer models. Controlled by a remote control unit or bar code reader, these Level I players lend themselves to teacher-mediated presentations in large group instruction and are often accompanied by a bar-coded teacher guide with lesson plans. **Level II** players are industrial models with improved access time, programmable memory, and the ability to read a program track on the disc. Level II players are rarely used in education. **Level III** players are designed to interface with a computer and to operate under its control. Level III software packages contain both videodiscs and computer program discs. In addition to full searching capabilities, the software often allows the user to assemble information into a unique presentation. Students can experience truly interactive lessons and have their performance data stored in the computer.

Feature films, simulations, and visual databases containing still images, including maps, sound, and motion sequences, are found on videodiscs and can be used in many educational settings. Language arts teachers have used the CAV versions of some of the action-adventure Indiana Jones movies as a tool to teach and examine screen writing. Simulation software such as Tom Snyder Productions' *The Great Solar System Rescue* involves students in scientist and historian roles as they work together to solve problems. *The National Gallery of Art* by Videodisc Publishing is a visual database containing still images of works by the great masters, as well as a guided tour of the gallery. It has been **repurposed;** that is, educators and other users use its content in ways different from the original intent in order to teach the basic concepts of visual design. *Communism and the Cold War* and *Martin Luther King,* both by ABC News Interactive, are examples of multimedia visual databases. By using still images, recorded speeches, and video clips from its vast archives, ABC has compiled resources containing a wealth of information for teachers to present and students to examine and manipulate to construct their own understanding of complex issues.

CD-Audio. The **CD-audio** (compact disc-audio) digital format, introduced in 1983, has achieved phenomenal success, with millions of players installed all over the world. In only a few years it made record players obsolete. It has supplied the economy of scale and research and development funds that have contributed to the development of CD-ROM and other compact disc formats.

Photo-CD. Eastman Kodak Company has developed and marketed **photo-CD** technology to consumers. Anyone can walk in off the street at a location that handles the service, drop off up to 100 color slides or negatives, and have them scanned into a photo-CD at a reasonable cost. Played back in a photo-CD player or in most CD-ROM drives, the images can be viewed on a monitor or projected onto a screen.

Libraries are creating large image databases by scanning fragile manuscripts and publications, maps, drawings, and photographs into what they regard as a stable, long-life medium. Universities, school districts, and individual schools with large slide collections are looking at this technology as an inexpensive and practical way to convert slides to an electronic form for archival and instructional purposes. Computer software by Kodak, Aldus, and other publishers makes it possible to index the images, view thumbnail representations in a slide sorter format, prescribe their subsequent viewing in a specific sequence, and create keyword searching capabilities.

CD-ROM. This much-publicized medium, the **CD-ROM** (compact disk-read only memory), was introduced in 1985, two years after the introduction of the CD-audio. It was initially seen primarily as a publishing or database medium aimed at users who needed relatively low-cost mass storage of information and rapid access and retrieval. Grolier, Compton, and World Book are some of the electronic encyclopedias available in this format. The technology has since blossomed into a powerful interactive multimedia tool.

A CD-ROM is a digital format disc that measures only 4.75 inches but can contain approximately 650 megabytes of data, the equivalent of approximately 300,000 typewritten pages of text. Text and graphic information can be displayed on a monitor screen by a CD-ROM drive attached as a peripheral device to a computer. In 1998 approximately 90 percent of computers manufactured included an internal CD-ROM drive. Although the medium began as a read-only technology, as its name implies, CD-Recordable (CD-R) and CD-Rewriteable (CD-RW) are two recording formats now readily available.

DVD. Digital Versatile Disc (**DVD**) is one of the most exciting incarnations of the digital disk medium. With a 4.70-inch diameter, it physically resembles the CD-ROM. While the CD-ROM can accept 650 MB of data, the DVD stores up to 17 GB (17,000 MB). It is produced in a number of different configurations—playback only single or dual layered, single or double sided, and record once and record many. The multiple configurations are designed to address the needs of different market segments ranging from data storage to the housing of feature films. A DVD can present a feature film with video superior to a videodisc and up to eight tracks of Dolby AC-3 surround sound audio channels and 32 tracks of subtitle channels. Due to the DVD's large storage capacity, a film can include a number of different takes of the same scene and multiple endings from which the viewer can choose with the navigation control provided.

Applications of Multimedia Hardware in Education

More and more classrooms are acquiring the equipment to allow teachers to use multimedia presentations as a method of instruction and to support student development of multimedia projects. Because these technologies are interesting, interactive, multidimensional, and student-controlled, they are ideally suited for educational purposes. Learners are engaged by the exciting technology, and they can explore information at their own pace and according to their own interests and needs.

The optical disk technologies have gained widespread acceptance as media for classroom instruction. Once a price/performance breakthrough occurs in large video screen, flat screen, and video projection, optical disk technologies will become universally accepted. The DVD player will replace the 16 mm motion picture film projector and the filmstrip projector. The video cassette will continue in use for a time, due to its local production characteristics, until recordable disks become cost effective. The 35 mm slide may become an endangered species as digital still camera technology is improved and becomes more affordable.

The CD-ROM medium is extremely accurate, compact, durable, and cost effective. Search time for any point on the disk is approximately one to three seconds. Low-volume publishing, public access catalogs, and library archives are logical applications of write-once discs. Already, thousands of CD-ROM products—including computer software, ready reference tools, encyclopedias, storybooks, indexes, and abstracts—have been published. As refinements improve the search and access times, the CD-ROM and its derivatives will become increasingly valuable information access tools in the library and in the classroom as electronic publishing media.

MULTIMEDIA AUTHORING TOOLS

Multimedia technologies allow users to experience information in many ways, including allowing them to interact with this information by creating, or authoring, programs and presentations combining original or ready-made text, graphics, and video clips. Multimedia technologies give the teacher or student control of powerful tools in the exploration and creation of information. A camcorder, digital camera, optical scanner, CD-ROM drive, videodisc player, and video cassette recorder all become potential information-gathering and composing tools. Multimedia tools allow a student or teacher to compose a complex statement that might include computer-generated sound, graphics, and animation, along with sound and visual forms stored in another medium such as videodisc, videotape, or CD-ROM.

Because multimedia involves the combination of more than one medium into a form of communication, there are many different types of multimedia productions and, thus, a variety of programs that help users to create multimedia products and presentations are available.

Desktop Presentation

Desktop presentation is the design, creation, and display of textual and graphic information under the control of a personal computer and so may be considered a form of multimedia. It has gained favor in boardrooms and business and community meetings, as well as in elementary, secondary, and college classrooms. Desktop presentation is gradually replacing traditional overhead transparencies and slide shows as a medium of projected visual information. To take advantage of this new electronic medium, the user must have access to presentation software that permits the creation or import of text and graphic images and their subsequent organization and display. The medium also requires appropriate hardware such as a computer and projector to display the images to the selected audience.

Presentation Software. Presentation software such as *Microsoft PowerPoint™* and *Aldus Persuasion™* provide the user with word processing, outlining, drawing, graphing, and presentation management tools. They also readily accept existing material originally prepared by other word processor, spreadsheet, and graphics programs. In addition to projecting visuals on a screen under software control, the user can print outlines of the presentation, speaker's notes, and handouts.

The software usually allows the user to switch among four different views as the presentation is being created. The illustration of those four views, shown in Figure 12–6 and Figure 12–7, were prepared using *Microsoft PowerPoint™* and are representative of those created by other desktop presentation programs.

The *slide view* shows a single visual and allows the user to type text and draw shapes, as illustrated in the right-hand panel of Figure 12–6. Material created with word processors, graphics programs, and spreadsheets can be imported into most desktop presentation programs. Professionally designed templates, including borders, bullets, and gradient fills, are provided to the user. Graphics elements such as

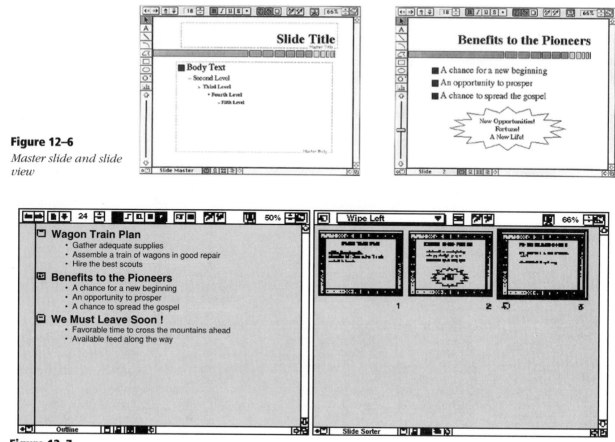

Figure 12–6

Master slide and slide view

Figure 12–7

Outline view and slide sorter view

the starburst shown in the right-hand panel of Figure 12–6 can be created easily to grab the viewer's attention. The presentation management tool is a unique element provided by this software. This tool allows the user to create a slide master, shown in the left panel of Figure 12–6, to format all of the visuals in the presentation. It saves the user considerable time because the slide master eliminates the need to re-format text or recreate repetitive elements such as the patterned border composed of gradient bars used in both panels of Figure 12–6.

The *outline view,* shown in the left panel of Figure 12–7, displays all of the title and body text of the entire presentation. As the user types in titles and text, the soft-ware creates the slides. As in any outline, the user can move paragraphs and head-ers up or down a level.

The *slide sorter view,* shown in the right-hand panel of Figure 12–7, allows the user to view miniature replicas of the slides and arrange them in any desired order. Notice the visual titled "Benefits to the Pioneers," shown in Figure 12–6, was created as the second slide and labeled as such in the lower part of its screen. Examining

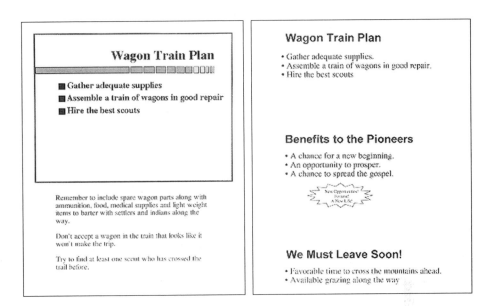

Figure 12–8

Notes and handouts printed from the presentation program

Figure 12–7, notice that it is the second slide in the sequence. While in the slide sorter view, it could be moved to any other position. Visuals can also be easily copied in this view to be used in other presentations.

The presentation management tool allows the user to select transition effects from a wide variety of **wipes** and **dissolves** between visuals. A wipe is a transition effect that allows a second visual to gradually replace the first visual being viewed. The visuals in the presentation shown in Figure 12–7 employ a *wipe left,* as indicated at the top of the right-hand panel. The following visual will enter the screen at the right and move leftward across the preceding visual. Other common wipes include a scroll, acting either vertically from top or bottom of the screen or from side to side; a *barn door,* acting horizontally from or toward the center of the screen; a *venetian blind,* acting as its name implies by breaking up the image in horizontal slats and introducing the new one; and an *iris,* which is a circular effect acting from or toward the center of the screen.

The *notes view* permits the user to create speaker's notes as the rest of the presentation is being created. These notes, as shown in Figure 12–8, contain a reduced image of the appropriate visual and can be printed. Handouts can be printed with usually one, three, or six visuals per page. Printing three visuals per page (as shown in the right-hand panel of Figure 12–8) leaves ample room for the audience to take their own notes on the handout provided.

Following the guidelines in Figure 12–9 will ensure a more effective presentation. Remember that the visual dimension is an important part of the presentation but you, as the presenter, are the most significant element.

Desktop Presentation as a Tool. Desktop presentation, with its ability to design, create, and display information under the control of a personal computer, is a tool that

- Begin and end your presentation with a blank screen.
- Use of generous margins will help focus attention on content.
- Use of a single background or frame will unify the presentation.
- Limit yourself to two or three colors on one screen.
- Use bright colors to emphasize important points.
- Use color contrasts effectively (e.g., yellow on blue is highly visible, while red on black is barely readable).
- Limit yourself to two typefaces in one presentation.
- Use an attention-grabbing title screen.
- Use single words and short phrases on the screen to focus attention on the details provided orally.
- Check carefully for spelling/typing errors.
- Use all uppercase letters only in major headings and make them a slightly larger size.
- Place headings at the same location in successive screens.
- Use dingbats (bullets, check marks, or other symbols) to organize lists.
- Use drop shadows and gradient fills for interesting visual effects.
- Use transition effects (wipes and dissolves), which add a graceful style to your presentation and help your audience to follow your train of thought.

Figure 12–9

Guidelines for preparing effective presentation graphics

extends the capability of the user to communicate. This electronic medium requires users to access software that permits them to design and create the message and to use appropriate hardware to display the message effectively. The presentation, once created, may be saved in a single file on disk, making it a very portable presentation indeed. Once again, as we note decreasing equipment size and increasing portability, we see evidence of the paradigm shifts described in Chapter 1: compare a presenter carrying file folders full of overhead transparencies or carousel trays full of slides to one carrying a floppy disk in a pocket or purse.

Hypermedia Authoring Tools

HyperCard™, a program introduced by Apple Computer, is said to have opened the door to multimedia as we know it today. The program has now been joined by a number of others, most prominent among them *ToolBook*™ and *Linkway*™ for the Windows operating system, and *HyperStudio*™, which works on both the Macintosh and Windows platforms. These programs afford the novice user the satisfaction of creating a multimedia product. Other high-end, sophisticated, and expensive authoring programs such as *Macromedia Director*™ are more useful to experienced and professional multimedia programmers.

"Students use *HyperCard*™ to draw maps of Alaska identifying geographical regions of the state, significant topographical features such as mountain ranges and bodies of water, animal distribution, population centers and cultural groups. Some students scan images and record sound into their *HyperCard*™ stack. I encourage them to then write adventure stories that provide multiple pathways and optional endings."

Fred Ross, 6th Grade Teacher
Bering Strait School District, Unalakleet, AK

Figure 12–10 presents various multimedia applications created in *HyperStudio*™. The *HyperStudio*™ home page is located at the top center. Top-left is a geography stack on Australia; top-right is a look at the people of Rwanda; bottom-left and bottom-center are examples of electronic portfolios; bottom-right is a storybook created

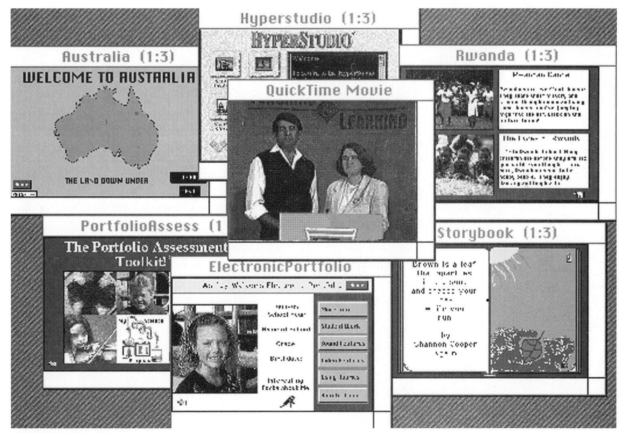

Figure 12–10

A variety of applications created in HyperStudio (Courtesy of Roger Wagner Publishing Inc.)

by elementary students that is complete with picture and with text that can be read aloud by the computer; in the center of this collage is a *QuickTime*™ movie welcoming people to the 1996 NECC conference in Minneapolis. Not only does *Hyper-Studio*™ allow the user to create buttons that link to the World Wide Web through *Netscape*™, but it is designed to let users publish their multimedia projects over the World Wide Web as well. A *HyperStudio*™ window can be embedded in a web page or the complete *HyperStudio*™ created display can be an entire Internet document. In many ways, multimedia is a marriage of technologies that allows information to be presented locally to an individual or to groups and globally to anyone accessing the World Wide Web.

HTML and HTML Editors

Web pages written in HTML, discussed in the previous chapter, can be viewed as multimedia. They can contain text, images, animations, and movies and can link to other sources of information. They, in fact, may resemble desktop presentations, with the added power of hypertext. They communicate information to the user in a multidimensional fashion with clickable links to other sources. HTML editors such as *Microsoft Front Page*™ and *Claris Home Page*™ make quick work of web page construction. Examine Figure 12–11, a simple illustration similar to one in the previous chapter. We see how both text and graphic images can be included on a web page. The command <IMG SRC="ball.gif"><AHREF="http://www.wlma.org/default.asp">Go to WLMA </A> produces text preceded by a graphic on the line, and it establishes a link to another web site at its address.

Interactive multimedia and hypermedia are not only presentation tools for commercially prepared material, but they are tools with which the teacher can custom prepare information of a local or immediate nature. Most important, they are tools students can use to gather their own information, construct their own knowledge, and communicate their ideas effectively.

Application of Multimedia Authoring Tools in Education

Multimedia authoring can be approached from the teacher's perspective and from the student's. The teacher can select and create material, addressing instructional needs ranging from discrete projects aimed at specific facts and concepts to be taught to complete lessons. A chemistry teacher might design a multimedia periodic table of the elements that would allow a user to select an element; identify its atomic number, atomic weight, and discoverer; see an illustration of its atomic structure; then see a picture of the discoverer and read a brief biography. An English teacher might create a simple multimedia program that would present the student with lesson objectives, ask specific questions to focus the student's attention, and give the student a brief introduction to a work of Shakespeare being studied and a link to the *Complete Works of William Shakespeare* web site (http://www.thetech.mit.edu/Shakespeare/works.html). A teacher of English to Speakers of Other Languages

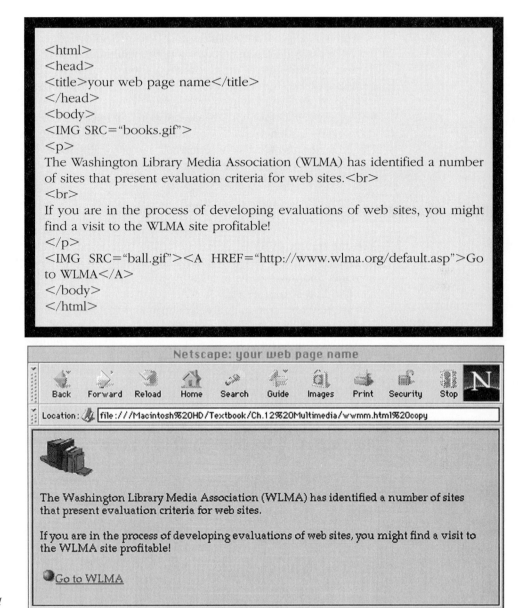

```
<html>
<head>
<title>your web page name</title>
</head>
<body>
<IMG SRC="books.gif">
<p>
The Washington Library Media Association (WLMA) has identified a number
of sites that present evaluation criteria for web sites.<br>
<br>
If you are in the process of developing evaluations of web sites, you might
find a visit to the WLMA site profitable!
</p>
<IMG SRC="ball.gif"><A HREF="http://www.wlma.org/default.asp">Go
to WLMA</A>
</body>
</html>
```

Figure 12–11

Web page generated by preceding HTML text

(ESOL) might create a multimedia vocabulary program that would allow a student to see a word and hear it pronounced. An image of an object representing the word might also be displayed. At the simplest authoring level, a teacher of any subject at any grade level might create bookmarks appropriate to the World Wide Web browser being used that would allow students to interact with multimedia web sites related to current lessons being taught.

From the student's perspective, multimedia authoring presents a rich environment in which to explore information and construct knowledge. As an example, students might be assigned the task of developing a multimedia project describing the early settlement and subsequent development of their community. The resulting product might be text gleaned from official records, pictures found in a museum or library, and audio clips from live interviews with senior citizens, accompanied by their photographs. This chapter will close with the description of a Master's degree thesis project in which elementary students created multimedia products dealing with immigrants to the United States and famous Americans. It is compelling testimony to the power of multimedia when placed in the hands of students.

VIRTUAL REALITY

Virtual reality (VR) is a term referring to computer-based technologies ranging from sophisticated 3-D simulations to full immersion experiences in which the participants find themselves in a highly interactive, multisensory, artificial environment so vivid that it appears real. It is the ultimate multimedia experience, with elements so carefully and convincingly synchronized that computer-generated audio and visual messages appear to be real.

Virtual reality offers us the opportunity to explore reality in a new way. It is difficult to understand how extremely exciting VR is until one has had the opportunity to experience it. Imagine being able to fly through the air or to walk around on the ocean floor, without ever leaving home! This certainly has the potential to be very powerful technology.

How Does One Experience Virtual Reality?

At the low end, non-immersion VR experiences (though more sophisticated, more engaging and more interactive) are not unlike other computer simulations in which the user is presented with text, graphics, and sound and allowed to navigate through a simulated environment. At the high end, full-immersion VR experiences are achieved by using equipment that controls all visual and auditory input. Virtual reality is often delivered to the user by a head-mounted display consisting of a helmet or goggles with integrated sensors and additional sensors attached to gloves and other clothing worn by the user. The sensors provide feedback to the computer in order to modify the simulated environment.

The head-mounted display takes the form of a helmet, with earphones and miniature video screens positioned directly in front of the user's eyes. Slightly different scenes are sent to each eye screen, thus producing 3-D images. The "surround sound" effect is similar to that used in movie theaters and home entertainment centers. The helmet blocks out all other surrounding visual and auditory input, thus heightening the illusions resulting from the data sent directly by the computer. More sophisticated VR equipment also includes gloves to wear. At times, even full body suits are employed. These pieces of equipment interpret the movements of the wearer (as does the helmet) and cause the computer to create scenes that change in response to the movement of the user. As you might guess, this form of virtual reality requires a great deal of computing power and a phenomenal amount of programming. The remarkable increase in the power of affordable computers is one factor contributing to the rapid advances made by VR during the past few years.

Virtual Reality and Communication

Novak (cited in Schmitt, 1993, p. 86) states that one of the most characteristic differences between full-immersion virtual reality and other forms of representation is that, in virtual reality, information "surrounds" the participant. The notion of being inside the communication medium, or channel, is prevalent in the virtual reality literature.

Three characteristics of communication in this type of virtual reality stand out as being very different from those of traditional models of communication. First, as previously mentioned, participants in virtual reality are perceived to be in the center of the communication medium, or channel, instead of being situated outside the communication medium and sending information through it. Second, virtual reality participants not only communicate with other participants simultaneously, but they also communicate with themselves. Third, sources of noise in traditional communication may also be noise in virtual reality or may be sensual links to the real world that make virtual reality seem more real. Traditional models of communication do not capture these differences.

Figure 12–12 depicts a new model of communication, created by Sylvia Sandoz (1994), that captures these differences of communication in virtual reality. It portrays the participant or participants inside the communication medium, inside virtual reality. The white space in Figure 12–12 outside the communication medium represents reality. The more immersed the senses are, the more virtual reality appears to be real. The white space at the center of the circle is what Sutherland (1965, p. 507) calls the point of perfect presence, in which the virtual world "looks real, acts real, sounds real, feels real." If virtual reality achieves perfection, participants do not recognize the difference between reality and virtual reality; virtual reality, according to Furriness (Miller, 1992, p. 14), is "just like you're walking into another world, and you're perceiving it as if it becomes reality itself."

The second difference between traditional communication and communication in full-immersion virtual reality is that participants communicate with themselves, as well as with others. In virtual reality, the communication medium (for example, a computer) is no longer just a means of connecting sender and receiver. The focus of attention, according to Steuer (1992, p. 78), is on the relationship "between an individual who is both a sender and a receiver, and on the mediated environment with which he or she interacts. Information is not transmitted from sender to receiver; rather, mediated environments are created and then experienced." In other words, participants in immersive virtual reality are in constant communication with the medium itself, the computer, and themselves as the object of their communication.

The third difference between traditional communication and communication in full-immersion virtual reality is that participants may experience the connection to

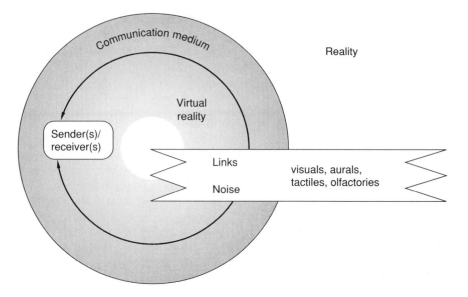

Figure 12–12

Sandoz model of communication in virtual reality

reality through the senses as noise that distracts from the sense of reality or as a link that adds to a sense of reality.

To a participant in a virtual world of the 1804 Lewis and Clark expedition, noise might be a passerby in the real world commenting on the status of Social Security or the latest space mission. Noise might also be the literal noise of airplane traffic sounds from a nearby real airport or the fumes of diesel fuel from a nearby real factory. "Noise need not be senseless; perfectly good information, even an organized message, can act like noise when it interferes with or disturbs reception of some signal" (Klapp, 1986, p. 84).

How real are the sounds in virtual reality? How real are the visuals? Can the participants become so engaged that they forget they are not experiencing something real? When they move their heads, does the environment change? Tactile feelings have a sense of reality as well. When a participant picks up an object, does she feel the proper amount of resistance or weight in the object?

Just as our senses can be sources of noise in virtual reality communication, so, too, can they be links to reality that make virtual reality seem more real. Real-time sounds from nearby co-participants can add to the sense of reality when playing a virtual game. Grabbing a physically real set of bicycle handles adds to the feeling of a virtual bike ride through the Swiss Alps. Chewing gum or smelling hot dogs adds to the sense of playing virtual big league baseball.

The sixth sense, psychology, is another consideration. Theater patrons agree to ignore the backstage, risers, and stagehands. With a computerized virtual world, according to Pimentel and Teixeira (1993, p. 157), participants enter into the same "conspiracy" and agree to forget the computer, the software, the head tracker, the glove and goggles.

In virtual reality, we communicate through all our own senses, and our own senses determine the amount of noise or how linked we are to reality. "It is an irony of the information society that information gets in its own way—or, as one might put it, communication becomes noise to its own signal" (Klapp, 1986, p. 85). According to Figure 12–12, the connection between reality and virtual reality is the senses. Inside the connector, the horizontal gray area depicts noise, and the horizontal white area depicts links between reality and virtual reality. Whether what we sense is noise that detracts from the sense of reality or links that add to the sense of reality depends on the specific application of virtual reality.

Virtual Reality Authoring Tools

Full-immersion VR tools are still the province of the well-funded virtual reality laboratories; however, authoring tools that create sophisticated simulations have entered the market and are becoming more affordable. These 3-D modeling tools have navigation controls that allow you to move through a screen image and examine it from every perspective. *Virtus VR™*, an inexpensive, entry-level program, and the more powerful *Virtus Walkthrough Pro™* (illustrated in Figures 12–13 and 12–14) are pro-

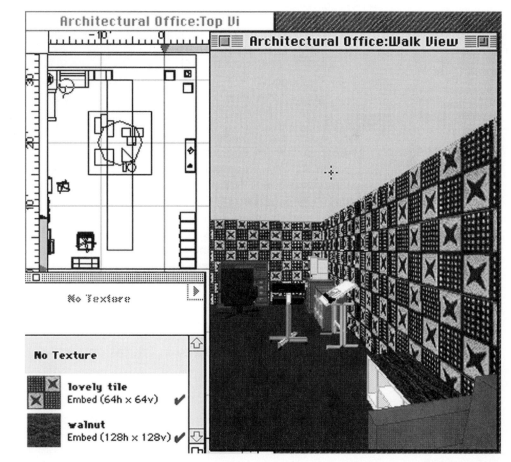

Figure 12–13

A distant view in Walkthrough Pro™, showing three windows

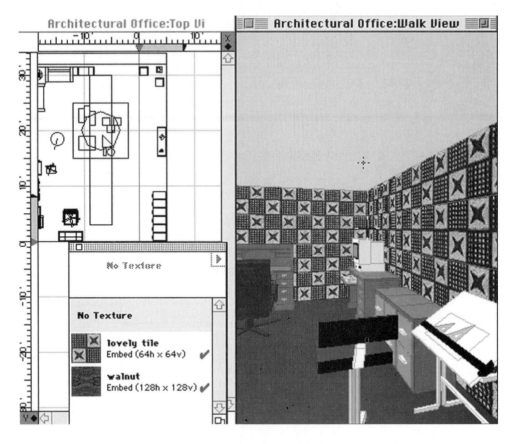

Figure 12–14

A near view as the viewer navigates through the scene in Walkthrough Pro™

grams that allow the user to easily create 3-D worlds. Into the program's 2-D window, you simply drag basic 3-D shapes from numerous galleries supplied with the programs and combine these to build complex objects, structures, and models. For even more realism, you can add surface features and textures that are provided or create your own. You can also create translucent and transparent surfaces for objects, including doors and windows. You see your designs instantly rendered in a companion 3-D window, where you can also use your mouse to navigate quickly and fluidly through and explore your world from any perspective. *Virtus 3-D Website Builder*™ provides the user with everything needed to create 3-D VRML worlds on the Internet.

Applications of Virtual Reality in Education

Non-immersion VR is now present in many classrooms. The role of full-immersion virtual reality in the classroom for the future remains uncertain, largely due to the huge technical and financial challenges that form of virtual reality now presents. If developments in VR technology make it viable for classroom use, the possibilities are astonishing. Since virtual reality allows users to explore and experience the simulated surroundings as if they were reality, students could use VR technologies to explore St. Petersburg for a Russian language class, to participate in a Civil War battle for a history class, to deep-sea dive for a marine biology lab, or to simulate the feeling of performing a difficult gymnastic maneuver for an Olympic athletic training program. Designing virtual worlds for education may become a whole new field of specialization!

In some ways, virtual reality is even better than reality: we can stop it, replay it, and stretch the limits of our own physical reality. For example, virtual reality could allow us to explore microscopic worlds inside bacteria, or unreachable worlds in and beyond our own solar system. Virtual reality might allow students to overcome physical disabilities or limitations as they explore these new worlds. Virtual reality also allows users to translate abstract ideas into a form that can be perceived and manipulated. As you can imagine, educational applications of VR, though mainly in the future, might be found in a number of disciplines and could be applied to instruction and learning in a variety of ways.

Students might work collaboratively to build virtual worlds with their classmates. Portfolio assessments in the future might include virtual worlds created by students. "Over their years in school, students could create a universe of learning worlds that reflected the evolution of their skills and the pattern of their conceptual growth. Evaluating comprehension and competence would become experiential as well as analytical, as teachers explored the worlds of thought constructed by their students" (Bricken & Byrne, 1992, p. 11).

The promise of a technology such as virtual reality can be both exciting and frustrating—exciting to reflect on the potential, frustrating to contemplate the inherent funding problems. Obviously, virtual reality technologies are expensive to develop and expensive to run. Most desktop computers don't have nearly enough computing power to operate virtual reality programs. Realizing that most teachers don't even have a telephone in their classrooms, expensive technologies always seem to be in the distant future. Take away the television set, the VCR, the stereo system, and the computer and printer from a home and you will have made it a much more sterile and information-poor environment. Attempt to do the same to a classroom, and you will probably have little effect on it, since those items are usually not there to begin with.

MULTIMEDIA IN A CONSTRUCTIVIST CLASSROOM

Susan K. Arnold (1996) set out to prove that using multimedia technology as a tool for accessing information and demonstrating knowledge would improve self-directedness in learners. Her research took place in a suburban elementary school of 14 mixed-age classrooms, with an average of 26 students in each class. Her sample population consisted of 51 students in two 4th-/5th-grade classes. The students were placed in two heterogeneous groups, with consideration given to balancing the variables of grade level and students with special needs.

The groups were assigned a four-week research project on the topic of United States immigration. Group A was taught how to use electronic technology to retrieve

	More When Using Technology (%)	More When Not Using Technology (%)
Effective Work Habits		
Focused attention on research	73%	27%
Used time wisely	69	31
Set goals each day	69	31
Had better work habits	67	33
Followed a Work Plan		
Enjoyed researching and gathering materials	57	43
Did a better job finding resources	62	38
Hardest work	65	35
Best-quality work	76	24
Self-reflection		
Felt responsible for getting work done	72	28
Project that communicated information best	73	27
Project liked doing best	90	10
Proudest of project	79	21

Figure 12–15

Technology's impact on student self-directedness

information and produce a multimedia report in *HyperStudio*™. Group B was restricted from using electronic technology. At the end of four weeks, the groups were assigned another four-week research project, this time on famous Americans. Group A was restricted from using electronic technology and Group B was taught how to use electronic technology to produce a multimedia report. At the end of the eight weeks, the students presented the results of their projects to their peers, teachers, parents, and invited guests.

The analysis of the data focused on differences within each group, not on differences across the two groups. Class mean scores using the Oregon Department of Education Student Self-Directed Learning Scoring Guide showed substantial improvement when students had access to electronic technology. The table presented as Figure 12–15 summarizes multimedia technology's impact on the students.

Students took a good deal of pride in the multimedia presentations they had prepared. Students who had been identified as "At Risk" were observed being significantly more involved during the electronic technology treatment and exhibiting a higher degree of personal responsibility. These are the feelings students had about their exposure to multimedia technology, captured in their own words (Arnold, 1996):

"I really took time to do a good job. I stayed in at breaks to finish it."
"I worked longer on the technology project and it wasn't just slopped together."
"It's like it's easier to stick to the project."

"My tech project shows my hardest work. It looks a heck of a lot better. I worked hard to make it neat, interesting, and fun for the person looking at it."
"My technology project looks more professional."
"When I use technology I feel . . . powerful and different. Learning's more fun."
"I feel privileged because in other generations people were not able to do this. We're lucky!"

Multimedia technology can be a catalyst for change, helping teachers alter their approach to teaching and learning from passive learning to active learning.

Technology can lead teachers to develop more learner-centered environments. Students learned more than was expected and also developed new competencies like the ability to collaborate, to recognize and analyze problems as systems, to acquire and use large amounts of information, and to apply technology to solve real world problems. (Dwyer, 1996).

SUMMARY

Multimedia employs more than one way of conveying information in a multisensory manner. Multimedia computer programs are used to control the presentation of video information from external sources such as videotape and videodisc, as well as graphic, audio, and textual information from CD-ROM. Hypermedia uses a nonlinear method of conveying multimedia information.

Optical storage formats employ a laser beam that reads a precise series of pits and lands on the disc. Common formats include videodisc, CD-ROM, CD-audio, photo-CD, and DVD. A 12-inch videodisc can contain up to 54,000 different images per side and two continuous audio tracks. The information may be displayed as still pictures, drawings, or up to 120 minutes of live video and audio. Videodiscs are classified as either extended-play CLV (constant linear velocity) or frame-addressable CAV (constant angular velocity).

Up to 100 color slides or negatives can be scanned into a photo-CD and played back in a photo-CD player or in most CD-ROM drives. Computer software makes it possible to index the images, view thumbnail representations in a slide sorter format, prescribe their subsequent viewing in a specific sequence, and create keyword searching capabilities.

The CD-ROM, a digital format disc that can contain approximately 650 megabytes of data, was initially seen as a publishing or database medium aimed at users who needed relatively low-cost mass storage of information. With graphics and sound added to the text data, the technology has blossomed into a powerful interactive multimedia tool.

Digital versatile disc can store up to 17 GB on a 4.70-inch-diameter disk produced in a number of different configurations designed to address the needs of different market segments. A DVD can present a feature film with video superior to that of a videodisc, up to eight tracks of Dolby AC-3 surround sound audio channels, and 32 tracks of subtitle channels.

Multimedia authoring tools allow students and teachers to create and compose desktop presentations, hypertext and hypermedia documents, web pages, and other multimedia productions. These creations might include computer-generated sound, graphics, and animation, along with sound and visual forms stored in another medium such as videodisc, videotape, or CD-ROM.

Virtual reality (VR) is the ultimate multimedia experience. In its immersive mode, it is a computer-generated simulated environment delivered to the user by a head-mounted display with integrated sensors and additional ones attached to items of clothing worn by the user. This artificial environment, or virtual reality, created by computer-based technology is highly interactive, multisensory, and vivid enough for it to seem to the participants almost as if it were reality. Communication in virtual reality is very different from traditional models of communication. Educational applications for virtual reality abound, although financial and technological obstacles currently make classroom use impractical.

Multimedia technology can be a catalyst for change, helping teachers to alter their approach to teaching and learning from passive learning to active learning. Students take a good deal of pride in preparing multimedia presentations. Students' self-directedness and other study and learning habits may show substantial improvement when students have access to multimedia technology.

CHAPTER EXERCISES

1. Prepare a desktop presentation that demonstrates at least 10 of the 15 guidelines for effective desktop presentations given in this chapter.
2. Using the HTML script presented in Figure 12–11 as a template, adapt the script to a lesson in geography.
3. Using an authoring program such as *HyperCard*™, *Digital Chisel*™, or *ToolBook*™, create a family tree. Scan photographs into your project and record the sound of each member's name. Go back at least as far as your great-grandparents.
4. Evaluate a multimedia program from your school's software collection. Was it appropriate for the multimedia format? Did it take full advantage of the format? Did its complexity interfere with its effective use? Can you suggest a better way to convey the same information?
5. Choose a CD-ROM encyclopedia or other CD-ROM product and demonstrate it to a colleague.
6. Do a library search for the five most recent articles on virtual reality. What do the authors believe is the apparent impact on education? When are they predicting this impact will be felt in any meaningful way?

GLOSSARY

button A visible object or an invisible area of the screen, often covering images or text, that can be programmed using a scripting language to perform certain actions such as linking to additional information or controlling an external device.

CAV (constant angular velocity) A frame-addressable videodisc format whose tracks are recorded as concentric circles with radial data sectors.

CD-audio (compact disc-audio) A digital audio format introduced in 1983 that has achieved a phenomenal success, with millions of players installed all over the world.

CD-ROM (compact disk-read only memory) The 4.75-inch digital optical disk storage medium capable of containing approximately 650 megabytes of data was initially seen primarily as a publishing or database medium aimed at users who needed relatively low-cost mass storage of information and rapid access and retrieval.

CLV (constant linear velocity) An extended play videodisc format whose track is recorded as a spiral divided into data sectors of equal length.

desktop presentation Software that facilitates the organization of text and graphics into computer screens, with the intention that the user will project them to an audience.

dissolve A transition effect between visuals. The original visual fades into another one and is replaced by it.

DVD Digital versatile disc is an optical digital disk medium that can store up to 17 GB on a 4.70-inch-diameter disk produced in a number of different configurations—playback only single or dual layered, single or double sided, and record once and record many.

Level I A videodisc classification of mostly consumer models providing still frame, chapter and frame addressability, and two-channel audio. They lend themselves to teacher-mediated presentations in large group instruction.

Level II Industrial models of videodiscs, with improved access time, programmable memory, and the ability to read a program track on the disc. They allow students to interact independently with the instructional content on the disc through a keypad and bar code reader.

Level III Videodisc players designed to interface with a computer and to operate under its control. Students can experience truly interactive lessons and have their performance data stored in the computer.

multimedia A technique that conveys information in a multisensory manner. It might include the use of textual, graphic, audio, and video materials to convey information to the user, who would interact with it by reading, listening, and observing still and moving images.

photo-CD Eastman Kodak Company developed this technology, which allows up to 100 color slides or negatives to be scanned onto an optical disk. Played back in a Photo-CD player or in most CD-ROM drives, the images can be viewed on a monitor or projected onto a screen.

repurpose To use computer programs to use content (usually stored on a videodisc) in ways different from its original intent.

videodisc An optical storage technology composed of a 12-inch disc capable of storing up to 54,000 different images per side and two continuous audio tracks. The information may be displayed as still pictures or up to 120-minute sequences of live video and audio.

virtual reality (VR) A computer-generated simulated environment delivered by a head-mounted display with integrated sensors attached to items of clothing worn by the user.

wipe A transition effect between visuals. One visual appears to slide over another, replacing it.

REFERENCES & SUGGESTED READINGS

Arnold, S. (1996). *Effects of integrative technology on student self-directedness at Mountain View Elementary School.* Unpublished thesis for a Master of Education degree in Information Technology. Western Oregon University.

Barron, A. E. (1993, March). The marriage of computers and TV. *Media and Methods, 29*(3), 10.

Benesky, J., & Waber, J. (1997, May). Virtual laboratories in the sciences. *Syllabus 10*(9), 20–22, 37.

Biocca, F. (1992). Virtual reality technology: A tutorial. *Journal of Communication, 42*(4), 23–72.

Bricken, M., & Byrne, C. M. (1992). *Summer students in virtual reality: A pilot study on educational applications of virtual reality technology.* Seattle: Washington University Technology Center.

Dale, E. (1969). Audio-visual methods in teaching (3rd ed). New York: Holt, Rinehart and Winston, 108.

D'Ignazio, F. (1997, September). Create a web page in a swamp! *Learning and Leading with Technology, 25*(1), 46–49.

Dwyer, D. (1996, Winter). Apple classrooms of tomorrow, the first ten years. *Apple Education Digest.* (http://www.info.apple.com/education/acot.menu.html)

Kasman Valenza, J. (1997, May-June). How to choose an encyclopedia. *Electronic Learning, 16*(6), 50–53.

Klapp, O. E., (1986). *Overload and boredom: Essays on the quality of life in the information society.* Westport, CT: Greenwood Press.

Lanier, J., & Biocca, F. (1992, Autumn). An insider's view of the future of virtual reality. *Journal of Communication, 42*(4), 150–172.

Lee, J. R., & Patterson, W. R. (1997, February). It's showtime: Six hints for PowerPoint presentations. *Learning and Leading with Technology, 24*(5), 6–12.

Lynch, P. (1994, November/December). The evolving face of multimedia. *Syllabus, 8*(3), 48–50.

Miller, C. (1992, November). Online interviews: Dr. Thomas A. Furness, III, virtual reality pioneer. *Online, 16*(6), 14–27.

Moeller, B., & Hupert, N. (1997, May-June). Reading in the age of multimedia. *Electronic Learning, 16*(6), 54.

Nugent, W. R. (1991). Virtual reality: Advanced imaging special effects let you roam in cyberspace. *Journal of the American Society for Information Science, 42*(8), 609–617.

Pantelidis, V. S. (1993, April). Virtual reality in the classroom. *Educational Technology, 33*(4), 23–27.

Pimentel, K., & Teixeira, K. (1993). *Virtual reality: Through the new looking glass.* New York: Intel/Windcrest/McGraw-Hill.

Powell, G. (1997, May). Documenting multimedia: Well-taken steps for educational developers. *Syllabus, 10*(9), 16–18.

Salpeter, J. (1992, April). Breakthroughs in Digital Video. *Technology & Learning, 12*(7), 66–74.

Sandoz, S. (1994). *Innovation in virtual reality is about the power of the mind.* Unpublished manuscript, Western Oregon University.

Schmitt, G. N. (1993). Virtual reality in architecture. In N. M. Thalmann & D. Thalmann (eds.), *Virtual worlds and multimedia* (pp. 85–97). Chichester, England: John Wiley & Sons.

Sorge, D. H., Campbell, J. P., & Russell, J. D. (1993, April/May). Evaluating interactive video: Software and hardware. *Tech Trends, 38*(10), 19–26.

Sprague, D. (1996, May). Virtual reality and precollege education: Where are we today? *Learning and Leading with Technology, 23*(8), 10–12.

Steuer, J. (1992, Autumn). Defining virtual reality: Dimensions determining tele-presence. *Journal of Communication, 42*(4), 73–93.

Sutherland, I. (1965). *The ultimate display.* Proceedings of the International Federation of Information Processing Congress, 2, 506–508.

Thornburg, D. D. (1991). *Education, technology, and paradigms of change for the 21st century.* San Carlos, CA: Starsong Publications.

Welsh, T. (1997, January/February). From multimedia to multiple-media: Designing computer-based course materials for the information age. *Techtrends, 42*(1), 17–23.

Woodward, J. (1992, June). *Virtual reality and its potential use in special education: Identifying emerging issues and trends in technology for special education.* Washington, DC: Special Education Programs. ERIC 350 766.

Chapter 13

Managing a
Software Collection

ADVANCE ORGANIZER

1. Where are the sources for locating software?

2. Why is it important to evaluate software?

3. What should be considered in rating software?

4. What should be considered in the selection of software?

5. How can the acquisition of software be facilitated?

6. How should a software collection be managed? That is, how might a software collection be treated in much the same way as a book collection, with periodic assessment, weeding, and promotion of its use?

Collection management is a term that describes the process by which libraries acquire a wide range of materials in a variety of formats to meet the information needs of teachers and students. The term is well suited to describing the responsibilities and activities related to the evaluation, selection, acquisition, maintenance, and promotion of computer software. This chapter will focus on examining the many factors that contribute to the process of selecting software that is compatible with a school's philosophy, goals, and objectives. A process of locating, evaluating, selecting, and managing software will be discussed. Evaluation guidelines and sample worksheets will be developed. A system will be discussed for the management of a software collection to ensure its currency and optimal access by teachers and students.

THE ELEMENTS OF SOFTWARE COLLECTION MANAGEMENT

Collection management, as described in the introduction to this chapter, is a series of processes and procedures, which together result in the evaluation, selection, acquisition, processing, organization, preservation, effective use, and even the eventual withdrawal of materials from a library's collection. These processes do not exist in isolation from each other or from other operations in a school; rather, they are a direct outgrowth of its mission and philosophy.

Figure 13–1 illustrates the interrelationship of these elements. Knowledge of the school's underlying mission and an awareness of the learning goals for its students are fundamental to developing the best possible software collection. Knowledge of the existing collection gained by a thorough assessment provides the base from which to work. Selection policies guide the development of the collection. Selection

Figure 13–1

*The components of
collection
management*

Figure 13–2

The process of building a collection

procedures include an awareness of selection tools such as journal reviews and selection sources such as educational vendors, as well as the evaluation of the software prior to selection. Acquisition policies and procedures guide the cataloging, classification, and processing of the software once it arrives in the school to ensure maximum accessibility. Maintenance policies and procedures include weeding of the software collection and discarding of items that have outlived their usefulness. Promotion of the collection's use assumes that the collection exists for the benefit of all students and all teachers. It is an effort to assure that all are aware of new acquisitions as well as understand possible applications of current holdings. Promotion may take the form of notices of software arrivals, but it may also entail some inservice work with teachers to demonstrate software and to discuss its potential applications.

Figure 13–2 illustrates four elements in the process of collection development: identifying sources along with product information and reviews, evaluating the product, selecting the product for adoption within a given setting, and acquiring the software. Once software is located, its evaluation and selection for instructional use require the same professional skills that library media specialists and classroom teachers already perform so well when identifying needs, analyzing content, matching style, and constructing an environment for learning. Acquisition includes the usual value considerations of cost, timeliness of delivery, and after-sales support by the vendor.

Identification of Software Sources

Earlier chapters have dealt with learning theories and with the need to understand, in general, software classifications. When searching for software, keep in mind what it is you wish to accomplish with the software. In order to have sufficient software to offer support to many subject areas at various grade levels, a school will make a sizable investment in time and money. The software selected must be intrinsically of good quality and able to be used effectively in the curriculum.

Gaining access to software for evaluation is no insignificant matter. The following are some likely places to look for information on software.

Educational Software Vendors. Some companies that had been marketing general curriculum materials are now specializing in computer software. These vendors are familiar with schools and many use strict selection policies of their own in order to present the best products from a number of publishers. They employ staff trained in teaching and in instructional materials. They exhibit at professional educational conferences and demonstrate software at inservice meetings. Some of these vendors print catalogs listing software by subject area and by computer make and model. The better ones offer "on approval" purchasing, and a few even arrange for limited previewing of the software. They are prepared to offer support after the sale as well. Remember, however, that sales is their first objective and professional good judgment must be used in examining their promotional materials. These vendors are not the most objective source of information about the products they are selling.

Software Publishers. Many companies (textbook publishers included) print catalogs listing their software by topic. Very few, however, offer a preview of their programs before purchase. Some of the companies may have sample disks, which they will send to help you with your selection. Companies are reluctant to send out products for review because of the ease with which they can be copied. Books and other materials cost almost as much to duplicate as would purchasing another item from the company. Software, however, can be copied with very little investment of time or money. If a product is copied illegally, then the company has lost some of its investment in research and production. According to the Software Publishers Association (SPA), one-quarter to one-third of all software used in K–12 grades in this country is illegal (Salvador, 1994). This is a significant problem. Some misguided users blame copyright infringement on inadequate budget resources. They fail to recognize copyright violation as the theft that it is. Rampant violations can endanger the profitability and even the continued existence of small producers, many of whom have provided schools with truly innovative and useful software.

Some school districts have established centers for software review where publishers and/or vendors send products. Teachers are invited to visit these centers to review the software. Stringent safeguards are usually in place to assure that illegal copies are not made. The centers provide an excellent opportunity for publishers to display their latest products and for teachers to use software before having to purchase it.

Most large software packages involve a great deal of time to create, and only by getting a fair return on this investment can the companies continue to produce quality materials. The educational community must take the responsibility to handle software in good faith. If a company does send out software for preview, it is usually done under an agreement, with the previewer accepting responsibility to see that the product's copyright is protected. If you obtain software from a publisher, make sure you know the return policy before you order. Some software publishers are listed in Appendix N of this text.

Software Clearinghouses. There are several clearinghouses for the exchange of **freeware,** which is in the **public domain.** These are items that are not protected by copyright and may be duplicated. Clearinghouses often make available **shareware,** software that can be tried out first and then duplicated for a nominal cost. For example, the Oregon Education Computing Consortium makes both freeware and shareware available to its members. Explore the availability of software exchanges in your area.

Local User Groups and Electronic Bulletin Boards. Freeware is widely circulated among user groups, simply through exchanging floppy disks. Specific clubs exist for each major brand of computer in most parts of the country. Ask your hardware dealer for a list of local groups. If you do not want to invest the time in a user group or the local groups are not oriented to your needs, another possible source of freeware and shareware is an electronic bulletin board. Hundreds of these services have sprung up across the country and are available by dialing up the service from your computer and modem, choosing the program you want, and retrieving it over the telephone line.

Freeware and shareware exchanges can be major contributors to the spread of computer **viruses.** A virus is a computer program that installs itself in the user's system software or hard disk. It can replicate itself, change the execution of another program, and carry out instructions it contains. Some viruses are rather benign but others have the potential of wreaking major havoc by destroying systems and files on the disk. They are usually spread from computer to computer when users download files or exchange floppy disks.

When might you suspect a virus infection? Suspect a virus if you notice any pronounced change in the way your computer behaves. Do programs take a longer time to open? Do they run more slowly? Does your system suddenly crash? Is there a sudden reduction of hard disk space? Do new error messages appear? Fortunately, **virus protection programs** are available from several publishers. One type prevents viruses from being installed on your hard drive by scanning floppy disks; another repairs your drive by eradicating existing viruses before they can do more damage. With the constant advent of new viruses, virus protection programs are now sold on an annual subscription basis.

Local Computer Stores. Although local computer stores may not cater directly to the educational market, they may have a small selection of software that could be demonstrated to you. Even some of the software that they carry to meet business and home use can be useful in the classroom. Examine the software and get some ideas on how it might be used. Read the user's guide and any additional material. Run the software. Find out what kind of equipment it will run on, how much internal memory is required, and what additional hardware, if any, is needed to run the software. Keep in mind that the salesperson may know a lot about games but very little about education.

Computer Magazines and Professional Journals. Computer journals and magazines carry advertisements and critical reviews of a broad range of available products. Read the reviews and look for articles that discuss the kind of software in which you are interested. Be on the lookout for articles that delve into a specific type of program such as word processing and that compare, feature by feature, the leading products. Major technology journals of interest to the library/media specialist and classroom teacher are listed in Appendix O of this text.

Regional Education Support Groups. Regional educational laboratories, education service districts, institutions of teacher education with resource centers, state departments of education, and computing consortia are actively collecting and reviewing software for the purpose of making this information available to schools for inspection. Visit one of these organizations and review the software it has on hand.

Other Schools. Heed the old advertising slogan "Ask the person who owns one." A visit, phone call, or e-mail message to teachers in nearby schools, inquiring about software in specific subject areas, may yield some valuable information. Ask questions such as "What software addresses this topic?" "How do you like it?" "Do students find it interesting?" "Is it easy to use?" "Have you had any problems with it?" and "Do you know of anything better on the market?" Remember that answers are opinions, however, and that these views may not fit your particular situation. Once you have identified particular software, it is your responsibility to proceed with a systematic evaluation.

Conferences. Almost all professional education conferences now have vendors displaying software along with traditional curriculum materials. Also, many of the conference sessions are devoted to making effective use of software in teaching as it pertains to the interest group of the conference.

Software Evaluation

We must keep in mind that the fundamental reason for using computer software is to enhance teaching and learning. The fundamental reason for software evaluation is to see if it fits your educational goals. D'Ignazio (1992, pp. 54–55) states,

> Technology has the potential to dramatically improve the performance of teachers and students, and enrich the learning environment. However, in order to produce these outcomes, technology must be used to support the "best practices" for teaching and learning.

Technology must be used by teachers to create a classroom that encourages:

- Heightened student attention, engagement, and enthusiasm for learning
- Inspired teaching
- Students taking responsibility for their learning and for coaching fellow students
- Student authoring, publishing, and presentations
- Cooperative learning
- Problem solving, critical thinking, questioning, and analysis
- Collaborative inquiry, research, and investigation

When evaluating software, keep some kind of permanent record that describes the product and lists its features and potential applications. Keeping a record of the evaluation serves two purposes. The first purpose is to allow you to refine the criteria and guidelines needed to assess the quality and appropriateness of the software. The second is to allow you to use the information from the evaluation in the school's electronic resource guides to media available in the school or in the public access catalog of the school library's automated system if the software is purchased.

Some of the criteria for evaluation are common to all software, while some of the evaluative criteria are specific to types of software: drill and practice, tutorial, simulation, or tool. The following sections will consider the evaluation process, first according to general criteria, and then according to criteria related to software type.

General Criteria. Familiarize yourself with the total software package. Read the instructions to the teacher and to the user. Look over the manuals, if available. Pay attention to the organization and layout of the written material.

Run the program, following the written or on-screen directions, and see if the program leads you through the material in a well-organized fashion. Notice if the program will let you correct mistakes or if it will trap data entry errors. Can you exit the program at any point without difficulty? Is the information accurate? How well are the displays organized?

After you are familiar with the intent of the program, examine the guidelines in this section, which attempt to address the soundness of the software. The actual worth of the program is determined by the school's curriculum needs. A program can be very good technically but may not develop the needed goals, or it may be of fair technical quality but very good in terms of its approach to subject and content.

Many programs can be used in a variety of settings. Group interaction, whether as an entire class or as a small group of students in a lab setting, can encourage communication and sharing, which leads to a broader range of ideas. Team interaction can occur in either a cooperative or competitive situation. Individual interaction focused on gathering information for a group promotes cooperation and teamwork, enhancing the development of problem-solving techniques. When reviewing software, consider the possible settings in which the program may be used.

Many factors are viewed differently, depending on the classification of the software as drill and practice, tutorial, simulation, or one of the construction tools such as word processors and databases. The following general guidelines will help to measure the soundness of a program and to gather information about a piece of software in the drill and practice, tutorial, and simulation formats.

General Evaluation Guidelines for Educational Software

1. Documentation
   a. Is a manual included?
   b. Are the instructions clear and easy to read?
   c. Are goals and objectives clearly stated?
   d. Are suggested lesson plans or activities included?
   e. Are other resource materials included?
2. Ease of use
   a. Is minimum knowledge needed to run the program?
   b. Are potential errors trapped?
   c. Is text easily readable on the monitor screen?
   d. Can the user skip on-screen directions?
   e. Can the student use the program without teacher intervention?
3. Content
   a. Is the content appropriate to the curriculum?
   b. Is the content accurate?
   c. Is the content free of age, gender, and ethnic discrimination?
   d. Is the presentation of the information interesting and does it encourage a high degree of student involvement?
   e. Is the content free of grammar and punctuation errors?
   f. In a simulation, is the content realistic?
4. Performance
   a. Does the program reach its stated goal?
   b. Is the goal worthwhile?
   c. Does the program follow sound educational techniques?
   d. Does the program make proper and effective use of graphics and sound?
   e. Does the program present appropriate reinforcement for correct replies?
   f. Does the program handle incorrect responses appropriately?
5. Versatility
   a. Can the program be used in a variety of ways?
   b. Can the user control the rate of presentation?
   c. Can the user control the sequence of the lesson?
   d. Can the user control the level of difficulty?
   e. Can the user review previous information?
   f. Can the user enter and exit at various points?
   g. In a tutorial, is the user tested and placed at the proper entry level?
   h. In a tutorial, is there effective remedial branching in the instruction?
   i. In a simulation, can the instructor change random and control factors?
6. Data collection
   a. Is the program's data collection and management system easy to use?
   b. Can student data be summarized in tables and charts?
   c. Is the student's privacy and data security ensured?

Evaluating the Use of Graphics and Sound. As we contemplate general characteristics in the evaluation of educational software, we must look beyond text as the carrier of the message. The computer as a tool for instruction and learning must first gain a student's attention and then hold that interest to satisfy a curiosity. Addressing the student's interest by using the computer's capabilities of graphics and sound yields the optimum presentation of the software's message in a drill and practice, tutorial, or simulation format. The use of graphics and sound has become so ubiquitous in educational software that it deserves special consideration in the evaluation process.

Use of Sound. Sound can enhance the learning experience by adding a degree of realism and by holding the user's attention. It can be used as a reward or reinforcement. Sound can help to highlight key concepts. Music and speech synthesis are important factors in some software. Conversely, sound can be distracting in a classroom or in a room full of computers. The ability to turn sound on or off is desirable. If sound is important to the concept being presented, the user should be able to direct it to an external connection, rather than to the computer's built-in speaker, to permit the use of headphones.

Use of Graphics. Learning theorists stress the importance of graphic representation as a means of simplifying complex interactions of verbal and nonverbal communication. A picture contributes an image to be stored in memory for later retrieval. This function is critical to learning.

Graphics included in computer-assisted instruction have the same impact on the student. In a review of visual research, Francis Dwyer (1978) concluded that a moderate amount of realism in a visual results in the maximum amount of learning. Too little realism may not offer enough visual clues, and too much may distract the viewer. Graphics in software are often used to focus student attention. Studies have shown, however, that visual stimuli used to attract attention may not be the most effective in sustaining attention (Dwyer, 1978, p. 156). High-resolution computer graphics offering a moderate degree of realism have the potential to maximize learning. Graphics must support the ideas being communicated without detracting from the instructional objective of the activity. Some very poor programs have been marketed that pair graphic symbols with unrelated text or that animate a concept improperly, making the lesson needlessly confusing. These program flaws must be detected in the evaluation process.

The graphic design of text must be considered in combination with visual presentation. Screen layout and design are important in maintaining student attention and interest. The screen should not be overcrowded and should present only one major idea at a time. Animation extends the descriptive impact of the concept being communicated by showing the logical sequence of development. In reviewing basic math materials found in products of three large commercial software publishers, Francis Fisher (1982) found examples of terrible graphics design, inappropriate use of sound, and other misapplications of computer technology. Although significant improvements have been made since Fisher's initial research, his findings are still applicable as an element of evaluation.

The program in Figure 13–3 responds to a wrong answer with a confusing screen display. What response is the question "How many are there?" supposed to elicit? The number of empty circles? The number of filled circles? The total number of circles? Is it likely that students who cannot add 7 and 2 in the first place will be able

Figure 13–3

Example of confusing screen display

Figure 13–4

Inappropriate use of sound

Figure 13–5

Example of poor allocation of screen area

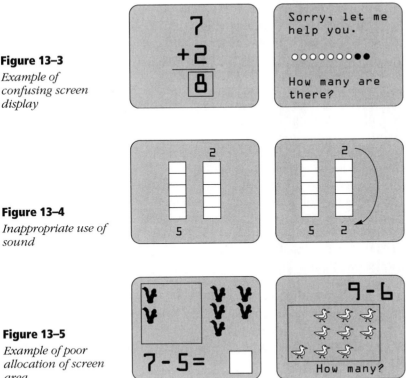

to figure out the intended connection between empty circles and the first number in the problem and filled circles and the second number? Such students can and probably will get the answer faster by counting on their fingers than by puzzling over these complicated, poorly organized instructions.

In the right screen of Figure 13–4, the number 2 travels downward, accompanied by musical sound effects. This attention-getter is totally irrelevant to the instruction and serves only to distract some youngsters needlessly.

Figure 13–5 illustrates a poor use of the screen area. In the screen to the left, five squirrels have left the box. The two remaining squirrels are located directly above the number 7. The answer box (in which the user is supposed to enter 2) is placed under the five squirrels. The potential confusion here is caused by a designer working against the advantages of the medium. Instead of using the screen space to illustrate the subtraction process plainly in terms of numbers and related squirrel symbols, the designer created a visual juxtaposition of actual minuend with the subtrahend symbolized by the two squirrels and the minuend symbolized by the five squirrels with the intended answer. The screen to the right also has a poorly placed, misleading question that appears to be asking how many are in the box. In evaluating software, be alert for such misuses of graphics capability.

An Evaluation Instrument for CAI Software. Having familiarized ourselves with general criteria and guidelines for the evaluation of educational software and the evaluation of graphics and sound, we must attempt to develop a process for the evaluation of CAI software. A effective instrument is at the heart of a successful process. Just as one set of curricular materials is not expected to meet all the needs of all students, one type of software cannot be expected to address all needs. One "standard" list of criteria will not measure all the necessary elements of good CAI software in the areas of drill and practice, tutorial, and simulation. A reliable list is the set of characteristics that comprises the events of a good lesson in a particular learning situation. A "best fit" happens when the teacher skillfully matches instructional needs with elements in a software program.

An evaluation instrument must provide for the recording of descriptive information about the software being evaluated, as well as a listing of performance criteria. The descriptive elements listed in Figure 13–6 are presented for your consideration.

Once the software is described, it must be examined and rated against performance criteria. Reflecting on the general evaluation guidelines previously presented, a criterion section could be developed that would examine some common traits, as well as allow for the specific characteristics of drill and practice, tutorial, and simulation software to be analyzed.

There is no single correct way to evaluate CAI software. An instrument could be developed that would include only broad guidelines and allow the evaluator considerable leeway in interpreting and applying them. On the other hand, an instrument might have a long list of specifics and a complex scoring system, leaving little to the judgment of the evaluator. Think of an evaluation instrument as a communication device that describes and assesses the value of a given software item. It must convey an accurate impression of the software while being easy and convenient to use. A cumbersome evaluation instrument will be seen as more trouble than it's

```
Program title: _____

Vendor name & address: _____

Vendor phone:_____ Program cost:_____

Computer and operating system requirements: _____

Internal memory needed:_____ Disk space required: __

Other required equipment:_____

Content area: _____ (e.g., mathematics)

Topic:_____ (e.g., common fractions)

Grade level:_____

Brief description of program:_____

_____

Supplementary materials included:_____

Program goals:_____

Time for estimated program execution in minutes:_____
```

Figure 13–6

Descriptive data about CAI software

worth to potential evaluators and, therefore, will be of little use. Four different software evaluation forms are presented for your study in Appendix A of this text. Although all are meant to be used in evaluating drill and practice, tutorial, and simulation software, note the similarities and differences in their design.

An Evaluation Instrument for Word Processing. As with previously examined types of software, an evaluation instrument must provide for the recording of descriptive information about the software being evaluated, as well as a listing of performance criteria. The descriptive elements presented in Figure 13–7 are appropriate for word processors, spreadsheets, and databases.

Once the software is described, it must be examined and rated against performance criteria specific to word processors. The general categories to be explored would include ease of use, sophistication of features, and usefulness of editing functions. The two most important questions to answer are "What will it be used for?" and "Who will be using it?" The tasks it will be expected to perform determine which features are most important. The intended user will determine the needed editing functions and relate them directly to the ease of use expected.

Review of Word Processor Features. The following are some features readily found on a number of word processors currently on the market. The evaluation form that is developed should contain reference to these and perhaps to other features as well.

column formatting Some word processors allow the user to format a page in multiple columns. Columns can be parallel or newspaper-style, with text flowing from the bottom of one column to the top of the adjacent one.

footer A footer is a brief message that may include a date, time, or page display that is automatically added to the bottom of each page.

header A header, similar to a footer, can be automatically added to the top of each page.

help screens Help screens present information to the user about the operation of the word processor and its functions as the need arises.

hyphenation The hyphenation feature generates a hyphen at the most appropriate syllable break in a word at the end of a line.

Figure 13–7

Descriptive data about word processors, spreadsheets, and databases

Program title: _____

Vendor name & address: _____

Program cost:_____

Computer and operating system requirements: _____

Internal memory needed:_____Disk space required: _____

Other required equipment: _____

Software type: _____ (e.g., word processor) _____

Supplementary materials included: _____

import This feature allows the user to insert graphics or other file types into a document.

index An index feature allows a user to mark words that are then automatically copied to an index at the end of the document.

mail merge A feature that allows the merging of data in one file to the proper place in another document.

outlining An integrated outliner allows the user to create an outline of the document and to expand or collapse various levels.

pagination Once a user sets the page length of the document by prescribing top and bottom margins on a specified size of paper, this feature allows a word processor to automatically generate page breaks, indicate them on the screen, number pages, and renumber them when editing is performed.

preview document The better programs allow document editing in this page view and closely approach a WYSIWYG (What You See Is What You Get) state when printed.

speller A spell-checking feature allows the user to compare each word in a document with a known list in the speller's database.

thesaurus A selected word is compared with a list in the thesaurus, and a number of synonyms are suggested to avoid undue repetitions.

Review of Editing Functions. The following are the most often used editing functions and are commonly found in many word processors.

copy This command allows the duplication of selected text or graphics to a storage area in temporary memory.

cut This command allows the removal of selected text or graphics to a storage area in temporary memory.

delete The removal or erasure of text can be accomplished in a number of ways. The remaining text is automatically rearranged properly, with word wrap and page breaks being taken into account.

find and replace This feature allows the user to find and, if desired, to replace a particular word or phrase by searching for it in the document.

paste This command allows whatever is stored in temporary memory to be duplicated and inserted into the document at the location of the cursor.

Remember that word processing programs are available either as individual programs or as integrated software that may also contain a spreadsheet, a file manager, graphics, and telecommunications components. Stand-alone programs are usually more powerful and feature-laden than similar programs that are part of integrated packages. An evaluation form is presented in Appendix B of this text. When examining it, you might find it useful to review the descriptions presented here and in Chapter 6.

An Evaluation Instrument for Spreadsheets. The descriptive information recorded about the word processing software being evaluated, as shown in Figure 13–7, is appropriate to the evaluation of spreadsheets as well. The spreadsheet is a tool uniquely suited to arrange and display data in a matrix of rows and columns. It can store text, values, and formulas that perform a wide range of calculations. The evaluation of spreadsheets should examine both the power and the ease with which the tool may be employed.

Review of Spreadsheet Features. The following are some features readily found on a number of spreadsheets currently on the market. The evaluation form that is developed should contain reference to these and other features as well.

cell formatting Along with the usual font formats and alignment, spreadsheets often provide a wide range of formats for decimal values, currency, time, and date.

charting Spreadsheets may generate a wide variety of charts such as area, bar, column, line, and pie. Some programs also create pictograms.

deletes/inserts Columns and rows may be able to be deleted or inserted, with any affected formulas adjusting automatically.

display options The user may control whether or not gridlines, column and row headings, and values or formulas are displayed.

filling cells automatically Once an entry is made in a cell, spreadsheets usually allow the user to replicate the entry across a row to the right or down a column.

functions Spreadsheets may have 100 or more built-in routines, called functions, in categories such as business, date, logical, statistical, and mathematics.

grid labeling A convention has emerged in which rows are identified numerically and columns are identified alphabetically.

page and view formatting The user may be able to set forced page breaks and be able to designate the specific area to be printed. The screen should be split into panes, or views, in order to constantly display the same information at the top or at the left edge. The user should be able to lock the position of rows or columns used as titles, and these titles should be able to print on every page in a manner similar to headers and footers.

protecting data The user can usually lock cells in order to protect data or formulas from being changed accidentally.

sorting Ranges of cells may be able to be sorted by rows or by columns. Multiple-level, or nested, sorts are very useful.

Again, it is important to note that spreadsheets are available either as individual programs or as integrated software packages. Stand-alone programs are usually more powerful and have a greater number of features than similar programs that are part of integrated packages. An evaluation form is presented in Appendix C of this text. When examining it, you might find it useful to review the descriptions presented here and in Chapter 8.

An Evaluation Instrument for Databases. The descriptive information recorded about the word processing software being evaluated, as shown in Figure 13–7, is appropriate to the evaluation of databases as well. The database manager is a tool uniquely suited to store, access, and organize data in order to display information in an "on-line" screen fashion or as printed reports. It can store text, values, and formulas that perform a wide range of calculations in a record and can effectively summarize information across a number of records. The evaluation of a database manager should examine both the power and the ease with which the tool may be employed.

Review of Database Features. The following are some features readily found on a number of database managers currently on the market. The evaluation form that is developed should contain reference to these and other functions as well.

accuracy control Database managers should include the ability to restrict or evaluate data entry to ensure its accuracy (e.g., a number field meant to record a student's GPA and restricted to data entry between 0 and 4 would not allow a decimal to be typed in the wrong place, resulting in an entry of 35.0).

data entry automation Data such as a serial number or the date might be automatically entered when a new record is created. In order to simplify and control data entry, a layout might include checkboxes, pop-up lists, or buttons to be clicked with the mouse rather than requiring data always to be entered through the keyboard.

field definition Fields should be able to be defined as text, number (value), calculation, and summary. Some programs include other fields such as date and time.

file linkage Some flat file managers emulate relational database managers by allowing the user to create links between files so that data can be exchanged automatically.

finding records The user should be able to find records using the Boolean constructs of AND, OR, and NOT, as well as the operators < (less than), > (greater than), and = (exact match).

layout The better database managers allow the user a great deal of control in designing the data layouts (forms or views). Several programs include a number of preformatted layouts, along with graphics tools to enhance their appearance.

sorting The user should be able to sort the entire file or a found set of records in ascending or descending order. Multiple-level, or nested, sorts are very useful. They allow records to be sorted first by the contents of one field (e.g., last name) and then by the contents of another field (e.g., first name).

As is the case for word processors and spreadsheets, database managers are available either as individual programs or as part of integrated software packages. Stand-alone programs are usually more powerful and more feature-laden than similar programs that are part of integrated packages. An evaluation form is presented in Appendix D of this text. When examining it, you might find it useful to review the descriptions presented here and in Chapter 9.

Software Selection

The importance of the use of computer software to locate information is directly proportional to the increase in the amount of knowledge required to function effectively in today's society. Teachers and students are making better use of a greater variety of all forms of media in instruction and learning. Computer software is a resource that can be used by itself or in conjunction with other instructional materials. The increased impact of curriculum materials, including educational software, dramatically underlines the significance of the evaluation and selection of high-quality materials. Software that may be effective in one setting may not be useful in another, even if it covers the same concepts. It is important to have a process for determining the quality and content of materials with respect to the needs of the student.

Evaluation is used to assess the quality of the software product. Selection takes evaluation a step further by matching the quality of the software and its cost to the specific needs of your school. This can be accomplished in several ways. In the case of an inexpensive or highly specific stand-alone program, the individual making the evaluation may complete the process by recommending purchase. When a more substantial purchase is contemplated or the software under consideration is applicable in a variety of settings, the collective wisdom, experience, and training present in a team of educators may be valuable in order to better analyze collected evaluations and arrive at a decision regarding selection. Individual teacher requests should certainly play a role in shaping a software collection, but requests should be measured against current software availability in the collection. Notice should be given to all subject areas, but the areas of greatest need and use (based on an understanding of a particular school user community) should be emphasized. Decisions will always take into account costs and budgets, software currently in the collection, equipment presently available or needing to be purchased, number of machines and number of students per machine, and computer literacy of the staff. The important issue in each case should be the "best fit" between the needs of students and teachers and the features of the software.

Teachers have the final word on instructional use and must use the characteristics of a good learning situation as the criteria to measure the value of the software package. Since district needs and student characteristics vary, professional judgment on what elements are present or missing in relation to an instructional situation is the only feasible "standard for evaluation." This judgment also determines what elements need to be supplied in the learning environment or what adaptations need to be made to the software.

The selection process requires documentation of decisions made. Software evaluation, selection, and acquisition are closely related, and an efficient documentation process should relate to each phase. If a school has an automated library system in place, such a system might well provide the best means of documenting selection decisions. If not, as software is selected, a software inventory database could be designed.

Figure 13–8 suggests data fields in a sample selection screen layout for a software database that would capture relevant information describing software that was selected for purchase. Libraries call information entered at this point the "shelf list record." Data recorded on the descriptive portion of the evaluation form could be entered in the selection screen of the database.

Should you be interested in replicating the record-keeping processes of selection, acquisition, and access described in this chapter, Appendix M of this text contains the complete file description of the software database designed in *FileMaker Pro™*. You can create this file using either the Macintosh or Windows version of the program and apply it to your own use.

Title [   ]   Version # [   ]

Publisher [   ]   Copyright Date [   ]

Vendor Name [   ]

Street Address [   ]

City, ST, ZIP [   ]

Vendor Phone # [   ]   Technical Support # (if different) [   ]

Computer and OS requirements [   ]

RAM needed [   ]   Hard disk space [   ]

License [   ]   Number of Users [   ]

Grade Level [   ]   Cost: [   ]

Description [   ]

Software Type

○ D&P   ○ Tut   ○ Sim   ○ Multi   ○ WP   ○ SS   ○ DB   ○ Gr   ○ Comm   ○ Other

Subject Area

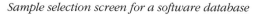
○ Foreign Language ○ Language Arts ○ Math ○ Science ○ Social Studies

Figure 13–8

Sample selection screen for a software database

Software Acquisition

After the software is selected for purchase, some of the data recorded in the selection step could then be used in the acquisition phase and later to facilitate student and teacher access to information about the software and to promote the software's use. A sample acquisition screen layout is presented as Figure 13–9. Data in the shaded boxes would have been recorded at the time of the selection. The P.O. #,

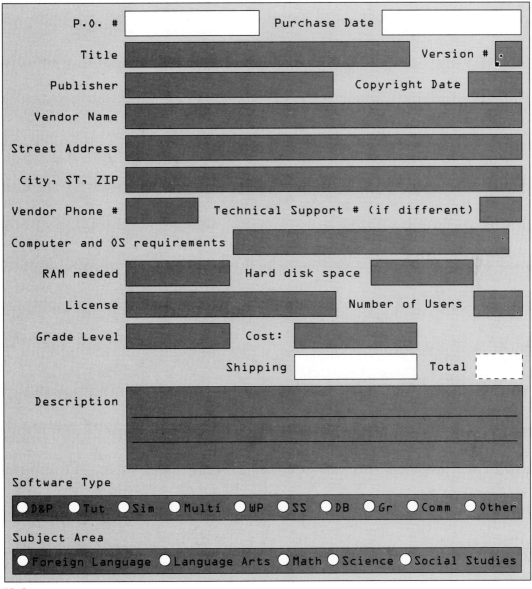

Figure 13–9

Sample acquisition screen for a software database

Purchase Date, and Shipping fields would be entered as the software was ordered. The computer would calculate the total cost.

Before sending the order, the person doing the purchasing might wish to do some cost comparisons, remembering that the price, along with the quality of service provided by the vendor, is the true determiner of value. A consideration of vendor service should include the timeliness of delivery, the customer's right to return prod-

Figure 13–10

The process of sustaining a collection

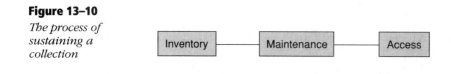

ucts that do not perform as expected, the vendor's willingness to demonstrate software, and the vendor's technical support by telephone. Should a different vendor be chosen, the Vendor Name and the Address fields of that particular software record would be edited.

Purchase considerations might include deciding whether to buy a single copy, multiple copies (often called a lab pack), or a site license that would grant unlimited use at one location. When purchasing lab packs or a site license, the necessary number of manuals should also be ordered.

SUSTAINING A SOFTWARE COLLECTION

As indicated in Figure 13–10, the process of supporting a collection can be thought of as the three functions necessary to sustain a viable and effective collection of software: (1) inventory, (2) maintenance, and (3) access. These three functions might differ very little from those applied to all other print and nonprint formats of instructional materials in the school library.

Software Collection Inventory

As previously mentioned, school librarians use the term *shelf list* to denote the inventory they maintain of books, films, videos, kits, and all other forms of media. This concept should be extended to computer software. It makes very little sense to treat the inventory of software in a manner different from other formats. Granted, physical access to software is different and it doesn't circulate in a manner similar to some other formats. However, its intellectual access requirements are identical. It should be found by searching the library's automated system or card catalog.

Once software has been ordered and received from the vendor, it should be verified against the purchase order, checked to see that it runs properly, and marked for ownership. Backup disks should be copied for archival purposes and must be stored in a secure place, not circulated. The software should then be cataloged and classified to ensure the intellectual access recently mentioned and then entered into the school's software inventory or into the library's shelf list or automated system.

The main purposes of maintaining a software inventory are accountability and control. The expenditure of public funds demands a reasonable accounting. Current and future selections should be compared against the content and scope of the current collection. An effective inventory will identify software location in order to facilitate its circulation and maximize its use.

Building on the software database designed to record selection and acquisition data, Figure 13–11 shows shaded boxes that already contain data. Cataloging and

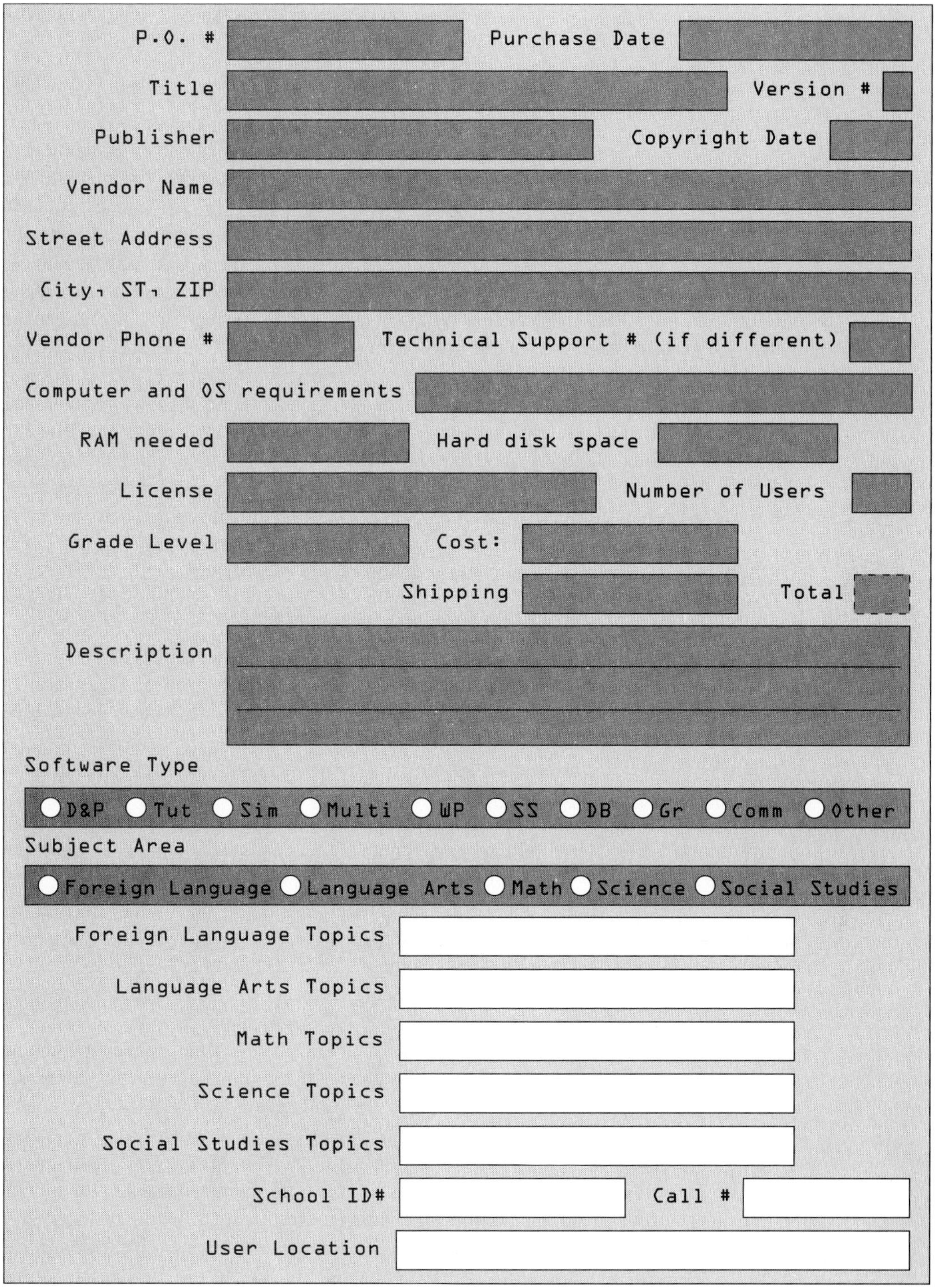

| P.O. # | | Purchase Date | |

| Title | | Version # | |

| Publisher | | Copyright Date | |

Vendor Name

Street Address

City, ST, ZIP

| Vendor Phone # | | Technical Support # (if different) | |

Computer and OS requirements

| RAM needed | | Hard disk space | |

| License | | Number of Users | |

| Grade Level | | Cost: | |

| | | Shipping | | Total | |

Description

Software Type

○ D&P ○ Tut ○ Sim ○ Multi ○ WP ○ SS ○ DB ○ Gr ○ Comm ○ Other

Subject Area

○ Foreign Language ○ Language Arts ○ Math ○ Science ○ Social Studies

Foreign Language Topics

Language Arts Topics

Math Topics

Science Topics

Social Studies Topics

| School ID# | | Call # | |

User Location

Figure 13–11

Sample inventory screen for a software database

classification yield the Call # and Topics fields in the specific subject areas. The School ID #, if any, will be assigned and User Location data, identifying where the software will be housed permanently or on a long-term basis, are now added to the record of each software item being inventoried.

The entire software collection need not be housed in one central location; in fact, it might be more effective if the collection were dispersed to locations in close proximity to greatest potential use, as long as one centralized catalog of holdings is maintained to provide ease of access by everyone. Some software would undoubtedly reside in the library media center and in the computer lab, while other software would be better housed in the science lab or the foreign language classroom. Care needs to be taken that teachers understand that the software purchased by the school is for the use of all teachers and students, not just those in a particular classroom.

Circulation of software is somewhat different from that of other library media materials. Circulation systems in school libraries are sophisticated programs designed to handle a high volume of materials being checked in and out. Software circulation, on the other hand, tends to be of a very low volume and of infrequent occurrence. Often copies are legitimately loaded onto hard disk drives or file servers. Software is often checked out on a long-term basis to locations of greatest potential use in the school. Teachers and students, however, do not generally check out software to take home, since the legal number of copies must be controlled.

The concept of computer software circulation is really one of inventory. Effective inventory control dictates that software records be centralized to minimize needless duplication and to facilitate sharing among teachers and instructional programs. In a large setting, centralized cataloging of software also provides a reference source for future acquisitions.

Software Collection Maintenance

Collection maintenance is essential to sustain currency, relevance, and balance in a software collection. It's easy for a collection to become unnecessarily large and cumbersome as software is added and none is discarded. As well-designed and more effective software is acquired, older software in the collection should be replaced. The collection should be weeded periodically to remove software that is dated, is functioning poorly, or has not been used for a long time. Maintenance of the software collection should be approached as both an ongoing and a periodic process. An ongoing assessment of the software collection will reveal dated, faulty, or cumbersome materials that are no longer effective, prompting their removal and a search for replacement products. Periodically, the entire collection should be assessed so that it can be examined as a whole and any changing needs addressed.

Unique problems are encountered when a significant portion of the collection is loaded on hard drives or on a central file server. Who has the responsibility to decide what software is placed on hard drives? This should not be left up to individual users. Many schools, lacking full-time computer coordinators, have assigned this task to the library media specialist. In many parts of the country, the word *technology* has not only crept into this person's job description but has been made part of his or her professional title. It follows, then, that this person should also be responsible for periodically purging software that has become outdated or has fallen into disuse. It is also important to monitor version numbers of software. Usually, as software upgrades are purchased, old versions are removed from use to simplify the situation for the users. New versions are backward-compatible with prior ones. Launching the new version and opening a file created by a previous one usually result in the file being updated to the new version.

To make the best use of budget resources, assure compatibility, and simplify staff training needs, a school will often decide to support only one word processing, spreadsheet, and database program. The choice is often to support an integrated package such as *ClarisWorks™* or *Microsoft Works™*.

Software Collection Access

The goal of collection access is to match the software to the user as effectively and efficiently as possible. Many schools have installed sophisticated library automation systems. Software records should be entered into these systems. This would provide one central point for information to be retrieved for all print and nonprint formats. If a school does not have a library automation system or chooses not to enter software records, a further refinement of the database begun at the selection stage might be effective.

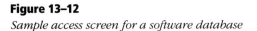

Title	
Publisher	
Software Type	
Subject Area	
◯ Foreign Language ◯ Language Arts ◯ Math ◯ Science ◯ Social Studies	
Foreign Language Topics	
Language Arts Topics	
Math Topics	
Science Topics	
Social Studies Topics	
Location	Call #

Figure 13–12

Sample access screen for a software database

At this stage, all of the information has been entered into the software database. The task now is to retrieve information by doing a search (Find) on any field present in Figure 13–12. The sample access screen layout presented contains only the information judged relevant to the user. Individual software items can be located, with all pertinent information displayed on the screen. A software catalog may be organized by subject area and specific topics and printed as a hard copy.

The responsibility for collection development often rests with the school library media specialist. It is this person's obligation to promote the collection's effective use by teachers and students. This can be done by circulating or posting memos featuring particular software, especially new acquisitions. Bibliographies pertinent to specific topics or events might be posted. One-on-one consulting relative to an individual's need is perhaps the most effective way of ensuring good use of the collection.

SUMMARY

Collection management describes the processes and procedures by which libraries acquire materials to meet the information needs of teachers and students. The term is well suited to describing the responsibilities and activities related to the evaluation, selection, acquisition, processing, organization, maintenance, promotion, and effective use of computer software.

The process of software selection consists of finding sources along with product information and reviews, evaluating the product, and then selecting the product for adoption in a given setting. One "standard" list of evaluative criteria will not measure all of the necessary elements of good software. An instrument to evaluate software must allow the recording of both descriptive and evaluative information. It is a communication device that describes and assesses a software item. It must convey an accurate impression of the software while itself being easy and convenient to use. Information from the completed evaluation form could be included in the public access catalog of the school library's automated system or stored in another database format.

When evaluating word processors, spreadsheets, and databases, the general categories to be explored include its ease of use, the sophistication of its features, and the usefulness of its functions. The tasks it will be expected to perform determine which features are most important. The intended user will determine the needed functions and relate them directly to the ease of use expected.

Once software has been ordered and received, it should be verified against the purchase order, checked to see that it runs properly, and entered into the school's software inventory. Backup disks should be copied for archival purposes and must be stored in a secure place, not circulated. Effective inventory control dictates that software records are centralized to minimize needless duplication and to facilitate sharing among instructional programs. Centralized records also provide a reference source for future acquisitions.

Effective collection maintenance preserves currency, relevance, and balance in a software collection. As more effective software is acquired, it should replace older software in the collection. The collection should be weeded periodically to remove software that is dated, is functioning poorly, or has not been used for a long time. The process of collection assessment allows you to base acquisitions on the quality of the material and with an eye to complementing the existing collection.

The goal of collection access is to match the software to the user as effectively and efficiently as possible. For schools that have installed sophisticated library automation systems, software records should be entered. This would provide one central point for information to be retrieved for all print and nonprint formats. If a school does not have a library automation system or chooses not to enter software records, a specific software database might be effective.

The school library media specialist or whoever is responsible for collection management should promote the software collection's effective use by teachers and students. This can be done by circulating or posting bibliographies and memos featuring particular software, especially new acquisitions. Personal attention related to an individual's need is perhaps the most effective way of ensuring good use of the collection.

CHAPTER EXERCISES

1. Review the sample evaluation forms in Appendix A. Develop your own form for the evaluation of software in the area of drill and practice, tutorial, and simulation.

2. Locate advertisements for a popular computer program. Compare the ad to a review of the program. Is the ad misleading? What functions does the ad highlight? What does the review say about these functions?

3. Reviewing catalogs of instructional materials publishers, list 10 titles of materials available in videodisc and/or CD-ROM formats and identify their subject area, grade level, systems requirements, and cost.

4. Using a published review of a program, fill out the form you designed as a result of your study of the sample evaluation forms in Appendix A. Are there items on your form that cannot be answered from the review?

5. Run a program and evaluate it, using the form you designed. Comment on the process of reviewing. Was it frustrating or rewarding? How long did it take you to evaluate the program thoroughly?

6. Using a published review of a spreadsheet, fill out the appropriate evaluation form found in Appendix C. Are there items on the form that cannot be answered from the review?

7. Using a published review of a database management program, fill out the appropriate form found in Appendix D. Are there items on the form that cannot be answered from the review?

8. Operate a word processor with which you are not very familiar and evaluate it, using the form found in Appendix B. Comment on the process of reviewing. How long did it take you to evaluate the program thoroughly?

9. Determine the evaluative system used by two different magazines or journals that publish software reviews. In each case, who does the reviewing? Is the

review based on student use of the program? Describe the strengths and shortcomings of both publications' reviewing systems.

10. While there are ideal ways to evaluate and acquire software, what constraints do you see in a school situation that might interfere with carrying out the process in an optimum way?

11. You have just acquired a new software program at your school. Describe how you would promote its use.

GLOSSARY

collection management The processes and procedures of evaluation, selection, acquisition, processing, organization, and maintenance of computer software or other materials.

freeware Software available without charge.

public domain Not protected by copyright; may be duplicated.

shareware Software available at minimal charge, with payment usually on the honor system.

virus A potentially damaging program that surreptitiously installs itself in the user's system software or hard disk. Viruses are often spread when users download files or exchange floppy disks.

virus protection program Software that prevents viruses from being copied to your hard drive and/or repairs your drive by eradicating existing viruses before they can do more damage.

REFERENCES & SUGGESTED READINGS

Barba, R. H. (1990, May). Examining computer configurations: Mini labs. *The Computing Teacher,* 8–13.

D'Ignazio, F. (1992, August/September). Are you getting your money's worth? *The Computing Teacher,* 54–55.

Dwyer, F. M. (1978). *Strategies for improving visual learning.* State College, PA: Learning Services, 33, 156.

Fetner, C., & Johnson, K. (1990, March/April). Selecting software—Who me? *The Computing Teacher,* 12–15.

Fisher, F. D. (1982, Summer). Computer assisted education: What's not happening. *Journal of Computer-Based Instruction, 9*(1), 19–27.

Maddux, C. D. (1991, October). Integration versus computer labs: An either/or proposition? *Educational Technology, 31*(1), 36–40.

Maxwell, J. R., & Lamon, W. E. (1992, August/September). Computer viruses: Pathology and detection. *The Computing Teacher,* 12–15.

Powell, N., & Bushing, M. (1992). *Collection assessment manual* (4th ed.). Lacey, WA: Western Library Network.

Salpeter, J. (1993, September). The multimedia encyclopedias face off. *Technology & Learning, 14*(1), 30–38.

Salvador, R. (1994, September). Copyright and wrong. *Electronic Learning, 14*(1), 32–33, 86.

Wedman, J. F. (1986, November). Making software more useful. *The Computing Teacher, 13*(3) 11–14.

Afterword

Today's information technologies provide us a glimpse into our educational future. They are serving as a catalyst for school reform. With the thought that innovations in technology allow us to dream about the potential of tomorrow's education, I will close with the following story told by Melanie Wallis (1997, pp. 2–9), an elementary school library media specialist, as she looks into the future.

The school day had already begun when the small group of visitors entered the building. They are teachers who had come to observe Community School, an elementary school which had received many awards and accolades for innovative teaching. The school manager greeted them near the entrance.

"Welcome to our school. We'll begin with a tour of the facility, and I'll try to fill you in on aspects of our program as we go."

The manager led the teachers down a short hallway and paused at the intersection of a larger one branching off in both directions. "One difference between our school and traditional schools is that Community School has redefined the role of the principal. As school manager, I oversee the condition and use of the facility; serve as the chair of the personnel committee; coordinate scheduling; facilitate the professional, paraprofessional, and clerical staff; and work as a liaison to parents and the community through our site council. Educational leadership is provided by a team consisting of the information technologist, the lead teachers and the child-care director.

"Here we are at the hub of our school—the information technology center."

The group entered a very large octagonal room through an archway. In the middle of the room was a low, octagonal desk. The center was lined with smaller rooms, computer stations, bookshelves, and a sunken stage with an interactive 3-D wall screen. Children and adults were working, conversing and reading individually and in small groups around the room. There was a purposeful hum of activity.

"The technology center is our pride and joy," beamed the manager. "We believe that we couldn't get along without it. You'll notice the smaller rooms off to your left. Those are our production rooms, used for various projects our learners are working on. We have multimedia capabilities, including sound recording, animation, video, and holographic imaging. Two of the rooms have virtual reality stations for interaction and production. Virtual reality has been the most popular feature of the technology center for quite some time." The manager chuckled. "It's all we can do to get the parents out at closing time."

The visitors walked past the production rooms toward the stage, where a class of older children was viewing the construction of a space dome on the wall-sized 3-D imaging screen. The manager turned toward the visitors.

"If you'll look toward the far side of the room, you'll see our book stacks, which includes our optical disk collections as well. Although some people would have us dispense [with] books altogether, we obviously disagree. We like to give the kids lots of experiences with the books so they're exposed to a medium that encourages them to use their imagination."

The visitors noticed a few computer stations next to the book stacks. The manager explained that those were primarily used as backup stations. Once learners enter the Intermediate Unit of the school, they are each issued laptop computers at the beginning of the school year that connect to an infrared network throughout the school campus for on-line information searching and satellite downlinks. The information technology center is also connected to the Regional Information Center, through which it accesses the Worldwide Info Network. From the classrooms, their homes or the school, students and adults could communicate with people or databases at information centers around the world. The school provides the necessary equipment for those students' families who are without personal information terminals.

A woman approached them from the computer stations. "Hello, I'm the Information Technologist. The manager told me you were coming and were curious about our program. I'm in charge of this center, which serves the children and staff as well as their parents and other members of the community. My staff consists of two information specialists, a technician, and several assistants. The information specialists and I work with the lead teachers to develop curriculum and plan appropriate learning opportunities for the children. I also coordinate the community outreach program and the volunteer program. Since we're open 12 hours each day except for Sunday, it takes quite a few people to keep things operating smoothly!" She looked up as another group of children entered the center. "You'll have to excuse me. Here comes the robotics team I'm scheduled to work with."

The manager spoke. "Let's walk out to the classroom area, while I address scheduling." They exited the center through the same doorway they had entered. "As the director mentioned, we are open from 7:00 a.m. until seven at night. Students are scheduled for a core block of time during the mornings and afternoons which they spend working with their core teacher, working on cooperative team investigations, individualized learning modules, and individual investigations and projects. Enrichment and extension classes are scheduled before and after their core, or they may schedule individual work time with their teacher, mentor or in the technology center. Lunch and snacks are provided, and of course, the students get daily recreation and fitness time!"

The manager continued talking as the tour group walked down the hallway which encircled the Information Technology Center. "The technology center is the largest room in our school and you probably noticed that it was eight-sided. This surrounding hallway opens into eight wings radiating from the center. You entered the building through the smallest wing which houses the administrative component. Flanking the administrative wing are the community health center and the childcare facility. Both have their own independent directors who coordinate with me.

"The health center has a separate entrance, and serves the entire community as well as the school. It is a primary care unit fully staffed with physicians and nurses. One feature which benefits us is the KidsKare area. It's a group of rooms, each decorated with a different theme, for kids who are contagious. It gives parents an option on those days

when their child can't be at school, but isn't sick enough to need to be home in bed. Children can even keep up with their classrooms' activities with two-way interactive video!

"The adults on staff at the care unit are also integrated into our educational program as mentors, volunteers, and resource people. Several groups of children have done fascinating research projects about aspects of the clinic and its operation. They spent up to a week observing and even participating in the clinic's routines as part of their fact-gathering stage.

"If you'll look to your left, you'll see the childcare facility which includes infants through age six and directs a portion of the before and after school program. The childcare center's mission is to provide a broad range of developmentally appropriate activities to stimulate and encourage curiosity, creativity, and critical thinking skills. They also provide parenting classes on subjects such as discipline and nutrition." The visitors were able to catch a glimpse of brightly painted walls and children's artwork before the manager ushered them on.

"Here is our community gym and fitness center. The students have priority during the day, but it is heavily used by the entire community. Fitness specialists instruct the children and plan daily activities. Each child's progress is carefully monitored and the program is adjusted accordingly. The specialists even use virtual reality to help the kids master new skills—that really keeps them motivated!"

The manager checked his watch. "It's almost lunch time. The wing directly opposite us, on the other side of the technology center, houses our cafeteria and food preparation facilities. That wing also has our auditorium and the music practice rooms." He grinned as he motioned the visitors on. "We'll be getting to that side of the building at just about the right time!"

The group of visitors was now standing with their backs toward the second archway into the Information Technology Center, having gone halfway around the building. Directly in front of them, and to the left and the right were the three classroom wings of the school. Between each of the radiating wings were windows and doorways opening onto gardens.

"I see you've noticed our horticulture laboratory, more commonly referred to as 'The Gardens,'" the manager said, following the gazes of a number of the group. "Plots of land are provided for students and their families, as well as for student groups. It's been quite a success!

"Now, I'd like to tell you about our educational program. We serve 450 full-time students, and another 200 children who come part-time or are home-schooled and connected to our network. The three wings are organized by the ages and learning characteristics of the children. The Early Childhood Unit to your left is for four- through seven-year-olds. The focus for them is on socialization, verbal communication, cooperative skills, and the exploration of objects and ideas. No formal reading or writing is taught, but the foundation is firmly established through developmentally appropriate activities. When a child shows competence in the focus areas, and demonstrates that he or she is moving into the concrete operations stage of development, they are moved to the Primary Unit."

The visitors followed the school manager down the hall of the Primary Unit. Doorways on each side opened into rooms of various sizes. Some had tables and chairs, with a few students' desks in groups or scattered singly about. Other rooms had couches and kid-sized rocking chairs. Each room contained several computer stations with multimedia capabilities. Children and adults were busily occupied in each of the rooms with a variety of activities. A teacher was making notes on his pen-based personal digital assistant. The manager commented, "The PDAs sure help teachers jot down anecdotal records and progress information as they interact with the learners. That information is sent over the infrared network and stored in the student's permanent file."

The manager stopped to show the group some of the children's work displayed in the hallway. "The children in this unit focus on developing their reading, writing, speaking and critical thinking skills. The fundamentals of mathematics are taught using manipulatives and problem-solving activities. We strive to develop the whole child here, including ample time for the arts. That's one reason the extended day is so beneficial for everyone."

He smiled and nodded at an adult in one of the rooms. "Each of our units is headed by a lead teacher, supported by the full and part-time teachers, along with assistants and volunteers. The children in the Primary Unit range in age from six to nine years. As in the other units, they are assigned to one core teacher with whom they spend most of their time. They stay with that same teacher for two to three years, although they also are instructed by the other teachers for various projects. The teachers work together as a team to evaluate each child and determine the best educational program. The children are in mixed age groupings which change according to the activities throughout the day."

The group exited the Primary Unit, proceeding to the next wing. The children they now saw were older, but equally involved with a variety of activities and projects. The manager continued his presentation. "The children are moved at their own rate into the Intermediate Unit, which includes ages nine to twelve. One of the main criteria for moving into the Intermediate Unit is the ability of the child to set goals and work without as much direct adult supervision. The focus of this unit is helping the child move from concrete operations to formal operations. Critical thinking and problem solving skills are applied to all areas of the curriculum. Students are encouraged to investigate a broad range of topics and ideas, develop areas of expertise and present their findings to their peers. We expect students to do more than just reporting others' research. They also design and carry out their own scientific investigations, and apply their learning to new situations. By the time they leave us, they are quite capable of structuring their own learning! We strive to teach them skills in learning to last a lifetime."

The group of teachers continued down the hall toward the cafeteria. The manager stopped them before they went in. "Our tour is officially over. Enjoy your lunch, and feel free to observe in the classrooms during the afternoon. I hope you'll be taking back some useful information to your own schools."

Source: Wallis, M. (1997). *A future learning environment.* Unpublished report, Western Oregon University.

Appendixes

DESCRIPTION FORM

The information in the following form is descriptive of software being evaluated. The form is to be used in conjunction with the seven sample evaluation forms that follow (Appendixes A through D) and is meant to be attached to them.

Program title: _____ Version: _____

Publisher: _____

Vendor name and address: _____

Sales phone #: _____ Technical support #: _____

Program cost: $_____ Site license cost: $_____ # Users: _____

Computer and OS requirements: _____

RAM needed: _____ Hard disk space required:_____

Other required equipment: _____

Tutorial: _____ Drill & Practice: _____ Simulation: _____ Multimedia:_____

Content area: _____ Specific topic(s): _____

Grade level: _____

WP _____ SS _____ DB _____ Graphics _____ Other _____

Supplementary materials included: _____

Special features:_____

_____

_____

EVALUATION FORM #1: EDUCATIONAL SOFTWARE

The following is a checklist to refresh your memory regarding important aspects of computer software. Read the entire list before evaluating the software; then check the appropriate items after using the software. Use the summary evaluation section to record your overall impressions of the program.

General Criteria Applicable to All Categories

____ 1. Content is accurate	____ 11. Reinforces/rewards user appropriately
____ 2. Content is appropriate to meet goals	____ 12. Teacher able to modify the content
____ 3. Instructions are clear	____ 13. Keeps records of student progress
____ 4. Program executes reliably	____ 14. No age, gender, or ethnic discrimination
____ 5. Program is easy to use	____ 15. Sound can be controlled
____ 6. Format is interactive	____ 16. Computer used effectively
____ 7. High level of interest maintained	____ 17. Has suggested activities
____ 8. User establishes the pace	____ 18. Support materials are effective
____ 9. Progression in levels of difficulty	____ 19. Program is cost-effective
____10. Handles incorrect responses appropriately	

Additional Criteria Specific to Tutorial Programs

____ 1. Variety in presentation
____ 2. Logical, sequential concept development
____ 3. Frequent testing
____ 4. Positive reinforcement
____ 5. Conditional branching
____ 6. Limits frequency of incorrect responses

Additional Criteria Specific to Simulations

____ 1. Clear directions
____ 2. Appropriate graphics
____ 3. Simple keyboard/mouse use
____ 4. Realistic situation for role playing
____ 5. Results predicated upon user input
____ 6. Promotes problem solving

Summary Evaluation (E = excellent, VG = very good, G = good, F = fair, P = poor):

Appropriateness	E	VG	G	F	P
Performance	E	VG	G	F	P
Documentation	E	VG	G	F	P
Ease of use	E	VG	G	F	P
Overall rating	E	VG	G	F	P

Recommend for purchase? _____

Comments: _____

_____

Evaluator's name: _____

EVALUATION FORM #2: EDUCATIONAL SOFTWARE

The following is a checklist regarding important aspects of computer software. Read the entire list before evaluating the software; then mark a "+" for each item present and adequate after using the software. Count the number of "+" and mark the number of stars in the rating section to record your overall impression of the program.

General Criteria Applicable to All Categories
____ 1. Content is accurate
____ 2. Content is appropriate to meet goals
____ 3. Instructions are clear
____ 4. Program executes reliably
____ 5. Program is easy to use
____ 6. Format is interactive
____ 7. High level of interest maintained
____ 8. User establishes the pace
____ 9. Progression in levels of difficulty
____10. Handles incorrect responses appropriately

____ 11. Reinforces/rewards user appropriately
____ 12. Teacher able to modify
____ 13. Keeps records of student progress
____ 14. No age, gender, or ethnic discrimination
____ 15. Sound can be controlled
____ 16. Computer used effectively
____ 17. Has suggested activities
____ 18. Support materials are effective
____ 19. Program is cost-effective

Additional Criteria Specific to Tutorial Programs
____ 1. Variety in presentation
____ 2. Logical, sequential concept development
____ 3. Frequent testing
____ 4. Positive reinforcement
____ 5. Conditional branching
____ 6. Limits frequency of incorrect responses

Additional Criteria Specific to Simulations
____ 1. Clear directions
____ 2. Appropriate graphics
____ 3. Simple keyboard/mouse use
____ 4. Realistic situation for role playing
____ 5. Results predicated upon user input
____ 6. Promotes problem solving

Rating Criteria

Count number of "+" on form for both general and specific category guidelines. Mark rating line with appropriate number of stars.

****   = 22 or more
***   = 18–21
**   = 14–17
*   = 13 or less

Comments: _____

_____

_____

Evaluator's name:_____

Rating:_____

EVALUATION FORM #3: EDUCATIONAL SOFTWARE

The following is a checklist to refresh your memory regarding important aspects of computer software. Read the entire list before evaluating the software; then mark yes or no by the appropriate items after using the software. Record your overall impressions of the program.

Interaction

_____ 1. User can stop and reenter at same place
_____ 2. User can see score at any time
_____ 3. User can select level of difficulty
_____ 4. Program can set level through testing

_____ 5. User can review past mistakes
_____ 6. User proceeds at own pace
_____ 7. Testing occurs periodically during program
_____ 8. Program can have more than one user

Content

_____ 1. Appropriate subject matter
_____ 2. Appropriate for grade level suggested
_____ 3. No age, gender, or ethnic discrimination
_____ 4. Can reteach principles
_____ 5. Meets objectives—teaches what it should
_____ 6. Applicable to more than one subject

_____ 7. Presents accurate information
_____ 8. Program is interesting
_____ 9. Program is involving
_____10. Program is realistic
_____11. Program is educationally sound

Format

_____ 1. Clear documentation
_____ 2. Written instructions are short and concise
_____ 3. Program uses reinforcement
    _____ through sound
    _____ through graphics
    _____ through animation
    _____ through text

_____ 4. Program uses graphics appropriately
_____ 5. Program format is consistent with objectives
_____ 6. Program makes full use of computer's ability

General remarks: _____

_____

_____

Cost-effectiveness (Is program worth the cost?):_____

Recommend for purchase?_____ **Evaluator's name:** _____

EVALUATION FORM #4: EDUCATIONAL SOFTWARE

The following is a checklist regarding important aspects of computer software. Read the entire list before evaluating the software; then circle the score from 5 to 0 by the appropriate items after using the software. Each item has a multiplier to place a relative value on that characteristic. Multiply the score you circled by the given multiplier. Add the extended scores and record the total as your overall impression of the program.

Rating 5 = strong agreement, 0 = strong disagreement

Content

5 4 3 2 1 0 2 x 5 ____ Content is accurate
5 4 3 2 1 0 2 x 5 ____ Content has educational value
5 4 3 2 1 0 2 x 5 ____ Free of age, gender, or ethnic bias

Instructional Quality

5 4 3 2 1 0 x 4 ____ Purpose is well defined
5 4 3 2 1 0 x 4 ____ Achieves its defined purpose
5 4 3 2 1 0 x 4 ____ Learner controls rate of presentation
5 4 3 2 1 0 x 3 ____ Presentation is clear and logical
5 4 3 2 1 0 x 3 ____ Support materials are effective
5 4 3 2 1 0 x 2 ____ Appropriate level of difficulty
5 4 3 2 1 0 x 2 ____ Graphics and sound are used effectively
5 4 3 2 1 0 x 2 ____ Feedback is effective
5 4 3 2 1 0 x 1 ____ Stimulates creativity
5 4 3 2 1 0 x 1 ____ Can be modified for students with special needs
5 4 3 2 1 0 x 1 ____ Support materials are comprehensive

Technical Quality

5 4 3 2 1 0 x 5 ____ Appropriately uses computer capabilities
5 4 3 2 1 0 x 4 ____ Information displays are effective
5 4 3 2 1 0 x 3 ____ User can easily and independently operate program
5 4 3 2 1 0 x 3 ____ Reliable in normal use

Total score: _____

Excellent = 270+; Very good = 269–224; Good = 223–168; Poor = 167–112; Unacceptable = less than 112

General remarks: _____

_____

_____

Recommend for purchase?_____

Evaluator's name:_____

EVALUATING WORD PROCESSORS

EVALUATION FORM #5

Once the software is described, such as in the Description Form of Appendix A, it must be examined and rated against performance criteria specific to word processors. Read the entire checklist before evaluating the software; then enter your rating *score* from 3 to 0 and the *weight* (importance) to you. The weight is a multiplier to place a relative value on that criterion.

	Score (3–0)	Weight (3–1)
Documentation		
The manual is designed for easy reference with table of contents, tabs, and an index	____	____
Quick reference card is useful	____	____
The instructions are clear and easy to read	____	____
The tutorial is effective	____	____

Ease of Use and Support

	Score	Weight
Minimum learning time required to run the program	____	____
Context-sensitive help screens are effective	____	____
Support (3 = free, unlimited; 2 = toll call; 1 = limited time)	____	____

Features and Functions

Rate these criteria with:
   3 = excellent implementation
   2 = adequate implementation
   1 = poor implementation
   0 = missing
Use a weight value of:
   3 = very important
   2 = somewhat important
   1 = not important

Total the rating column and the weight column. Multiply the rating total by the weight total to get the raw score. Multiply the weight total by 3 to get the possible score. Divide the raw score by the possible score to get a percentage.

	Score	Weight
Cursor control	____	____
Block moves	____	____
Column formatting	____	____
Find and replace	____	____
Header and footer	____	____
Hyphenation	____	____
Index	____	____
Mail merge	____	____
Outlining	____	____
Preview	____	____
Spelling checker	____	____
Dictionary	____	____
Grammar checker	____	____
Thesaurus	____	____
Split screen	____	____
Undo last move	____	____
Undo last delete	____	____
WYSIWYG screen	____	____
Rating and weight totals:	____	____

Raw (rating total X weight total) score: ____
Possible (3 X weight total) score: ____
Percentage (raw/possible score): ____

Recommend for purchase? _____

Evaluator's name: _____

EVALUATION FORM #6

Once the software is described, such as in the Description Form of Appendix A, it must be examined and rated against performance criteria specific to spreadsheets. Read the entire checklist before evaluating the software; then enter your rating *score* from 3 to 0 and the *weight* (importance) to you. The weight is a multiplier to place a relative value on that criterion.

	Score (3–0)	Weight (3–1)
Documentation		
The manual is designed for easy reference with table of contents, tabs, and an index	____	____
Quick reference card is useful	____	____
The instructions are clear and easy to read	____	____
The tutorial is effective	____	____
Ease of Use and Support		
Minimum learning time required to run the program	____	____
Context-sensitive help screens are effective	____	____
Support (3 = free, unlimited; 2 = toll call; 1 = limited time)	____	____

Features and Functions

Rate these criteria with:		Score	Weight
3 = excellent implementation	Sufficient matrix size	____	____
2 = adequate implementation	Flexible import/export features	____	____
1 = poor implementation	Adequate data entry safeguards	____	____
0 = missing	Adequate cell protection	____	____
Use a weight value of:	Useful math & date/time functions	____	____
3 = very important	Useful statistics functions	____	____
2 = somewhat important	Useful financial functions	____	____
1 = not important	Adequate cell format control	____	____
	Adequate column/row size controls	____	____
	Good page and view format controls	____	____
Total the rating column and	Print area controls	____	____
the weight column. Multiply	Fast nested ascend/descend sorts	____	____
the rating total by the weight	Flexible header and footer	____	____
total to get the raw score.	Split screen	____	____
Multiply the weight total by 3	Powerful graph generator	____	____
to get the possible score.	Sufficient number of graph types	____	____
Divide the raw score by the	WYSIWYG preview	____	____
possible score to get a percentage.	Automatic save	____	____
	Rating and weight totals:	____	____
	Raw (rating total X weight total) score: ____		
	Possible (3 X weight total) score: ____		
	Percentage (raw/possible score): ____		

Recommend for purchase? _____

Evaluator's name: _____

EVALUATING DATABASE MANAGERS

EVALUATION FORM #7

Once the software is described, such as in the Description Form of Appendix A, it must be examined and rated against performance criteria specific to database managers. Read the entire checklist before evaluating the software; then enter your rating *score* from 3 to 0 and the *weight* (importance) to you. The weight is a multiplier to place a relative value on that criterion.

	Score (3–0)	Weight (3–1)
Documentation		
The manual is designed for easy reference with table of contents, tabs, and an index	___	___
Quick reference card is useful	___	___
The instructions are clear and easy to read	___	___
The tutorial is effective	___	___

Ease of Use and Support

	Score	Weight
Minimum learning time required to run the program	___	___
Context-sensitive help screens are effective	___	___
Support (3 = free, unlimited; 2 = toll call; 1 = limited time)	___	___

Features and Functions

Rate these criteria with:
  3 = excellent implementation
  2 = adequate implementation
  1 = poor implementation
  0 = missing
Use a weight value of:
  3 = very important
  2 = somewhat important
  1 = not important

Total the rating column and the weight column. Multiply the rating total by the weight total to get the raw score. Multiply the weight total by 3 to get the possible score. Divide the raw score by the possible score to get a percentage.

	Score	Weight
Sufficient file and record size	___	___
Relational/lookup capability	___	___
Flexible import/export features	___	___
Data entry automation	___	___
Adequate data entry safeguards	___	___
Adequate password protection	___	___
Flexible layout design	___	___
Flexible report definition	___	___
Powerful graphics tools	___	___
Useful math & date/time functions	___	___
Useful statistics functions		
Import into picture fields	___	___
Supports AND, OR, NOT and range, exact, and wildcard searches	___	___
Nested ascend/descend sorts	___	___
Adequate speed in searches & sorts	___	___
Reports allow subtotals/totals	___	___
WYSIWYG report preview	___	___
Automatic save	___	___
Rating and Weight Totals:	___	___

Raw (rating total X weight total) score: ___
Possible (3 X weight total) score: ___
Percentage (raw/possible score): ___

Recommend for purchase? _____

Evaluator's name: _____

- Select a suitable typeface to enhance readability and the expression of your words.

- Use sans serif typefaces for headlines and titles. Used sparingly, they have a simplicity that commands attention. Large amounts, such as in body text, are difficult to read. Sans serif typefaces are best used in a large size.

- Use serif typefaces for body text. The decorations on the letters help to guide the reader's eye movement from one letter to the next, thereby helping the reader to perceive words rather than letters.

- Use ornate text for special visual effects.

- Avoid mixing typefaces within a document, except for a distinct purpose. Rarely should you mix more than two typefaces in the same document.

- Select a letter size appropriate to the message and its intended impact. Consider that not all output is intended for 8 1/2-by-11-inch paper. Consider the optimum viewing distance and the medium (e.g., a minimum of 18 point size should be used for overhead transparencies and 24 point or larger for presentation slide shows).

- Allow ample leading (space) between lines of text so that ascenders and descenders do not touch.

- Use style (plain, **bold**, *italic*, outline, shadow, underline) for emphasis.

- Allow plenty of space around a block of text. A block of text takes up space, so be sure to consider it in your overall design.

BASIC RULES FOR DESIGNING OVERHEAD TRANSPARENCIES

- Use landscape (horizontal) rather than portrait (vertical) orientation for your layout.

- Lettering must be at least 1/4 inch high (18 point) and should be simple, bold, and easy to read. This will allow the projected screen image of the text to be viewed comfortably from the rear of a typical classroom.

- Lettering and drawings should be large enough to fill most of the transparency sheet, leaving enough blank space to emphasize the design elements.

- Color should be used where appropriate. Different colors can be used to highlight key words by separating the components of the transparency into two masters and printing them in different colors of thermal film.

- Text should be kept to a minimum and should present only an outline or key points rather than specific details. Key points might be bulleted or presented as a list. Key words can be emphasized by using bold, underline, or italics but avoid a mixture of the elements. Remember that this is an ephemeral medium in that, once a projector is turned off, the projected information is gone. Significant text and detail require a printed hard copy in the hands of the students.

- Divide a complex topic into "overlay cells" so that the concept may be presented in a logical sequence. "Overlay" transparencies allow items to be added in a progressive fashion to develop the finished product or complete idea.

SELECTION GUIDELINES FOR CHARTS AND GRAPHS

Line graphs are ideal for displaying a continuous event or trends over time (e.g., growth or decline over time). The rise and fall of the line on a graph easily portrays the fluctuations in value. Multiple trends can be compared simultaneously by plotting more than one line on the graph.

Area graphs are variations of line graphs and are successful at depicting amount or volume. A line is plotted and the area below it is filled in with a selected pattern. Each data set creates a band, or area, with each area stacked on the preceding one. These graphs can be eye-catching, but since they show cumulative results they can be more difficult to understand.

Column graphs (vertical columns) and bar graphs (horizontal bars) present changes in a dependent variable over an independent variable and are excellent ways of comparing multiple variables to a common variable (e.g., different performances during the same time frame). However, they lack the feeling of continuity displayed by a line graph. At times, column graphs and line graphs can be combined effectively to present both discrete and incremental views of the data. More elaborate graphs adding another variable can be created by stacking the columns/bars.

Pie charts are the ideal way to display part-to-the-whole relationships, or percentages. The size of each slice shows that segment's share of the entire pie. A segment (pie slice) may even be dragged away from the center for emphasis and the chart displayed in three dimensions.

GUIDELINES FOR EFFECTIVE PRESENTATION GRAPHICS

- Begin and end your presentation with a blank screen.

- Use generous margins to help focus attention on content.

- Use a single background or frame to unify the presentation.

- Keep any background text or graphics simple and restrict them to the same screen position.

- Limit yourself to two or three colors on one screen.

- Use bright colors to emphasize important points.

- Use color contrasts effectively (e.g., yellow on blue is highly visible, while red on black is barely readable).

- Limit yourself to two typefaces in one presentation.

- For maximum visibility, choose a type size of 24 points or larger.

- Use an attention-grabbing title screen.

- Use single words and short phrases on the screen to focus attention on the details provided orally.

- Use all uppercase letters only in major headings and make them a slightly larger size.

- Place headings at the same location in successive screens.

- Use dingbats (bullets, check marks, or other symbols) to organize lists.

- Use drop shadows and gradient fills for interesting visual effects.

- Use transition effects (wipes and dissolves) that create a graceful style and help your audience to follow your train of thought. Avoid mixing too many types of transition effects, since this could be distracting to the viewer.

- Check carefully for spelling/typing errors.

NETWORK COMMUNICATION ETIQUETTE (NETIQUETTE)

- Compose all but brief messages off-line to minimize network traffic.

- Limit each message to one topic and keep it succinct.

- Use subject headings that are very descriptive.

- Reply promptly to messages received.

- When replying, restate enough of the message to clearly identify context.

- Delete messages once you have read them.

- Don't be vulgar or offensive.

- Don't attempt to represent yourself as someone you are not.

- Don't criticize ("flame") others on the network.

- Supply clues if you are intending to write using humor, irony, sarcasm, or emotion. Your intent may not be obvious to the reader. Using all uppercase in a word or phrase SHOUTS.
  Try :-) for a sideways smile or ;-) for a wink.

- Use a signature footer that includes your name, school, and e-mail address.

- Practice safe communications. Don't spread viruses! Check downloaded executable files.

- Consider yourself a guest on the system and behave accordingly.

ACCESS POLICIES AND PARENT/GUARDIAN CONSENT FORM

School District 4J
Eugene Public Schools
200 North Monroe
Eugene, Oregon 97402-4295

IMPORTANT INFORMATION ABOUT STUDENT
USE OF ELECTRONIC MAIL AND THE INTERNET
August 1996

School District 4J is continuing to expand the use of Internet services on our electronic network (4JNet). The Internet is a global network that provides your child with access to a wide range of information from throughout the world and allows your child to communicate with people worldwide. 4J's purpose in providing Internet services is to assist in preparing your child for success in the 21st Century. Our network was made possible when you helped fund our 1992 bond request to provide computers in classrooms, libraries, and labs.

It is possible that your child may find material on the Internet that you consider objectionable. District 4J's *Guidelines for Accessing 4JNet* prohibit access to material that is inappropriate in the school environment. Although your student's use of the Internet while at school will be supervised by staff, we cannot guarantee that your child will not gain access to inappropriate materials. We encourage you to have a discussion with your child about your values and how they should guide his/her activities while using the Internet. When school resumes, Internet access through 4JNet will not be available via modem.

Your child may also have access to the district e-mail system, with your permission, at school and through a dial-up modem from home. You will be responsible for monitoring your child's activities when he or she accesses the system from home. You must specifically authorize your child's individual e-mail account by returning the *4JNet Account Agreement* signed by you and your child to your school. Please note that inappropriate use of e-mail will not be tolerated and students risk losing their accounts.

4JNet Services

1. **The World Wide Web** provides an incredible amount of good, useful information in the form of text, graphics, photographs, video, and sound. The Web is used in the classroom to extend teaching and learning, as well as being a valuable research tool. There are real advantages to being able to access such valuable resources on the Internet. However, without an e-mail account, a student will not be able to legitimately correspond easily with other people on the Internet.

2. **E-Mail** allows students to communicate with people throughout the world. In addition to using e-mail to communicate with individuals, students will also be able to subscribe to listservs, an Internet-based program for group communication to which participants must subscribe. Students use listservs to engage in group discussions related to educational projects.

<u>Individual E-Mail Accounts</u>: Secondary students may be provided with individual e-mail accounts with written parental or guardian agreement. A signed *4JNet Student Account Agreement* must be returned to the school indicating that the student and parent agree to follow 4J's *Guidelines for Accessing 4JNet*. These agreements are available either at your school or from Computing and Information Services at the Education Center (687-3329).

<u>Classroom Accounts</u>: Elementary students will be granted e-mail access only through a classroom account requested by a teacher. Elementary students may be provided with an individual account under special circumstances at the request of their teacher and with the approval of their parent as described above. A signed *4JNet Student Account Agreement* will be required for an elementary student to have an individual e-mail account.

3. **File Transfer Protocol** (FTP) allows users to download large files and computer software. The provisions of 4J's *Guidelines for Accessing 4JNet* apply to FTP, just as to all other Internet use.

4. **Newsgroups** are discussion groups that are similar to listservs and may be available to students. However, the District will only provide access to selected newsgroups that relate to subjects that are appropriate to our educational purpose.

5. **Internet Relay Chat** (IRC) provides the capability of engaging in "real-time" discussions and may be available to students. However, the District will provide access to IRC only for specifically defined educational activities.

These procedures are being followed as Internet resources are being integrated into the classroom.

• We are providing all staff with information about the Internet and its uses and possible misuses so that they can discuss these issues with students. Staff inservice about use of the network also includes information about teaching students how to use the Internet appropriately.

• We have established clear rules and set boundaries for students. Your student's school will have copies of 4J's *Guidelines for Accessing 4JNet* and *Netiquette* (online etiquette). The existing guidelines are under review and an updated Student Acceptable Use Policy is being developed.

We are helping teachers to learn about the appropriate use of the Internet and advising them about how to use this technology with students to extend teaching and learning. Your school may schedule information meetings which include a live demonstration on the Internet and the opportunity to explore the Internet on your own. Contact your school principal teachers to learn more about how this educational resource is being used at your school.

For more information about how 4JNet is being used to extend teaching and learning, contact Sheryl Steinke, Library Services, at 687-3280, or Jack Turner, Computing and Information Services, at 687-6950. They can also be contacted via e-mail:
steinke@4j.lane.edu
turner@4j.lane.edu

GUIDELINES FOR ACCESSING 4JNET
The Eugene School District's Electronic Network

4JNet is to be used in a responsible, efficient, ethical and legal manner and in accordance with the mission of School District 4J. Users must agree to these guidelines prior to using 4JNet, including receiving a district E-mail account. Failure to adhere to these guidelines may likely result in the suspension or revocation of the privilege of network access.

GUIDELINES

1. The following individuals are authorized to use 4JNet.

    1. All 4J employees and school board members may be issued an individual E-mail account.

    2. Secondary students, with the written consent of their parent or guardian, may be issued an individual E-mail account.

    3. Elementary students have access to 4JNet only under their teacher's direct supervision using a classroom account. Individual elementary students are not generally issued E-mail accounts. **Exception**: Identified elementary students may be issued an individual E-mail account with the written consent of a sponsoring educator and their parent.

    4. Others who request Guest Accounts from Computing and Information Services (CIS) **may** be issued E-mail accounts based on their need and the availability of space.

2. The use of 4JNet is intended to extend learning and teaching. Network users are encouraged to develop uses which meet their individual learning and teaching needs and to take advantage of the network's many useful functions, including World Wide Web, electronic mail, newsgroups, listservs, bulletin boards, and access to Gopher, Telnet and FTP resources.

3. The following uses of 4JNet are unacceptable and may result in suspension or revocation of network privileges.

    1. Violation of School Board Policy, District Administrative Rules, or any provision in the district **Student Rights and Responsibilities Handbook**.

    2. The use of profanity, obscenity or other language that may be offensive to another user.

    3. Reposting of personal communications without the author's prior consent.

    4. Copying commercial software or other material in violation of federal copyright laws.

    5. Use of the network for financial gain, commercial activity, or illegal activity.

    6. Accessing another person's individual account without prior consent or accessing a restricted account without the prior consent of the responsible administrator or teacher.

4. 4JNet will limit the newsgroups that are available to elementary and secondary students so that they will only have access to those newsgroups that are appropriate to their instructional level and age.

5. Users must avoid spreading computer viruses, and all downloaded files must be virus-checked. Deliberate attempts to degrade or disrupt system performance is a violation of law.

6. Teachers are expected to provide guidance and supervision of students who use 4JNet in the following ways:

   1. Teachers and other supervising adults should discuss the appropriate use of 4JNet and Internet with their students, monitor their use, and intervene if the resource is not being used appropriately.

   2. Computers that allow access to Internet should be placed in areas supervised by adults.

7. Students should report any inappropriate material they access to a teacher, other staff persons, or their parents. Students are not to share inappropriate materials or their sources with other students.

8. The person in whose name an account is issued is responsible at all times for its proper use. Passwords should never be shared with another person and should be changed frequently.

NETIQUETTE

Users of E-mail and other network services should be aware of the common expectations or etiquette that users expect from one another.

1. E-mail messages are not guaranteed to be private. The system operator of 4JNet has access to all mail in order to maintain the system.

2. When sending E-mail, make your "subject" as descriptive as possible.

3. Do not post the personal addresses or phone numbers of students or colleagues.

4. Check your E-mail frequently and delete after reading it. Be aware that read or sent E-mail messages are automatically deleted after 30 days to ensure adequate disk space on the network.

5. Proofread and edit messages before they are sent, but be tolerant of errors in messages from others.

6. Be careful when using sarcasm and humor: without face-to-face communication, a joke may not be taken the way it was intended.

7. Do not publicly criticize or "flame" others.

8. Protect the privacy of other people.

9. Messages written in all caps are difficult to read and are the network equivalent of shouting.

Computing and Information Services
Lane County School District No. 4J, Eugene, Oregon
August 1996

Return to 4J Computing and Information Services
200 N. Monroe
Eugene, OR 97402
CIS will return a copy of this completed form to the building computer rep.

4J NET STUDENT ACCOUNT AGREEMENT

Student Section

❏ Check here if new account
❏ Check here if renewing account
Current USERNAME_____

Student Name_____Grade_____

Student Signature_____

School_____

I have read the *Guidelines for Accessing 4JNet*, and I agree to follow the guidelines/rules contained in this policy. I understand that if I violate the policy my account with 4JNET can be terminated and I may face other disciplinary measures as specified in the *Guidelines*, or in the District's *Student Rights and Responsibilities Handbook*.

Elementary students **only** require a 4J educator's signature.

4J Educator's Signature_____ Date_____

****

Parent or Guardian Section

I have read the information provided by Eugene 4J on student access to 4JNET. If dial-up access is provided from our home, I accept responsibility for at-home supervision.

I will instruct my child regarding any values against accessing materials that I have in addition to the restrictions set forth in the *Guidelines for Accessing 4JNet*, and I will emphasize to my child the importance of following the guidelines for student responsibility on the Internet.

Parent or Guardian Name_____Date_____

Parent or Guardian Signature_____Date _____

Home Address_____Phone_____

****

This space reserved for System Administrator

Assigned User Name:_____Assigned Temporary Password: _____

TELECOMPUTING RESOURCES: EDUCATIONAL NETWORKS

AT&T Learning Network
P.O. Box 4012
Bridgewater, NJ 98807-4012
800-367-7225

FrEd Mail
Al Rogers
P.O. Box 243
Bonita, CA 91902
619-475-4852

GTE Educational Services
SpecialNet
8505 Freeport Pkwy., Suite 600
Irving, TX 75063-9990
800-659-3000

K12 Net
Janet Murray
Wilson High School
1151 SW Vermont St.
Portland, OR 97219
503-280-5280 x450

National Geographic Kids Network
National Geographic Society Educational Services
P.O. Box 98019
Washington, DC 20090
800-368-2728

A SAMPLE OF WWW SITES

Sites preceded by a star (*) are ones referenced in the text. Remember that the World Wide Web is a dynamic entity. Some of the web sites identified below may have moved location or gone out of existence. Happy surfing!

SOCIAL STUDIES

C.I.A. World Factbook
> http://www.odci.gov/cia/publications

National Geographic Society
> http://www.nationalgeographic.com

Maps, atlases, and geographic references
> http://www.cgrer.uiowa.edu/servers/servers_references.html

*A 21st Century Schoolhouse
> http://www.viser.net/gs21/twensch.htm

Tiger Mapping Service
> http://www.tiger.census.gov

U.S. Gazetteer
> http://www.tiger.census.gov/cgi-bin/gazetteer

U.S. Census Data
> http://www.census.gov

Gateway to Canadian Geography
> http://www.ellesmere.ccm.emr.ca/wwwnais/wwwnais.html

Canadian Government Information
> http://www.info.ic.gc.ca/opengov

Gateway to World History
> http://www.neal.ctstateu.edu/history/world_history/world_history.html

African American Mosaic
> http://www.lcweb.loc.gov/exhibits/African.American/intro.html

The Native American Experience
> http://www.csulb.edu/gc/libarts/am-indian/nae

Japan Information
> http://www.gan.ncc.go.jp/11/JAPAN/History

The Viking Network
> http://www.odin.nls.no/viking/vnethome.htm

The Thomas Register
> http://www.thomas.loc.gov

The Smithsonian Institution
> http://www.si.edu/start.htm

CBS News Up To The Minute
> http://www.uttm.com

Canadian Broadcasting Corporation Resources
> http://www.cbc.ca/whatsnew/educat1.html

China News page
> http://www.hk.net/~drummond/miles/china.html

CNN's Interactive Site
     http://www.cnn.com
Voice of America
     http://www.voa.gov

SCIENCE

San Diego Zoo
     http://www.sandiego zoo.org
Dinosaurs
     http://www.bvis.uic.edu/museum
National Wildlife Federation
     http://www.nwf.org/nwf
Discovery Channel Online
     http://www.discovery.com/area/nature.html
Christa McAuliffe Project
     http://www.bev.net/education/schools/mbeeks/ca/index.html
NASA K-12 Initiatives
     http://www.quest.arc.nasa.gov
NASA Space Shuttle Archives
     http://www.shuttle.nasa.gov
Lewis Research Center Learning Technologies K–12 Home Page
     http://www.lerc.nasa.gov/WWW/K-12
Exploring the Environment
     http://www.cotf.edu/ETE
Environmental Education Resources for Students
     http://www.envirolink.org/enviroed/students.html
Geosciences Web Server
     http://www.covis.nwu.edi/Geosciences/index.html
Newton's Apple (PBS)
     http://www.ericir.syr.edu/Newton/welcome.html
Science for the Millenium
     http://www.ncsa.uiuc.edu/Cyberia/Expo
Science Daily
     http://www.sciencedaily.com
Volcano World
     http://www.volcano.und.nodak.edu

MATHEMATICS

Math Parent Handbook
     http://www.hmco.com/school/math/res/parentbk
Math Magic
     http://www.forum.swarthmore.edu/mathmagic
Mega Math Activities
     http://www.cs.uidaho.edu/~casey931/mega-math

Mega Math Glossary
    http://www.c3.lanl.gov/mega-math/gloss/gloss.html
Mathematics Archives
    http://www.archives.math.utk.edu/tutorials.html
Mathematica Demonstration
    http://www.wri.com/demo
Lewis Research Center Learning Technologies K–12 Home Page
    http://www.lerc.nasa.gov/WWW/K-12

ENGLISH LANGUAGE ARTS

*Children's Literature Web Guide
    http://www.ucalgary.ca/~dkbrown
*KidPub WWW Publishing
    http://www.kidpub.org/kidpub
*Complete Works of William Shakespeare
    http://www.the-tech.mit.edu/Shakespeare/works.html
The Young Writers Club
    http://www.cs.bilkent.edu/tr/~david/derya/ywc.html
ERIC Clearinghouse on Reading
    http://www.indiana.edu/~eric_rec
Poetry Archive
    http://www.english-www.hss.cmu.edu/Poetry.html
APA Publication Manual Crib Sheet
    http://www.gasou.edu/psychweb/tipsheet/apacrib.html
MLA Style Citations of Electronic Sources
    http://www.cas.usf.edu/english/walker/mla.html

ART

Online Visual Literacy Project
    http://www.pomona.edu/visual-lit/intro/intro.html
The Art Room
    http://www.sunsite.unc.edu/cisco/art.html
Crayola Art Education
    http://www.crayola.com/art_education
Free Crafting Materials
    http://www.ppi-free.com
Vatican Exhibit
    http://www.ncsa.uiuc.edu/SDG/Experimental/vatican.exhibit/Vatican.exhibit.html
Canadian Students Creative Art Project
    http://www.rsc2.carleton.ca/NSTW

MUSIC

The Music Educator's Home Page
http://www.athena.athenanet.net/~wslow/index.html
Internet Music Resources Guide
http://www.teleport.com/~celinec/music.shtml
Hotlist for Music Educators
http://www.sln.fi.edu/tfi/hotlists/music.html

TEACHER RESOURCES

*Evaluating Web Sites
http://www.wlma.org/libint/evalweb.htm
*Collaborative Lesson Archive
http://faldo.atmos.uiuc.edu/CLA
*Louisiana Challenge Grant Lessons Resources
http://www.challenge.state.la.us/k12act/index.html
U.S. Department of Education
http://www.ed.gov
Guide to U.S. Department of Education Programs
http://www.ed.gov/programs.html#guide
Educator's Virtual Library
http://www.byu.edu/acd1/ed/coe/vlibrary/vlibrary.html
Educational Guide to the Web
http://www.cs.uidaho.edu/~connie/interests.html
Teachers Net
http://www.teachers.net
Teachers Helping Teachers
http://www.pacificnet.net/~mandel
Online Internet Institute
http://www.prism.prs.k12.nj.us:70/0/WWW/OII/OIIhome.html
Annenberg/CPB Learners Online
http://www.learner.org
Library of Congress Home Page
http://www.loc.gov
Subject Curriculum Guide
http://www.byu.edu/acd1/ed/InSci/Projects/WWWSubjectGuide.html
National Teachers' Enhancement Network
http://www.montana.edu/80/~wwwxs
Yahoo™
http://www.yahoo.com
AltaVista™
http://www.altavista.digital.com
MetaCrawler™
http://www.metacrawler.cs.washington.edu

SOFTWARE DATABASE TEMPLATE

Field Name	Field Type	Formula/Entry Option
Title	Text	
Version #	Text	
Publisher	Text	
Copyright Date	Number	Range: 1985 . . . 2010
Vendor Name	Text	
Vendor Street Address	Text	
City, ST, ZIP	Text	
Vendor Phone #	Text	
Technical Support Phone #	Text	
Computer/OS	Text	
RAM Needed	Text	
Hard Disk Space Needed	Text	

Software License	Text	Value List:
		    Single User
		    Multiple User
		    Site License

Number of Licensed Users	Number	
Cost	Number	

Grade Level	Text	Value List:
		    Pri
		    Int
		    MS
		    HS
		    Fac

Program Description	Text	

Type of Software	Text	Value List:
		    Drill & Practice
		    Tutorial
		    Simulation
		    Multimedia
		    Word processor
		    Spreadsheet
		    Database
		    Communication
		    Other

Subject Area	Text	Value List:
		    Foreign Language
		    Language Arts
		    Math
		    Science
		    Social Studies

Language Other Than English	Text	Value List:
		    French
		    German
		    Japanese
		    Spanish

Purchase Order #	Text	
Purchase Date	Date	
Shipping Cost	Number	
TOTAL	Calculation	= Cost + Shipping

Field Name	Field Type	Formula/Entry Option

Foreign Language Topics	Text	Value List:
		    Conversation
		    Culture
		    Grammar
		    Vocabulary

Language Arts Topics	Text	Value List:
		    Capitals
		    Consonants
		    Literature
		    Paragraphs
		    Prefix
		    Punctuation
		    Reading
		    Sentence Structure
		    Spelling
		    Suffix
		    Vowels
		    Writing

Math Topics	Text	Value List:
		    Addition, Simple
		    Addition, 2 place
		    Addition, > 2 place
		    Subtraction, Simple
		    Subtraction, 2 place
		    Subtraction, > 2 place
		    Place Value
		    Multiplication, Simple
		    Multiplication, > 1 digit multiplier
		    Division, Simple
		    Division, > 1 digit divisor
		    Fractions
		    Decimals
		    Story problems, Simple
		    Story problems, Complex
		    Time
		    Money
		    Pre-algebra
		    Algebra
		    Geometry
		    Trigonometry
		    Calculus

Science Topics	Text	Value List:
		    Astronomy
		    Biology
		    Chemistry
		    Earth Science
		    Geology
		    Physical Science
		    Physics

Social Studies Topics	Text	Value List: American History Geography Government Economics Mapping Regions World History
School ID #	Text	
Call #	Text	
User Location	Text	
Inventory Value	Summary	= Total of Cost
Average Age	Summary	= Mean of Copyright Date

Notes:

Copyright Date   This field is prescribed as a number in order to be able to calculate an average. The range is limited to years that would be reasonable numbers (e.g., 1985 to 2010).

Software License   As with other fields in this database, a value list is suggested to ensure data entry consistency. Controlling the data entry will facilitate doing searches later on.

Inventory Value   A summary field that can reveal the value of the entire holdings represented in the database. It may also be used to show the value of any portion (e.g., MS, Simulation, Science, or Physics) of the database. This could yield useful assessment information.

Average Age   A summary field that can reveal the average age (based on copyright, not purchase date) of the entire holdings represented in the database. It may also be used to show the average age of any portion (e.g., MS, Simulation, Science, or Physics) of the database. This also could yield useful assessment information.

Broderbund Software
17 Paul Drive
San Rafael, CA 94903
800-521-6263 (sales and customer service)
415-492-3500 (technical support)
Policies: 30-day preview, 60-day return, 90-day replacement, unlimited support

Claris Corporation
Box 58168
Santa Clara, CA 95052
408-727-8227 (sales and customer service)
800-735-7393 (technical support—recorded answers to frequently asked questions)
408-727-9054 (technical support—Macintosh)
408-727-9004 (technical support—Windows)
Policies: Unlimited support, on-line support (Claris CR@aol.com)

Compton's New Media
Division of Encyclopedia Britannica
2320 Camino Vida Roble
Carlsbad, CA 92009
800-862-2206 (sales and customer service)
619-929-2626 (technical support)
Policies: 30-day return, unlimited support

Davidson & Associates
P.O. Box 2961
Torrance, CA 90509
800-545-7677 (sales and customer service)
800-545-6141 (technical support)
Policies: 3-day money-back guarantee, unlimited support

Discis Knowledge Research
90 Sheppard Avenue East, Seventh Floor
Toronto, Ontario M2N SW9, Canada
800-567-4321 (sales and customer service)
800-567-4321 or 904-886-7273 (technical support)
Policies: Unlimited guarantee, unlimited support

Grolier Electronic Publishing
Sherman Turnpike
Danbury, CT 06816
800-356-5590 (sales and customer service)
800-356-5590 (technical support)
Policies: 30-day money back guarantee, unlimited support

Intellimation
P.O. Box 1922, Cremona Drive
Santa Barbara, CA 93116
800-346-8355 (sales and customer service)
800-346-8355 (technical support)
Policies: 30-day money back guarantee, unlimited support

Microsoft Corporation
One Microsoft Way
Redmond, WA 98052
800-426-9400 (sales and customer service)
206-454-2030 (technical support)
Policies: 90-day money-back guarantee, unlimited support

Minnesota Educational Computing Corporation (MECC)
6160 Summit Drive North
Minneapolis, MN 55430
800-685-6322 (sales and customer service)
800-685-6322 (technical support)
Policies: 30-day money-back guarantee

Optical Data Corporation
30 Technology Drive
Warren, NJ 07059
800-524-2481 (sales and customer service)
800-524-2481 (technical support)
Policies: 30-day money-back guarantee

Sunburst Communications
P.O. Box 100
Pleasantville, NY 10570-0100
800-321-7511 (sales and customer service)
800-321-7511 (technical support)
Policies: 45-day preview, 100% lifetime replacement, 1-year money-back guarantee, unlimited support, online support (sunburst4@aol.com)

Tom Snyder Productions
80 Coolidge Hill Road
Watertown, MA 02172
800-342-0236 (sales and customer service)
800-342-0236 x255 (technical support)
www.teachsp.com
Policies: 30-day preview, 100% lifetime money-back guarantee, online support (chiptsp@aol.com)

Voyager Company
1351 Pacific Coast Highway
Santa Monica, CA 90401
800-446-2001 (sales and customer service)
914-591-5500 (technical support)
Policies: 30-day money-back guarantee, unlimited support

ZTEK Company
P.O. Box 1055
Louisville, KY 402012
[ZTEK is a reseller as well as a publisher. It provides support for all of its products.]
800-247-1603 (sales and customer service and technical support)
Policies: 30-day money-back guarantee, unlimited support, online support (ZTEK@applelink.apple.com)

TECHNOLOGY JOURNALS AND MAGAZINES

The following magazines and journals contain software reviews, as well as "how to" articles. A selection of these would form the core of an excellent collection of periodicals for a school library. This textbook's author's favorite, *Learning and Leading with Technology*, is of consistently high quality, with practical articles founded on a sound theory base.

CD-ROM Professional
462 Danbury Road
Wilton, CT 06897

Classroom Computer Learning
5615 West Carmel Rd.
Cicero, IL 60650

Computers in the Schools
Haworth Press
10 Alice Street
Binghamton, NY 13904

Ed-Tech Review
Association for the Advancement of Computing in Education
P.O. Box 2966
Charlottesville, VA 22902

Educational Technology
Educational Technology Publishing
140 Sylvan Ave.
Englewood Cliffs, NJ 07632

Educators' Tech Exchange
Edutech, Inc.
P.O. Box 51760
Pacific Grove, CA 93950

Electronic Learning
P.O. Box 2041
Mahopa, NY 10541

Information Technology and Libraries
50 East Huron Street
Chicago, IL 60611

Journal of Educational Computing Research
Baywood Publishing
26 Austin Avenue
Amityville, NY 11701

Learning and Leading with Technology
International Society for Technology in Education
1787 Agate St.
Eugene, OR 97403-1923

Learning
Box 2580
Boulder, CO 80322

Library Hi-Tech Journal
Pierian Press
P.O. Box 1808
Ann Arbor, MI 48106

Macworld
Macworld Communications Inc.
501 Second Street
San Francisco, CA 94107

Media & Methods
1429 Walnut St.
Philadelphia, PA 10102

New Media
P.O. Box 1771
Riverton, NJ 08077-9771

PC World
PC World Communications Inc.
555 DeHaro St.
San Francisco, CA 94107

Teaching and Computers
P.O. Box 2040
Mahopac, NY 10541

Technology & Learning
Peter Li, Inc.
2451 East River Rd.
Dayton, OH 45439

The following are primarily review journals:
Booklist
50 East Huron St.
Chicago, IL 60611

The Digest of Software Reviews
301 West Mesa
Fresno, CA 93704

EPIE Micro-courseware Profiles
EPIE and Consumer's Union
Box 839
Water Mill, NY 11976

Library Software Review
520 Riverside Ave.
Westport, CT 06877

School Library Journal
Box 13706
Philadelphia, PA 19101

School Library Media Quarterly
50 East Huron St.
Chicago, IL 60611

Whole Earth Review
P.O. Box 27956
San Diego, CA 92128

Wilson Library Bulletin
900 University Ave.
Bronx, NY 10452

PROFESSIONAL ASSOCIATIONS PROMOTING THE USE OF TECHNOLOGY

The following national and international associations contribute valuable information to their members' professional development through publications and conferences. The reader is encouraged to find statewide associations that would contribute as well.

Association for Computing Machinery (ACM)
1133 Avenue of the Americas
New York, NY 10036
212-265-6300

Association for Development of Computer-Based Instructional Systems (ADCIS)
Western Washington Computer Center
Bellingham, WA 98225
206-676-2860

Association for Educational Communication and Technology (AECT)
1126 16th Street NW
Washington, DC 20036
202-833-4186

Association for Educational Data Systems (AEDS)
1201 16th Street NW
Washington, DC 20036
202-833-4100

International Society for Technology in Education (ISTE)
1787 Agate St.
Eugene, OR 97403
503-686-4414

Index